Justice and Economic Distribution

Second Edition

Justice
and
Economic Distribution

John Arthur

William H. Shaw

Prentice Hall
Englewood Cliffs, New Jersey 07632

Library of Congress Cataloging-in-Publication Data

Justice and economic distribution / [edited by] JOHN ARTHUR, WILLIAM
    H. SHAW.—2nd ed.
       p.   cm.
    Includes bibliographical references.
    ISBN 0-13-514241-5
    1. Distributive justice.   I. Arthur, John, [date].   II. Shaw,
 William H., [date].
 HB771.J87   1991
 330—dc20   90-48333

Editorial/production supervision: *Edith Riker/Joanne Riker*
Cover design: *Ben Santora*
Prepress buyer: *Herb Klein*
Manufacturing buyer: *David Dickey*

Printed in the United States of America

10 9 8 7 6 5 4 3 2 1

ISBN   0-13-514241-5

Prentice-Hall International (UK) Limited, *London*
Prentice-Hall of Australia Pty. Limited, *Sydney*
Prentice-Hall Canada Inc., *Toronto*
Prentice-Hall Hispanoamericana, S.A., *Mexico*
Prentice-Hall of India Private Limited, *New Delhi*
Prentice-Hall of Japan, Inc., *Tokyo*
Simon & Schuster Asia Pte. Ltd., *Singapore*
Editora Prentice-Hall do Brasil, Ltda., *Rio de Janeiro*

CONTENTS

PREFACE

The vast disparities in wealth and styles of life between virtual neighbors in the same society often seem incredible. How, it is natural to ask, can it be just or fair that some persons are barely able to meet even their minimum nutritional needs, while others spend hundreds of dollars a month heating their private swimming pools? Perhaps even more striking than this is the fact that so many take this state of affairs to be normal, never questioning its legitimacy. Yet, in other contexts, the fairness of society's economic arrangements is an issue about which people feel strongly. Individuals argue, agitate, campaign, organize, lobby, and fight over the justice of the allocation of economic goods and bads. Are taxes fair? Is welfare a rip-off? What about farm subsidies? Do corporations deserve their huge profits, or their executives and owners such large salaries and other benefits? Lying behind political disputes, frequently, are rival claims and assumptions about economic justice, and examining these leads one to philosophy. Today, certainly, the problem of what constitutes a just economic distribution is central to social and political philosophy.

This anthology is an attempt to bring together in a single volume the ideas of some of the most perceptive and interesting contemporary writers on this subject. Inspired by an undergraduate seminar taught by the editors, the first edition of this book utilized the three-way theoretical debate among Rawls, Nozick, and the utilitarians Smart and Hare to introduce students to the topic of economic justice. The volume also included original essays by eight other authors that pursued various normative and methodological issues raised by this debate. The book's reception over the years has pleased us: It has seen several printings; people we respect tell us they use it in their classrooms; and the professional literature frequently cites its essays. But in the thirteen years since the first edition, the need to revise and update *Justice and Economic Distribution* has become clear.

Although we have re-edited and expanded our selection from Rawls's *A Theory of Justice*, Part I retains its original organization. Part II, however, has been revised and reorganized, and contains more essays. A new section, which includes selections from the work of MacIntyre, Sandel, and Walzer, is devoted to the communitarian challenge to liberal theories of justice, a challenge that has been the most important development in political philosophy since the previous edition. Although the other two sections of Part II focus on the same array of topics as before, they now include important new essays on economic desert, the market, and global justice.

In this new edition of *Justice and Economic Distribution*, we have endeavored, as before, to strike a balance between philosophical sophistication on the one hand and the needs of philosophy students on the other. We have sought essays that avoid needless technicality and recondite issues. But the readings are not easy because the issues they address are not easy. Our introductory essay and the shorter introductions to each of the sections, however, are designed to provide sufficient background for introductory students to follow the major arguments, at least in broad outline.

John Arthur
William H. Shaw

ON THE PROBLEM
OF ECONOMIC JUSTICE

The problem of economic justice can be expressed with remarkable simplicity: On what basis should economic goods and services be distributed? Answers to this question, however, are as numerous as those to any important philosophical issue. Some (libertarians) believe that the operation of a free market guarantees justice. Others (utilitarians) hold that the needs or interests of people should be of primary concern. Still others look to how much is deserved, as measured by labor time, effort, or contribution, as the basis for distribution. Equal distribution, since it seems to reflect the common humanity shared by all, is also viewed by many to be the core of economic justice. The philosophical problem is to decide which among these and other positions is in fact superior, and to give reasons for one's conclusion that will convince others.

This volume is an attempt to help us resolve the issue of economic justice. The very existence of such an anthology, however, reflects an important fact about recent events in the philosophical world: Issues of social justice have been close to center stage for two decades. That this is so will not seem surprising to nonphilosophers, but it was not so many years ago that political philosophy was declared by its former practitioners to be dead. The announcement of its passing, however, startled no one because its illness had been widely acknowledged to be terminal, and philosophers had already turned their attentions elsewhere.

The disease with which political philosophy was presumed to have been stricken had been diagnosed much earlier as a congenital ailment of all moral theory. Logical positivism classified as meaningless any proposition that was neither verifiable by empirical evidence nor true by definition and so relegated ethical and political theory to the realm of nonsense, along with poetry, metaphysics, and other emotional ejaculations. No serious philosopher, so it was thought, need waste his or her time on social or moral philosophy. This advice was not entirely heeded, and philosophers, under the influence of so-called ordinary language philosophy, began to turn their attention to the analysis of the key terms of ethical discourse. Philosophy could have something to say about morality, but still one should not expect too much. In particular, it was said, one should not expect philosophy to provide any substantive answers to the hard questions of ethics and social policy. There is a logic to moral and social discourse, but the truth of these matters cannot be known; indeed there is no real truth to know because in the end it is all a matter of individual emotional preference.

A rejection of the narrow horizons of logical positivism and a close attention to actual linguistic practice—both products of ordinary language philosophy—did, however, guide some away from this dead end. Philosophers looked more carefully at the nature of ethical discourse and were forced to abandon their noncognitivism (that is, the belief that ethical claims can be neither correct nor incorrect) for an appreciation of the real and legitimate role that reasoning and argument play in moral and political philosophy and of the possibility of reaching philosophical answers to the pressing questions of those topics.

Gradually in the late 1950s and then throughout the 1960s, articles, anthologies, and books appeared as interest was restored in substantive political philosophy. John Rawls's *A Theory of Justice*, published in 1971, marked a watershed, as growing attention to social philosophy evolved into a major concern of the discipline. While philosophers now explore confidently such topics as preferential hiring, health care delivery, and civil disobedience, among many others, a central concern of social and political philosophy has been, and remains, that of economic justice. This is not surprising since it is an issue that lies at the heart of all philosophizing about society: What constitutes a just distribution of the benefits and burdens of economic life?

THE CONCEPT OF JUSTICE

Justice is an old concept with a rich history, a concept that is fundamental to any discussion of how society ought to be organized. Philosophical concern with it goes back at least to ancient Greece. For Plato and some of his contemporaries, justice seems to have been the paramount virtue or, more precisely, the sum of virtue with regard to our relations with others. "Justice" had the ring of "righteousness," and to know an act was just was to know it was right. Although there is still a sense in which to do what is just is to do what is right, philosophers today generally distinguish justice from the whole of morality.

To claim something is "unjust" is a more specific complaint than to say it is "bad" or "immoral." I may be rude to you, behave selfishly, sleep with your spouse, and engage in a variety of other naughty or immoral behavior without—it seems—being unjust to you. On the other hand, an act that is unjust might be morally justified on the whole, as when the necessities of war require denial of legal due process to a traitor. We can make sense of the thought that the act is unjust but, on balance, still should be done. This suggests that in speaking of justice or injustice we are discussing only one sphere of the moral picture. In general, however, an injustice is acceptable only if it can be shown that the consequence of not committing it would be very bad indeed, and to know something is unjust is to have a good reason to think it is wrong overall.

If justice is a part of morality, what sorts of facts make an act unjust rather than simply wrong in general? Consider someone who is locked up for criticizing the government; here liberty has been violated and an injustice done. Similarly, if someone else is punished for a crime he did not commit or is singled out from his philosophy class and required to write twice as many papers as the others, then we naturally speak of injustice.

What seems to be going on is that talk of justice or injustice focuses on at least one of several related ideas. First, a claim that one is treated unjustly often suggests that one's moral rights have been violated—in particular, that one has been made to suffer some burden one had a right to avoid or has been denied some benefit one had a right to possess. If we agree to go into business together and you back out without justification, costing me time and money, then you have violated a right of mine and I may well claim that you have treated me unjustly.

Second, the term injustice is often used to mean unfairness. Justice frequently concerns the treatment of members of groups or else looks backwards to the compensating of prior injuries, demanding fairness in our handling of such situations. Exactly what fairness requires is hard to say, and different standards may well be applied to the same case. If Nixon committed high crimes and misdemeanors, he is justly impeached under the Constitution. If Presidents Kennedy and Johnson committed equally heinous acts, then Nixon suffers a comparative injustice since he was singled out. On the other hand, our treatment of Nixon and other white-collar lawbreakers is unjust, although this time for the opposite reason, when compared to the stiffer sentences meted out to "common" criminals for less grave offenses.

Injustice in one sense of unfairness occurs when like cases are not treated in the same fashion. Following Aristotle, many philosophers believe that we are required, as a formal principle of justice, to treat similar cases alike except where there is some relevant difference. This principle emphasizes the role of impartiality and consistency in justice, but it is purely formal because we are not told which differences are relevant and which are not. Satisfying this formal requirement, furthermore, does not guarantee that justice is done; for example, by treating like cases similarly a judge can administer non-arbitrarily a law (like an apartheid regulation in South Africa) which is in fact unjust. (Similarly it may be noted that a fair procedure can lead to unjust results, as when a guilty man is mistakenly acquitted by an honest jury, or vice versa, as when the police unscrupulously trick a person who turns out to be guilty into confessing.)

Related to Aristotle's fairness requirement is a third idea commonly bound up with the concept of justice, namely, that of equality. "All persons are morally equal," it is said, and so justice is frequently held to require that our treatment of them reflect this fact. While Aristotle's formal principle of justice does not say whether we are to assume equality of treatment until some difference between cases is shown or to assume the opposite until some relevant similarities are demonstrated, a claim of injustice based on equality is meant to place the burden of proof on those who would endorse unequal treatment.

The demand that equality be respected, though still abstract, does have more content than the two previously mentioned aspects of justice. Even so, to claim simply that all persons are equal is not to establish a relationship between justice and economic distribution. We all believe that *some* differences in the treatment of persons are consistent with equality (punishment, for example), and neither respect for equality nor the requirement of equal treatment implies by itself an egalitarian distribution of economic goods.

Despite equality, then, individual circumstances—in particular, what a person has done—make a difference. We think it is unfair, for example, when a guilty person goes free or an innocent person hangs, regardless of how others have been treated, because the first fails to get his or her due and the second suffers an undeserved fate. This suggests that justice sometimes involves, as a fourth aspect, something beyond equal or even impartial treatment: Justice requires that individuals get what they deserve. But what do people deserve? A substantive theory of justice is needed to answer this as well as to explain when a failure to get what one deserves is a failure of justice. (For example, if I study hard for the exam, while Roger with his photographic memory goofs off all term, it may seem that I deserve to pass more than he. But when Roger breezes through the test and I fail, have I been done an injustice?) Nonetheless, the idea of desert, however it is fleshed out, is frequently tied up with discourse about justice.

SOCIAL AND ECONOMIC JUSTICE

Justice, then, is an important subclass of morality in general, a subclass which generally involves appeals to the overlapping notions of rights, fairness, equality, and desert. Justice is not the only virtue an individual or a social institution can pursue, and many of the most difficult moral dilemmas arise when the requirements of justice conflict with other goods or obligations.

Within the general category of justice, however, further distinctions must be drawn. In particular, many cases of injustice are not instances of *social* injustice. Consider, for example, parents who permit only their favorite daughter to attend college, when it is within their means to send all their children. They behave unfairly, but the injustice in question is not a social injustice. While justice is in a sense a social virtue, since it is a characteristic of our relations with others, the concept of social justice is not used to capture this simple fact. Rather, social justice refers to the *structure* and *policies* of a society, to its political, legal, economic, and social institutions. (Are they fair? Do they violate rights? Do they reflect the equality of citizens?) Thus a constitutional structure that gives undue influence to one group is unjust, as is a policy requiring the registration of Jews. Both cases involve the shared institutions of a society; they are failures of social justice. A corrupt judge who abuses the legal system by throwing an innocent into jail perpetrates a grievous injustice, but such an individual transgression is not a matter of social injustice unless the social system in question tolerates or encourages such corruption.

Justice in general and social justice in particular involve the distribution of benefits and burdens, but distributive justice has come to be synonymous with economic justice, that is, with the distribution of *economic* benefits and burdens. Social justice includes but is not identical to economic justice, although both are concerned in part with how to distribute things that people care about. Political powers and liberties may be distributed unjustly, yet this is not a problem of economic justice as such (unless, perhaps, the political injustice in question results from a particular economic distribution).

Distinguishing the distribution of economic from other social goods goes only part of the way toward defining our subject. Worldwide poverty and starvation, for example, raise serious moral problems involving the distribution of economic goods, yet these problems are not obviously ones of economic *justice* at all. How can this be if, as some philosophers maintain, there is no revelant moral difference between aiding a person in your own town and helping someone overseas?

Some, of course, think that for one person to have more than another is intrinsically unjust, but disparity of wealth itself cannot be the source of the injustice. (Only in a cosmic or poetic sense is it unjust for me to thrive on my Iowa farm while you barely eke out an existence in the Yukon.) If we are to speak of justice at all, there must be some relation between the parties by virtue of which a right is violated or an unfairness done. And furthermore, if we are to speak of hunger overseas as being a matter of social or, more specifically, economic justice for us, the situation must reflect upon the policies or structure of our society as a whole. (Other moral considerations, of course, may oblige us to assist those in need outside our own country, if justice does not.)

However, even if foreign poverty were a matter of economic justice for some wealthy country (perhaps because it enjoys an economically exploitative relation with the countries in question or because its hoarding of resources violates some right of theirs), there would still be the issue of the justice of its own economic institutions as this affects its citizens. The joint enterprises and shared institutions of a society, the economic interrelatedness and mutual dependence of its citizens, and the fact that its members often view themselves as a community of persons who share certain aims and ideals suggest that the question of intra-societal economic distribution is different from moral problems concerning relations between persons in separate societies. In addition, it may be, as some philosophers think, that resolving the former issue will shed light on the latter, just as, in ge·

determining the requirements of justice will take us some way toward understanding our overall moral obligation. In any case, intra-societal economic distribution is the concern of most writers in this volume.

Finally, it is worth noting that the philosophical problem of economic justice is distinct from the numerous empirical problems discussed by economists. The latter are largely concerned to predict outcomes of various economic policies. Important examples are the effect of monetary and fiscal policy on prices and employment, and of tax schedules on capital investment, spending, and saving. Now obviously any philosopher should consider such factors in arguing for a particular conception of economic justice, at least to the extent of ensuring that implementation of a certain philosophy will not have a disastrous economic impact. Still, the point to emphasize here is that the two questions (economic justice and the impact of policies) are distinct. Just as a theory of economic justice must take economics into account, so also it is important that economists should consider philosophy. What use is predicting the effect of policies until it is known what end ought to be sought or what justice requires?

DIFFERENT APPROACHES

How, then, ought economic costs and benefits to be distributed? Although some answers, like "according to race or sex," can surely be ruled out, there is still a wide range of principles that have been offered in answer to this question. Distribution has been recommended in accordance with equality, need, and effort, to name only a few.

Strict equality of income may appear superficially attractive. Yet distribution of society's product according to this criterion would ignore what seem to be morally relevant differences: For example, some people have dependents to feed or large medical bills to pay. A satisfactory principle of equality will surely require that individual circumstances and needs be respected, not denied.

Distribution according to need, however, ignores the question of how much is deserved. A lazy student may need a passing grade more than a diligent one, but his need hardly seems a just basis for his passing. Similarly, that Jones worked hard and Smith did not would seem to be important in determining a just distribution of income. In addition, since no society could hope to satisfy every whim of every person, notorious problems are posed by trying to compare needs between individuals or by trying to discriminate between basic needs and secondary ones (or "true" needs and "false" ones).

Questions of merit and desert are discussed further in Part II, but it is clear that while effort, ability, contribution, or moral merit may seem plausible as a basis of distribution in some circumstances, each faces problems when elevated to *the* principle of economic justice. This has led some philosophers to deny that any single principle of distribution will suffice. Combining two or more criteria, however, into a more complicated principle seems almost as arbitrary—which criteria should one choose and which are to be weighed more heavily? As a result, other philosophers have denied that there is a solution to the issue of distributive justice. The problem is so complicated, they seem to say, that we had best leave things alone.

This skeptical conclusion is inescapable if we continue only to juxtapose or combine simple principles of distribution. The answer will come only if one has recourse to a more general normative theory that provides a theoretical reason to justify a particular economic distribution.

Utilitarianism is one such theory. According to it, the rightness of an action or social policy is determined by its total consequences for all concerned, measured in terms of happiness (or satisfied desires). Justice is not a consideration that is independent of this general principle, and utilitarians would demur to the categorization of justice as a specific realm within morality as a whole. For them there is only one moral issue: Which course of action promotes the greatest sum of happiness for all concerned? Accordingly, the best distribution of economic goods is that which produces more happiness than any other. Which system actually provides this optimal distribution is an empirical question for social scientists to resolve.

Although utilitarianism in its various guises has been popular for over a century, it has been thought by many to be seriously flawed. Utilitarianism, some philosophers charge, does not take seriously enough the differences between persons. The happiness of each person should not count equally in the total, without regard to his or her past behavior. Further, an increase in total happiness might be unfairly purchased at the price of the pain of some innocent individual.

John Rawls is among those contemporary philosophers unhappy with utilitarianism, and his social contract approach is an effort to find an alternative theoretical basis for determining social and economic justice. We are to imagine ourselves in a hypothetical situation, choosing the principles of distribution that will then serve to govern all members of society. In Rawls's view, such a choice should be made without knowledge of one's own race, religion, or social position in order to insure the fairness of the result. It is a hypothetical thought experiment which, he argues, guarantees that whatever principles are chosen are just. Rawls gives the term "difference principle" to the choice which, he contends, would be made by his social contracters—namely, that economic goods should be distributed equally unless an unequal distribution would work to the benefit of all, especially the worst off. Justice for Rawls is not the only focal point of morality, but it is the first virtue of social institutions.

Even philosophers who are dissatisfied with Rawls's approach, his principles of justice, or both acknowledge that he has raised the level of discourse in political philosophy to a new height. Robert Nozick is one of those philosophers, and his disagreements with Rawls set the stage for the discussion of economic justice in this volume. Agreeing only with Rawls's repudiation of utilitarianism, Nozick's libertarian philosophy operates with a radically different conception of the relation of the individual to society. Liberty is the cardinal political virtue. Justice ensures the right of individuals not to be coerced, to be free from the interference of others. Beyond this, justice insists upon little. Whatever economic arrangements individuals freely consent to are just, and Nozick's entitlement theory holds simply that a distribution is just if it results, via gifts or voluntary exchanges, from a prior just distribution. The type of economic system which justice requires is a laissez-faire, free-market system.

This conclusion is rejected by both J. J. C. Smart and R. M. Hare, who present the case for utilitarianism. Although they argue from vastly different theoretical perspectives, they unite in defending utilitarian theory in the face of the rival approaches of Rawls and Nozick. Part I of this book thus presents three major approaches to economic justice that have been exceptionally influential in contemporary political philosophy. Part II proceeds to explore various issues raised by this clash of perspectives, probe shortcomings in the leading theories, and suggest alternative positions. First, however, it will be useful to offer some further, more general reflections on the debate.

REMARKS ON METHODOLOGY

There are three general questions that may be asked about a theory which tries to resolve a moral dispute of this sort. The first is, of course, What answer does the theory offer—what principle of distribution does it recommend? The governing criterion could be one that looks to the past behavior of individuals (effort), their present situation (need), their choices (market distribution), or their structural relations (the difference principle or equality), among other possibilities. Justice might be thought to require a certain distributive result or only a particular process or method of distribution.

There is more than one way, it should be noted, to defend a particular principle or organization of distribution. For example, contemporary libertarians argue for an unregulated, capitalistic market society in terms of rights or liberty, while nineteenth-century friends of laissez faire appealed more to utilitarian considerations. Similarly, Rawls concedes that one might affirm his contract approach but eschew the difference principle, or vice versa.

In evaluating a particular theory one must examine, secondly, how it approaches the problem of choosing a criterion of distribution. For instance, does the theory recommend that one decide how goods ought to be distributed according to the consequences of the distribution, or does it take the acknowledgment of rights or the following of certain moral rules as essential? The former, teleological, view (sometimes called "consequentialism") would contend that the right or just principle is to be chosen on the basis of its having the best consequences. Of course, any such theory, if it is ever to get off the ground, also needs to specify which consequences are good and should be aimed at. Utilitarianism is the best known and most widely accepted teleological theory; it holds, as we said before, that maximization of happiness is the goal that should be pursued. Other teleological views might wish to promote some other end—for example, religious faithfulness or human excellence—and would argue for criteria of distribution that realize that good.

The other type of approach that a theory might adopt is a "deontological" one. Here, rather than justifying a distribution pattern by appealing to its consequences, the theory claims that rules (or alternatively, rights of persons) ought to be respected in distributing economic goods. As with the dispute among teleological theories over what good to promote, deontologists disagree widely over which rights or rules are to count and how much. Some may value greatly the right to inherit property, for example, while others discount it in favor of principles that emphasize the importance of work as a means to acquire income justly.

Depending on whether the theory one accepts is teleological (looking to realize the best outcome) or deontological (protecting rights or following moral rules) in its approach, one will perceive economic justice very differently. Of the major approaches included here, only utilitarianism is fully teleological while libertarianism and Rawls's social contract are deontological theories.

The third question that it is useful to keep in mind when considering a particular theory of justice is the basis on which it defends its answer. Philosophers have argued in favor of their theories, and thus the specific principles of distribution that those theories endorse, in very different ways.

One approach, as we have seen, is that of Rawls's hypothetical social contract. But why should principles chosen by imaginary persons in a hypothetical original position carry any weight with real persons in a real society? Rawls's basic answer is that the initial position, as he describes it, represents a situation of fairness; upon philosophical reflection we will come to agree, he believes, that what rational self-interested persons decide under these conditions does illuminate the nature of justice. Furthermore, the principles chosen accord well with our considered intuitions about justice. The theoretical construction that generates Rawls's principles is thus anchored in our existing judgments of what constitutes justice.

Nozick, it seems, has rather different intuitions about justice and a contrasting vision of the purpose and role of society. The right not to have others interfere in one's life is taken as fundamental. Whatever persons consent to is just, and any coercion is illegitimate. The relevant standard of comparison for evaluating social institutions is an imaginary state of nature, a prepolitical world of autonomous individuals. Persons are seen as having certain natural rights, including the right to property, which are logically prior to society and which must be respected if we are to treat individuals as ends in themselves and not means in the projects of others. While Rawls's social contract emphasizes the fairness of the society established in contract, Nozick and other libertarians see as just those arrangements which result from the uncoerced choices and agreements of actual individuals. Such a theory begins with a strong intuition about the primacy of liberty and then paints an attractive picture of the world in which the right of noncoercion is treated as the basic good. On the strength of this, libertarians hope to persuade us to revise some of our previous ideas about what justice requires in the economic realm.

Both Rawls and Nozick rely on moral intuitions to some extent, and Smart defends utilitarianism solely by appeal to our natural feelings of benevolence, which should, in his view, lead us to adopt the utilitarian principle. But what is "intuition"? Intuitions, as contemporary moral philosophers use the term, are essentially moral attitudes or judgments that we feel fairly sure are correct. These may be of two types: intuitions about particular cases (taking your neighbor's car without consent in order to go to the January sales is wrong) or about general moral principles (theft is wrong). Intuitions are used to arrive at answers to disputed problems like economic justice by showing that a certain principle is more consistent with our intuitions about particular cases than any alternative, and then employing that principle in turn to resolve moral issues about which our intuitions are uncertain. In this way our given moral beliefs are extended to cover more difficult cases. On the other hand, very firm intuitions about individual cases may be used to jettison a generally plausible moral principle when it is discovered to conflict with these particular judgments.

Many moral philosophers today see ethical theory as a matter of working back and forth between our moral intuitions about particular cases and the general principles that account for those particular judgments or are themselves intuitively attractive, in order to weave our moral thinking into a coherent and consistent web. R. M. Hare, however, rejects this approach, taking an essentially skeptical view of moral intuition as a basis for moral theory. Such attitudes, learned at society's knee, as it were, are subject to all the prejudices and inconsistencies ever held by a parent.

Hare argues that by paying close attention to the uses and logical implications of ethical language, we can go a long way toward resolving moral issues like that of economic justice. An understanding of the functioning of moral language and of the requirements of logical consistency supports a utilitarian approach which can, when supplemented by certain factual claims, lead us to affirm egalitarian conclusions concerning economic distribution.

We have, then, several very different approaches to distributive justice, and choosing between rival methods and theories is not easy. At various points in each essay, the writer provides some justification for the claim that conclusions reached by his theoretical method are for that reason worthy of belief. These arguments are all-important in evaluating each alternative. Furthermore, considerations are advanced against competing theories and rival approaches. Thus Hare argues against reliance on intuition, Nozick against social contract theory, and both Rawls and Nozick against utilitarianism.

We can see now that each theory is a complex blend of specific normative conclusions about economic justice, more general normative principles, and rather abstract metaethical considerations. So in our effort to determine what is a just distribution of economic benefits and burdens—and to justify our conclusion—we are led back to very serious and profound philosophical issues. The place to begin answering for ourselves the problem of economic justice is with a study of the three major contemporary approaches to the issue presented in Part I.

PART I
The Major Approaches

THE SOCIAL CONTRACT

Social contract is the name given to an important tradition in political philosophy, one with roots in ancient Greek and medieval thought but which blossomed in the seventeenth and eighteenth centuries. Hobbes, Locke, Rousseau, Kant, and others, all in rather different ways, used the notion of a social contract. It was also an important part of the political view of the writers of the Declaration of Independence.

Traditionally, social contract theorists have hypothesized the existence of a presocial, prepolitical stage of human existence, a "state of nature" prior to the uniting of individuals in society. These autonomous persons are then seen as coming together to determine the principles and organizational form of their social union—that is, to agree on a social contract. Individuals with certain rights and interests are, in this view, logically prior to society, and society is in turn the result of the covenant of these individuals. The legitimacy of government derives, thus, from the consent of the governed, and the social contract approach provides a vehicle for attempting to specify the proper role of government, its purpose and limits.

John Rawls, as we have mentioned, returns to the social contract tradition in an effort to develop a conception of justice, and indeed a basis for political philosophy, which does not rest solely on intuition, yet is distinct from utilitarianism. For him, the contract is only a *hypothetical* construction. Neither a prehistorical state of nature nor an actual contract situation is suggested. He is concerned, rather, with what principles free and rational persons would choose to govern their basic social and political institutions if they were brought together in an imaginary "original position" for this purpose.

In Rawls's view, society is to be seen as a "cooperative venture for mutual advantage," and one should imagine the individuals in the hypothetical original position as choosing, in an initial situation of equality and fairness, those principles most in accord with their rational self-interest. These people do not choose the principles they do because they believe them to be just. They are concerned with their share of the primary social goods (including wealth, power, self-respect, and liberty) and seek to look after their own interests. The principles chosen are principles of justice because they would be chosen by such persons under the (fair) conditions of the original position.

These conditions are elaborated by Rawls in the following selections. One crucial feature of the original position is that its participants are ignorant of their personal characteristics and endowments, their social position, and their historical period. If the procedure is to be fair, none of these things, argues Rawls, should be known. This "veil of ignorance" makes the decision impartial and, thus, unanimity possible. Since the conditions and constraints on the original position are, in Rawls's view, fair, the principles chosen have a certain justification. In addition, the principles are thought by Rawls to conform with our considered convictions or intuitions about justice.

Under conditions of ignorance, a rational person in the original position would reason conservatively. Not knowing his or her particular situation, one would wish to reduce one's loss in the event of the worst possible outcome. Thus, Rawls contends, a person in the original position would choose the general principle that all social values—including liberty, income, and opportunity—be distributed equally unless an unequal distribution of these goods is to everyone's advantage. Under appropriate conditions of material well-being, the general conception yields to the "special conception" of justice, composed of two principles. The first, which has priority over the second, calls for as extensive a system of equal liberty as possible. The second guarantees equality of opportunity and requires that any social and economic inequalities benefit the least advantaged. Contrary to utilitarianism, it is not enough that inequalities increase the total social good; they must work to the favor of the least advantaged members of society.

A virtue of the two principles, according to Rawls, is their acceptability once the veil of ignorance is lifted. In contrast again to utilitarianism, they are thought by him to be principles to which the participants could remain committed no matter what their situation in society. Their implementation would result in both a stable society and one that promotes the self-respect of its citizens. The type of economic system that would be best in this society is, Rawls says, for social scientists to determine; but he does believe that a regime of either welfare capitalism or democratic socialism could realize his two principles of justice.

John Rawls
A Theory of Justice

AN OVERVIEW OF THE THEORY

The Subject of Justice

Many different kinds of things are said to be just and unjust: not only laws, institutions, and social systems, but also particular actions of many kinds, including decisions, judgments, and imputations. We also call the attitudes and dispositions of persons, and persons themselves, just and unjust. Our topic, however, is that of social justice. For us the primary subject of justice is the basic structure of society, or more exactly, the way in which the major social institutions distribute fundamental rights and duties and determine the division of advantages from social cooperation. By major institutions I understand the political constitution and the principal economic and social arrangements. Thus the legal protection of freedom of thought and liberty of conscience, competitive markets, private property in the means of production, and the monogamous family are examples of major social institutions. Taken together as one scheme, the major institutions define men's rights and duties and influence their life-prospects, what they can expect to be and how well they can hope to do. The basic structure is the primary subject of justice because its effects are so profound and present from the start. The intuitive notion here is that this structure contains various social positions and that men born into different positions have different expectations of life determined, in part, by the political system as well as by economic and social circumstances. In this way the institutions of society favor certain starting places over others. These are especially deep inequalities. Not only are they pervasive, but they affect men's initial chances in life; yet they cannot possibly be justified by an appeal to the notions of merit or desert. It is these inequalities, presumably inevitable in the basic structure of any society, to which the principles of social justice must in the first instance apply. These principles, then, regulate the choice of a political constitution and the main elements of the economic and social system. The justice of a social scheme depends essentially on how fundamental rights and duties are assigned and on the economic opportunities and social conditions in the various sectors of society. . . .

The Main Idea of the Theory of Justice

My aim is to present a conception of justice which generalizes and carries to a higher level of abstraction the familiar theory of the social contract as found, say, in Locke, Rousseau, and Kant.[1] In order to do this we are not to think of the original contract as one to enter a particular society or to set up a particular form of government. Rather, the guiding idea is that the principles of justice for the basic structure of society are the object of the original agreement. They are the principles that free and rational persons concerned to further their own interests would accept in an initial position of equality as defining the fundamental terms of their association. These principles are to regulate all further agreements: they specify the kinds of social cooperation that can be entered into and the forms of government that can be established. This way of regarding the principles of justice I shall call justice as fairness.

Thus we are to imagine that those who engage in social cooperation choose together, in one joint act, the principles which are to assign basic rights and duties and to determine the division of social benefits. Men are to decide in advance how they are to regulate their claims against one another and what is to be the foundation charter of their society. Just as each person must decide by rational reflection what constitutes his good, that is, the system of ends which it is rational for him to pursue, so a group of persons must decide once and for all what is to count among them as just and unjust. The choice which rational men would make in this hypothetical situation of equal liberty, assuming for the present that this choice problem has a solution, determines the principles of justice.

In justice as fairness the original position of equality corresponds to the state of nature in the traditional theory of the social contract. This original position is not, of course, thought of as an actual historical state of affairs, much less as a primitive condition of culture. It is understood as a purely hypothetical situation characterized so as to lead to a certain conception of justice.[2] Among the essential features of this situation is that no one knows his place in society, his class position or social status, nor does any one know his fortune in the distribution of natural assets and abilities, his intelligence, strength, and the like. I shall even assume that the parties do not know their conceptions of the good or their special psychological propensities. The principles of justice are chosen behind a veil of ignorance. This ensures that no one is advantaged or disadvantaged in the choice of principles by the outcome of natural chance or the contingency of social circumstances. Since all are similarly situated and no one is able to design principles to favor his particular condition, the principles of justice are the result of a fair agreement or bargain. For given the circumstances of the original position, the symmetry of everyone's relations to each other, this initial situation is fair between individuals as moral persons, that is, as rational beings with their own ends and capable, I shall assume, of a sense of justice. The original position is, one might say, the appropriate initial status quo, and thus the fundamental agreements reached in it are fair. This explains the propriety of the name "justice as fairness": it conveys the idea that the principles of justice are agreed to in an initial situation that is fair. The name does not mean that the concepts of justice and fairness are the same, any more than the phrase "poetry as metaphor" means that the concepts of poetry and metaphor are the same.

Justice as fairness begins, as I have said, with one of the most general of all choices which persons might make together, namely, with the choice of the first principles of a conception of justice which is to regulate all subsequent criticism and reform of institutions. Then, having chosen a conception of justice, we can suppose that they are to choose a constitution and a legislature to enact laws, and so on, all in accordance with the principles of justice initially agreed upon. Our social situation is just if it is such that by this sequence of hypothetical agreements we would have contracted into the general system of rules which defines it. Moreover, assuming that the original position does determine a set of principles (that is, that a particular conception of justice would be chosen), it will then be true that whenever social institutions satisfy these principles those engaged in them can say to one another that they are cooperating on terms to which they would agree if they were free and equal persons whose relations with respect to one another were fair. They could all view their arrangements as meeting the stipulations which they would acknowledge in an initial situation that embodies widely accepted and reasonable constraints on the choice of principles. The general recognition of this fact would provide the basis for a public acceptance of the corresponding principles of justice. No society can, of course, be a scheme of cooperation which men enter voluntarily in a literal sense; each person finds himself placed at birth in some particular position in some particular society, and the nature of this position materially affects his life prospects. Yet a society satisfying the principles of justice as fairness comes as close as a society can to being a voluntary scheme, for it meets the principles which free and equal persons would assent to under circumstances that are fair. In this sense its members are autonomous and the obligations they recognize self-imposed.

One feature of justice as fairness is to think of the parties in the initial situation as rational and mutually disinterested. This does not mean that the parties are egoists, that is, individuals with only certain kinds of interests, say in wealth, prestige, and domination. But they are conceived as not taking an interest in one another's interests. They are to presume that even their spiritual aims may be opposed, in the way that the aims of those of different religions may be opposed. Moreover, the concept of rationality must be interpreted as far as possible in the narrow sense, standard in economic theory, of taking the most effective means to given ends. I shall modify this concept to some extent, as explained later, but one must try to avoid introducing into it any controversial ethical elements. The initial situation must be characterized by stipulations that are widely accepted.

In working out the conception of justice as fairness one main task clearly is to determine which principles of justice would be chosen in the original position. To do this we must describe this situation in some detail and formulate with care the problem of choice which it presents. These matters I shall take up in the immediately succeeding chapters. It may be observed, however, that once the principles of justice are thought of as arising from an original agreement in a situation of equality, it is an open question whether the principle of utility would be acknowledged. Offhand it hardly seems likely that persons who view themselves as equals, entitled to press their claims upon one another, would agree to a principle which may require lesser life prospects for some simply for the sake of a greater sum of advantages enjoyed by others. Since each desires to protect his interests, his capacity to advance his conception of the good, no one has a reason to acquiesce in an enduring loss for himself in order to bring about a greater net balance of satisfaction. In the absence of strong and lasting benevolent impulses, a rational man would not accept a basic structure merely because it maximized the algebraic sum of advantages irrespective of its permanent effects on his own basic rights and interests. Thus it seems that the principle of utility is incompatible with the conception of social cooperation among equals for mutual advantage. It appears to be inconsistent with the idea of reciprocity implicit in the notion of a well-ordered society. Or, at any rate, so I shall argue.

I shall maintain instead that the persons in the initial situation would choose two rather different principles: the first requires equality in the assignment of basic rights and duties, while the second holds that social and economic inequalities, for example inequalities of wealth and authority, are just only if they result in compensating benefits for everyone, and in particular for the least advantaged members of society. These principles rule out justifying institutions on the grounds that the hardships of some are offset by a greater good in the aggregate. It may be expedient but it is not just that some should have less in order that others may prosper. But there is no injustice in the greater benefits earned by a few provided that the situation of persons not so fortunate is thereby improved. The intuitive idea is that since everyone's well-being depends upon a scheme of cooperation without which no one could have a satisfactory life, the division of advantages should be such as to draw forth the willing cooperation of everyone taking part in it, including those less well situated. Yet this can be expected only if reasonable terms are proposed. The two principles mentioned seem to be a fair agreement on the basis of which those better endowed, or more fortunate in their social position, neither of which we can be said to deserve, could expect the willing cooperation of others when some workable scheme is a necessary condition of the welfare of all. Once we decide to look for a conception of justice that nullifies the accidents of natural endowment and the contingencies of social circumstance as counters in quest for political and economic advantage, we are led to these principles. They express the result of leaving aside those aspects of the social world that seem arbitrary from a moral point of view.

The problem of the choice of principles, however, is extremely difficult. I do not expect the answer I shall suggest to be convincing to everyone. It is, therefore, worth noting from the outset that justice as fairness, like other contract views, consists of two parts: (1) an interpretation of the initial situation and of the problem of choice posed there, and (2) a set of principles which, it is argued, would be agreed to. One may accept the first part of the theory (or some variant thereof), but not the other, and conversely. The concept of the initial contractual situation may seem reasonable although the particular principles proposed are rejected. To be sure, I want to maintain that the most appropriate conception of this situation does lead to principles of justice contrary to utilitarianism and perfectionism, and therefore that the contract doctrine provides an alternative to these views. Still, one may dispute this contention even though one grants that the contractarian method is a useful way of studying ethical theories and of setting forth their underlying assumptions.

Justice as fairness is an example of what I have called a contract theory. Now there may be an objection to the term "contract" and related expressions, but I think it will serve reasonably well. Many words have misleading connotations which at first are likely to confuse. The terms "utility" and "utilitarianism" are surely no exception. They too have unfortunate suggestions which hostile critics have been willing to exploit; yet they are clear enough for those prepared to study utilitarian doctrine. The same should be true of the term "contract" applied to moral theories. As I have mentioned, to understand it one has to keep in mind that it implies a certain level of abstraction. In particular, the content of the relevant agreement is not to enter a given society or to adopt a given form of government, but to accept certain moral principles. Moreover, the undertakings referred to are purely hypothetical: a contract view holds that certain principles would be accepted in a well-defined initial situation.

The merit of the contract terminology is that it conveys the idea that principles of justice may be conceived as principles that would be chosen by rational persons, and that in this way conceptions of justice may be explained and justified. The theory of justice is a part, perhaps the most significant part, of the theory of rational choice. Furthermore, principles of justice deal with conflicting claims upon the advantages won by social cooperation; they apply to the relations among several persons or groups. The word "contract" suggests this plurality as well as the condition that the appropriate division of advantages must be in accordance with principles acceptable to all parties. The condition of publicity for principles of justice is also connoted by the contract phraseology. Thus, if these principles are the outcome of an agreement, citizens have a knowledge of the principles that others follow. It is characteristic of contract theories to stress the public nature of political principles. Finally there is the long tradition of the contract doctrine. Expressing the tie with this line of thought helps to define ideas and accords with natural piety. There are then several advantages in the use of the term "contract." With due precautions taken, it should not be misleading. . . .

The Original Position and Justification

I have said that the original position is the appropriate initial status quo which insures that the fundamental agreements reached in it are fair. This fact yields the name "justice as fairness." It is clear, then, that I want to say that one conception of justice is more reasonable than another, or justifiable with respect to it, if rational persons in the initial situation would choose its principles over those of the other for the role of justice. Conceptions of justice are to be ranked by their acceptability to persons so circumstanced. Understood in this way the question of justification is settled by working out a problem of deliberation: we have to ascertain which principles it would be rational to adopt given the contractual situation. This connects the theory of justice with the theory of rational choice.

If this view of the problem of justification is to succeed, we must, of course, describe in some detail the nature of this choice problem. A problem of rational decision has a definite answer only if we know the beliefs and interests of the parties, their relations with respect to one another, the alternatives between which they are to choose, the procedure whereby they make up their minds, and so on. As the circumstances are presented in different ways, correspondingly different principles are accepted. The concept of the original position, as I shall refer to it, is that of the most philosophically favored interpretation of this initial choice situation for the purposes of a theory of justice.

But how are we to decide what is the most favored interpretation? I assume, for one thing, that there is a broad measure of agreement that principles of justice should be chosen under certain conditions. To justify a particular description of the initial situation one shows that it incorporates these commonly shared presumptions. One argues from widely accepted but weak premises to more specific conclusions. Each of the presumptions should by itself be natural and plausible; some of them may seem innocuous or even trivial. The aim of the contract approach is to establish that taken together they impose significant bounds on acceptable principles of justice. The ideal outcome would be that these conditions determine a unique set of principles; but I shall be satisfied if they suffice to rank the main traditional conceptions of social justice.

One should not be misled, then, by the somewhat unusual conditions which characterize the original position. The idea here is simply to make vivid to ourselves the restrictions that it seems reasonable to impose on arguments for principles of justice, and therefore on these principles themselves. Thus it seems reasonable and generally acceptable that no one should be advantaged or disadvantaged by natural fortune or social circumstances in the choice of principles. It also seems widely agreed that it should be impossible to tailor principles to the circumstances of one's own case. We should insure further that particular inclinations and aspirations, and persons' conceptions of their good do not affect the principles adopted. The aim is to rule out those principles that it would be rational to propose for acceptance, however little the chance of success, only if one knew certain things that are irrelevant from the standpoint of justice. For example, if a man knew that he was wealthy, he might find it rational to advance the principle that various taxes for welfare measures be counted unjust; if he knew that he was poor, he would most likely propose the contrary principle. To represent the desired restrictions one imagines a situation in which everyone is deprived of this sort of information. One excludes the knowledge of those contingencies which sets men at odds and allows them to be guided by their prejudices. In this manner the veil of ignorance is arrived at in a natural way. This concept should cause no difficulty if we keep in mind the constraints on arguments that it is meant to express. At any time we can enter the original position, so to speak, simply by following a certain procedure, namely, by arguing for principles of justice in accordance with these restrictions.

It seems reasonable to suppose that the parties in the original position are equal. That is, all have the same rights in the procedure for choosing principles; each can make proposals, submit reasons for their acceptance, and so on. Obviously the purpose of these conditions is to represent equality between human beings as moral persons, as creatures having a conception of their good and capable of a sense of justice. The basis of equality is taken to be similarity in these two respects. Systems of ends are not ranked in value; and each man is presumed to have the requisite ability to understand and to act upon whatever principles are adopted. Together with the veil of ignorance, these conditions define the principles of justice as those which rational persons concerned to advance their interests would consent to as equals when none are known to be advantaged or disadvantaged by social and natural contingencies.

There is, however, another side to justifying a particular description of the original position. This is to see if the principles which would be chosen match our considered convictions of justice or extend them in an acceptable way. We can note whether applying these principles would lead us to make the same judgments about the basic structure of society which we now make intuitively and in which we have the greatest confidence; or whether, in cases where our present judgments are in doubt and given with hesitation, these principles offer a resolution which we can affirm on reflection. There are questions which we feel sure must be answered in a certain way. For example, we are confident that religious intolerance and racial discrimination are unjust. We think that we have examined these things with care and have reached what we believe is an impartial judgment not likely to be distorted by an excessive attention to our own interests. These convictions are provisional fixed points which we presume any conception of justice must fit. But we have much less assurance as to what is the correct distribution of wealth and authority. Here we may be looking for a way to remove our doubts. We can check an interpretation of the initial situation, then, by the capacity of its principles to accommodate our firmest convictions and to provide guidance where guidance is needed.

In searching for the most favored description of this situation we work from both ends. We begin by describing it so that it represents generally shared and preferably weak conditions. We then see if these conditions are strong enough to yield a significant set of principles. If not, we look for further premises equally reasonable. But if so, and these principles match our considered convictions of justice, then so far well and good. But presumably there will be discrepancies. In this case we have a choice. We can either modify the account of the initial situation or we can revise our existing judgments, for even the judgments we take provisionally as fixed points are liable to revision. By going back and forth, sometimes altering the conditions of the contractual circumstances, at others withdrawing our judgments and conforming them to principle, I assume that eventually we shall find a description of the initial situation that both expresses reasonable conditions and yields principles which match our considered judgments duly pruned and adjusted. This state of affairs I refer to as reflective equilibrium[3]. It is an equilibrium because at last our principles and judgments coincide; and it is reflective since we know to what principles our judgments conform and the premises of their derivation. At the moment everything is in order. But this equilibrium is not necessarily stable. It is liable to be upset by further examination of the conditions which should be imposed on the contractual situation and by particular cases which may lead us to revise our judgments. Yet for the time being we have done what we can to render coherent and to justify our convictions of social justice. We have reached a conception of the original position.

I shall not, of course, actually work through this process. Still, we may think of the interpretation of the original position that I shall present as the result of such a hypothetical course of reflection. It represents the attempt to accommodate within one scheme both reasonable philosophical conditions on principles as well as our considered judgments of justice. In arriving at the favored interpretation of the initial situation there is no point at which an appeal is made to self-evidence in the traditional sense either of general conceptions or particular convictions. I do not claim for the principles of justice proposed that they are necessary truths or derivable from such truths. A conception of justice cannot be deduced from self-evident premises or conditions on principles; instead, its justification is a matter of the mutual support of many considerations, of everything fitting together into one coherent view.

A final comment. We shall want to say that certain principles of justice are justified because they would be agreed to in an initial situation of equality. I have emphasized that this original position is purely hypothetical. It is natural to ask why, if this agreement is never actually entered into, we should take any interest in these principles, moral or otherwise. The answer is that the conditions embodied in the description of the original position are ones that we do in fact accept. Or if we do not, then perhaps we can be persuaded to do so by philosophical reflection. Each aspect of the contractual situation can be given supporting grounds. Thus what we shall do is to collect together into one conception a number of conditions on principles that we are ready upon due consideration to recognize as reasonable. These constraints express what we are prepared to regard as limits on fair terms of social cooperation. One way to look at the idea of the original position, therefore, is to see it as an expository device which sums up the meaning of these conditions and helps us to extract their consequences. On the other hand, this conception is also an intuitive notion that suggests its own elaboration, so that led on by it we are drawn to define more clearly the standpoint from which we can best interpret moral relationships. We need a conception that enables us to envision our objective from afar: the intuitive notion of the original position is to do this for us. . . .

The Veil of Ignorance

The idea of the original position is to set up a fair procedure so that any principles agreed to will be just. The aim is to use the notion of pure procedural justice as a basis of theory. Somehow we must nullify the effects of specific contingencies which put men at odds and tempt them to exploit social and natural circumstances to their own advantage. Now in order to do this I assume that the parties are situated behind a veil of ignorance. They do not know how the various alternatives will affect their own particular case and they are obliged to evaluate principles solely on the basis of general considerations.[1]

It is assumed, then, that the parties do not know certain kinds of particular facts. First of all, no one knows his place in society, his class position or social status; nor does he know his fortune in the distribution of natural assets and abilities, his intelligence and strength, and the like. Nor, again, does anyone know his conception of the good, the particulars of his rational plan of life, or even the special features of his psychology such as his aversion to risk or liability to optimism or pessimism. More than this, I assume that the parties do not know the particular circumstances of their own society. That is, they do not know its economic or political situation, or the level of civilization and culture it has been able to achieve. The persons in the original position have no information as to which generation they belong. These broader restrictions on knowledge are appropriate in part because questions of social justice arise between generations as well as within them, for example, the question of the appropriate rate of capital saving and of the conservation of natural resources and the environment of nature. There is also, theoretically anyway, the question of a reasonable genetic policy. In these cases too, in order to carry through the idea of the original position, the parties must not know the contingencies that set them in opposition. They must choose principles the consequences of which they are prepared to live with whatever generation they turn out to belong to.

As far as possible, then, the only particular facts which the parties know is that their society is subject to the circumstances of justice and whatever this implies. It is taken for granted, however, that they know the general facts about human society. They understand political affairs and the principles of economic theory; they know the basis of social organization and the laws of human psychology. Indeed, the parties are presumed to know whatever general facts affect the choice of the principles of justice. There are no limitations on general information, that is, on general laws and theories, since conceptions of justice must be adjusted to the characteristics of the systems of social cooperation which they are to regulate, and there is no reason to rule out these facts. It is, for example, a consideration against a conception of justice that in view of the laws of moral psychology, men would not acquire a desire to act upon it even when the institutions of their society satisfied it. For in this case there would be difficulty in securing the stability of social operation. It is an important feature of a conception of justice that it should generate its own support. That is, its principles should be such that when they are embodied in the basic structure of society men tend to acquire the corresponding sense of justice. Given the principles of moral learning, men develop a desire to act in accordance with its principles. In this case a conception of justice is stable. This kind of general information is admissible in the original position.

The notion of the veil of ignorance raises several difficulties. Some may object that the exclusion of nearly all particular information makes it difficult to grasp what is meant by the original position. Thus it may be helpful to observe that one or more persons can at any time enter this position, or perhaps, better, simulate the deliberations of this hypothetical situation, simply by reasoning in accordance with the appropriate restrictions. In arguing for a conception of justice we must be sure that it is among the permitted alternatives and satisfies the stipulated formal constraints. No considerations can be advanced in its favor unless they would be rational ones for us to urge were we to lack the kind of knowledge that is excluded. The evaluation of principles must proceed in terms of the general consequences of their public recognition and universal application, it being assumed that they will be complied with by everyone. To say that a certain conception of justice would be chosen in the original position is equivalent to saying that rational deliberation satisfying certain conditions and restrictions would reach a certain conclusion. If necessary, the argument to this result could be set out more formally. I shall, however, speak throughout in terms of the notion of the original position. It is more economical and suggestive, and brings out certain essential features that otherwise one might easily overlook. . . .

Thus there follows the very important consequence that the parties have no basis for bargaining in the usual sense. No one knows his situation in society nor his natural assets, and therefore no one is in a position to tailor principles to his advantage. We might imagine that one of the contractees threatens to hold out unless the others agree to principles favorable to him. But how does he know which principles are especially in his interests? The same holds for the formation of coalitions: if a group were to decide to band together to the disadvantage of the others, they would not know how to favor themselves in the choice of principles. Even if they could get everyone to agree to their proposal, they would have no assurance that it was to their advantage, since they cannot identify themselves either by name or description. . . .

The restrictions on particular information in the original position are, then, of fundamental importance. Without them we would not be able to work out any definite theory of justice at all. We would have to be content with a vague formula stating that justice is what would be agreed to without being able to say much, if anything, about the substance of the agreement itself. The formal constraints of the concept of right, those applying to principles directly, are not sufficient for our purpose. The veil of ignorance makes possible a unanimous choice of a particular conception of justice. Without these limitations on knowledge the bargaining problem of the original position would be hopelessly complicated. Even if theoretically a solution were to exist, we would not, at present anyway, be able to determine it. . . .

The Rationality of the Parties

I have assumed throughout that the persons in the original position are rational. In choosing between principles each tries as best he can to advance his interests. But I have also assumed that the parties do not know their conception of the good. This means that while they know that they have some rational plan of life, they do not know the details of this plan, the particular ends and interests which it is calculated to promote. How, then, can they decide which conceptions of justice are most to their advantage? Or must we suppose that they are reduced to mere guessing? To meet this difficulty, I postulate. . . that they would prefer more primary social goods rather than less [i.e., rights and liberties, powers and opportunities, income and wealth and self-respect]. . . . Of course, it may turn out once the veil of ignorance is removed, that some of them for religious or other reasons may not, in fact, want more of these goods. But from the standpoint of the original position, it is rational for the parties to suppose that they do want a larger share, since in any case they are not compelled to accept more if they do not wish to nor does a person suffer from a greater liberty. Thus even though the parties are deprived of information about their particular ends, they have enough knowledge to rank the alternatives. They know that in general they must try to protect their liberties, widen their opportunities, and enlarge their means for promoting their aims whatever these are. Guided by the theory of the good and the general facts of moral psychology, their deliberations are no longer guesswork. They can make a rational decision in the ordinary sense. . . .

The assumption of mutually disinterested rationality, then, comes to this: the persons in the original position try to acknowledge principles which advance their system of ends as far as possible. They do this by attempting to win for themselves the highest index of primary social goods, since this enables them to promote their conception of the good most effectively whatever it turns out to be. The parties do not seek to confer benefits or to impose injuries on one another; they are not moved by affection or rancor. Nor do they try to gain relative to each other; they are not envious or vain. Put in terms of a game, we might say: they strive for as high an absolute score as possible. They do not wish a high or a low score for their opponents, nor do they seek to maximize or minimize the difference between their successes and those of others. The idea of a game does not really apply, since the parties are not concerned to win but to get as many points as possible judged by their own system of ends. . . .

Once we consider the idea of a contract theory it is tempting to think that it will not yield the principles we want unless the parties are to some degree at least moved by benevolence, or an interest in one another's interests. . . . Now the combination of mutual disinterest and the veil of ignorance achieves the same purpose as benevolence. For this combination of conditions forces each person in the original position to take the good of others into account. In justice as fairness, then, the effects of good will are brought about by several conditions working jointly. The feeling that this conception of justice is egoistic is an illusion fostered by looking at but one of the elements of the original position. Furthermore, this pair of assumptions has enormous advantages over that of benevolence plus knowledge. As I have noted, the latter is so complex that no definite theory at all can be worked out. Not only are the complications caused by so much information insurmountable, but the motivational assumption requires clarification. For example, what is the relative strength of benevolent desires? In brief, the combination of mutual disinterestedness plus the veil of ignorance has the merits of simplicity and clarity while at the same time insuring the effects of what are at first sight morally more attractive assumptions. And if it is asked why one should not postulate benevolence with the veil of ignorance the answer is that there is no need for so strong a condition. Moreover, it would defeat the purpose of grounding the theory of justice on weak stipulations, as well as being incongruous with the circumstances of justice. . . .

THE PRINCIPLES OF JUSTICE

Two Principles of Justice

I shall now state in a provisional form the two principles of justice that I believe would be chosen in the original position. In this section I wish to make only the most general comments, and therefore the first formulation of these principles is tentative. As we go on I shall run through several formulations and approximate step by step the final statement to be given much later. I believe that doing this allows the exposition to proceed in a natural way.

The first statement of the two principles reads as follows.

> First: each person is to have an equal right to the most extensive basic liberty compatible with a similar liberty for others.
> Second: social and economic inequalities are to be arranged so that they are both (a) reasonably expected to be to everyone's advantage, and (b) attached to positions and offices open to all.

There are two ambiguous phrases in the second principle, namely "everyone's advantage" and "equally open to all." Determining their sense more exactly will lead to a second formulation of the principle. . . .

By way of general comment, these principles primarily apply, as I have said, to the basic structure of society. They are to govern the assignment of rights and duties and to regulate the distribution of social and economic advantages. As their formulation suggests, these principles presuppose that the social structure can be divided into two more or less distinct parts, the first principle applying to the one, the second to the other. They distinguish between those aspects of the social system that define and secure the equal liberties of citizenship and those that specify and establish social and economic inequalities. The basic liberties of citizens are, roughly speaking, political liberty (the right to vote and to be eligible for public office) together with freedom of speech and assembly; liberty of conscience and freedom of thought; freedom of the person along with the right to hold (personal) property; and freedom from arbitrary arrest and seizure as defined by the concept of the rule of law. These liberties are all required to be equal by the first principle, since citizens of a just society are to have the same basic rights.

The second principle applies, in the first approximation, to the distribution of income and wealth and to the design of organizations that make use of differences in authority and responsibility, or chains of command. While the distribution of wealth and income need not be equal, it must be to everyone's advantage, and at the same time, positions of authority and offices of command must be accessible to all. One applies the second principle by holding positions open, and then, subject to this constraint, arranges social and economic inequalities so that everyone benefits.

These principles are to be arranged in a serial order with the first principle prior to the second. This ordering means that a departure from the institutions of equal liberty required by the first principle cannot be justified by, or compensated for, by greater social and economic advantages. The distribution of wealth and income, and the hierarchies of authority, must be consistent with both the liberties of equal citizenship and equality of opportunity.

It is clear that these principles are rather specific in their content, and their acceptance rests on certain assumptions that I must eventually try to explain and justify. A theory of justice depends upon a theory of society in ways that will become evident as we proceed. For the present, it should be observed that the two principles (and this holds for all formulations) are a special case of a more general conception of justice that can be expressed as follows.

> All social values—liberty and opportunity, income and wealth, and the bases of self-respect—are to be distributed equally unless an unequal distribution of any, or all, of these values is to everyone's advantage.

Injustice, then, is simply inequalities that are not to the benefit of all. Of course, this conception is extremely vague and requires interpretation.

As a first step, suppose that the basic structure of society distributes certain primary goods, that is, things that every rational man is presumed to want. These goods normally have a use whatever a person's rational plan of life. For simplicity, assume that the chief primary goods at the disposition of society are rights and liberties, powers and opportunities, income and wealth. (Later on in Part Three the primary good of self-respect has a central place.) These are the social primary goods. Other primary goods such as health and vigor, intelligence and imagination, are natural goods; although their possession is influenced by the basic structure, they are not so directly under its control. Imagine, then, a hypothetical initial arrangement in which all the social primary goods are equally distributed: everyone has similar rights and duties, and income and wealth are evenly shared. This state of affairs provides a benchmark for judging improvements. If certain inequalities of wealth and organizational powers would make everyone better off than in this hypothetical starting situation, then they accord with the general conception.

Now it is possible, at least theoretically, that by giving up some of their fundamental liberties men are sufficiently compensated by the resulting social and economic gains. The general conception of justice imposes no restrictions on what sort of inequalities are permissible; it only requires that everyone's position be improved. We need not suppose anything so drastic as consenting to a condition of slavery. Imagine instead that men forego certain political rights when the economic returns are significant and their capacity to influence the course of policy by the exercise of these rights would be marginal in any case. It is this kind of exchange which the two principles as stated rule out; being arranged in serial order they do not permit exchanges between basic liberties and economic and social gains. The serial ordering of principles expresses an underlying preference among primary social goods. When this preference is rational so likewise is the choice of these principles in this order. . . .

The fact that the two principles apply to institutions has certain consequences. Several points illustrate this. First of all, the rights and liberties referred to by these principles are those which are defined by the public rules of the basic structure. Whether men are free is determined by the rights and duties established by the major institutions of society. Liberty is a certain pattern of social forms. The first principle simply requires that certain sorts of rules, those defining basic liberties, apply to everyone equally and that they allow the most extensive liberty compatible with a like liberty for all. The only reason for circumscribing the rights defining liberty and making men's freedom less extensive than it might otherwise be is that these equal rights as institutionally defined would interfere with one another.

Another thing to bear in mind is that when principles mention persons, or require that everyone gain from an inequality, the reference is to representative persons holding the various social positions, or offices, or whatever, established by the basic structure. Thus in applying the second principle I assume that it is possible to assign an expectation of well-being to representative individuals holding these positions. This expectation indicates their life prospects as viewed from their social station. In general, the expectations of representative persons depend upon the distribution of rights and duties throughout the basic structure. When this changes, expectations change. I assume, then, that expectations are connected: by raising the prospects of the representative man in one position we presumably increase or decrease the prospects of representative men in other positions. Since it applies to institutional forms, the second principle (or rather the first part of it) refers to the expectations of representative individuals. As I shall discuss below, neither principle applies to distributions of particular goods to particular individuals who may be identified by their proper names. The situation where someone is considering how to allocate certain commodities to needy persons who are known to him is not within the scope of the principles. They are meant to regulate basic institutional arangements. We must not assume that there is much similarity from the standpoint of justice between an administrative allotment of goods to specific persons and the appropriate design of society.

Now the second principle insists that each person benefit from permissible inequalities in the basic structure. This means that it must be reasonable for each relevant representative man defined by this structure, when he views it as a going concern, to prefer his prospects with the inequality to his prospects without it. One is not allowed to justify differences in income or organizational powers on the ground that the disadvantages of those in one position are outweighed by the greater advantages of those in another. Much less can infringements of liberty be counterbalanced in this way. Applied to the basic structure, the principle of utility would have us maximize the sum of expectations of representative men (weighted by the number of persons they represent, on the classical view); and this would permit us to compensate for the losses of some by the gains of others. Instead, the two principles require that everyone benefit from economic and social inequalities. It is obvious, however, that there are indefinitely many ways in which all may be advantaged when the initial arrangement of equality is taken as a benchmark. How then are we to choose among these possibilities? The principles must be specified so that they yield a determinate conclusion. I now turn to this problem.

Interpretations of the Second Principle

I have already mentioned that since the phrases "everyone's advantage" and "equally open to all" are ambiguous, both parts of the second principle have two natural senses. Because these senses are independent of one another, the principle has four possible meanings. Assuming that the first principle of equal liberty has the same sense throughout, we then have four interpretations of the two principles. These are indicated in the table on page 28.

I shall sketch in turn these three interpretations: the system of natural liberty, liberal equality, and democratic equality. In some respects this sequence is the more intuitive one, but the sequence via the interpretation of natural aristocracy is not without interest and I shall comment on it briefly. In working out justice as fairness, we must decide which interpretation is to be preferred. I shall adopt that of democratic equality, explaining in this chapter what this notion means. The argument for its acceptance in the original position does not begin until the next chapter.

| | "Everyone's advantage" | |
"Equally Open"	Principle of Efficiency	Difference Principle
Equality as careers open to talents	System of Natural Liberty	Natural Aristocracy
Equality as equality of fair opportunity	Liberal Equality	Democratic Equality

The first interpretation (in either sequence) I shall refer to as the system of natural liberty. In this rendering the first part of the second principle is understood as the principle of efficiency adjusted so as to apply to institutions or, in this case, to the basic structure of society; and the second part is understood as an open social system in which, to use the traditional phrase, careers are open to talents. I assume in all interpretations that the first principle of equal liberty is satisfied and that the economy is roughly a free market system, although the means of production may or may not be privately owned. The system of natural liberty asserts, then, that a basic structure satisfying the principle of efficiency and in which positions are open to those able and willing to strive for them will lead to a just distribution. Assigning rights and duties in this way is thought to give a scheme which allocates wealth and income, authority and responsibility, in a fair way whatever this allocation turns out to be. The doctrine includes an important element of pure procedural justice which is carried over to the other interpretations.

At this point it is necessary to make a brief digression to explain the principle of efficiency. . . . The principle holds that a configuration is efficient whenever it is impossible to change it so as to make some persons (at least one) better off without at the same time making other persons (at least one) worse off. Thus a distribution of a stock of commodities among certain individuals is efficient if there exists no redistribution of these goods that improves the circumstances of at least one of these individuals without another being disadvantaged. The organization of production is efficient if there is no way to alter inputs so as to produce more of some commodity without producing less of another. For if we could produce more of one good without having to give up some of another, the larger stock of goods could be used to better the circumstances of some persons without making that of others any worse. These applications of the principle show that it is, indeed, a principle of efficiency. A distribution of goods or a scheme of production is inefficient when there are ways of doing still better for some individuals without doing any worse for others. I shall assume that the parties in the original position accept this principle to judge the efficiency of economic and social arrangements. . . .

There are, however, many configurations that are efficient. For example, the distributions in which one person receives the entire stock of commodities is efficient, since there is no rearrangement that will make some better off and none worse off. . . .

Now these reflections show only what we knew all along, that is, that the principle of efficiency cannot serve alone as a conception of justice.[5] Therefore it must be supplemented in some way. Now in the system of natural liberty the principle of efficiency is constrained by certain background institutions: when these constraints are satisfied, any resulting efficient distribution is accepted as just. The system of natural liberty selects an efficient distribution roughly as follows. Let us suppose that we know from economic theory that under the standard assumptions defining a competitive market economy, income and wealth will be distributed in an efficient way, and that the particular efficient distribution which results in any period of time is determined by the initial distribution of assets, that is, by the initial distribution of income and wealth, and of natural talents and abilities. With each initial distribution, a definite efficient outcome is arrived at. Thus it turns out that if we are to accept the outcome as just, and not merely as efficient, we must accept the basis upon which over time the initial distribution of assets is determined.

In the system of natural liberty the initial distribution is regulated by the arrangements implicit in the conception of careers open to talents (as earlier defined). These arrangements presuppose a background of equal liberty (as specified by the first principle) and a free market economy. They require a formal equality of opportunity in that all have at least the same legal rights of access to all advantaged social positions. But since there is no effort to preserve an equality, or similarity, of social conditions, except insofar as this is necessary to preserve the requisite background institutions, the initial distribution of assets for any period of time is strongly influenced by natural and social contingencies. The existing distribution of income and wealth, say, is the cumulative effect of prior distributions of natural assets—that is, natural talents and abilities—as these have been developed or left unrealized, and their use favored or disfavored over time by social circumstances and such chance contingencies as accident and good fortune. Intuitively, the most obvious injustice of the system of natural liberty is that it permits distributive shares to be improperly influenced by these factors so arbitrary from a moral point of view.

The liberal interpretation, as I shall refer to it, tries to correct for this by adding to the requirement of careers open to talents the further condition of the principle of fair equality of opportunity. The thought here is that positions are to be not only open in a formal sense, but that all should have a fair chance to attain them. Offhand it is not clear what is meant, but we might say that those with similar abilities and skills should have similar life chances. More specifically, assuming that there is a distribution of natural assets, those who are at the same level of talent and ability, and have the same willingness to use them, should have the same prospects of success regardless of their initial place in the social system, that is, irrespective of the income class into which they are born. In all sectors of society there should be roughly equal prospects of culture and achievement for everyone similarly motivated and endowed. The expectations of those with the same abilities and aspirations should not be affected by their social class.

The liberal interpretation of the two principles seeks, then, to mitigate the influence of social contingencies and natural fortune on distributive shares. To accomplish this end it is necessary to impose further basic structural conditions on the social system. Free market arrangements must be set within a framework of political and legal institutions which regulates the overall trends of economic events and preserves the social conditions necessary for fair equality of opportunity. The elements of this framework are familiar enough, though it may be worthwhile to recall the importance of preventing extensive accumulations of property and wealth and of maintaining equal opportunities of education for all. Chances to acquire cultural knowledge and skills should not depend upon one's class position, and so the school system, whether public or private, should be designed to even out class barriers.

While the liberal conception seems clearly preferable to the system of natural liberty, intuitively it still appears defective. For one thing, even if it works to perfection in eliminating the influence of social contingencies, it still permits the distribution of wealth and income to be determined by the natural distribution of abilities and talents. Within the limits allowed by the background arrangements, distributive shares are decided by the outcome of the natural lottery; and this outcome is arbitrary from a moral perspective. There is no more reason to permit the distribution of income and wealth to be settled by the distribution of natural assets than by historical and social fortune. Furthermore, the principle of fair opportunity can be only imperfectly carried out, at least as long as the institution of the family exists. The extent to which natural capacities develop and reach fruition is affected by all kinds of social conditions and class attitudes. Even the willingness to make an effort, to try, and so to be deserving in the ordinary sense is itself dependent upon happy family and social circumstances. It is impossible in practice to secure equal chances of achievement and culture for those similarly endowed, and therefore we may want to adopt a principle which recognizes this fact and also mitigates the arbitrary effects of the natural lottery itself. That the liberal conception fails to do this encourages one to look for another interpretation of the two principles of justice.

Before turning to the conception of democratic equality, we should note that of natural aristocracy. On this view no attempt is made to regulate social contingencies beyond what is required by formal equality of opportunity, but the advantages of persons with greater natural endowments are to be limited to those that further the good of the poorer sectors of society. The aristocratic ideal is applied to a system that is open, at least from a legal point of view, and the better situation of those favored by it is regarded as just only when less would be had by those below, if less were given to those above.[6] In this way the idea of *noblesse oblige* is carried over to the conception of natural aristocracy.

Now both the liberal conception and that of natural aristocracy are unstable. For once we are troubled by the influence of either social contingencies or natural chance on the determination of distributive shares, we are bound, on reflection, to be bothered by the influence of the other. From a moral standpoint the two seem equally arbitrary. So however we move away from the system of natural liberty, we cannot be satisfied short of the democratic conception. This conception I have yet to explain. And, moreover, none of the preceding remarks are an argument for this conception, since in a contract theory all arguments, strictly speaking, are to be made in terms of what it would be rational to choose in the original position. But I am concerned here to prepare the way for the favored interpretation of the two principles so that these criteria, especially the second one, will not strike the reader as too eccentric or bizarre. I have tried to show that once we try to find a rendering of them which treats everyone equally as a moral person, and which does not weight men's share in the benefits and burdens of social cooperation according to their social fortune or their luck in the natural lottery, it is clear that the democratic interpretation is the best choice among the four alternatives. With these comments as a preface, I now turn to this conception.

Democratic Equality and the Difference Principle

The democratic interpretation, as the table suggests, is arrived at by combining the principle of fair equality of opportunity with the difference principle. This principle removes the indeterminateness of the principle of efficiency by singling out a particular position from which the social and economic inequalities of the basic structure are to be judged. Assuming the framework of institutions required by equal liberty and fair equality of opportunity, the higher expectations of those better situated are just if and only if they work as part of a scheme which improves the expectations of the least advantaged members of society. The intuitive idea is that the social order is not to establish and secure the more attractive prospects of those better off unless doing so is to the advantage of those less fortunate. . . .

To illustrate the difference principle, consider the distribution of income among social classes. Let us suppose that the various income groups correlate with representative individuals by reference to whose expectations we can judge the distribution. Now those starting out as members of the entrepreneurial class in a property-owning democracy, say, have a better prospect than those who begin in the class of unskilled laborers. It seems likely that this will be true even when the social injustices which now exist are removed. What, then, can possibly justify this kind of initial inequality in life prospects? According to the difference principle, it is justifiable only if the difference in expectation is to the advantage of the representative man who is worse off, in this case the representative unskilled worker. The inequality in expectation is permissible only if lowering it would make the working class even more worse off. Supposedly, given the rider in the second principle concerning open positions, and the principle of liberty generally, the greater expectations allowed to entrepreneurs encourages them to do things which raise the long-term prospects of the laboring class. Their better prospects act as incentives so that the economic process is more efficient, innovation proceeds at a faster pace, and so on. Eventually the resulting material benefits spread throughout the system and to the least advantaged. I shall not consider how far these things are true. The point is that something of this kind must be argued if these inequalities are to be just by the difference principle. . . .

. . . And therefore, as the outcome of the last several sections, the second principle is to read as follows.

> Social and economic inequalities are to be arranged so that they are both (a) to the greatest benefit of the least advantaged and (b) attached to offices and positions open to all under conditions of fair equality of opportunity.

Finally, it should be observed that the difference principle, or the idea expressed by it, can easily be accommodated to the general conception of justice. In fact, the general conception is simply the difference principle applied to all primary goods including liberty and opportunity and so no longer constrained by other parts of the special conception. This is evident from the earlier brief discussion of the principles of justice. These principles in serial order are, as I shall indicate from time to time, the form that the general conception finally assumes as social conditions improve. This question ties up with that of the priority of liberty which I shall discuss later on. For the moment it suffices to remark that in one form or another the difference principle is basic throughout. . . .

The Tendency to Equality

I wish to conclude this discussion of the two principles by explaining the sense in which they express an egalitarian conception of justice. Also I should like to forestall the objection to the principle of fair opportunity that it leads to a callous meritocratic society. In order to prepare the way for doing this, I note several aspects of the conception of justice that I have set out.

First we may observe that the difference principle gives some weight to the considerations singled out by the principle of redress. This is the principle that undeserved inequalities call for redress; and since inequalities of birth and natural endowment are undeserved, these inequalities are to be somehow compensated for.[7] Thus the principle holds that in order to treat all persons equally, to provide genuine equality of opportunity, society must give more attention to those with fewer native assets and to those born into the less favorable social positions. The idea is to redress the bias of contingencies in the direction of equality. In pursuit of this principle greater resources might be spent on the education of the less rather than the more intelligent, at least over a certain time of life, say the earlier years of school.

Now the principle of redress has not to my knowledge been proposed as the sole criterion of justice, as the single aim of the social order.

It is plausible as most such principles are only as a prima facie principle, one that is to be weighed in the balance with others. For example, we are to weigh it against the principle to improve the average standard of life, or to advance the common good. But whatever other principles we hold, the claims of redress are to be taken into account. It is thought to represent one of the elements in our conception of justice. Now the difference principle is not of course the principle of redress. It does not require society to try to even out handicaps as if all were expected to compete on a fair basis in the same race. But the difference principle would allocate resources in education, say, so as to improve the long-term expectation of the least favored. If this end is attained by giving more attention to the better endowed, it is permissible; otherwise not. And in making this decision, the value of education should not be assessed only in terms of economic efficiency and social welfare. Equally if not more important is the role of education in enabling a person to enjoy the culture of his society and to take part in its affairs, and in this way to provide for each individual a secure sense of his own worth.

Thus although the difference principle is not the same as that of redress, it does achieve some of the intent of the latter principle. It transforms the aims of the basic structure so that the total scheme of institutions no longer emphasizes social efficiency and technocratic values. We see then that the difference principle represents, in effect, an agreement to regard the distribution of natural talents as a common asset and to share in the benefits of this distribution whatever it turns out to be. Those who have been favored by nature, whoever they are, may gain from their good fortune only on terms that improve the situation of those who have lost out. The naturally advantaged are not to gain merely because they are more gifted, but only to cover the costs of training and education and for using their endowments in ways that help the less fortunate as well. No one deserves his greater natural capacity nor merits a more favorable starting place in society. But it does not follow that one should eliminate these distinctions. There is another way to deal with them. The basic structure can be arranged so that these contingencies work for the good of the least fortunate. Thus we are led to the difference principle if we wish to set up the social system so that no one gains or loses from his arbitrary place in the distribution of natural assets or his initial position in society without giving or receiving compensating advantages in return.

In view of these remarks we may reject the contention that the injustice of institutions is always imperfect because the distribution of natural talents and the contingencies of social circumstance are unjust, and this injustice must inevitably carry over to human arrangements. Occasionally this reflection is offered as an excuse for ignoring injustice, as if the refusal to acquiesce in injustice is on a par with being unable to accept death. The natural distribution is neither just nor unjust; nor is it unjust that men are born into society at some particular position. These are simply natural facts. What is just and unjust is the way that institutions deal with these facts. Aristocratic and caste societies are unjust because they make these contingencies the ascriptive basis for belonging to more or less enclosed and privileged social classes. The basic structure of these societies incorporates the arbitrariness found in nature. But there is no necessity for men to resign themselves to these contingencies. The social system is not an unchangeable order beyond human control but a pattern of human action. In justice as fairness men agree to share one another's fate. In designing institutions they undertake to avail themselves of the accidents of nature and social circumstance only when doing so is for the common benefit. The two principles are a fair way of meeting the arbitrariness of fortune; and while no doubt imperfect in other ways, the institutions which satisfy these principles are just.

A further point is that the difference principle expresses a conception of reciprocity. It is a principle of mutual benefit. We have seen that, at least when chain connection holds, each representative man can accept the basic structure as designed to advance his interests. The social order can be justified to everyone, and in particular to those who are least favored; and in this sense it is egalitarian. But it seems necessary to consider in an intuitive way how the condition of mutual benefit is satisfied. Consider any two representative men A and B, and let B be the one who is less favored. Actually, since we are most interested in the comparison with the least favored man, let us assume that B is this individual. Now B can accept A's being better off since A's advantages have been gained in ways that improve B's prospects. If A were not allowed his better position, B would be even worse off than he is. The difficulty is to show that A has no grounds for complaint. Perhaps he is required to have less than he might since his having more would result in some loss to B. Now what can be said to the more favored man? To begin with, it is clear that the well-being of each depends on a scheme of social cooperation without which no one could have a satisfactory life. Secondly, we can ask for the willing cooperation of everyone only if the terms of the scheme are reasonable. The difference principle, then, seems to be a fair basis on which those better endowed, or more fortunate in their social circumstances, could expect others to collaborate with them when some workable arrangement is a necessary condition of the good of all.

There is a natural inclination to object that those better situated deserve their greater advantages whether or not they are to the benefit of others. At this point it is necessary to be clear about the notion of desert. It is perfectly true that given a just system of cooperation as a scheme of public rules and the expectations set up by it, those who, with the prospect of improving their condition, have done what the system announces that it will reward are entitled to their advantages. In this sense the more fortunate have a claim to their better situation; their claims are legitimate expectations established by social institutions, and the community is obligated to meet them. But this sense of desert presupposes the existence of the cooperative scheme; it is irrelevant to the question whether in the first place the scheme is to be designed in accordance with the difference principle or some other criterion.

Perhaps some will think that the person with greater natural endowments deserves those assets and the superior character that made their development possible. Because he is more worthy in this sense, he deserves the greater advantages that he could achieve with them. This view, however, is surely incorrect. It seems to be one of the fixed points of our considered judgments that no one deserves his place in the distribution of native endowments, any more than one deserves one's initial starting place in society. The assertion that a man deserves the superior character that enables him to make the effort to cultivate his abilities is equally problematic; for his character depends in large part upon fortunate family and social circumstances for which he can claim no credit. The notion of desert seems not to apply to these cases. Thus the more advantaged representative man cannot say that he deserves and therefore has a right to a scheme of cooperation in which he is permitted to acquire benefits in ways that do not contribute to the welfare of others. There is no basis for his making this claim. From the standpoint of common sense, then, the difference principle appears to be acceptable both to the more advantaged and to the less advantaged individual. Of course, none of this is strictly speaking an argument for the principle, since in a contract theory arguments are made from the point of view of the original position. But these intuitive considerations help to clarify the nature of the principle and the sense in which it is egalitarian. . . .

THE REASONING LEADING TO THE TWO PRINCIPLES

It seems clear from these remarks that the two principles are at least a plausible conception of justice. The question, though, is how one is to argue for them more systematically. Now there are several things to do. One can work out their consequences for institutions and note their implications for fundamental social policy. In this way they are tested by a comparison with our considered judgments of justice. . . . But one can also try to find arguments in their favor that are decisive from the standpoint of the original position. In order to see how this might be done, it is useful as a heuristic device to think of the two principles as the maximin solution to the problem of social justice. There is an analogy between the two principles and the maximin rule for choice under uncertainty.[8] This is evident from the fact that the two principles are those a person would choose for the design of a society in which his enemy is to assign him his place. The maximin rule tells us to rank alternatives by their worst possible outcomes: we are to adopt the alternative the worst outcome of which is superior to the worst outcomes of the others. The persons in the original position do not, of course, assume that their initial place in society is decided by a malevolent opponent. As I note below, they should not reason from false premises. The veil of ignorance does not violate this idea, since an absence of information is not misinformation. But that the two principles of justice would be chosen if the parties were forced to protect themselves against such a contingency explains the sense in which this conception is the maximin solution. And this analogy suggests that if the original position has been described so that it is rational for the parties to adopt the conservative attitude expressed by this rule, a conclusive argument can indeed be constructed for these principles. Clearly the maximin rule is not, in general, a suitable guide for choices under uncertainty. But it is attractive in situations marked by certain special features. My aim, then, is to show that a good case can be made for the two principles based on the fact that the original position manifests these features to the fullest possible degree, carrying them to the limit, so to speak.

Consider the gain-and-loss table below. It represents the gains and losses for a situation which is not a game of strategy. There is no one playing against the person making the decision; instead he is faced with several possible circumstances which may or may not obtain. Which circumstances happen to exist does not depend upon what the person choosing decides or whether he announces his moves in advance. The numbers in the table are monetary values (in hundreds of dollars) in comparison with some initial situation. The gain (g) depends upon the individual's decision (d) and the circumstances (c). Thus $g = f(d, c)$. Assuming that there are three possible decisions and three possible circumstances, we might have this gain-and-loss table.

Decisions	Circumstances		
	C_1	C_2	C_3
d_1	−7	8	12
d_2	−8	7	14
d_3	5	6	8

The maximin rule requires that we make the third decision. For in this case the worst that can happen is that one gains five hundred dollars, which is better than the worst for the other actions. If we adopt one of these we may lose either eight or seven hundred dollars. Thus, the choice of d_3 maximizes $f(d,c)$ for that value of c, which for a given d, minimizes f. The term "maximin" means the *maximum minimorum*; and the rule directs our attention to the worst that can happen under any proposed course of action, and to decide in the light of that.

Now there appear to be three chief features of situations that give plausibility to this unusual rule.[9] First, since the rule takes no account of the likelihoods of the possible circumstances, there must be some reason for sharply discounting estimates of these probabilities. Offhand, the most natural rule of choice would seem to be to compute the expectation of monetary gain for each decision and then to adopt the course of action with the highest prospect. . . . Thus it must be, for example, that the situation is one in which a knowledge of likelihoods is impossible, or at best extremely insecure. In this case it is unreasonable not to be skeptical of probabilistic calculations unless there is no other way out, particularly if the decision is a fundamental one that needs to be justified to others.

The second feature that suggests the maximin rule is the following: the person choosing has a conception of the good such that he cares very little, if anything, for what he might gain above the minimum stipend that he can, in fact, be sure of by following the maximin rule. It is not worthwhile for him to take a chance for the sake of a further advantage, especially when it may turn out that he loses much that is important to him. This last provision brings in the third feature, namely, that the rejected alternatives have outcomes that one can hardly accept. The situation involves grave risks. Of course these features work most effectively in combination. The paradigm situation for following the maximin rule is when all three features are realized to the highest degree. This rule does not, then, generally apply, nor of course is it self-evident. Rather, it is a maxim, a rule of thumb, that comes into its own in special circumstances. Its application depends upon the qualitative structure of the possible gains and losses in relation to one's conception of the good, all this against a background in which it is reasonable to discount conjectural estimates of likelihoods.

It should be noted, as the comments on the gain-and-loss table say, that the entries in the table represent monetary values and not utilities. This difference is significant since for one thing computing expectations on the basis of such objective values is not the same thing as computing expected utility and may lead to different results. The essential point though is that in justice as fairness the parties do not know their conception of the good and cannot estimate their utility in the ordinary sense. In any case, we want to go behind de facto preferences generated by given conditions. Therefore expectations are based upon an index of primary goods and the parties make their choice accordingly. The entries in the example are in terms of money and not utility to indicate this aspect of the contract doctrine.

Now, as I have suggested, the original position has been defined so that it is a situation in which the maximin rule applies. In order to see this, let us review briefly the nature of this situation with these three special features in mind. To begin with, the veil of ignorance excludes all but the vaguest knowledge of likelihoods. The parties have no basis for determining the probable nature of their society, or their place in it. Thus they have strong reasons for being wary of probability calculations if any other course is open to them. They must also take in account the fact that their choice of principles should seem reasonable to others, in particular their descendants, whose rights will be deeply affected by it. There are further grounds for discounting that I shall mention as we go along. For the present it suffices to note that these considerations are strengthened by the fact that the parties know very little about the gain-and-loss table. Not only are they unable to conjecture the likelihoods of the various possible circumstances, they cannot say much about what the possible circumstances are, much less enumerate them and foresee the outcome of each alternative available. Those deciding are much more in the dark than the illustration by a numerical table suggests. It is for this reason that I have spoken of an analogy with the maximin rule.

Several kinds of arguments for the two principles of justice illustrate the second feature. Thus, if we can maintain that these principles provide a workable theory of social justice, and that they are compatible with reasonable demands of efficiency, then this conception guarantees a satisfactory minimum. There may be, on reflection, little reason for trying to do better. Thus much of the argument . . . is to show, by their application to the main questions of social justice, that the two principles are a satisfactory conception. These details have a philosophical purpose. Moreover, this line of thought is practically decisive if we can establish the priority of liberty, the lexical ordering of the two principles. For this priority implies that the persons in the original position have no desire to try for greater gains at the expense of the equal liberties. The minimum assured by the two principles in lexical order is not one that the parties wish to jeopardize for the sake of greater economic and social advantages. . . . I present the case for this ordering [elsewhere].

Finally, the third feature holds if we can assume that other conceptions of justice may lead to institutions that the parties would find intolerable. For example, it has sometimes been held that under some conditions the utility principle (in either form) justifies, if not slavery or serfdom, at any rate serious infractions of liberty for the sake of greater social benefits. We need not consider here the truth of this claim, or the likelihood that the requisite conditions obtain. For the moment, this contention is only to illustrate the way in which conceptions of justice may allow for outcomes which the parties may not be able to accept. And having the ready alternative of the two principles of justice which secure a satisfactory minimum, it seems unwise, if not irrational, for them to take a chance that these outcomes are not realized.

So much, then, for a brief sketch of the features of situations in which the maximin rule comes into its own and of the way in which the arguments for the two principles of justice can be subsumed under them. . . . These principles would be selected by the rule. The original position clearly exhibits these special features to a very high degree in view of the fundamental character of the choice of a conception of justice. These remarks about the maximin rule are intended only to clarify the structure of the choice problem in the original position. They depict its qualitative anatomy. The arguments for the two principles will be presented more fully as we proceed. . . .

Some Main Grounds for the Two Principles of Justice

In this section my aim is to use the conditions of publicity and finality to give some of the main arguments for the two principles of justice. I shall rely upon the fact that for an agreement to be valid, the parties must be able to honor it under all relevant and foreseeable circumstances. There must be a rational assurance that one can carry through. The arguments I shall adduce fit under the heuristic schema suggested by the reasons for following the maximin rule. That is, they help to show that the two principles are an adequate minimum conception of justice in a situation of great uncertainty. Any further advantages that might be won by the principle of utility, or whatever, are highly problematical, whereas the hardships if things turn out badly are intolerable. It is at this point that the concept of a contract has a definite role: it suggests the condition of publicity and sets limits upon what can be agreed to. Thus justice as fairness uses the concept of contract to a greater extent than the discussion so far might suggest.

The first confirming ground for the two principles can be explained in terms of what I earlier referred to as the strains of commitment. I said that the parties have a capacity for justice in the sense that they can be assured that their undertaking is not in vain. Assuming that they have taken everything into account, including the general facts of moral psychology, they can rely on one another to adhere to the principles adopted. Thus they consider the strains of commitment. They cannot enter into agreements that may have consequences they cannot accept. They will avoid those that they can adhere to only with great difficulty. Since the original agreement is final and made in perpetuity, there is no second chance. In view of the serious nature of the possible consequences, the question of the burden of commitment is especially acute. A person is choosing once and for all the standards which are to govern his life prospects. Moreover, when we enter an agreement we must be able to honor it even should the worst possibilities prove to be the case. Otherwise we have not acted in good faith. Thus the parties must weigh with care whether they will be able to stick by their commitment in all circumstances. Of course, in answering this question they have only a general knowledge of human psychology to go on. But this information is enough to tell which conception of justice involves the greater stress.

In this respect the two principles of justice have a definite advantage. Not only do the parties protect their basic rights but they insure themselves against the worst eventualities. They run no chance of having to acquiesce in a loss of freedom over the course of their life for the sake of a greater good enjoyed by others, an undertaking that in actual circumstances they might not be able to keep. Indeed, we might wonder whether such an agreement can be made in good faith at all. Compacts of this sort exceed the capacity of human nature. How can the parties possibly know, or be sufficiently sure, that they can keep such an agreement? Certainly they cannot base their confidence on a general knowledge of moral psychology. To be sure, any principle chosen in the original position may require a large sacrifice for some. The beneficiaries of clearly unjust institutions (those founded on principles which have no claim to acceptance) may find it hard to reconcile themselves to the changes that will have to be made. But in this case they will know that they could not have maintained their position anyway. Yet should a person gamble with his liberties and substantive interests hoping that the application of the principle of utility might secure him a greater well-being, he may have difficulty abiding by his undertaking. He is bound to remind himself that he had the two principles of justice as an alternative. If the only possible candidates all involved similar risks, the problem of the strains of commitment would have to be waived. This is not the case, and judged in this light the two principles seem distinctly superior.

A second consideration invokes the condition of publicity as well as that of the constraints on agreements. I shall present the argument in terms of the question of psychological stability. Earlier I stated that a strong point in favor of a conception of justice is that it generates its own support. When the basic structure of society is publicly known to satisfy its principles for an extended period of time, those subject to these arrangements tend to develop a desire to act in accordance with these principles and to do their part in institutions which exemplify them. A conception of justice is stable when the public recognition of its realization by the social system tends to bring about the corresponding sense of justice. Now whether this happens depends, of course, on the laws of moral psychology and the availability of human motives. I shall discuss these matters later on. At the moment we may observe that the principle of utility seems to require a greater identification with the interests of others than the two principles of justice. Thus the latter will be a more stable conception to the extent that this identification is difficult to achieve. When the two principles are satisfied, each person's liberties are secured and there is a sense defined by the difference principle in which everyone is benefited by social cooperation. Therefore we can explain the acceptance of the social system and the principles it satisfies by the psychological law that persons tend to love, cherish, and support whatever affirms their own good. Since everyone's good is affirmed, all acquire inclinations to uphold the scheme.

When the principle of utility is satisfied, however, there is no such assurance that everyone benefits. Allegiance to the social system may demand that some should forgo advantages for the sake of the greater good of the whole. Thus the scheme will not be stable unless those who must make sacrifices strongly identify with interests broader than their own. But this is not easy to bring about. The sacrifices in question are not those asked in times of social emergency when all or some must pitch in for the common good. The principles of justice apply to the basic structure of the social system and to the determination of life prospects. What the principle of utility asks is precisely a sacrifice of these prospects. We are to accept the greater advantages of others as a sufficient reason for lower expectations over the whole course of our life. This is surely an extreme demand. In fact, when society is conceived as a system of cooperation designed to advance the good of its members, it seems quite incredible that some citizens should be expected, on the basis of political principles, to accept lower prospects of life for the sake of others. It is evident then why utilitarians should stress the role of sympathy in moral learning and the central place of benevolence among the moral virtues. Their conception of justice is threatened with instability unless sympathy and benevolence can be widely and intensely cultivated. Looking at the question from the standpoint of the original position, the parties recognize that it would be highly unwise if not irrational to choose principles which may have consequences so extreme that they could not accept them in practice. They would reject the principle of utility and adopt the more realistic idea of designing the social order on a principle of reciprocal advantage. We need not suppose, of course, that persons never make substantial sacrifices for one another, since moved by affection and ties of sentiment they often do. But such actions are not demanded as a matter of justice by the basic structure of society.

Furthermore, the public recognition of the two principles gives greater support to men's self-respect and this in turn increases the effectiveness of social cooperation. Both effects are reasons for choosing these principles. It is clearly rational for men to secure their self-respect. A sense of their own worth is necessary if they are to pursue their conception of the good with zest and to delight in its fulfillment. Self-respect is not so much a part of any rational plan of life as the sense that one's plan is worth carrying out. Now our self-respect normally depends upon the respect of others. Unless we feel that our endeavors are honored by them, it is difficult if not impossible for us to maintain the conviction that our ends are worth advancing. Hence for this reason the parties would accept the natural duty of mutual respect which asks them to treat one another civilly and to be willing to explain the grounds of their actions, especially when the claims of others are overruled. Moreover, one may assume that those who respect themselves are more likely to respect each other and conversely. Self-contempt leads to contempt of others and threatens their good as much as envy does. Self-respect is reciprocally self-supporting.

Thus a desirable feature of a conception of justice is that it should publicly express men's respect for one another. In this way they insure a sense of their own value. Now the two principles achieve this end. For when society follows these principles, everyone's good is included in a scheme of mutual benefit and this public affirmation in institutions of each man's endeavors supports men's self-esteem. The establishment of equal liberty and the operation of the difference principle are bound to have this effect. The two principles are equivalent, as I have remarked, to an undertaking to regard the distribution of natural abilities as a collective asset so that the more fortunate are to benefit only in ways that help those who have lost out. I do not say that the parties are moved by the ethical propriety of this idea. But there are reasons for them to accept this principle. For by arranging inequalities for reciprocal advantage and by abstaining from the exploitation of the contingencies of nature and social circumstance within a framework of equal liberty, persons express their respect for one another in the very constitution of their society. In this way they insure their self-esteem as it is rational for them to do.

Another way of putting this is to say that the principles of justice manifest in the basic structure of society men's desire to treat one another not as means only but as ends in themselves. I cannot examine Kant's view here. Instead I shall freely interpret it in the light of the contract doctrine. The notion of treating men as ends in themselves and never as only a means obviously needs an explanation. There is even a question whether it is possible to realize. How can we always treat everyone as an end and never as a means only? Certainly we cannot say that it comes to treating everyone by the same general principles, since this interpretation makes the concept equivalent to formal justice. On the contract interpretation treating men as ends in themselves implies at the very least treating them in accordance with the principles to which they would consent in an original position of equality. For in this situation men have equal representation as moral persons who regard themselves as ends and the principles they accept will be rationally designed to protect the claims of their person. The contract view as such defines a sense in which men are to be treated as ends and not as means only.

But the question arises whether there are substantive principles which convey this idea. If the parties wish to express this notion visibly in the basic structure of their society in order to secure each man's rational interest in his self-respect, which principles should they choose? Now it seems that the two principles of justice achieve this aim: for all have an equal liberty and the difference principle explicates the distinction between treating men as a means only and treating them also as ends in themselves. To regard persons as ends in themselves in the basic design of society is to agree to forgo those gains which do not contribute to their representative expectations. By contrast, to regard persons as means is to be prepared to impose upon them lower prospects of life for the sake of the higher expectations of others. Thus we see that the difference principle, which at first appears rather extreme, has a reasonable interpretation. If we further suppose that social cooperation among those who respect each other and themselves as manifest in their institutions is likely to be more effective and harmonious, the general level of expectations, assuming we could estimate it, may be higher when the two principles of justice are satisfied than one might otherwise have thought. The advantage of the principle of utility in this respect is no longer so clear.

The principle of utility presumably requires some to forgo greater life prospects for the sake of others. . . .

CLASSICAL UTILITARIANISM

There are many forms of utilitarianism, and the development of the theory has continued in recent years. I shall not survey these forms here, nor take account of the numerous refinements found in contemporary discussions. My aim is to work out a theory of justice that represents an alternative to utilitarian thought generally and so to all of these different versions of it. I believe that the contrast between the contract view and utilitarianism remains essentially the same in all these cases. Therefore I shall compare justice as fairness with utilitarianism in order to bring out the underlying differences in the simplest way. With this end in mind, the kind of utilitarianism I shall describe here is the strict classical doctrine which receives perhaps its clearest and most accessible formulation in Sidgwick. The main idea is that society is rightly ordered, and therefore just, when its major institutions are arranged so as to achieve the greatest net balance of satisfaction summed over all the individuals belonging to it. . . .

The two main concepts of ethics are those of the right and the good; the concept of a morally worthy person is, I believe, derived from them. The structure of an ethical theory is, then, largely determined by how it defines and connects these two basic notions. Now it seems that the simplest way of relating them is taken by teleological theories: the good is defined independently from the right, and then the right is defined as that which maximizes the good. More precisely, those institutions and acts are right which of the available alternatives produce the most good, or at least as much good as any of the other institutions and acts open as real possibilities (a rider needed when the maximal class is not a singleton). Teleological theories have a deep intuitive appeal since they seem to embody the idea of rationality. It is natural to think that rationality is maximizing something and that in morals it must be maximizing the good. Indeed, it is tempting to suppose that it is self-evident that things should be arranged so as to lead to the most good.

It is essential to keep in mind that in a teleological theory the good is defined independently from the right. This means two things. First, the theory accounts for our considered judgments as to which things are good (our judgments of value) as a separate class of judgments intuitively distinguishable by common sense, and then proposes the hypothesis that the right is maximizing the good as already specified. Second, the theory enables one to judge the goodness of things without referring to what is right. For example, if pleasure is said to be the sole good, then presumably pleasures can be recognized and ranked in value by criteria that do not presuppose any standards of right, or what we would normally think of as such. Whereas if the distribution of goods is also counted as a good, perhaps a higher order one, and the theory directs us to produce the most good (including the good of distribution among others), we no longer have a teleological view in the classical sense. The problem of distribution falls under the concept of right as one intuitively understands it, and so the theory lacks an independent definition of the good. The clarity and simplicity of classical teleological theories derives largely from the fact that they factor our moral judgments into two classes, the one being characterized separately while the other is then connected with it by a maximizing principle.

Teleological doctrines differ, pretty clearly, according to how the conception of the good is specified. If it is taken as the realization of human excellence in the various forms of culture, we have what may be called perfectionism. This notion is found in Aristotle and Nietzsche, among others. If the good is defined as pleasure, we have hedonism; if as happiness, eudaimonism, and so on. I shall understand the principle of utility in its classical form as defining the good as the satisfaction of desire, or perhaps better, as the satisfaction of rational desire. This accords with the view in all essentials and provides, I believe, a fair interpretation of it. The appropriate terms of social cooperation are settled by whatever in the circumstances will achieve the greatest sum of satisfaction of the rational desires of individuals. It is impossible to deny the initial plausibility and attractiveness of this conception.

The striking feature of the utilitarian view of justice is that it does not matter, except indirectly, how this sum of satisfactions is distributed among individuals any more than it matters, except indirectly, how one

man distributes his satisfactions over time. The correct distribution in either case is that which yields the maximum fulfillment. Society must allocate its means of satisfaction whatever these are, rights and duties,
opportunities and privileges, and various forms of wealth, so as to achieve
this maximum if it can. But in itself no distribution of satisfaction is better
than another except that the more equal distribution is to be preferred to
break ties. It is true that certain common sense precepts of justice, particularly those which concern the protection of liberties and rights, or which
express the claims of desert, seem to contradict this contention. But from a
utilitarian standpoint the explanation of these precepts and of their seemingly stringent character is that they are those precepts which experience
shows should be strictly respected and departed from only under exceptional circumstances if the sum of advantages is to be maximized. Yet, as
with all other precepts, those of justice are derivative from the one end of
attaching the greatest balance of satisfaction. Thus there is no reason in
principle why the greater gains of some should not compensate for the
lesser losses of others; or more importantly, why the violation of the liberty
of a few might not be made right by the greater good shared by many. It
simply happens that under most conditions, at least in a reasonably advanced stage of civilization, the greatest sum of advantages is not attained
in this way. No doubt the strictness of common sense precepts of justice
has a certain usefulness in limiting men's propensities to injustice and to
socially injurious actions, but the utilitarian believes that to affirm this
strictness as a first principle of morals is a mistake. For just as it is rational
for one man to maximize the fulfillment of his system of desires, it is right
for a society to maximize the net balance of satisfaction taken over all of its
members.

The most natural way, then, of arriving at utilitarianism (although
not, of course, the only way of doing so) is to adopt for society as a whole
the principle of rational choice for one man. . . . On this conception of
society separate individuals are thought of as so many different lines along
which rights and duties are to be assigned and scarce means of satisfaction
allocated in accordance with rules so as to give the greatest fulfillment of
wants. The nature of the decision made by the ideal legislator is not,
therefore, materially different from that of an entrepreneur deciding how
to maximize his profit by producing this or that commodity, or that of a
consumer deciding how to maximize his satisfaction by the purchase of this
or that collection of goods. In each case there is a single person whose
system of desires determines the best allocation of limited means. The
correct decision is essentially a question of efficient administration. This
view of social cooperation is the consequence of extending to society the
principle of choice for one man, and then, to make this extension work,
conflating all persons into one through the imaginative acts of the impartial sympathetic spectator. Utilitarianism does not take seriously the distinction between persons. . . .

The last contrast that I shall mention now is that utilitarianism is a
teleological theory whereas justice as fairness is not. By definition, then,
the latter is a deontological theory, one that either does not specify the

good independently from the right, or does not interpret the right as maximizing the good. (It should be noted that deontological theories are defined as non-teleological ones, not as views that characterize the right-ness of institutions and acts independently from their consequences. All ethical doctrines worth our attention take consequences into account in judging rightness. One which did not would simply be irrational, crazy.) Justice as fairness is a deontological theory in the second way. For if it is assumed that the persons in the original position would choose a principle of equal liberty and restrict economic and social inequalities to those in everyone's interests, there is no reason to think that just institutions will maximize the good. (Here I suppose with utilitarianism that the good is defined as the satisfaction of rational desire.) Of course, it is not impossible that the most good is produced but it would be a coincidence. The ques-tion of attaining the greatest net balance of satisfaction never arises in justice as fairness; this maximum principle is not used at all.

There is a further point in this connection. In utilitarianism the satisfaction of any desire has some value in itself which must be taken into account in deciding what is right. In calculating the greatest balance of satisfaction it does not matter, except indirectly, what the desires are for. We are to arrange institutions so as to obtain the greatest sum of satisfac-tions; we ask no questions about their source or quality but only how their satisfaction would affect the total of well-being. Social welfare depends directly and solely upon the levels of satisfaction or dissatisfaction of indi-viduals. Thus if men take a certain pleasure in discriminating against one another, in subjecting others to a lesser liberty as a means of enhancing their self-respect, then the satisfaction of these desires must be weighed in our deliberations according to their intensity, or whatever, along with other desires. If society decides to deny them fulfillment, or to suppress them, it is because they tend to be socially destructive and a greater welfare can be achieved in other ways.

In justice as fairness, on the other hand, persons accept in advance a principle of equal liberty and they do this without a knowledge of their more particular ends. They implicitly agree, therefore, to conform their conceptions of their good to what the principles of justice require, or at least not to press claims which directly violate them. An individual who finds that he enjoys seeing others in positions of lesser liberty understands that he has no claim whatever to this enjoyment. The pleasure he takes in other's deprivations is wrong in itself: it is a satisfaction which requires the violation of a principle to which he would agree in the original position. The principles of right, and so of justice, put limits on which satisfactions have value; they impose restrictions on what are reasonable conceptions of one's good. In drawing up plans and in deciding on aspirations men are to take these constraints into account. Hence in justice as fairness one does not take men's propensities and inclinations as given, whatever they are, and then seek the best way to fulfill them. Rather, their desires and aspira-tions are restricted from the outset by the principles of justice which specify the boundaries that men's systems of ends must respect. We can express this by saying that in justice as fairness the concept of right is prior to that of the good. A just social system defines the scope within which individuals must develop their aims, and it provides a framework of rights and opportunities and the means of satisfaction within and by the use of which these ends may be equitably pursued. The priority of justice is accounted for, in part, by holding that the interests requiring the violation of justice have no value. Having no merit in the first place, they cannot override its claims. . . .

APPLICATIONS OF THE TWO PRINCIPLES

Fair Equality of Opportunity and Pure Procedural Justice

. . . Now I have said that the basic structure is the primary subject of justice. This means, as we have seen, that the first distributive problem is the assignment of fundamental rights and duties and the regulation of social and economic inequalities and of the legitimate expectations founded on these. Of course, any ethical theory recognizes the importance of the basic structure as a subject of justice, but not all theories regard its importance in the same way. In justice as fairness society is interpreted as a cooperative venture for mutual advantage. The basic structure is a public system of rules defining a scheme of activities that leads men to act together so as to produce a greater sum of benefits and assigns to each certain recognized claims to a share in the proceeds. What a person does depends upon what the public rules say he will be entitled to, and what a person is entitled to depends on what he does. The distribution which results is arrived at by honoring the claims determined by what persons undertake to do in the light of these legitimate expectations.

These considerations suggest the idea of treating the question of distributive shares as a matter of pure procedural justice. The intuitive idea is to design the social system so that the outcome is just whatever it happens to be, at least so long as it is within a certain range. The notion of pure procedural justice is best understood by a comparison with perfect and imperfect procedural justice. To illustrate the former, consider the simplest case of fair division. A number of men are to divide a cake: assuming that the fair division is an equal one, which procedure, if any, will give this outcome? Technicalities aside, the obvious solution is to have one man divide the cake and get the last piece, the others being allowed their pick before him. He will divide the cake equally, since in this way he assures for himself the largest share possible. This example illustrates the two characteristic features of perfect procedural justice. First, there is an independent criterion for what is a fair division, a criterion defined separately from and prior to the procedure which is to be followed. And second, it is possible to devise a procedure that is sure to give the desired outcome. Of course, certain assumptions are made here, such as that the man selected can divide the cake equally, wants as large a piece as he can get, and so on. But we can ignore these details. The essential thing is that there is an independent standard for deciding which outcome is just and a procedure guaranteed to lead to it. Pretty clearly, perfect procedural justice is rare, if not impossible, in cases of much practical interest.

Imperfect procedural justice is exemplified by a criminal trial. The desired outcome is that the defendant should be declared guilty if and only if he has committed the offense with which he is charged. . . . Even though the law is carefully followed, and the proceedings fairly and properly conducted, it may reach the wrong outcome. An innocent man may be found guilty, a guilty man may be set free. In such cases we speak of a miscarriage of justice: the injustice springs from no human fault but from a fortuitous combination of circumstances which defeats the purpose of the legal rules. The characteristic mark of imperfect procedural justice is that while there is an independent criterion for the correct outcome, there is no feasible procedure which is sure to lead to it.

By contrast, pure procedural justice obtains when there is no independent criterion for the right result: instead there is a correct or fair procedure such that the outcome is likewise correct or fair, whatever it is, provided that the procedure has been properly followed. This situation is illustrated by gambling. If a number of persons engage in a series of fair bets, the distribution of cash after the last bet is fair, or at least not unfair, whatever this distribution is. . . . What makes the final outcome of betting fair, or not unfair, is that it is the one which has arisen after a series of fair gambles. A fair procedure translates its fairness to the outcome only when it is actually carried out.

In order, therefore, to apply the notion of pure procedural justice to distributive shares it is necessary to set up and to administer impartially a just system of institutions. Only against the background of a just basic structure, including a just political constitution and a just arrangement of economic and social institutions, can one say that the requisite just procedure exists. In Part Two I shall describe in some detail a basic structure that has the necessary features. Its various institutions are explained and connected with the two principles of justice. The intuitive idea is familiar. Suppose that law and government act effectively to keep markets competitive, resources fully employed, property and wealth (especially if private ownership of the means of production is allowed) widely distributed by the appropriate forms of taxation, or whatever, and to guarantee a reasonable social minimum. Assume also that there is fair equality of opportunity underwritten by education for all; and that the other equal liberties are secured. Then it would appear that the resulting distribution of income and the pattern of expectations will tend to satisfy the difference principle. In this complex of institutions, which we think of as establishing social justice in the modern state, the advantages of the better situated improve the condition of the least favored. Or when they do not, they can be adjusted to do so, for example, by setting the social minimum at the appropriate level. As these institutions presently exist they are riddled with grave injustices. But there presumably are ways of running them compatible with their basic design and intention so that the difference principle is satisfied consistent with the demands of liberty and fair equality of opportunity. It is this fact which underlies our assurance that these arrangements can be made just.

It is evident that the role of the principle of fair opportunity is to insure that the system of cooperation is one of pure procedural justice. Unless it is satisfied, distributive justice could not be left to take care of itself, even within a restricted range. Now the great practical advantage of pure procedural justice is that it is no longer necessary in meeting the demands of justice to keep track of the endless variety of circumstances and the changing relative positions of particular persons. . . .

The Four-Stage Sequence

. . . We may think of the political process as a machine which makes social decisions when the views of representatives and their constituents are fed into it. A citizen will regard some ways of designing this machine as more just than others. So a complete conception of justice is not only able to assess laws and policies but it can also rank procedures for selecting which political opinion is to be enacted into law. . . . The citizen accepts a certain constitution as just, and he thinks that certain traditional procedures are appropriate, for example, the procedure of majority rule duly circumscribed. Yet since the political process is at best one of imperfect procedural justice, he must ascertain when the enactments of the majority are to be complied with and when they can be rejected as no longer binding. In short, he must be able to determine the grounds and limits of political duty and obligation. Thus a theory of justice has to deal with [several] types of questions, and this indicates that it may be useful to think of the principles as applied in a several-stage sequence.

At this point, then, I introduce an elaboration of the original position. So far I have supposed that once the principles of justice are chosen the parties return to their place in society and henceforth judge their claims on the social system by these principles. But if several intermediate stages are imagined to take place in a definite sequence, this sequence may give us a schema for sorting out the complications that must be faced. Each stage is to represent an appropriate point of view from which certain kinds of questions are considered. (The idea of a four-stage sequence is suggested by the United States Constitution and its history.) Thus I suppose that after the parties have adopted the principles of justice in the original position, they move to a constitutional convention. Here they are to decide upon the justice of political forms and choose a constitution: they are delegates, so to speak, to such a convention. Subject to the constraints of the principles of justice already chosen, they are to design a system for the constitutional powers of government and the basic rights of citizens. It is at this stage that they weigh the justice of procedures for coping with diverse political views. Since the appropriate conception of justice has been agreed upon, the veil of ignorance is partially lifted. The persons in the convention have, of course, no information about particular individuals: they do not know their own social position, their place in the distribution of natural attributes, or their conception of the good. But in addition to an understanding of the principles of social theory, they now know the relevant general facts about their society, that is, its natural circumstances and resources, its level of economic advance and political culture, and so on. They are no longer limited to the information implicit in the circumstances of justice. Given their theoretical knowledge and the appropriate general facts about their society, they are to choose the most effective just constitution, the constitution that satisfies the principles of justice and is best calculated to lead to just and effective legislation.

At this point we need to distinguish two problems. Ideally a just constitution would be a just procedure arranged to insure a just outcome. The procedure would be the political process governed by the constitution, the outcome the body of enacted legislation, while the principles of justice would define an independent criterion for both procedure and outcome. In pursuit of this ideal of perfect procedural justice, the first problem is to design a just procedure. To do this the liberties of equal citizenship must be incorporated into and protected by the constitution. These liberties include those of liberty of conscience and freedom of thought, liberty of the person, and equal political rights. The political system, which I assume to be some form of constitutional democracy, would not be a just procedure if it did not embody these liberties.

Clearly any feasible political procedure may yield an unjust outcome. In fact, there is no scheme of procedural political rules which guarantees that unjust legislation will not be enacted. In the case of a constitutional regime, or indeed of any political form, the ideal of perfect procedural justice cannot be realized. The best attainable scheme is one of imperfect procedural justice. Nevertheless some schemes have a greater tendency than others to result in unjust laws. The second problem, then, is to select from among the procedural arrangements that are both just and feasible those which are most likely to lead to a just and effective legal order. Once again this is Bentham's problem of the artificial identification of interests, only here the rules (just procedure) are to be framed to give legislation (just outcome) likely to accord with the principles of justice rather than the principle of utility. To solve this problem intelligently requires a knowledge of the beliefs and interests that men in the system are liable to have and of the political tactics that they will find it rational to use given their circumstances. The delegates are assumed, then, to know these things. Provided they have no information about particular individuals including themselves, the idea of the original position is not affected.

In framing a just constitution I assume that the two principles of justice already chosen define an independent standard of the desired outcome. If there is no such standard, the problem of constitutional design is not well posed, for this decision is made by running through the feasible just constitutions (given, say, by enumeration on the basis of social theory) looking for the one that in the existing circumstances will most probably result in effective and just social arrangements. Now at this point we come to the legislative stage, to take the next step in the sequence. The justice of laws and policies is to be assessed from this perspective. Proposed bills are judged from the position of a representative legislator who, as always, does not know the particulars about himself. Statutes must satisfy not only the principles of justice but whatever limits are laid down in the constitution. By moving back and forth between the stages of the constitutional convention and the legislature, the best constitution is found.

Now the question whether legislation is just or unjust, especially in connection with economic and social policies, is commonly subject to reasonable differences of opinion. In these cases judgment frequently depends upon speculative political and economic doctrines and upon social theory generally. Often the best that we can say of a law or policy is that it is at least not clearly unjust. The application of the difference principle in a precise way normally requires more information than we can expect to have and, in any case, more than the application of the first principle. It is often perfectly plain and evident when the equal liberties are violated. These violations are not only unjust but can be clearly seen to be unjust: the injustice is manifest in the public structure of institutions. But this state of affairs is comparatively rare with social and economic policies regulated by the difference principle.

I imagine then a division of labor between stages in which each deals with different questions of social justice. This division roughly corresponds to the two parts of the basic structure. The first principle of equal liberty is the primary standard for the constitutional convention. Its main requirements are that the fundamental liberties of the person and liberty of conscience and freedom of thought be protected and that the political process as a whole be a just procedure. Thus the constitution establishes a secure common status of equal citizenship and realizes political justice. The second principle comes into play at the stage of the legislature. It dictates that social and economic policies be aimed at maximizing the long-term expectations of the least advantaged under conditions of fair equality of opportunity, subject to the equal liberties being maintained. At this point the full range of general economic and social facts is brought to bear. The second part of the basic structure contains the distinctions and hierarchies of political, economic, and social forms which are necessary for efficient and mutually beneficial social cooperation. Thus the priority of the first principle of justice to the second is reflected in the priority of the constitutional convention to the legislative stage.

The last stage is that of the application of rules to particular cases by judges and administrators, and the following of rules by citizens generally. At this stage everyone has complete access to all the facts. No limits on knowledge remain since the full system of rules has now been adopted and applies to persons in virtue of their characteristics and circumstances. . . .

Equal Liberty of Conscience

. . . Now it seems that equal liberty of conscience is the only principle that the persons in the original position can acknowledge. They cannot take chances with their liberty by permitting the dominant religious or moral doctrine to persecute or to suppress others if it wishes. Even granting (what may be questioned) that it is more probable than not that one will turn out to belong to the majority (if a majority exists), to gamble in this way would show that one did not take one's religious or moral convictions seriously, or highly value the liberty to examine one's beliefs. Nor on the other hand, could the parties consent to the principle of utility. In this case their freedom would be subject to the calculus of social interests and they would be authorizing its restriction if this would lead to a greater net balance of satisfaction. Of course, as we have seen, a utilitarian may try to argue from the general facts of social life that when properly carried out the computation of advantages never justifies such limitations, at least under reasonably favorable conditions of culture. But even if the parties were persuaded of this, they might as well guarantee their freedom straightway by adopting the principle of equal liberty. There is nothing gained by not doing so, and to the extent that the outcome of the actuarial calculation is unclear a great deal may be lost. Indeed, if we give a realistic interpretation to the general knowledge available to the parties, they are forced to reject the utilitarian principle. These considerations have all the more force in view of the complexity and vagueness of these calculations (if we can so describe them) as they are bound to be made in practice. . . .

Toleration and the Common Interest

Justice as fairness provides, as we have now seen, strong arguments for an equal liberty of conscience. I shall assume that these arguments can be generalized in suitable ways to support the principle of equal liberty. Therefore the parties have good grounds for adopting this principle. It is obvious that these considerations are also important in making the case for the priority of liberty. From the perspective of the constitutional convention these arguments lead to the choice of a regime guaranteeing moral liberty and freedom of thought and belief, and of religious practice, although these may be regulated as always by the state's interest in public order and security. The state can favor no particular religion and no penalties or disabilities may be attached to any religious affiliation or lack thereof. The notion of a confessional state is rejected. Instead, particular associations may be freely organized as their members wish, and they may have their own internal life and discipline subject to the restriction that their members have a real choice of whether to continue their affiliation. The law protects the right of sanctuary in the sense that apostasy is not recognized, much less penalized, as a legal offense, any more than is having no religion at all. In these ways the state upholds moral and religious liberty.

Liberty of conscience is limited, everyone agrees, by the common interest in public order and security. This limitation itself is readily derivable from the contract point of view. First of all, acceptance of this limitation does not imply that public interests are in any sense superior to moral and religious interests; nor does it require that government view religious matters as things indifferent or claim the right to suppress philosophical beliefs whenever they conflict with affairs of state. The government has no authority to render associations either legitimate or illegitimate any more than it has this authority in regard to art and science. These matters are simply not within its competence as defined by a just constitution. Rather, given the principles of justice, the state must be understood as the association consisting of equal citizens. It does not concern itself with philosophical and religious doctrine but regulates individuals' pursuit of their moral and spiritual interests in accordance with principles to which they themselves would agree in an initial situation of equality. By exercising its powers in this way the government acts as the citizens' agent and satisfies the demands of their public conception of justice. Therefore the notion of the omnicompetent laicist state is also denied, since from the principles of justice it follows that government has neither the right nor the duty to do what it or a majority (or whatever) wants to do in questions of morals and religion. Its duty is limited to underwriting the conditions of equal moral and religious liberty.

Granting all this, it now seems evident that, in limiting liberty by reference to the common interest in public order and security, the government acts on a principle that would be chosen in the original position. For in this position each recognizes that the disruption of these conditions is a danger for the liberty of all. This follows once the maintenance of public order is understood as a necessary condition for everyone's achieving his ends whatever they are (provided they lie within certain limits) and for his fulfilling his interpretation of his moral and religious obligations. To restrain liberty of conscience at the boundary, however inexact, of the state's interest in public order is a limit derived from the principle of the common interest, that is, the interest of the representative equal citizen. The government's right to maintain public order and security is an enabling right, a right which the government must have if it is to carry out its duty of impartially supporting the conditions necessary for everyone's pursuit of his interests and living up to his obligations as he understands them.

Furthermore, liberty of conscience is to be limited only when there is a reasonable expectation that not doing so will damage the public order which the government should maintain. This expectation must be based on evidence and ways of reasoning acceptable to all. It must be supported by ordinary observation and modes of thought (including the methods of rational scientific inquiry where these are not controversial) which are generally recognized as correct. Now this reliance on what can be established and known by everyone is itself founded on the principles of justice. It implies no particular metaphysical doctrine or theory of knowledge. For this criterion appeals to what everyone can accept. It represents an agreement to limit liberty only by reference to a common knowledge and understanding of the world. Adopting this standard does not infringe upon anyone's equal freedom. On the other hand, a departure from generally recognized ways of reasoning would involve a privileged place for the views of some over others, and a principle which permitted this could not be agreed to in the original position. Furthermore, in holding that the consequences for the security of public order should not be merely possible or in certain cases even probable, but reasonably certain or imminent, there is again no implication of a particular philosophical theory. Rather this requirement expresses the high place which must be accorded to liberty of conscience and freedom of thought. . . .

Toleration of the Intolerant

Let us now consider whether justice requires the toleration of the intolerant, and if so under what conditions. There are a variety of situations in which this question arises. Some political parties in democratic states hold doctrines that commit them to suppress the constitutional liberties whenever they have the power. Again, there are those who reject intellectual freedom but who nevertheless hold positions in the university. It may appear that toleration in these cases is inconsistent with the principles of justice, or at any rate not required by them. I shall discuss the matter in connection with religious toleration. With appropriate alterations the argument can be extended to these other instances.

Several questions should be distinguished. First, there is the question whether an intolerant sect has any title to complain if it is not tolerated; second, under what conditions tolerant sects have a right not to tolerate those which are intolerant; and last, when they have the right not to tolerate them, for what ends it should be exercised. Beginning with the first question, it seems that an intolerant sect has no title to complain when it is denied an equal liberty. At least this follows if it is assumed that one has no title to object to the conduct of others that is in accordance with principles one would use in similar circumstances to justify one's actions toward them. A person's right to complain is limited to violations of principles he acknowledges himself. A complaint is a protest addressed to another in good faith. It claims a violation of a principle that both parties accept. Now, to be sure, an intolerant man will say that he acts good faith and that he does not ask anything for himself that he denies to others. His view, let us suppose, is that he is acting on the principle that God is to be obeyed and the truth accepted by all. This principle is perfectly general and by acting on it he is not making an exception in his own case. As he sees the matter, he is following the correct principle which others reject.

The reply to this defense is that, from the standpoint of the original position, no particular interpretation of religious truth can be acknowledged as binding upon citizens generally; nor can it be agreed that there should be one authority with the right to settle questions of theological doctrine. Each person must insist upon an equal right to decide what his religious obligations are. He cannot give up this right to another person or institutional authority. In fact, a man exercises his liberty in deciding to accept another as an authority even when he regards this authority as infallible, since in doing this he in no way abandons his equal liberty of conscience as a matter of constitutional law. For this liberty as secured by justice is imprescriptible: a person is always free to change his faith and this right does not depend upon his having exercised his powers of choice regularly or intelligently. . . .

Let us suppose, then, that an intolerant sect has no title to complain of intolerance. We still cannot say that tolerant sects have the right to suppress them. For one thing, others may have a right to complain. They may have this right not as a right to complain on behalf of the intolerant, but simply as a right to object whenever a principle of justice is violated. For justice is infringed whenever equal liberty is denied without sufficient reason. The question, then, is whether being intolerant of another is grounds enough for limiting someone's liberty. To simplify things, assume that the tolerant sects have the right not to tolerate the intolerant in at least one circumstance, namely, when they sincerely and with reason believe that intolerance is necessary for their own security. This right follows readily enough since, as the original position is defined, each would agree to the right of self-preservation. Justice does not require that men must stand idly by while others destroy the basis of their existence. Since it can never be to men's advantage, from a general point of view, to forgo the right of self-protection, the only question, then, is whether the tolerant have a right to curb the intolerant when they are of no immediate danger to the equal liberties of others.

Suppose that, in some way or other, an intolerant sect comes to exist within a well-ordered society accepting the two principles of justice. How are the citizens of this society to act in regard to it? Now certainly they should not suppress it simply because the members of the intolerant sect could not complain were they to do so. Rather, since a just constitution exists, all citizens have a natural duty of justice to uphold it. We are not released from this duty whenever others are disposed to act unjustly. A more stringent condition is required: there must be some considerable risks to our own legitimate interests. Thus just citizens should strive to preserve the constitution with all its equal liberties as long as liberty itself and their own freedom are not in danger. They can properly force the intolerant to respect the liberty of others, since a person can be required to respect the rights established by principles that he would acknowledge in the original position. But when the constitution itself is secure, there is no reason to deny freedom to the intolerant.

The question of tolerating the intolerant is directly related to that of the stability of a well-ordered society regulated by the two principles. We can see this as follows. It is from the position of equal citizenship that persons join the various religious associations, and it is from this position that they should conduct their discussions with one another. Citizens in a free society should not think one another incapable of a sense of justice unless this is necessary for the sake of equal liberty itself. If an intolerant sect appears in a well-ordered society, the others should keep in mind the inherent stability of their institutions. The liberties of the intolerant may persuade them to a belief in freedom. This persuasion works on the psychological principle that those whose liberties are protected by and who benefit from a just constitution will, other things equal, acquire an allegiance to it over a period of time. So even if an intolerant sect should arise, provided that it is not so strong initially that it can impose its will straightway, or does not grow so rapidly that the psychological principle has no time to take hold, it will tend to lose its intolerance and accept liberty of conscience. This is the consequence of the stability of just institutions, for stability means that when tendencies to injustice arise other forces will be called into play that work to preserve the justice of the whole arrangement. Of course, the intolerant sect may be so strong initially or growing so fast that the forces making for stability cannot convert it to liberty. This situation presents a practical dilemma which philosophy alone cannot resolve. Whether the liberty of the intolerant should be limited to preserve freedom under a just constitution depends on the circumstances. The theory of justice only characterizes the just constitution, the end of political action by reference to which practical decisions are to be made. In pursuing this end the natural strength of free institutions must not be forgotten. . . .

Some Remarks about Economic Systems

. . . Political economy is importantly concerned with the public sector and the proper form of the background institutions that regulate economic activity, with taxation and the rights of property, the structure of markets, and so on. An economic system regulates what things are produced and by what means, who receives them and in return for which contributions, and how large a fraction of social resources is devoted to saving and to the provision of public goods. Ideally all of these matters should be arranged in ways that satisfy the two principles of justice. But we have to ask whether this is possible and what in particular these principles require.

To begin with, it is helpful to distinguish between two aspects of the public sector; otherwise the difference between a private-property economy and socialism is left unclear. The first aspect has to do with the ownership of the means of production. The classical distinction is that the size of the public sector under socialism (as measured by the fraction of total output produced by state-owned firms and managed either by state officials or by workers' councils) is much larger. In a private-property economy the number of publicly owned firms is presumably small and in any event limited to special cases such as public utilities and transportation.

A second quite different feature of the public sector is the proportion of total social resources devoted to public goods. The distinction between public and private goods raises a number of intricate points, but the main idea is that a public good has two characteristic features, indivisibility and publicness. That is, there are many individuals, a public so to speak, who want more or less of this good, but if they are to enjoy it at all must each enjoy the same amount. The quantity produced cannot be divided up as private goods can and purchased by individuals according to their preferences for more and less. There are various kinds of public goods depending upon their degree of indivisibility and the size of the relevant public. The polar case of a public good is full indivisibility over the whole society. A standard example is the defense of the nation against (unjustified) foreign attack. All citizens must be provided with this good in the same amount; they cannot be given varying protection depending on their wishes. The consequence of indivisibility and publicness in these cases is that the provision of public goods must be arranged for through the political process and not through the market. Both the amount to be produced and its financing need to be worked out by legislation. Since there is no problem of distribution in the sense that all citizens receive the same quantity, distribution costs are zero.

Various features of public goods derive from these two characteristics. First of all, there is the free-rider problem. Where the public is large and includes many individuals, there is a temptation for each person to try to avoid doing his share. This is because whatever one man does his action will not significantly affect the amount produced. He regards the collective action of others as already given one way or the other. If the public good is produced his enjoyment of it is not decreased by his not making a contribution. If it is not produced his action would not have changed the situation anyway. A citizen receives the same protection from foreign invasion regardless of whether he has paid his taxes. Therefore in the polar case trade and voluntary agreements cannot be expected to develop.

It follows that arranging for and financing public goods must be taken over by the state and some binding rule requiring payment must be enforced. Even if all citizens were willing to pay their share, they would presumably do so only when they are assured that others will pay theirs as well. Thus once citizens have agreed to act collectively and not as isolated individuals taking the actions of the others as given, there is still the task of tying down the agreement. The sense of justice leads us to promote just schemes and to do our share in them when we believe that others, or sufficiently many of them, will do theirs. But in normal circumstances a reasonable assurance in this regard can only be given if there is a binding rule effectively enforced. Assuming that the public good is to everyone's advantage, and one that all would agree to arrange for, the use of coercion is perfectly rational from each man's point of view. Many of the traditional activities of government, insofar as they can be justified, can be accounted for in this way. The need for the enforcement of rules by the state will still exist even when everyone is moved by the same sense of justice. The characteristic features of essential public goods necessitate collective agreements, and firm assurance must be given to all that they will be honored.

Another aspect of the public goods situation is that of externality. When goods are public and indivisible, their production will cause benefits and losses to others which may not be taken into account by those who arrange for these goods or who decide to produce them. Thus in the polar case, if but a part of the citizenry pays taxes to cover the expenditure on public goods, the whole society is still affected by the items provided. Yet those who agree to these levies may not consider these effects, and so the amount of public expenditure is presumably different from what it would be if all benefits and losses had been considered. The everyday cases are those where the indivisibility is partial and the public is smaller. Someone who has himself inoculated against a contagious disease helps others as well as himself; and while it may not pay him to obtain this protection, it may be worth it to the local community when all advantages are tallied up.

And, of course, there are the striking cases of public harms, as when industries sully and erode the natural environment. These costs are not normally reckoned with by the market, so that the commodities produced are sold at much less than their marginal social costs. There is a divergence between private and social accounting that the market fails to register. One essential task of law and government is to institute the necessary corrections.

It is evident, then, that the indivisibility and publicness of certain essential goods, and the externalities and temptations to which they give rise, necessitate collective agreements organized and enforced by the state. That political rule is founded solely on men's propensity to self-interest and injustice is a superficial view. For even among just men, once goods are indivisible over large numbers of individuals, their actions decided upon in isolation from one another will not lead to the general good. Some collective arrangement is necessary and everyone wants assurance that it will be adhered to if he is willingly to do his part. . . .

Having considered briefly . . . the public sector, I should like to conclude with a few comments about the extent to which economic arrangements may rely upon a system of markets in which prices are freely determined by supply and demand. Several cases need to be distinguished. All regimes will normally use the market to ration out the consumption goods actually produced. Any other procedure is administratively cumbersome, and rationing and other devices will be resorted to only in special cases. But in a free market system the output of commodities is also guided as to kind and quantity by the preferences of households as shown by their purchases on the market. Goods fetching a greater than normal profit will be produced in larger amounts until the excess is reduced. In a socialist regime planners' preferences or collective decisions often have a larger part in determining the direction of production. Both private-property and socialist systems normally allow for the free choice of occupation and of one's place of work. It is only under command systems of either kind that this freedom is overtly interfered with.

Finally, a basic feature is the extent to which the market is used to decide the rate of saving and the direction of investment, as well as the fraction of national wealth devoted to conservation and to the elimination of irremediable injuries to the welfare of future generations. Here there are a number of possibilities. A collective decision may determine the rate of saving while the direction of investment is left largely to individual firms competing for funds. In both a private-property as well as in a socialist society great concern may be expressed for preventing irreversible damages and for husbanding natural resources and preserving the environment. But again either one may do rather badly.

It is evident, then, that there is no essential tie between the use of free markets and private ownership of the instruments of production. The idea that competitive prices under normal conditions are just or fair goes back at least to medieval times. While the notion that a market economy is in some sense the best scheme has been most carefully investigated by so-called bourgeois economists, this connection is a historical contingency in that, theoretically at least, a socialist regime can avail itself of the advantages of this system. One of these advantages is efficiency. Under certain conditions competitive prices select the goods to be produced and allocate resources to their production in such a manner that there is no way to improve upon either the choice of productive methods by firms, or the distribution of goods that arises from the purchases of households. There exists no rearrangement of the resulting economic configuration that makes one household better off (in view of its preferences) without making another worse off. No further mutually advantageous trades are possible; nor are there any feasible productive processes that will yield more of some desired commodity without requiring a cutback in another. For if this were not so, the situation of some individuals could be made more advantageous without a loss for anyone else. The theory of general equilibrium explains how, given the appropriate conditions, the information supplied by prices leads economic agents to act in ways that sum up to achieve this outcome. Perfect competition is a perfect procedure with respect to efficiency. Of course, the requisite conditions are highly special ones and they are seldom if ever fully satisfied in the real world. Moreover, market failures and imperfections are often serious, and compensating adjustments must be made by the allocation branch. Monopolistic restrictions, lack of information, external economies and diseconomies, and the like must be recognized and corrected. And the market fails altogether in the case of public goods. But these matters need not concern us here. These idealized arrangements are mentioned in order to clarify the related notion of pure procedural justice. The ideal conception may then be used to appraise existing arrangements and as a framework for identifying the changes that should be undertaken.

A further and more significant advantage of a market system is that, given the requisite background institutions, it is consistent with equal liberties and fair equality of opportunity. Citizens have a free choice of careers and occupations. There is no reason at all for the forced and central direction of labor. Indeed, in the absence of some differences in earnings as these arise in a competitive scheme, it is hard to see how, under ordinary circumstances anyway, certain aspects of a command society inconsistent with liberty can be avoided. Moreover, a system of markets decentralizes the exercise of economic power. Whatever the internal nature of firms, whether they are privately or state owned, or whether they are run by entrepreneurs or by managers elected by workers, they take the prices of outputs and inputs as given and draw up their plans accordingly. When markets are truly competitive, firms do not engage in price wars or other contests for market power. In conformity with political decisions reached democratically, the government regulates the economic climate by adjusting certain elements under its control, such as the overall amount of investment, the rate of interest, and the quantity of money, and so on. There is no necessity for comprehensive direct planning. Individual households and firms are free to make their decisions independently, subject to the general conditions of the economy.

In noting the consistency of market arrangements with socialist institutions, it is essential to distinguish between the allocative and the distributive functions of prices. The former is connected with their use to achieve economic efficiency, the latter with their determining the income to be received by individuals in return for what they contribute. It is perfectly consistent for a socialist regime to establish an interest rate to allocate resources among investment projects and to compute rental charges for the use of capital and scarce natural assets such as land and forests. Indeed, this must be done if these means of production are to be employed in the best way. For even if these assets should fall out of the sky without human effort, they are nevertheless productive in the sense that when combined with other factors a greater output results. It does not follow, however, that there need be private persons who as owners of these assets receive the monetary equivalents of these evaluations. Rather these accounting prices are indicators for drawing up an efficient schedule of economic activities. Except in the case of work of all kinds, prices under socialism do not correspond to income paid over to private individuals. Instead, the income imputed to natural and collective assets accrues to the state, and therefore their prices have no distributive function.

It is necessary, then, to recognize that market institutions are common to both private-property and socialist regimes, and to distinguish between the allocative and the distributive function of prices. Since under socialism the means of production and natural resources are publicly owned, the distributive function is greatly restricted, whereas a private-property system uses prices in varying degrees for both purposes. Which of these systems and the many intermediate forms most fully answers to the requirements of justice cannot, I think, be determined in advance. There is presumably no general answer to this question, since it depends in large part upon the traditions, institutions, and social forces of each country, and its particular historical circumstances. The theory of justice does not include these matters. But what it can do is to set out in a schematic way the outlines of a just economic system that admits of several variations. The political judgment in any given case will then turn on which variation is most likely to work out best in practice. A conception of justice is a necessary part of any such political assessment, but it is not sufficient.

NOTES

1. As the text suggests, I shall regard Locke's *Second Treatise of Government*, Rousseau's *The Social Contract*, and Kant's ethical works beginning with *The Foundations of the Metaphysics of Morals* as definitive of the contract tradition. For all of its greatness, Hobbes's *Leviathan* raises special problems. A general historical survey is provided by J. W. Gough, *The Social Contract*, 2nd ed. (Oxford, The Clarendon Press, 1957), and Otto Gierke, *Natural Law and the Theory of Society*, trans. with an introduction by Ernest Barker (Cambridge, The University Press, 1934). A presentation of the contract view as primarily an ethical theory is to be found in G. R. Grice, *The Grounds of Moral Judgment* (Cambridge, The University Press, 1967). . . .
2. Kant is clear that the original agreement is hypothetical. See *The Metaphysics of*

Morals, pt. I *(Rechtslehre)*, especially §§47, 52; and pt. II of the essay "Concerning the Common Saying: This May Be True in Theory but It Does Not Apply in Practice," in *Kant's Political Writings*, ed. Hans Reiss and trans. by H. B. Nisbet (Cambridge: The University Press, 1970), pp. 73–87. . . .

3. The process of mutual adjustment of principles and considered judgments is not peculiar to moral philosophy. See Nelson Goodman, *Fact, Fiction, and Forecast* (Cambridge, Mass.: Harvard University Press, 1955), pp. 65–68, for parallel remarks concerning the justification of the principles of deductive and inductive inference.

4. The veil of ignorance is so natural a condition that something like it must have occurred to many. The closest express statement of it known to me is found in J. C. Harsanyi, "Cardinal Utility in Welfare Economics and in the Theory of Risk-Taking," *Journal of Political Economy*, vol. 61 (1953). Harsanyi uses it to develop a utilitarian theory. . . .

5. This fact is generally recognized in welfare economics, as when it is said that efficiency is to be balanced against equity. See for example Tibor Scitovsky, *Welfare and Competition* (London: George Allen and Unwin, 1952), pp. 60–69 and I. M. D. Little, *A Critique of Welfare Economics*, 2nd ed. (Oxford: The Clarendon Press, 1957), ch. VI. esp. pp. 112–116. See Sen's remarks on the limitations of the principle of efficiency, *Collective Choice and Social Welfare*, pp. 22, 24–26, 83–86.

6. This formulation of the aristocratic ideal is derived from Santayana's account of aristocracy in ch. IV of *Reason and Society* (New York: Charles Scribner, 1905), pp. 109f. He says, for example, "an aristocratic regimen can only be justified by radiating benefit and by proving that were less given to those above, less would be attained by those beneath them." I am indebted to Robert Rodes for pointing out to me that natural aristocracy is a possible interpretation of the two principles of justice and that an ideal feudal system might also try to fulfill the difference principle.

7. See Herbert Spiegelberg, "A Defense of Human Equality," *Philosophical Review*, vol. 53 (1944), pp. 101, 113–123; and D. D. Raphael, "Justice and Liberty," *Proceedings of the Aristotelian Society*, vol. 51 (1950–1951), pp. 187f.

8. An accessible discussion of this and other rules of choice under uncertainty can be found in W. J. Baumol, *Economic Theory and Operations Analysis*, 2nd ed. (Englewood Cliffs, N.J.: Prentice Hall, Inc., 1965), ch. 24. Baumol gives a geometric interpretation of these rules . . . See pp. 558–562. See also R. D. Luce and Howard Raiffa, *Games and Decisions* (New York: John Wiley and Sons, Inc., 1957), ch. XIII, for a fuller account.

9. Here I borrow from William Fellner, *Probability and Profit* (Homewood, Ill.: R. D. Irwin, Inc., 1965), pp. 140–142, where these features are noted.

LIBERTARIANISM

John Rawls, as we have seen, presents an elegant and powerful case for his theory of justice. Adopting his principles would require extensive changes in our national priorities, even if we retained a basically capitalistic system of production. Nonetheless, he does provide a revamped theoretical foundation for the dominant liberalism of our time, which is committed to personal liberty and to reducing social and economic inequalities. Thus it should not be surprising that his strongest critics should come from thinkers outside this political mainstream. Although a challenge to Rawls has arisen from the left, one of his most trenchant opponents has been Robert Nozick, a libertarian.

As a libertarian, Nozick places individual liberty at center stage as the prime political value. Nozick challenges the assumption, common to liberal political thought, that justice demands extensive economic redistribution. He denies that the state may legitimately tax us—take our money by threat of coercion—to accomplish that redistribution. As a defender of laissez-faire capitalism and a critic of governmental authority, Nozick stands along with many contemporary American conservatives in the tradition of the seventeenth- and eighteenth-century liberalism of John Locke and Adam Smith.

Nozick assumes, in accordance with this tradition, a perspective of individual rights—rights that may not be transgressed by others, either as individuals or collectively as the state. Commonly called Lockean, or negative, these rights constitute "side constraints" on the actions of others, ensuring a person's freedom from interference in the pursuit of his or her own life. They are negative because they require only that others refrain from acting in certain ways, in particular, that they refrain from interfering with us. Beyond this, no one is obliged to do anything positive for us; we have no right, for example, to expect others to provide us with satisfying work or with any material goods we might need. Each individual is to be seen as autonomous and responsible, and should be left to fashion his or her own life free from the interference of others—as long as this is compatible with the right of others to do the same. Only the acknowledgment of this almost absolute right to be free from coercion, argues Nozick, fully respects the distinctiveness of persons, each with a unique life to lead.

This framework of individual rights and corresponding duties constitutes the basis of what power the government may legitimately have. In Nozick's view, the only morally legitimate state is the so-called night-watchman state, one whose functions are restricted to protecting the negative rights of citizens, that is, to protect them against force, theft, fraud, and so on. Yet even this limited state is not obviously consistent with libertarian constraints, since consent is the only basis of political obligation (beyond that imposed by others' natural rights) and people have never expressly consented to the rule of government. Nozick's first task, then, is to justify his minimal state in the face of the anarchist claim that *no* government is morally legitimate. Nozick answers the anarchist by sketching how the minimal state could arise legitimately from a state of nature without violating the rights of any individual (by an invisible hand process, analogous to the invisible hand of Adam Smith's economics, in which the free choices of separate individuals, each pursuing his or her own private interest, promote a result—namely, the formation of a state—not intended by any one of them.) For this reason, the night-watchman state is morally acceptable.

Nozick claims further that this is the most extensive kind of state that can be justified, and rejects in particular the claim that a larger state is necessary in order to achieve justice in economic distribution. He argues for this by presenting his own libertarian conception of economic justice and by criticizing alternative views. In contrast to theories he calls end-state and patterned, Nozick proposes what he terms a historical entitlement theory of justice. End-state principles hold that distributive justice depends upon certain structural features of the situation (for example, which distribution results in the greatest utility), regardless of the origins of and entitlements to the distributed goods. By contrast, historical principles hold that past circumstances "can create differential entitlements or differential deserts to things." A principle is patterned, on the other hand, if it specifies that distribution is to vary along some natural (that is, biological or social) dimension, for example, according to I.Q. (or need or height). A patterned principle may be historical if it looks to past action, as in "distribute according to moral merit."

Nozick's entitlement theory is historical and unpatterned since it holds that a distribution is just if it arises from a prior just distribution by just means. Things may be acquired originally by one's taking something that belongs to no one else, if this does not make others worse off than before. There are a number of ways of legitimately transferring justly acquired objects; gift and voluntary exchange are among them—theft and blackmail are not. There is, however, no pattern to which a just distribution should conform. In the absence of force and fraud, people may do what they wish with their goods or holdings. A parent has the right, for example, to leave an inheritance for her daughter (or anyone else's for that matter). The daughter does not necessarily deserve her inheritance and the advantage in life which it gives her, any more than she merits her native intelligence. But, in Nozick's view, she would be entitled to both; neither is a social good that society is free to distribute. One has a right to acquire and dispose of one's property as one sees fit, and an individual is entitled to his personal talents and characteristics and to whatever property he can obtain with them, so long as the negative rights of others are not violated in the process.

To disturb the free market is to tread on liberty, and the redistribution of wealth through taxation, claims Nozick, is on a par with forced labor. Justice forbids it. Nozick further argues that any patterned principle of distribution will conflict with liberty. For whatever pattern is chosen, free people will exchange labor and goods and thus upset the pattern. Enforcement of patterned conceptions of justice is thus incompatible with liberty since any nonlibertarian society would have to "forbid capitalist acts between consenting adults."

Nozick's critique of Rawls also strengthens the case for the entitlement view. He emphasizes that social goods do not come into the world unattached, like manna from heaven. To focus exclusively on distribution, as he contends Rawls does, is to ignore production, to ignore the fact that those goods must be created by someone who in doing so establishes a title to them. Why should society be viewed as a cooperative project in the first place, or the talents and endowments of each person be seen as part of the collective assets of society to which all have a title? Indeed, the terms of Rawls's contract seem unfair to the well-endowed because their skill and talent are exploited by others in society. It is hardly unjust, argues Nozick, to let economic holdings vary with the abilities, interests, and endeavors of individuals. Rawls's whole procedure, he believes, is biased against the entitlement view because the model of the original position behind a veil of ignorance guarantees that an end-state principle will be chosen.

Robert Nozick
Anarchy, State, and Utopia

THE ENTITLEMENT THEORY

The minimal state is the most extensive state that can be justified. Any state more extensive violates people's rights. Yet many persons have put forth reasons purporting to justify a more extensive state. It is impossible within the compass of this book to examine all the reasons that have been put forth. Therefore, I shall focus upon those generally acknowledged to be most weighty and influential, to see precisely wherein they fail. In this chapter we consider the claim that a more extensive state is justified, because necessary (or the best instrument) to achieve distributive justice.
. . .
　　　The term "distributive justice" is not a neutral one. Hearing the term "distribution," most people presume that some thing or mechanism uses some principle or criterion to give out a supply of things. Into this process of distributing shares some error may have crept. So it is an open question, at least, whether *re*distribution should take place; whether we should do again what has already been done once, though poorly. However, we are not in the position of children who have been given portions of pie by someone who now makes last minute adjustments to rectify careless cutting. There is no *central* distribution, no person or group entitled to control all the resources, jointly deciding how they are to be doled out. What each person gets, he gets from others who give to him in exchange for something, or as a gift. In a free society, diverse persons control different resources, and new holdings arise out of the voluntary exchanges and actions of persons. There is no more a distributing or distribution of shares than there is a distributing of mates in a society in which persons choose whom they shall marry. The total result is the product of many individual decisions which the different individuals involved are entitled to make. . . . We shall speak of people's holdings; a principle of justice in holdings describes (part of) what justice tells us (requires) about holdings. I shall state first what I take to be the correct view about justice in holdings, and then turn to the discussion of alternate views.

From *Anarchy, State and Utopia*, Chapter 7, "Distributive Justice" (New York: Basic Books, 1974). Reprinted By permission. Some footnotes omitted.

The subject of justice in holdings consists of three major topics. The first is the *original acquisition of holdings*, the appropriation of unheld things. This includes the issues of how unheld things may come to be held, the process, or processes, by which unheld things may come to be held, the things that may come to be held by these processes, the extent of what comes to be held by a particular process, and so on. We shall refer to the complicated truth about this topic, which we shall not formulate here, as the principle of justice in acquisition. The second topic concerns the *transfer of holdings* from one person to another. By what processes may a person transfer holdings to another? How may a person acquire a holding from another who holds it? Under this topic come general descriptions of voluntary exchange, and gift and (on the other hand) fraud, as well as reference to particular conventional details fixed upon in a given society. The complicated truth about this subject (with placeholders for conventional details) we shall call the principle of justice in transfer. (And we shall suppose it also includes principles governing how a person may divest himself of a holding, passing it into an unheld state.)

If the world were wholly just, the following inductive definition would exhaustively cover the subject of justice in holdings.

1. A person who acquires a holding in accordance with the principle of justice in acquisition is entitled to that holding.
2. A person who acquires a holding in accordance with the principle of justice in transfer, from someone else entitled to the holding, is entitled to the holding.
3. No one is entitled to a holding except by (repeated) applications of 1 and 2.

The complete principle of distributive justice would say simply that a distribution is just if everyone is entitled to the holdings they possess under the distribution.

A distribution is just if it arises from another just distribution by legitimate means. The legitimate means of moving from one distribution to another are specified by the principle of justice in transfer. The legitimate first "moves" are specified by the principle of justice in acquisition.* Whatever arises from a just situation by just steps is itself just. The means of change specified by the principle of justice in transfer preserve justice. As correct rules of inference are truth-preserving, and any conclusion deduced via repeated application of such rules from only true premises is itself true, so the means of transition from one situation to another specified by the principle of justice in transfer are justice-preserving, and any situation actually arising from repeated transitions in accordance with the principle from a just situation is itself just. The parallel between justice-preserving transformations and truth-preserving transformations illumi-

---

*Applications of the principle of justice in acquisition may also occur as part of the move from one distribution to another. You may find an unheld thing now and appropriate it. Acquisitions also are to be understood as included when, to simplify, I speak only of transitions by transfers.

nates where it fails as well as where it holds. That a conclusion could have been deduced by truth-preserving means from premises that are true suffices to show its truth. That from a just situation a situation *could* have arisen via justice-preserving means does *not* suffice to show its justice. The fact that a thief's victims voluntarily *could* have presented him with gifts does not entitle the thief to his ill-gotten gains. Justice in holdings is historical; it depends upon what actually has happened. We shall return to this point later.

Not all actual situations are generated in accordance with the two principles of justice in holdings: the principle of justice in acquisition and the principle of justice in transfer. Some people steal from others, or defraud them, or enslave them, seizing their product and preventing them from living as they choose, or forcibly exclude others from competing in exchanges. None of these are permissible modes of transition from one situation to another. And some persons acquire holdings by means not sanctioned by the principle of justice in acquisition. The existence of past injustice (previous violations of the first two principles of justice in holdings) raises the third major topic under justice in holdings: the rectification of injustice in holdings. If past injustice has shaped present holdings in various ways, some identifiable and some not, what now, if anything, ought to be done to rectify these injustices? What obligations do the performers of injustice have toward those whose position is worse than it would have been had the injustice not been done? Or, than it would have been had compensation been paid promptly? How, if at all, do things change if the beneficiaries and those made worse off are not the direct parties in the act of injustice, but, for example, their descendants? Is an injustice done to someone whose holding was itself based upon an unrectified injustice? How far back must one go in wiping clean the historical slate of injustices? What may victims of injustice permissibly do in order to rectify the injustices being done to them, including the many injustices done by persons acting through their government? I do not know of a thorough or theoretically sophisticated treatment of such issues. Idealizing greatly, let us suppose theoretical investigation will produce a principle of rectification. This principle uses historical information about previous situations and injustices done in them (as defined by the first two principles of justice and rights against interference), and information about the actual course of events that flowed from these injustices, until the present, and it yields a description (or descriptions) of holdings in the society. The principle of rectification presumably will make use of its best estimate of subjunctive information about what would have occurred. . . .

The general outlines of the theory of justice in holdings are that the holdings of a person are just if he is entitled to them by the principles of justice in acquisition and transfer, or by the principle of rectification of injustice (as specified by the first two principles). If each person's holdings are just, then the total set (distribution) of holdings is just. To turn these general outlines into a specific theory we would have to specify the details of each of the three principles of justice in holdings: the principle of acquisition of holdings, the principle of transfer of holdings, and the principle of rectification of violations of the first two principles. I shall not attempt that task here. (Locke's principle of justice in acquisition is discussed below.)

Historical Principles and End-Result Principles

The general outlines of the entitlement theory illuminate the nature and defects of other conceptions of distributive justice. The entitlement theory of justice in distribution is *historical*; whether a distribution is just depends upon how it came about. In contrast, *current time-slice principles* of justice hold that the justice of a distribution is determined by how things are distributed (who has what) as judged by some *structural* principle(s) of just distribution. A utilitarian who judges between any two distributions by seeing which has the greater sum of utility and, if the sums tie, applies some fixed equality criterion to choose the more equal distribution, would hold a current time-slice principle of justice. As would someone who had a fixed schedule of trade-offs between the sum of happiness and equality. According to a current time-slice principle, all that needs to be looked at, in judging the justice of a distribution, is who ends up with what; in comparing any two distributions one need look only at the matrix presenting the distributions. No further information need be fed into a principle of justice. It is a consequence of such principles of justice that any two structurally identical distributions are equally just. (Two distributions are structurally identical if they present the same profile, but perhaps have different persons occupying the particular slots. My having ten and your having five, and my having five and your having ten are structurally identical distributions.) Welfare economics is the theory of current time-slice principles of justice. The subject is conceived as operating on matrices representing only current information about distribution. This, as well as some of the usual conditions (for example, the choice of distribution is invariant under relabeling of columns), guarantees that welfare economics will be a current time-slice theory, with all of its inadequacies.

Most persons do not accept current time-slice principles as constituting the whole story about distributive shares. They think it relevant in assessing the justice of a situation to consider not only the distribution it embodies, but also how that distribution came about. If some persons are in prison for murder or war crimes, we do not say that to assess the justice of the distribution in the society we must look only at what this person has, and that person has, and that person has, . . . at the current time. We think it relevant to ask whether someone did something so that he *deserved* to be punished, deserved to have a lower share. Most will agree to the relevance of further information with regard to punishments and penalties. Consider also desired things. One traditional socialist view is that workers are entitled to the product and full fruits of their labor; they have earned it; a distribution is unjust if it does not give the workers what they are entitled to. Such entitlements are based upon some past history. . . . [A] socialist rightly, in my view, holds onto the notions of earning, producing, entitlement, desert, and so forth, and he rejects current time-slice principles that look only to the structure of the resulting set of holdings. (The set of holdings resulting from what? Isn't it implausible that how holdings are produced and come to exist has no effect at all on who should hold what?) His mistake lies in his view of what entitlements arise out of what sorts of productive processes.

We construe the position we discuss too narrowly by speaking of *current* time-slice principles. Nothing is changed if structural principles operate upon a time sequence of current time-slice profiles and, for example, give someone more now to counterbalance the less he has had earlier. A utilitarian or an egalitarian or any mixture of the two over time will inherit the difficulties of his more myopic comrades. He is not helped by the fact that *some* of the information others consider relevant in assessing a distribution is reflected, unrecoverably, in past matrices. Henceforth, we shall refer to such unhistorical principles of distributive justice, including the current time-slice principles, as *end-result principles* or *end-state principles*.

In contrast to end-result principles of justice, *historical principles* of justice hold that past circumstances or actions of people can create differential entitlements or differential deserts to things. An injustice can be worked by moving from one distribution to another structurally identical one, for the second, in profile the same, may violate people's entitlements or deserts; it may not fit the actual history.

Patterning

The entitlement principles of justice in holdings that we have sketched are historical principles of justice. To better understand their precise character, we shall distinguish them from another subclass of the historical principles. Consider, as an example, the principle of distribution according to moral merit. This principle requires that total distributive shares vary directly with moral merit; no person should have a greater share than anyone whose moral merit is greater. (If moral merit could be not merely ordered but measured on an interval or ratio scale, stronger principles could be formulated.) Or consider the principle that results by substituting "usefulness to society" for "moral merit" in the previous principle. Or instead of "distribute according to moral merit," or "distribute according to usefulness to society," we might consider "distribute according to the weighted sum of moral merit, usefulness to society, and need," with the weights of the different dimensions equal. Let us call a principle of distribution *patterned* if it specifies that a distribution is to vary along with some natural dimension, weighted sum of natural dimensions, or lexicographic ordering of natural dimensions. And let us say a distribution is patterned if it accords with some patterned principle. (I speak of natural dimensions, admittedly without a general criterion for them, because for any set of holdings some artificial dimensions can be gimmicked up to vary along with the distribution of the set.) The principle of distribution in accordance with moral merit is a patterned historical principle, which specifies a patterned distribution. "Distribute according to I.Q." is a patterned principle that looks to information not contained in distributional matrices.

It is not historical, however, in that it does not look to any past actions creating differential entitlements to evaluate a distribution; it requires only distributional matrices whose columns are labeled by I.Q. scores. The distribution in a society, however, may be composed of such simple patterned distributions, without itself being simply patterned. Different sectors may operate different patterns, or some combination of patterns may operate in different proportions across a society. A distribution composed in this manner, from a small number of patterned distributions, we also shall term "patterned." And we extend the use of "pattern" to include the overall designs put forth by combinations of end-state principles.

Almost every suggested principle of distributive justice is patterned: to each according to his moral merit, or needs, or marginal product, or how hard he tries, or the weighted sum of the foregoing, and so on. The principle of entitlement we have sketched is *not* patterned. There is no one natural dimension or weighted sum or combination of a small number of natural dimensions that yields the distributions generated in accordance with the principle of entitlement. The set of holdings that results when some persons receive their marginal products, others win at gambling, others receive a share of their mate's income, others receive gifts from foundations, others receive interest on loans, others receive gifts from admirers, others receive returns on investment, others make for themselves much of what they have, others find things, and so on, will not be patterned. Heavy strands of patterns will run through it; significant portions of the variance in holdings will be accounted for by pattern-variables. If most people most of the time choose to transfer some of their entitlements to others only in exchange for something from them, then a large part of what many people hold will vary with what they held that others wanted. More details are provided by the theory of marginal productivity. But gifts to relatives, charitable donations, bequests to children, and the like, are not best conceived, in the first instance, in this manner. Ignoring the strands of pattern, let us suppose for the moment that a distribution actually arrived at by the operation of the principle of entitlement is random with respect to any pattern. Though the resulting set of holdings will be unpatterned, it will not be incomprehensible, for it can be seen as arising from the operation of a small number of principles. These principles specify how an initial distribution may arise (the principle of acquisition of holdings) and how distributions may be transformed into others (the principle of transfer of holdings). The process whereby the set of holdings is generated will be intelligible, though the set of holdings itself that results from this process will be unpatterned.

The writings of F. A. Hayek focus less than is usually done upon what patterning distributive justice requires. Hayek argues that we cannot know enough about each person's situation to distribute to each according to his moral merit (but would justice demand we do so if we did have this knowledge?); and he goes on to say, "our objection is against all attempts to impress upon society a deliberately chosen pattern of distribution, whether it be an order of equality or of inequality."[1] However, Hayek concludes that in a free society there will be distribution in accordance with value rather than moral merit; that is, in accordance with the perceived value of a person's actions and services to others. Despite his rejection of a patterned conception of distributive justice, Hayek himself suggests a pattern he thinks justifiable: distribution in accordance with the perceived benefits given to others, leaving room for the complaint that a free society does not realize exactly this pattern. Stating this patterned strand of a free capitalist society more precisely, we get "To each according to how much he benefits others who have the resources for benefiting those who benefit them." This will seem arbitrary unless some acceptable initial set of holdings is specified, or unless it is held that the operation of the system over time washes out any significant effects from the initial set of holdings. As an example of the latter, if almost anyone would have bought a car from Henry Ford, the supposition that it was an arbitrary matter who held the money then (and so bought) would not place Henry Ford's earnings under a cloud. In any event, *his* coming to hold it is not arbitrary. Distribution according to benefits to others *is* a major patterned strand in a free capitalist society, as Hayek correctly points out, but it is only a strand and does not constitute the whole pattern of a system of entitlements (namely, inheritance, gifts for arbitrary reasons, charity, and so on) or a standard that one should insist a society fit. Will people tolerate for long a system yielding distributions that they believe are unpatterned? No doubt people will not long accept a distribution they believe is *unjust.* People want their society to be and to look just. But must the look of justice reside in a resulting pattern rather than in the underlying generating principles? We are in no position to conclude that the inhabitants of a society embodying an entitlement conception of justice in holdings will find it unacceptable. Still, it must be granted that were people's reasons for transferring some of their holdings to others always irrational or arbitrary, we would find this disturbing. (Suppose people always determined what holdings they would transfer, and to whom, by using a random device.) We feel more comfortable upholding the justice of an entitlement system if most of the transfers under it are done for reasons. This does not mean necessarily that all deserve what holdings they receive. It means only that there is a purpose or point to someone's transferring a holding to one person rather than to another; that usually we can see what the transferrer thinks he's gaining, what cause he thinks he's serving, what goals he thinks he's helping to achieve, and so forth. Since in a capitalist society people often transfer holdings to others in accordance with how much they perceive these others benefiting them, the fabric constituted by the individual trans-

---

*We certainly benefit because great economic incentives operate to get others to spend much time and energy to figure out how to serve us by providing things we will want to pay for. It is not mere paradox mongering to wonder whether capitalism should be criticized for most rewarding and hence encouraging, not individualists like Thoreau who go about their own lives, but people who are occupied with serving others and winning them as customers. But to defend capitalism one need not think businessmen are the finest human types. (I do not mean to join here the general maligning of businessmen, either.) Those who think the finest should acquire the most can try to convince their fellows to transfer resources in accordance with *that* principle.

actions and transfers is largely reasonable and intelligible.* (Gifts to loved ones, bequests to children, charity to the needy also are nonarbitrary components of the fabric.) In stressing the large strand of distribution in accordance with benefit to others, Hayek shows the point of many transfers, and so shows that the system of transfer of entitlements is not just spinning its gears aimlessly. The system of entitlements is defensible when constituted by the individual aims of individual transactions. No overarching aim is needed, no distributional pattern is required.

To think that the task of a theory of distributive justice is to fill in the blank in "to each according to his————" is to be predisposed to search for a pattern; and the separate treatment of "from each according to his ————" treats production and distribution as two separate and independent issues. On an entitlement view these are *not* two separate questions. Whoever makes something, having bought or contracted for all other held resources used in the process (transferring some of his holdings for these cooperating factors), is entitled to it. The situation is *not* one of something's getting made, and there being an open question of who is to get it. Things come into the world already attached to people having entitlements over them. From the point of view of the historical entitlement conception of justice in holdings, those who start afresh to complete "to each according to his————" treat objects as if they appeared from nowhere, out of nothing. A complete theory of justice might cover this limit case as well; perhaps here is a use for the usual conceptions of distributive justice.

So entrenched are maxims of the usual form that perhaps we should present the entitlement conception as a competitor. Ignoring acquisition and rectification, we might say:

> From each according to what he chooses to do, to each according to what he makes for himself (perhaps with the contracted aid of others) and what others choose to do for him and choose to give him of what they've been given previously (under this maxim) and haven't yet expended or transferred.

This, the discerning reader will have noticed, has its defects as a slogan. So as a summary and great simplification (and not as a maxim with any independent meaning) we have:

> *From each as they choose, to each as they are chosen.*

How Liberty Upsets Patterns

It is not clear how those holding alternative conceptions of distributive justice can reject the entitlement conception of justice in holdings. For suppose a distribution favored by one of these non-entitlement conceptions is realized. Let us suppose it is your favorite one and let us call this distribution D_1; perhaps everyone has an equal share, perhaps shares vary in accordance with some dimension you treasure. Now suppose that Wilt Chamberlain is greatly in demand by basketball teams, being a great gate attraction. (Also suppose contracts run only for a year, with players being free agents.) He signs the following sort of contract with a team: In each home game, twenty-five cents from the price of each ticket of admission goes to him. (We ignore the question of whether he is "gouging" the owners, letting them look out for themselves.) The season starts, and people cheerfully attend his team's games; they buy their tickets, each time dropping a separate twenty-five cents of their admission price into a special box with Chamberlain's name on it. They are excited about seeing him play; it is worth the total admission price to them. Let us suppose that in one season one million persons attend his home games, and Wilt Chamberlain winds up with $250,000, a much larger sum than the average income and larger even than anyone else has. Is he entitled to this income? Is this new distribution D_2, unjust? If so, why? There is *no* question about whether each of the people was entitled to the control over the resources they held in D_1; because that was the distribution (your favorite) that (for the purposes of argument) we assumed was acceptable. Each of these persons *chose* to give twenty-five cents of their money to Chamberlain. They could have spent it on going to the movies, or on candy bars, or on copies of *Dissent* magazine, or of *Monthly Review*. But they all, at least one million of them, converged on giving it to Wilt Chamberlain in exchange for watching him play basketball. If D_1 was a just distribution, and people voluntarily moved from it to D_2 transferring parts of their shares they were given under D_1 (what was it for if not to do something with?), isn't D_2 also just? If the people were entitled to dispose of the resources to which they were entitled (under D_1), didn't this include their being entitled to give it to, or exchange it with, Wilt Chamberlain? Can anyone else complain on grounds of justice? Each other person already has his legitimate share under D_1. Under D_1, there is nothing that anyone has that anyone else has a claim of justice against. After someone transfers something to Wilt Chamberlain, third parties *still* have their legitimate shares; *their* shares are not changed. By what process could such a transfer among two persons give rise to a legitimate claim of distributive justice on a portion of what was transferred, by a third party who had no claim of justice on any holding of the others *before* the transfers?* To cut off objections irrelevant here, we might imagine the exchanges occurring in a socialist society, after hours. After playing whatever basketball he does in his daily work, or

---

*Might not a transfer have instrumental effects on a third party, changing his feasible options? (But what if the two parties to the transfer independently had used their holdings in this fashion?) I discuss this question below, but note here that this question concedes the point for distributions of ultimate intrinsic noninstrumental goods (pure utility experiences, so to speak) that are transferable. It also might be objected that the transfer might make a third party more envious because it worsens his position relative to someone else. I find it incomprehensible how this can be thought to involve a claim of justice. . . .

Here and elsewhere in this chapter, a theory which incorporates elements of pure procedural justice might find what I say acceptable, *if* kept in its proper place; that is, if background institutions exist to ensure the satisfaction of certain conditions on distributive shares. But if these institutions are not themselves the sum or invisible-hand result of people's voluntary (nonaggressive) actions, the constraints they impose require justification. At no point does *our* argument assume any background institutions more extensive than those of the minimal night-watchman state, a state limited to protecting persons against murder, assault, theft, fraud, and so forth.

doing whatever other daily work he does, Wilt Chamberlain decides to put in *overtime* to earn additional money. (First his work quota is set; he works time over that.) Or imagine it is a skilled juggler people like to see, who puts on shows after hours.

Why might someone work overtime in a society in which it is assumed their needs are satisfied? Perhaps because they care about things other than needs. I like to write in books that I read, and to have easy access to books for browsing at odd hours. It would be very pleasant and convenient to have the resources of Widener Library in my back yard. No society, I assume, will provide such resources close to each person who would like them as part of his regular allotment (under D_1). Thus, persons either must do without some extra things that they want, or be allowed to do something extra to get some of these things. On what basis could the inequalities that would eventuate be forbidden? Notice also that small factories would spring up in a socialist society, unless forbidden. I melt down some of my personal possessions (under D_1) and build a machine out of the material. I offer you, and others, a philosophy lecture once a week in exchange for your cranking the handle on my machine, whose products I exchange for yet other things, and so on. (The raw materials used by the machine are given to me by others who possess them under D_1, in exchange for hearing lectures.) Each person might participate to gain things over and above their allotment under D_1. Some persons even might want to leave their job in socialist industry and work full time in this private sector. I shall say something more about these issues in the next chapter. Here I wish merely to note how private property even in means of production would occur in a socialist society that did not forbid people to use as they wished some of the resources they are given under the socialist distribution D_1. The socialist society would have to forbid capitalist acts between consenting adults.

The general point illustrated by the Wilt Chamberlain example and the example of the entrepreneur in a socialist society is that no end-state principle or distributional patterned principle of justice can be continuously realized without continuous interference with people's lives. Any favored pattern would be transformed into one unfavored by the principle, by people choosing to act in various ways; for example, by people exchanging goods and services with other people, or giving things to other people, things the transferrers are entitled to under the favored distributional pattern. To maintain a pattern one must either continually interfere to stop people from transferring resources as they wish to, or continually (or periodically) interfere to take from some persons resources that others for some reason chose to transfer to them. (But if some time limit is to be set on how long people may keep resources others voluntarily transfer to them, why let them keep these resources for *any* period of time? Why not have immediate confiscation?) It might be objected that all persons voluntarily will choose to refrain from actions which would upset the pattern. This presupposes unrealistically (1) that all will most want to maintain the pattern (are those who don't, to be "reeducated" or forced to undergo "self-criticism"?), (2) that each can gather enough information about his own actions and the ongoing activities of others to discover which of his actions will upset the pattern, and (3) that diverse and far-flung persons can coordinate their actions to dovetail into the pattern. Compare the manner in which the market is neutral among persons' desires, as it reflects and transmits widely scattered information via prices, and coordinates persons' activities. . . .

Redistribution and Property Rights

Apparently, patterned principles allow people to choose to spend upon themselves, but not upon others, those resources they are entitled to (or rather, receive) under some favored distributional pattern D_1. For if each of several persons chooses to expend some of his D_1 resources upon one other person, then that other person will receive more than his D_1 share, disturbing the favored distributional pattern. Maintaining a distributional pattern is individualism with a vengeance! Patterned distributional principles do not give people what entitlement principles do, only better distributed. For they do not give the right to choose what to do with what one has; they do not give the right to choose to pursue an end involving (intrinsically, or as a means) the enhancement of another's position. To such views, families are disturbing; for within a family occur transfers that upset the favored distributional pattern. Either families themselves become units to which distribution takes place, the column occupiers (on what rationale?), or loving behavior is forbidden. We should note in passing the ambivalent position of radicals toward the family. Its loving relationships are seen as a model to be emulated and extended across the whole society, at the same time that it is denounced as a suffocating institution to be broken and condemned as a focus of parochial concerns that interfere with achieving radical goals. Need we say that it is not appropriate to enforce across the wider society the relationships of love and care appropriate within a family, relationships which are voluntarily undertaken?* Incidentally, love is an interesting instance of another relationship that is historical, in that (like justice) it depends upon what actually occurred. An adult may come to love another because of the other's characteristics; but it is the other person, and not the characteristics, that is loved. The love is not transferrable to someone else with the same characteristics, even to one who "scores" higher for these characteristics. And the love endures through changes of the characteristics that gave rise to it. One loves the particular person one actually encountered. Why love is historical, attach-

---

*One indication of the stringency of Rawls' difference principle, which we attend to in the second part of this chapter, is its inappropriateness as a governing principle even within a family of individuals who love one another. Should a family devote its resources to maximizing the position of its least well off and least talented child, holding back the other children or using resources for their education and development only if they will follow a policy through their lifetimes of maximizing the position of their least fortunate sibling? Surely not. How then can this even be considered as the appropriate policy for enforcement in the wider society? (I discuss below what I think would be Rawls' reply: that some principles apply at the macro level which do not apply to micro-situations.)

ing to persons in this way and not to characteristics, is an interesting and puzzling question.

Proponents of patterned principles of distributive justice focus upon criteria for determining who is to receive holdings; they consider the reasons for which someone should have something, and also the total picture of holdings. Whether or not it is better to give than to receive, proponents of patterned principles ignore giving altogether. In considering the distribution of goods, income, and so forth, their theories are theories of recipient justice; they completely ignore any right a person might have to give something to someone. Even in exchanges where each party is simultaneously giver and recipient, patterned principles of justice focus only upon the recipient role and its supposed rights. Thus discussions tend to focus on whether people (should) have a right to inherit, rather than on whether people (should) have a right to bequeath or on whether persons who have a right to hold also have a right to choose that others hold in their place. I lack a good explanation of why the usual theories of distributive justice are so recipient oriented; ignoring givers and transferrers and their rights is of a piece with ignoring producers and their entitlements. But why is it *all* ignored?

Patterned principles of distributive justice necessitate *re*distributive activities. The likelihood is small that any actual freely-arrived-at set of holdings fits a given pattern; and the likelihood is nil that it will continue to fit the pattern as people exchange and give. From the point of view of an entitlement theory, redistribution is a serious matter indeed, involving, as it does, the violation of people's rights. (An exception is those takings that fall under the principle of the rectification of injustices.) From other points of view, also, it is serious.

Taxation of earnings from labor is on a par with forced labor.* Some persons find this claim obviously true: taking the earnings of *n* hours labor is like taking *n* hours from the person; it is like forcing the person to work *n* hours for another's purpose. Others find the claim absurd. But even these, *if* they object to forced labor, would oppose forcing unemployed hippies to work for the benefit of the needy. And they would also object to forcing each person to work five extra hours each week for the benefit of the needy. But a system that takes five hours' wages in taxes does not seem to them like one that forces someone to work five hours, since it offers the person forced a wider range of choice in activities than does taxation in kind with the particular labor specified. (But we can imagine a gradation of systems of forced labor, from one that specifies a particular activity, to one that gives a choice among two activities, to . . . ; and so on up.) Furthermore, people envisage a system with something like a proportional tax on everything above the amount necessary for basic needs. Some think this does not force someone to work extra hours, since

---

*I am unsure as to whether the arguments I present below show that such taxation merely *is* forced labor; so that "is on a par with" means "is one kind of." Or alternatively, whether the arguments emphasize the great similarities between such taxation and forced labor, to show it is plausible and illuminating to view such taxation in the light of forced labor. This latter approach would remind one of how John Wisdom conceives of the claims of metaphysicians.

[Volunteering?]

[handwritten margin notes: "ppl who use their leisure time to work get their earnings taxed, should ppl who use their leisure time for pleasure also have to give some of that time to society?"]

there is no fixed number of extra hours he is forced to work, and since he can avoid the tax entirely by earning only enough to cover his basic needs. This is a very uncharacteristic view of forcing for those who *also* think people are forced to do something *whenever* the alternatives they face are considerably worse. However, *neither* view is correct. The fact that others intentionally intervene, in violation of a side constraint against aggression, to threaten force to limit the alternatives, in this case to paying taxes or (presumably the worse alternative) bare subsistence, makes the taxation system one of forced labor and distinguishes it from other cases of limited choices which are not forcings.[2]

The man who chooses to work longer to gain an income more than sufficient for his basic needs prefers some extra goods or services to the leisure and activities he could perform during the possible nonworking hours; whereas the man who chooses not to work the extra time prefers the leisure activities to the extra goods or services he could acquire by working more. Given this, if it would be illegitimate for a tax system to seize some of a man's leisure (forced labor) for the purpose of serving the needy, how can it be legitimate for a tax system to seize some of a man's goods for that purpose? Why should we treat the man whose happiness requires certain material goods or services differently from the man whose preferences and desires make such goods unnecessary for his happiness? Why should the man who prefers seeing a movie (and who has to earn money for a ticket) be open to the required call to aid the needy, while the person who prefers looking at a sunset (and hence need earn no extra money) is not? Indeed, isn't it surprising that redistributionists choose to ignore the man whose pleasures are so easily attainable without extra labor, while adding yet another burden to the poor unfortunate who must work for his pleasures? If anything, one would have expected the reverse. Why is the person with the nonmaterial or nonconsumption desire allowed to proceed unimpeded to his most favored feasible alternative, whereas the man whose pleasures or desires involve material things and who must work for extra money (thereby serving whomever considers his activities valuable enough to pay him) is constrained in what he can realize? Perhaps there is no difference in principle. And perhaps some think the answer concerns merely administrative convenience. (These questions and issues will not disturb those who think that forced labor to serve the needy or to realize some favored end-state pattern is acceptable.) In a fuller discussion we would have (and want) to extend our argument to include interest, entrepreneurial profits, and so on. Those who doubt that this extension can be carried through, and who draw the line here at taxation of income from labor, will have to state rather complicated patterned *historical* principles of distributive justice, since end-state principles would not distinguish *sources* of income in any way. It is enough for now to get away from end-state principles and to make clear how various patterned principles are dependent upon particular views about the sources or the illegitimacy or the lesser legitimacy of profits, interest, and so on; which particular views may well be mistaken.

What sort of right over others does a legally institutionalized end-state pattern give one? The central core of the notion of a property right in X, relative to which other parts of the notion are to be explained, is the right to determine what shall be done with X; the right to choose which of the constrained set of options concerning X shall be realized or attempted. The constraints are set by other principles or laws operating in the society; in our theory, by the Lockean rights people possess (under the minimal state). My property rights in my knife allow me to leave it where I will, but not in your chest. I may choose which of the acceptable options involving the knife is to be realized. This notion of property helps us to understand why earlier theorists spoke of people as having property in themselves and their labor. They viewed each person as having a right to decide what would become of himself and what he would do, and as having a right to reap the benefits of what he did . . . .

When end-result principles of distributive justice are built into the legal structure of a society, they (as do most patterned principles) give each citizen an enforceable claim to some portion of the total social product; that is, to some portion of the sum total of the individually and jointly made products. This total product is produced by individuals laboring, using means of production others have saved to bring into existence, by people organizing production or creating means to produce new things or things in a new way. It is on this batch of individual activities that patterned distributional principles give each individual an enforceable claim. Each person has a claim to the activities and the products of other persons, independently of whether the other persons enter into particular relationships that give rise to these claims, and independently of whether they voluntarily take these claims upon themselves, in charity or in exchange for something.

Whether it is done through taxation on wages or on wages over a certain amount, or through seizure of profits, or through there being a big *social pot* so that it's not clear what's coming from where and what's going where, patterned principles of distributive justice involve appropriating the actions of other persons. Seizing the results of someone's labor is equivalent to seizing hours from him and directing him to carry on various activities. If people force you to do certain work, or unrewarded work, for a certain period of time, they decide what you are to do and what purposes your work is to serve apart from your decisions. This process whereby they take this decision from you makes them a *part-owner* of you; it gives them a property right in you. Just as having such partial control and power of decision, by right, over an animal or inanimate object would be to have a property right in it.

End-state and most patterned principles of distributive justice institute (partial) ownership by others of people and their actions and labor. These principles involve a shift from the classical liberals' notion of self-ownership to a notion of (partial) property rights in *other* people.

Considerations such as these confront end-state and other patterned conceptions of justice with the question of whether the actions necessary to achieve the selected pattern don't themselves violate moral side constraints. Any view holding that there are moral side constraints on actions, that not all moral considerations can be built into end states that are to be achieved . . . , must face the possibility that some of its goals are not achievable by any morally permissible available means. An entitlement theorist will face such conflicts in a society that deviates from the principles of justice for the generation of holdings, if and only if the only actions available to realize the principles themselves violate some moral constraints. Since deviation from the first two principles of justice (in acquisition and transfer) will involve other persons' direct and aggressive intervention to violate rights, and since moral constraints will not exclude defensive or retributive action in such cases, the entitlement theorist's problem rarely will be pressing. And whatever difficulties he has in applying the principle of rectification to persons who did not themselves violate the first two principles are difficulties in balancing the conflicting considerations so as correctly to formulate the complex principle of rectification itself; he will not violate moral side constraints by applying the principle. Proponents of patterned conceptions of justice, however, often will face head-on clashes (and poignant ones if they cherish each party to the clash) between moral side constraints on how individuals may be treated and their patterned conception of justice that presents an end state or other pattern that *must* be realized.

May a person emigrate from a nation that has institutionalized some end-state or patterned distributional principle? For some principles (for example, Hayek's) emigration presents no theoretical problem. But for others it is a tricky matter. Consider a nation having a compulsory scheme of minimal social provision to aid the neediest (or one organized so as to maximize the position of the worst-off group); no one may opt out of participating in it. (None may say, "Don't compel me to contribute to others and don't provide for me via this compulsory mechanism if I am in need.") Everyone above a certain level is forced to contribute to aid the needy. But if emigration from the country were allowed, anyone could choose to move to another country that did not have compulsory social provision but otherwise was (as much as possible) identical. In such a case, the person's *only* motive for leaving would be to avoid participating in the compulsory scheme of social provision. And if he does leave, the needy in his initial country will receive no (compelled) help from him. What rationale yields the result that the person be permitted to emigrate, yet forbidden to stay and opt out of the compulsory scheme of social provision? If providing for the needy is of overriding importance, this does militate against allowing internal opting out; but it also speaks against allowing external emigration. (Would it also support, to some extent, the kidnapping of persons living in a place without compulsory social provision, who could be forced to make a contribution to the needy in your community?) Perhaps the crucial component of the position that allows emigration solely to avoid certain arrangements, while not allowing anyone internally to opt out of them, is a concern for fraternal feelings within the country. "We don't want anyone here who doesn't contribute, who doesn't care enough about the others to contribute." That concern, in this case, would have to be tied to the view that forced aiding tends to produce fraternal feelings between the aided and the aider (or perhaps merely to the view that the knowledge that someone or other voluntarily is not aiding produces unfraternal feelings).

ORIGINAL ACQUISITION

Locke's Theory of Acquisition

Before we turn to consider other theories of justice in detail, we must introduce an additional bit of complexity into the structure of the entitlement theory. This is best approached by considering Locke's attempt to specify a principle of justice in acquisition. Locke views property rights in an unowned object as originating through someone's mixing his labor with it. This gives rise to many questions. What are the boundaries of what labor is mixed with? If a private astronaut clears a place on Mars, has he mixed his labor with (so that he comes to own) the whole planet, the whole uninhabited universe, or just a particular plot? Which plot does an act bring under ownership? The minimal (possibly disconnected) area such that an act decreases entropy in that area, and not elsewhere? Can virgin land (for the purposes of ecological investigation by high-flying airplane) come under ownership by a Lockean process? Building a fence around a territory presumably would make one the owner of only the fence (and the land immediately underneath it).

Why does mixing one's labor with something make one the owner of it? Perhaps because one owns one's labor, and so one comes to own a previously unowned thing that becomes permeated with what one owns. Ownership seeps over into the rest. But why isn't mixing what I own with what I don't own a way of losing what I own rather than a way of gaining what I don't? If I own a can of tomato juice and spill it in the sea so that its molecules (made radioactive, so I can check this) mingle evenly throughout the sea, do I thereby come to own the sea, or have I foolishly dissipated my tomato juice? Perhaps the idea, instead, is that laboring on something improves it and makes it more valuable; and anyone is entitled to own a thing whose value he has created. (Reinforcing this, perhaps, is the view that laboring is unpleasant. If some people made things effortlessly, as the cartoon characters in *The Yellow Submarine* trail flowers in their wake, would they have lesser claim to their own products whose making didn't *cost* them anything?) Ignore the fact that laboring on something may make it less valuable (spraying pink enamel paint on a piece of driftwood that you have found). Why should one's entitlement extend to the whole object rather than just to the *added value* one's labor has produced? (Such reference to value might also serve to delimit the extent of ownership; for example, substitute "increases the value of" for "decreases entropy in" in the above entropy criterion.) No workable or coherent value-added property scheme has yet been devised, and any such scheme presumably would fall to objections (similar to those) that fell the theory of Henry George.

It will be implausible to view improving an object as giving full ownership to it, if the stock of unowned objects that might be improved is limited. For an object's coming under one person's ownership changes the situation of all others. Whereas previously they were at liberty (in Hohfeld's sense) to use the object, they now no longer are. This change in the situation of others (by removing their liberty to act on a previously unowned object) need not worsen their situation. If I appropriate a grain of sand from Coney Island, no one else may now do as they will with *that* grain of sand. But there are plenty of other grains of sand left for them to do the same with. Or if not grains of sand, then other things. Alternatively, the things I do with the grain of sand I appropriate might improve the position of others, counterbalancing their loss of the liberty to use that grain. The crucial point is whether appropriation of an unowned object worsens the situation of others.

Locke's proviso that there be "enough and as good left in common for others" (sect. 27) is meant to ensure that the situation of others is not worsened. (If this proviso is met is there any motivation for his further condition of nonwaste?) It is often said that this proviso once held but now no longer does. But there appears to be an argument for the conclusion that if the proviso no longer holds, then it cannot ever have held so as to yield permanent and inheritable property rights. Consider the first person Z for whom there is not enough and as good left to appropriate. The last person Y to appropriate left Z without his previous liberty to act on an object, and so worsened Z's situation. So Y's appropriation is not allowed under Locke's proviso. Therefore the next to last person X to appropriate left Y in a worse position, for X's act ended permissible appropriation. Therefore X's appropriation wasn't permissible. But then the appropriator two from last, W, ended permissible appropriation and so, since it worsened X's position, W's appropriation wasn't permissible. And so on back to the first person A to appropriate a permanent property right.

This argument, however, proceeds too quickly. Someone may be made worse off by another's appropriation in two ways: first, by losing the opportunity to improve his situation by a particular appropriation or any one; and second, by no longer being able to use freely (without appropriation) what he previously could. A *stringent* requirement that another not be made worse off by an appropriation would exclude the first way if nothing else counterbalances the diminution in opportunity, as well as the second. A *weaker* requirement would exclude the second way, though not the first. With the weaker requirement, we cannot zip back so quickly from Z to A, as in the above argument; for though person Z can no longer *appropriate*, there may remain some for him to *use* as before. In this case Y's appropriation would not violate the weaker Lockean condition. (With less remaining that people are at liberty to use, users might face more inconvenience, crowding, and so on; in that way the situation of others might be worsened, unless appropriation stopped far short of such a point.) It is arguable that no one legitimately can complain if the weaker provision is satisfied. However, since this is less clear than in the case of the more stringent proviso, Locke may have intended this stringent proviso by "enough and as good" remaining, and perhaps he meant the nonwaste condition to delay the end point from which the argument zips back.

Is the situation of persons who are unable to appropriate (there being no more accessible and useful unowned objects) worsened by a system allowing appropriation and permanent property? Here enter the various familiar social considerations favoring private property: it increases the social product by putting means of production in the hands of those who can use them most efficiently (profitably); experimentation is encouraged, because with separate persons controlling resources, there is no one person or small group whom someone with a new idea must convince to try it out; private property enables people to decide on the pattern and types of risks they wish to bear, leading to specialized types of risk bearing; private property protects future persons by leading some to hold back resources from current consumption for future markets; it provides alternate sources of employment for unpopular persons who don't have to convince any one person or small group to hire them, and so on. These considerations enter a Lockean theory to support the claim that appropriation of private property satisfies the intent behind the "enough and as good left over" proviso, *not* as a utilitarian justification of property. They enter to rebut the claim that because the proviso is violated no natural right to private property can arise by a Lockean process. The difficulty in working such an argument to show that the proviso is satisfied is in fixing the appropriate base line for comparison. Lockean appropriation makes people no worse off than they would be *how?* This question of fixing the baseline needs more detailed investigation than we are able to give it here. It would be desirable to have an estimate of the general economic importance of original appropriation in order to see how much leeway there is for differing theories of appropriation and of the location of the baseline. Perhaps this importance can be measured by the percentage of all income that is based upon untransformed raw materials and given resources (rather than upon human actions), mainly rental income representing the unimproved value of land, and the price of raw material *in situ*, and by the percentage of current wealth which represents such income in the past.*

We should note that it is not only persons favoring *private* property who need a theory of how property rights legitimately originate. Those believing in collective property, for example those believing that a group of persons living in an area jointly own the territory, or its mineral resources, also must provide a theory of how such property rights arise; they must show why the persons living there have rights to determine what is done with the land and resources there that persons living elsewhere don't have (with regard to the same land and resources).

The Proviso

Whether or not Locke's particular theory of appropriation can be spelled out so as to handle various difficulties, I assume that any adequate

---

*I have not seen a precise estimate. David Friedman, *The Machinery of Freedom* (N.Y.: Harper & Row, 1973), pp. xiv, xv, discusses this issue and suggests 5 percent of U.S. national income as an upper limit for the first two factors mentioned. However he does not attempt to estimate the percentage of current wealth which is based upon such income in the past. (The vague notion of "based upon" merely indicates a topic needing investigation.)

theory of justice in acquisition will contain a proviso similar to the weaker of the ones we have attributed to Locke. A process normally giving rise to a permanent bequeathable property right in a previously unowned thing will not do so if the position of others no longer at liberty to use the thing is thereby worsened. It is important to specify *this* particular mode of worsening the situation of others, for the proviso does not encompass other modes. It does not include the worsening due to more limited opportunities to appropriate (the first way above, corresponding to the more stringent condition), and it does not include how I "worsen" a seller's position if I appropriate materials to make some of what he is selling, and then enter into competition with him. Someone whose appropriation otherwise would violate the proviso still may appropriate provided he compensates the others so that their situation is not thereby worsened; unless he does compensate these others, his appropriation will violate the proviso of the principle of justice in acquisition and will be an illegitimate one.* A theory of appropriation incorporating this Lockean proviso will handle correctly the cases (objections to the theory lacking the proviso) where someone appropriates the total supply of something necessary for life.†

A theory which includes this proviso in its principle of justice in acquisition must also contain a more complex principle of justice in transfer. Some reflection of the proviso about appropriation constrains later actions. If my appropriating all of a certain substance violates the Lockean proviso, then so does my appropriating some and purchasing all the rest from others who obtained it without otherwise violating the Lockean proviso. If the proviso excludes someone's appropriating all the drinkable water in the world, it also excludes his purchasing it all. (More weakly, and messily, it may exclude his charging certain prices for some of his supply.) This proviso (almost?) never will come into effect; the more someone

---

*Fourier held that since the process of civilization had deprived the members of society of certain liberties (to gather, pasture, engage in the chase), socially guaranteed minimum provision for persons was justified as compensation for the loss (Alexander Gray, *The Socialist Tradition* (New York: Harper & Row, 1968), p. 188). But this puts the point too strongly. This compensation would be due those persons, if any, for whom the process of civilization was a *net loss*, for whom the benefits of civilization did not counterbalance being deprived of these particular liberties.

†For example, Rashdall's case of someone who comes upon the only water in the desert several miles ahead of others who also will come to it and appropriates it all. Hastings Rashdall, "The Philosophical Theory of Property," in *Property, its Duties and Rights* (London: MacMillan, 1915).

We should note Ayn Rand's theory of property rights ("Man's Rights" in *The Virtue of Selfishness* (New York: New American Library, 1964), p. 94), wherein these follow from the right to life, since people need physical things to live. But a right to life is not a right to whatever one needs to live; other people may have rights over these other things (see Chapter 3 of this book). At most, a right to life would be a right to have or strive for whatever one needs to live, provided that having it does not violate anyone else's rights. With regard to material things, the question is whether having it does violate any right of others. (Would appropriation of all unowned things do so? Would appropriating the water hole in Rashdall's example?) Since special considerations (such as the Lockean proviso) may enter with regard to material property, one *first* needs a theory of property rights before one can apply any supposed right to life (as amended above). Therefore the right to life cannot provide the foundation for a theory of property rights.

acquires of a scarce substance which others want, the higher the price of the rest will go, and the more difficult it will become for him to acquire it all. But still, we can imagine, at least, that something like this occurs: someone makes simultaneous secret bids to the separate owners of a substance, each of whom sells assuming he can easily purchase more from the other owners; or some natural catastrophe destroys all of the supply of something except that in one person's possession. The total supply could not be permissibly appropriated by one person at the beginning. His later acquisition of it all does not show that the original appropriation violated the proviso (even by a reverse argument similar to the one above that tried to zip back from Z to A). Rather, it is the combination of the original appropriation *plus* all the later transfers and actions that violates the Lockean proviso.

Each owner's title to his holding includes the historical shadow of the Lockean proviso on appropriation. This excludes his transferring it into an agglomeration that does violate the Lockean proviso and excludes his using it in a way, in coordination with others or independently of them, so as to violate the proviso by making the situation of others worse than their baseline situation. Once it is known that someone's ownership runs afoul of the Lockean proviso, there are stringent limits on what he may do with (what it is difficult any longer unreservedly to call) "his property." Thus a person may not appropriate the only water hole in a desert and charge what he will. Nor may he charge what he will if he possesses one, and unfortunately it happens that all the water holes in the desert dry up, except for his. This unfortunate circumstance, admittedly no fault of his, brings into operation the Lockean proviso and limits his property rights.* Similarly, an owner's property right in the only island in an area does not allow him to order a castaway from a shipwreck off his island as a trespasser, for this would violate the Lockean proviso.

Notice that the theory does not say that owners do have these rights, but that the rights are overridden to avoid some catastrophe. (Overridden rights do not disappear; they leave a trace of a sort absent in the cases under discussion.)[3] There is no such external (and *ad hoc?*) overriding. Considerations internal to the theory of property itself, to its theory of acquisition and appropriation, provide the means for handling such cases. . . .

The fact that someone owns the total supply of something necessary for others to stay alive does *not* entail that his (or anyone's) appropriation of anything left some people (immediately or later) in a situation worse than the baseline one. A medical researcher who synthesizes a new substance that effectively treats a certain disease and who refuses to sell except on his terms does not worsen the situation of others by depriving them of whatever he has appropriated. The others easily can possess the

*The situation would be different if his water hole didn't dry up, due to special precautions he took to prevent this. Compare our discussion of the case in the text with Hayek, *The Constitution of Liberty*, p. 136; and also with Ronald Hamowy, "Hayek's Concept of Freedom; A Critique," *New Individualist Review*, April 1961, pp. 28–31.

same materials he appropriated; the researcher's appropriation or purchase of chemicals didn't make those chemicals scarce in a way so as to
violate the Lockean proviso. Nor would someone else's purchasing the total
supply of the synthesized substance from the medical researcher. The fact
that the medical researcher uses easily available chemicals to synthesize the
drug no more violates the Lockean proviso than does the fact that the only
surgeon able to perform a particular operation eats easily obtainable food
in order to stay alive and to have the energy to work. This shows that the
Lockean proviso is not an "end-state principle"; it focuses on a particular
way that appropriative actions affect others, and not on the structure of
the situation that results.

. . . The theme of someone worsening another's situation by depriving him of something he otherwise would possess may also illuminate
the example of patents. An inventor's patent does not deprive others of an
object which would not exist if not for the inventor. Yet patents would
have this effect on others who independently invent the object. Therefore,
these independent inventors, upon whom the burden of proving independent discovery may rest, should not be excluded from utilizing their own
invention as they wish (including selling it to others). Furthermore, a
known inventor drastically lessens the chances of actual independent invention. For persons who know of an invention usually will not try to reinvent
it; and the notion of independent discovery here would be murky at best.
Yet we may assume that in the absence of the original invention, sometime
later someone else would have come up with it. This suggests placing a
time limit on patents, as a rough rule of thumb to approximate how long it
would have taken, in the absence of knowledge of the invention, for independent discovery.

I believe that the free operation of a market system will not actually run afoul of the Lockean proviso. . . . If this is correct, the proviso will
not . . . provide a significant opportunity for future state action. . . .

RAWLS' THEORY

We can bring our discussion of distributive justice into sharper focus by
considering in some detail John Rawls' recent contribution to the subject. *A
Theory of Justice* is a powerful, deep, subtle, wide-ranging, systematic work
in political and moral philosophy which has not seen its like since the
writings of John Stuart Mill, if then. It is a fountain of illuminating ideas,
integrated together into a lovely whole. Political philosophers must now
work within Rawls' theory or explain why not. . . . I permit myself to
concentrate here on disagreements with Rawls only because I am confident
that my readers will have discovered for themselves its many virtues.

Social Cooperation

I shall begin by considering the role of the principles of justice. Let us
assume, to fix ideas, that a society is a more or less self-sufficient association of persons who in their relations to one another recognize certain
rules of conduct as binding and who for the most part act in accordance

with them. Suppose further that these rules specify a system of cooperation designed to advance the good of those taking part in it. Then, although a society is a cooperative venture for mutual advantage, it is typically marked by a conflict as well as by an identity of interests. There is an identity of interests since social cooperation makes possible a better life for all than any would have if each were to live solely by his own efforts. There is a conflict of interests since persons are not indifferent as to how the greater benefits produced by their collaboration are distributed, for in order to pursue their ends they each prefer a larger to a lesser share. A set of principles is required for choosing among the various social arrangements which determine this division of advantages and for underwriting an agreement on the proper distributive shares. These principles are the principles of social justice: they provide a way of assigning rights and duties in the basic institutions of society and they define the appropriate distribution of the benefits and burdens of social cooperation.[4]

   . . . Why does social cooperation *create* the problem of distributive justice? Would there be no problem of justice and no need for a theory of justice, if there was no social cooperation at all, if each person got his share solely by his own efforts? If we suppose, as Rawls seems to, that this situation does *not* raise questions of distributive justice, then in virtue of what facts about social cooperation do these questions of justice emerge? What is it about social cooperation that gives rise to issues of justice? It cannot be said that there will be conflicting claims only where there is social cooperation; that individuals who produce independently and (initially) fend for themselves will not make claims of justice on each other. If there were ten Robinson Crusoes, each working alone for two years on separate islands, who discovered each other and the facts of their different allotments by radio communication via transmitters left twenty years earlier, could they not make claims on each other, supposing it were possible to transfer goods from one island to the next? Wouldn't the one with least make a claim on ground of need, or on the ground that his island was naturally poorest, or on the ground that he was naturally least capable of fending for himself? Mightn't he say that justice demanded he be given some more by the others, claiming it unfair that he should receive so much less and perhaps be destitute, perhaps starving? He might go on to say that the different individual noncooperative shares stem from differential natural endowments, which are not deserved, and that the task of justice is to rectify these arbitrary facts and inequities. Rather than its being the case that no one *will* make such claims in the situation lacking social cooperation, perhaps the point is that such claims clearly would be without merit. Why would they clearly be without merit? In the social noncooperation situation, it might be said, each individual deserves what he gets unaided by his own efforts; or rather, no one else can make a claim *of justice* against this holding. It is pellucidly clear in this situation who is entitled to what, so no theory of justice is needed. On this view social cooperation introduces a muddying of the waters that makes it unclear or indeterminate who is entitled to what. Rather than saying that no theory of justice applies to this noncooperative case (wouldn't it be unjust if someone stole another's products in the noncooperative situation?), I would say that it is a clear case of application of the correct theory of justice: the entitlement theory.

How does social cooperation change this so that the same entitlement principles that apply to the noncooperative cases become inapplicable or inappropriate to cooperative ones? It might be said that one cannot disentangle the contributions of distinct individuals who cooperate; everything is everyone's joint product. On this joint product, or on any portion of it, each person plausibly will make claims of equal strength; all have an equally good claim, or at any rate no person has a distinctly better claim than any other. Somehow (this line of thought continues), it must be decided how this total product of joint social cooperation (to which individual entitlements do not apply differentially) is to be divided up: this is the problem of distributive justice.

Don't individual entitlements apply to parts of the cooperatively produced product? First, suppose that social cooperation is based upon division of labor, specialization, comparative advantage, and exchange; each person works singly to transform some input he receives, contracting with others who further transform or transport his product until it reaches its ultimate consumer. People cooperate in making things but they work separately; each person is a miniature firm. The products of each person are easily identifiable, and exchanges are made in open markets with prices set competitively, given informational constraints, and so forth. In such a system of social cooperation; what is the task of a theory of justice? It might be said that whatever holdings result will depend upon the exchange ratios or prices at which exchanges are made, and therefore that the task of a theory of justice is to set criteria for "fair prices." This is hardly the place to trace the serpentine windings of theories of a just price. It is difficult to see why these issues should even arise here. People are choosing to make exchanges with other people and to transfer entitlements, with no restrictions on their freedom to trade with any other party at any mutually acceptable ratio. Why does such sequential social cooperation, linked together by people's voluntary exchanges, raise any special problems about how things are to be distributed? Why isn't the appropriate (a not inappropriate) set of holdings just the one which *actually occurs* via this process of mutually-agreed-to exchanges whereby people choose to give to others what they are entitled to give or hold? . . .

Terms of Cooperation and the Difference Principle

Another entry into the issue of the connection of social cooperation with distributive shares brings us to grips with Rawls' actual discussion. Rawls imagines rational, mutually disinterested individuals meeting in a certain situation, or abstracted from their other features not provided for in this situation. In this hypothetical situation of choice, which Rawls calls "the original position," they choose the first principles of a conception of justice that is to regulate all subsequent criticism and reform of their institutions. While making this choice, no one knows his place in society, his class position or social status, or his natural assets and abilities, his strength, intelligence, and so forth.

> The principles of justice are chosen behind a veil of ignorance. This ensures that no one is advantaged or disadvantaged in the choice of principles by the outcome of natural chance or the contingency of social circumstances. Since all are similarly situated and no one is able to design principles to favor his particular condition, the principles of justice are the result of a fair agreement or bargain.[5]

What would persons in the original position agree to?

> Persons in the initial situation would choose two . . . principles: the first requires equality in the assignment of basic rights and duties, while the second holds that social and economic inequalities, for example, inequalities of wealth and authority are just only if they result in compensating benefits for everyone, and in particular for the least advantaged members of society. These principles rule out justifying institutions on the grounds that the hardships of some are offset by a greater good in the aggregate. It may be expedient but it is not just that some should have less in order that others may prosper. But there is no injustice in the greater benefits earned by a few provided that the situation of persons not so fortunate is thereby improved. The intuitive idea is that since everyone's well-being depends upon a scheme of cooperation without which no one could have a satisfactory life, the division of advantages should be such as to draw forth the willing cooperation of everyone taking part in it, including those less well situated. Yet this can be expected only if reasonable terms are proposed. The two principles mentioned seem to be a fair agreement on the basis of which those better endowed, or more fortunate in their social position, neither of which we can be said to deserve, could expect the willing cooperation of others when some workable scheme is a necessary condition of the welfare of all.[6]

This second principle, which Rawls specifies as the difference principle, holds that the institutional structure is to be so designed that the worst-off group under it is at least as well off as the worst-off group (not necessarily the same group) would be under any alternative institutional structure. If persons in the original position follow the minimax policy in making the significant choice of principles of justice, Rawls argues, they will choose the difference principle. Our concern here is not whether persons in the position Rawls describes actually would minimax and actually would choose the particular principles Rawls specifies. Still, we should question why individuals in the original position would choose a principle that focuses upon groups, rather than individuals. Won't application of the minimax principle lead each person in the original position to favor maximizing the position of the worst-off *individual*? To be sure, this principle would reduce questions of evaluating social institutions to the issue of how the unhappiest depressive fares. Yet avoiding this by moving the focus to groups (or representative individuals) seems *ad hoc,* and is inadequately motivated for those in the individual position.[7] Nor is it clear which groups are appropriately considered; why exclude the group of depressives or alcoholics or the representative paraplegic? . . .

Rawls would have us imagine the worse-endowed persons say something like the following: "Look, better endowed: you gain by cooperating with us. If you want our cooperation you'll have to accept reasonable terms. We suggest these terms: We'll cooperate with you only if we get *as much as possible*. That is, the terms of our cooperation should give us that maximal share such that, if it was tried to give us more, we'd end up with less." How generous these proposed terms are might be seen by imagining that the better endowed make the almost symmetrical opposite proposal: "Look, worse endowed: you gain by cooperating with *us*. If you want our cooperation you'll have to accept reasonable terms. We propose these terms: We'll cooperate with you so long as *we* get as much as possible. That is, the terms of our cooperation should give us the maximal share such that, if it was tried to give us more, we'd end up with less." If these terms seem outrageous, as they are, why don't the terms proposed by those worse endowed seem the same? Why shouldn't the better endowed treat this latter proposal as beneath consideration, supposing someone to have the nerve explicitly to state it?

Rawls devotes much attention to explaining why those less well favored should not complain at receiving less. His explanation, simply put, is that because the inequality works for his advantage, someone less well favored shouldn't complain about it; he receives *more* in the unequal system than he would in an equal one. (Though he might receive still more in another unequal system that placed someone else below him.) But Rawls discusses the question of whether those *more* favored will or should find the terms satisfactory *only* in the following passage, where *A* and *B* are any two representative men with *A* being the more favored:

> The difficulty is to show that *A* has no grounds for complaint. Perhaps he is required to have less than he might since his having more would result in some loss to *B*. Now what can be said to the more favored man? To begin with, it is clear that the well-being of each depends on a scheme of social cooperation without which no one could have a satisfactory life. Secondly, we can ask for the willing cooperation of everyone only if the terms of the scheme are reasonable. The difference principle, then, seems to be a fair basis on which those better endowed, or more fortunate in their social circumstances, could expect others to collaborate with them when some workable arrangement is a necessary condition of the good of all.[8]

What Rawls imagines being said to the more favored men does *not* show that these men have no grounds for complaint, nor does it at all diminish the weight of whatever complaints they have. That the well-being of all depends on social cooperation without which no one could have a satisfactory life could also be said to the less well endowed by someone proposing any other principle, including that of maximizing the position of the best endowed. Similarly for the fact that we can ask for the willing cooperation of everyone only if the terms of the scheme are reasonable. The question is: What terms *would be* reasonable? What Rawls imagines being said thus far merely sets up his problem; it doesn't distinguish his proposed difference principle from the almost symmetrical counterproposal that we imagined the better endowed making, or from any other proposal. Thus, when Rawls continues, "The difference principle, then, seems to be a fair basis on which those best endowed, or more fortunate in their social circumstances, could expect others to collaborate with them when some workable arrangement is a necessary condition of the good of all," the presence of the "then" in his sentence is puzzling. Since the sentences which precede it are neutral between his proposal and any other proposal, the conclusion that the difference principle presents a fair basis for cooperation *cannot* follow from what precedes it in this passage. Rawls is merely repeating that it seems reasonable; hardly a convincing reply to anyone to whom it doesn't seem reasonable. Rawls has not shown that the more favored man A has no grounds for complaint at being required to have less in order that another B might have more than he otherwise would. And he can't show this, since A *does* have grounds for complaint. Doesn't he?

The Original Position and End-Result Principles

How can it have been supposed that these terms offered by the less well endowed are fair? Imagine a social pie somehow appearing so that *no one* has any claim at all on any portion of it, no one has any more of a claim than any other person; yet there must be unanimous agreement on how it is to be divided. Undoubtedly, apart from threats or holdouts in bargaining, an equal distribution would be suggested and found plausible as a solution. (It is, in Schelling's sense, a focal point solution.) If *somehow* the size of the pie wasn't fixed, and it was realized that pursuing an equal distribution somehow would lead to a smaller total pie than otherwise might occur, the people might well agree to an unequal distribution which raised the size of the least share. But in any actual situation, wouldn't this realization reveal something about differential claims on parts of the pie? Who is it that could make the pie larger, and would do it if given a larger share, but not if given an equal share under the scheme of equal distribution? To whom is an incentive to be provided to make this larger contribution? (There's no talk here of inextricably entangled joint product; it's known to *whom* incentives are to be offered, or at least to whom a bonus is to be paid after the fact.) Why doesn't this identifiable differential contribution lead to some differential entitlement?

If things fell from heaven like manna, and no one had any special entitlement to any portion of it, and no manna would fall unless all agreed to a particular distribution, and somehow the quantity varied depending on the distribution, then it is plausible to claim that persons placed so that they couldn't make threats, or hold out for specially large shares, would agree to the difference principle rule of distribution. But is *this* the appropriate model for thinking about how the things people produce are to be distributed? Why think the same results should obtain for situations where there *are* differential entitlements as for situations where there are not?

A procedure that founds principles of distributive justice on what rational persons who know nothing about themselves or their histories would agree to *guarantees that end-state principles of justice will be taken as fundamental*. Perhaps some historical principles of justice are derivable from end-state principles, as the utilitarian tries to derive individual rights, prohibitions on punishing the innocent, and so forth, from *his* end-state principle; perhaps such arguments can be constructed even for the entitlement principle. But no historical principle, it seems, could be agreed to in the first instance by the participants in Rawls' original position. For people meeting together behind a veil of ignorance to decide who gets what, knowing nothing about any special entitlements people may have, will treat anything to be distributed as manna from heaven.*

Suppose there were a group of students who have studied during a year, taken examinations, and received grades between 0 and 100 which they have not yet learned of. They are now gathered together, having no idea of the grade any one of them has received, and they are asked to allocate grades among themselves so that the grades total to a given sum (which is determined by the sum of the grades they actually have received from the teacher). First, let us suppose they are to decide jointly upon a particular distribution of grades; they are to give a particular grade to each identifiable one of them present at the meeting. Here, given sufficient restrictions on their ability to threaten each other, they probably would agree to each person receiving the same grade, to each person's grade being equal to the total divided by the number of people to be graded. Surely they would *not* chance upon the particular set of grades they already have received. Suppose next that there is posted on a bulletin board at their meeting a paper headed ENTITLEMENTS, which lists each person's name with a grade next to it, the listing being identical to the instructor's gradings. Still, this particular distribution will not be agreed to by those having done poorly. Even if they know what "entitlement" means (which perhaps we must suppose they don't, in order to match the absence of moral factors in the calculations of persons in Rawls' original position), why should they agree to the instructor's distribution? What self-interested reason to agree to it would they have?

Next suppose that they are unanimously to agree not to a *particular* distribution of grades, but rather to general principles to govern the distribution of grades. What principle would be selected? The equality principle, which gives each person the same grade, would have a prominent chance. And if it turned out that the total was variable depending upon how they divided it, depending on which of them got what grade, and a higher grade was desirable though they were not competing among each other (for example, each of them was competing for some position with the

---

*Do the people in the original position ever wonder whether *they* have the *right* to decide how everything is to be divided up? Perhaps they reason that since they are deciding this question, they must assume they are entitled to do so; and so particular people can't have particular entitlements to holdings (for then they wouldn't have the right to decide together on how all holdings are to be divided); and hence everything legitimately may be treated like manna from heaven.

members of separate distinct groups), then the principle of distributing grades so as to maximize the lowest grades *might* seem a plausible one. Would these people agree to the non-end-state *historical* principle of distribution: give people grades according to how their examinations were evaluated by a qualified and impartial observer?* If all the people deciding knew the particular distribution that would be yielded by this historical principle, they wouldn't agree to it. For the situation then would be equivalent to the earlier one of their deciding upon a particular distribution, in which we already have seen they would not agree to the entitlement distribution. Suppose then that the people do not know the particular distribution actually yielded by this historical principle. They cannot be led to select this historical principle because it looks just, or fair, to them; for no such notions are allowed to be at work in the original position. (Otherwise people would argue there, like here, about what justice requires.) Each person engages in a calculation to decide whether it will be in his own interests to accept this historical principle of distribution. Grades, under the historical principle, depend upon nature and developed intelligence, how hard the people have worked, accident, and so on, factors about which people in the original position know almost nothing. (It would be risky for someone to think that since he is reasoning so well in thinking about the principles, he must be one of the intellectually better endowed. Who knows what dazzling argument the others are reasoning their way through, and perhaps keeping quiet about for strategic reasons.) Each person in the original position will do something like assigning probability distributions to his place along these various dimensions. It seems unlikely that each person's probability calculations would lead to the historical-entitlement principle, in preference to every other principle. Consider the principle we may call the reverse-entitlement principle. It recommends drawing up a list of the historical entitlements in order of magnitude, and giving the most anyone is entitled to, to the person entitled to the least; the second most to the person entitled to the second least, and so on. Any probability calculations of self-interested persons in Rawls' original position, or any probability calculations of the students we have considered, will lead them to view the entitlement and the reverse-entitlement principles as ranked equally insofar as their own self-interest is concerned! (What calculations could lead them to view one of the principles as superior to the other?) Their calculations will not lead them to select the entitlement principle.

The nature of the decision problem facing persons deciding upon principles in an original position behind a veil of ignorance limits them to

*I do not mean to assume that all teachers are such, nor even that learning in universities should be graded. All I need is some example of entitlement, the details of which the reader will have some familiarity with, to use to examine decision making in the original position. Grading is a simple example, though not a perfect one, entangled as it is with whatever ultimate social purposes the ongoing practice serves. We may ignore this complication, for their selecting the historical principle on the grounds that it effectively serves those purposes would illustrate our point below that their fundamental concerns and fundamental principles are end-state ones.

end-state principles of distribution. The self-interested person evaluates any non end-state principle on the basis of how it works out for him; his calculations about any principle focus on how he ends up under the principle. (These calculations include consideration of the labor he is yet to do, which does not appear in the grading example except as the sunk cost of the labor already done.) Thus for any principle, an occupant of the original position will focus on the distribution D of goods that it leads to, or a probability distribution over the distributions $D_1, \ldots, D_n$, it may lead to, and upon his probabilities of occupying each position in each D; profile, supposing it to obtain. The point would remain the same if, rather than using personal probabilities, he uses some other decision rule of the sort discussed by decision theorists. In these calculations, the only role played by the principle is that of generating a distribution of goods (or whatever else they care about) or of generating a probability distribution over distributions of goods. Different principles are compared solely by comparing the alternative distributions they generate. Thus the principles drop out of the picture, and each self-interested person makes a choice among alternative end-state distributions. People in the original position either directly agree to an end-state distribution or they agree to a principle; if they agree to a principle, they do it solely on the basis of considerations about end-state distributions. The *fundamental* principles they agree to, the ones they can all converge in agreeing upon, *must* be end-state principles.

Rawls' construction is incapable of yielding an entitlement or historical conception of distributive justice. The end-state principles of justice yielded by his procedure might be used in an attempt to *derive*, when conjoined with factual information, historical-entitlement principles, as derivative principles falling under a nonentitlement conception of justice.[9] It is difficult to see how such attempts could derive and account for the *particular* convolutions of historical-entitlement principles. And any derivations from end-state principles of approximations of the principles of acquisition, transfer, and rectification would strike one as similar to utilitarian contortions in trying to derive (approximations of) usual precepts of justice; they do not yield the particular result desired, and they produce the wrong reasons for the sort of result they try to get. If historical-entitlement principles are fundamental, then Rawls' constructions will yield approximations of them at best; it will produce the wrong sorts of reasons for them, and its derived results sometimes will conflict with the precisely correct principles. The whole procedure of persons choosing principles in Rawls' original position presupposes that no historical-entitlement conception of justice is correct.

It might be objected to our argument that Rawls' procedure is designed to *establish* all facts about justice; there is no independent notion of entitlement, not provided by his theory, to stand on in criticizing his theory. But we do not need any *particular* developed historical-entitlement theory as a basis from which to criticize Rawls' construction. If *any* such fundamental historical-entitlement view is correct, then Rawls' theory is not. We are thus able to make this structural criticism of the type of theory Rawls presents and the type of principles it must yield, without first having formulated fully a particular historical-entitlement theory as an alternative to his. We would be ill advised to accept Rawls' theory and his construal of the problem as one of which principles would be chosen by rational self-interested individuals behind a veil of ignorance, unless we were sure that no adequate historical-entitlement theory was to be gotten.

Since Rawls' construction doesn't yield a historical or entitlement conception of justice, there will be some feature(s) of his construction in virtue of which it doesn't. Have we done anything other than focus upon the particular feature(s), and say that this makes Rawls' construction incapable in principle of yielding an entitlement or historical conception of justice? This would be a criticism without any force at all, for in this sense we would have to say that the construction is incapable in principle of yielding any conception other than the one it actually yields. It seems clear that our criticism goes deeper than this (and I hope it is clear to the reader); but it is difficult to formulate the requisite criterion of depth. Lest this appear lame, let us add that as Rawls states the root idea underlying the veil of ignorance, that feature which is the most prominent in excluding agreement to an entitlement conception, it is to prevent someone from tailoring principles to his own advantage, from designing principles to favor his particular condition. But not only does the veil of ignorance do this; it ensures that no shadow of entitlement considerations will enter the rational calculations of ignorant, nonmoral individuals constrained to decide in a situation reflecting some formal conditions of morality.* Perhaps, in a Rawls-*like* construction, some condition weaker than the veil of ignorance could serve to exclude the special tailoring of principles, or perhaps some other "structural-looking" feature of the choice situation could be formulated to mirror entitlement considerations. But as it stands there is no reflection of entitlement considerations in any form in the situation of those in the original position; these considerations do not enter even to be overridden or outweighed or otherwise put aside. Since no glimmer of entitlement principles is built into the structure of the situation of persons in the original position, there is no way these principles could be selected; and Rawls' construction is incapable in principle of yielding them. This is not to say, of course, that the entitlement principle (or "the principle of natural liberty") couldn't be *written* on the list of principles to be considered by those in the original position. Rawls doesn't do even this, perhaps because it is so transparently clear that there would be no point in including it to be considered *there*.

Macro and Micro

We noted earlier the objection which doubted whether there is any independent notion of entitlement. This connects with Rawls' insistence that the principles he formulates are to be applied only to the fundamental

---

*Someone might think entitlement principles count as specially tailored in a morally objectionable way, and so he might reject my claim that the veil of ignorance accomplishes more than its stated purpose. Since to specially tailor principles is to tailor them *unfairly* for one's own advantage, and since the question of the fairness of the entitlement principle is precisely the issue, it is difficult to decide which begs the question: my criticism of the strength of the veil of ignorance, or the defense against this criticism which I imagine in this note.

macrostructure of the whole society, and that no micro counterexample to them will be admissible. The difference principle is, on the face of it, *unfair* (though that will be of no concern to anyone deciding in the original position); and a wide gamut of counterexamples to it can be produced that focus on small situations that are easy to take in and manage. But Rawls does *not* claim the difference principle is to apply to every situation; only to the basic structure of the society. How are we to decide if it applies to that? Since we may have only weak confidence in our intuitions and judgments about the justice of the whole structure of society, we may attempt to aid our judgment by focusing on microsituations that we do have a firm grasp of. For many of us, an important part of the process of arriving at what Rawls calls "reflective equilibrium" will consist of thought experiments in which we try out principles in hypothetical microsituations. If, in our considered judgment, they don't apply there then they are not universally applicable. And we may think that since correct principles of justice *are* universally applicable, principles that fail for microsituations cannot be correct. Since Plato, at any rate, that has been our tradition; principles may be tried out in the large and in the small. Plato thought that writ large the principles are easier to discern; others may think the reverse.

Rawls, however, proceeds as though distinct principles apply to macro and micro contexts, to the basic structure of society and to the situations we can take in and understand. Are the fundamental principles of justice *emergent* in this fashion, applying only to the largest social structure yet not to its parts? Perhaps one thinks of the possibility that a whole social structure is just, even though none of its parts is, because the injustice in each part somehow balances out or counteracts another one, and the total injustice ends up being balanced out or nullified. But can a part satisfy the most fundamental principle of justice yet still clearly be unjust, apart from its failure to perform any supposed task of counterbalancing another existing injustice? Perhaps so, if a part involves some special domain. But surely a regular, ordinary, everyday part, possessing no very unusual features, should turn out to be just when it satisfies the fundamental principles of justice; otherwise, special explanations must be offered. One cannot say merely that one is speaking of principles to apply only to the fundamental structure, so that micro counter-examples do not tell. In virtue of what features of the basic structure, features not possessed by microcases, do special moral principles apply that would be unacceptable elsewhere?

There are special disadvantages to proceeding by focusing only on the intuitive justice of described complex wholes. For complex wholes are not easily scanned; we cannot easily keep track of everything that is relevant. The justice of a whole society may depend on its satisfying a number of distinct principles. These principles, though individually compelling (witness their application to a wide range of particular microcases), may yield surprising results when combined together. That is, one may be surprised at which, and only which, institutional forms satisfy all the principles. (Compare the surprise at discovering what, and only what, satisfies a number of distinct and individually compelling conditions of adequacy; and how illuminating such discoveries are.) Or perhaps it is one simple principle which is to be writ large, and what things look like when this is done is very surprising, at first. I am not claiming that new *principles* emerge in the large, but that how the old microprinciples turn out to be satisfied in the large may surprise. If this is so, then one should not depend upon judgments about the whole as providing the only or even the major body of data against which to check one's principles. One major path to changing one's intuitive judgments about some complex whole is through seeing the larger and often surprising implications of principles solidly founded at the micro level. Similarly, discovering that one's judgments are wrong or mistaken often surely will involve overturning them by stringent applications of principles grounded on the micro level. For these reasons it is undesirable to attempt to protect principles by excluding microtests of them.

The only reason I have thought of for discounting microtests of the fundamental principles is that microsituations have particular entitlements built into them. Of course, continues the argument, the fundamental principles under consideration will run afoul of these entitlements, for the principles are to operate at a deeper level than such entitlements. Since they are to operate at the level that underlies such entitlements, no microsituation that includes entitlements can be introduced as an example by which to test these fundamental principles. Note that this reasoning grants that Rawls' procedure assumes that no fundamental entitlement view is correct, that it assumes there is some level so deep that no entitlements operate that far down.

May all entitlements be relegated to relatively superficial levels? For example, people's entitlements to the parts of their own bodies? An application of the principle of maximizing the position of those worst off might well involve forcible redistribution of bodily parts ("You've been sighted for all these years; now one—or even both—of your eyes is to be transplanted to others"), or killing some people early to use their bodies in order to provide material necessary to save the lives of those who otherwise would die young. To bring up such cases is to sound slightly hysterical. But we are driven to such extreme examples in examining Rawls' prohibition on micro counterexamples. That not all entitlements in microcases are plausibly construed as superficial, and hence as illegitimate material by which to test our suggested principles, is made especially clear if we focus on those entitlements and rights that most clearly are not socially or institutionally based. On what grounds are such cases, whose detailed specifications I leave to the ghoulish reader, ruled inadmissible? On what grounds can it be claimed that the fundamental principles of justice need apply only to the fundamental institutional structure of a society? (And couldn't we build such redistributive practices concerning bodily parts or the ending of people's lives into the fundamental structure of a society?) . . .

Natural Assets and Arbitrariness

Rawls comes closer to considering the entitlement system in his discussion of what he terms the system of natural liberty:

The system of natural liberty selects an efficient distribution roughly as follows. Let us suppose that we know from economic theory that under the standard assumptions defining a competitive market economy, income and wealth will be distributed in an efficient way, and that the particular efficient distribution which results in any period of time is determined by the initial distribution of assets, that is, by the initial distribution of income and wealth, and of natural talents and abilities. With each initial distribution, a definite efficient outcome is arrived at. Thus it turns out that if we are to accept the outcome as just, and not merely as efficient, we must accept the basis upon which over time the initial distribution of assets is determined.

In the system of natural liberty the initial distribution is regulated by the arrangements implicit in the conception of careers open to talents. These arrangements presuppose a background of equal liberty (as specified by the first principle) and a free market economy. They require a formal equality of opportunity in that all have at least the same legal rights of access to all advantaged social positions. But since there is no effort to preserve an equality or similarity, of social conditions, except insofar as this is necessary to preserve the requisite background institutions, the initial distribution of assets for any period of time is strongly influenced by natural and social contingencies. The existing distribution of income and wealth, say, is the cumulative effect of prior distributions of natural assets—that is, natural talents and abilities—as these have been developed or left unrealized, and their use favored or disfavored over time by social circumstances and such chance contingencies as accident and good fortune. Intuitively, the most obvious injustice of the system of natural liberty is that it permits distributive shares to be improperly influenced by these factors so arbitrary from a moral point of view.[10]

Here we have *Rawls'* reason for rejecting a system of natural liberty: it "permits" distributive shares to be improperly influenced by factors that are so arbitrary from a moral point of view. These factors are: "prior distribution . . . of natural talents and abilities as these have been developed over time by social circumstances and such chance contingencies as accident and good fortune." Notice that there is no mention *at all* of how persons have chosen to develop their own natural assets. Why is that simply left out? Perhaps because such choices also are viewed as being the products of factors outside the person's control, and hence as "arbitrary from a moral point of view." "The assertion that a man deserves the superior character that enables him to make the effort to cultivate his abilities is equally problematic; for his character depends in large part upon fortunate family and social circumstances for which he can claim no credit."[11] (What view is presupposed here of character and its relation to action?) "The initial endowment of natural assets and the contingencies of their growth and nurture in early life are arbitrary from a moral point of view . . . the effort a person is willing to make is influenced by his natural abilities and skills and the alternatives open to him. The better endowed are more likely, other things equal, to strive conscientiously. . . ."[12] This line of argument can succeed in blocking the introduction of a person's autonomous choices and actions (and their results) only by attributing *everything* noteworthy about the person completely to certain sorts of "external" factors. So denigrating a person's autonomy and prime responsibility for his actions is a risky line to take for a theory that otherwise wishes to buttress the dignity and self-respect of autonomous beings; especially for a theory that founds so much (including a theory of the good) upon persons' choices. One doubts that the unexalted picture of human beings Rawls' theory presupposes and rests upon can be made to fit together with the view of human dignity it is designed to lead to and embody.

Before we investigate Rawls' reasons for rejecting the system of natural liberty, we should note the situation of those in the original position. The system of natural liberty is *one* interpretation of a principle that (according to Rawls) they do accept: social and economic inequalities are to be arranged so that they both are reasonably expected to be to everyone's advantage, and are attached to positions and offices open to all. It is left unclear whether the persons in the original position explicitly consider and choose among *all* the various interpretations of this principle, though this would seem to be the most reasonable construal. (Rawls' chart on page 124 listing the conceptions of justice considered in the original position does *not* include the system of natural liberty.) Certainly they explicitly consider one interpretation, the difference principle. Rawls does not state why persons in the original position who considered the system of natural liberty would reject it. Their reason cannot be that it makes the resulting distribution depend upon a *morally* arbitrary distribution of natural assets. What we must suppose, as we have seen before, is that the self-interested calculation of persons in the original position does not (and cannot) lead them to adopt the entitlement principle. We, however, and Rawls, base our evaluations on different considerations.

Rawls has explicitly *designed* the original position and its choice situation so as to embody and realize his negative reflective evaluation of allowing shares in holdings to be affected by natural assets: "Once we decide to look for a conception of justice that nullifies the accidents of natural endowment and the contingencies of social circumstance. . . ."[13] (Rawls makes many scattered references to this theme of nullifying the accidents of natural endowment and the contingencies of social circumstance.) . . .

Why shouldn't holdings partially depend upon natural endowments? (They will also depend on how these are developed and on the uses to which they are put.) Rawls' reply is that these natural endowments and assets, being undeserved, are "arbitrary from a moral point of view." . . .

The Positive Argument

We shall begin with the positive argument. How might the point that differences in natural endowments are arbitrary from a moral point of view function in an argument meant to establish that differences in holdings stemming from differences in natural assets ought to be nullified? We shall consider four possible arguments. . . .

Consider next argument B:

1. Holdings ought to be distributed according to some pattern that is not arbitrary from a moral point of view.
2. That persons have different natural assets *is* arbitrary from a moral point of view.

Therefore,

3. Holdings ought not to be distributed according to natural assets.

But differences in natural assets might be *correlated* with other differences that are not arbitrary from a moral point of view and that are clearly of some possible moral relevance to distributional questions. For example, Hayek argued that under capitalism distribution generally is in accordance with perceived service to others. Since differences in natural assets will produce differences in ability to serve others, there will be some correlation of differences in distribution with differences in natural assets. The principle of the system is *not* distribution in accordance with natural assets; but differences in natural assets will lead to differences in holdings under a system whose principle is distribution according to perceived service to others. . . .

I turn now to our final positive argument which purports to derive the conclusion that distributive shares shouldn't depend upon natural assets from the statement that the distribution of natural assets is morally arbitrary. This argument focuses on the notion of equality. Since a large part of Rawls' argument serves to justify or show acceptable a particular deviation from equal shares (some may have more if this serves to improve the position of those worst off), perhaps a reconstruction of his underlying argument that places equality at its center will be illuminating. Differences between persons (the argument runs) are arbitrary from a moral point of view if there is no moral argument for the conclusion that there ought to be the differences. Not all such differences will be morally objectionable. That there is no such moral argument will seem important only in the case of those differences we believe oughtn't to obtain unless there is a moral reason establishing that they ought to obtain. There is, so to speak, a presumption against certain differences that can be overridden (can it merely be neutralized?) by moral reasons; in the absence of any such moral reasons of sufficient weight, there ought to be equality. Thus we have argument D:

1. Holdings ought to be equal, unless there is a (weighty) moral reason why they ought to be unequal.
2. People do not deserve the ways in which they differ from other persons in natural assets; there is no moral reason why people ought to differ in natural assets.
3. If there is no moral reason why people differ in certain traits, then their actually differing in these traits does not provide, and cannot give rise to, a moral reason why they should differ in other traits (for example, in holdings).
4. Therefore people's differing in natural assets is not a reason why holdings ought to be unequal.
5. People's holdings ought to be equal unless there is some other moral reason (such as, for example, raising the position of those worst off) why their holdings ought to be unequal.

Statements similar to the third premiss will occupy us shortly. Here let us focus on the first premiss, the equality premiss. Why ought people's holdings to be equal, in the absence of special moral reason to deviate from equality? (Why think there *ought* to be *any* particular pattern in holdings?) Why is equality the rest (or rectilinear motion) position of the system, deviation from which may be caused only by moral forces? Many "arguments" for equality merely *assert* that differences between persons are arbitrary and must be justified. Often writers state a presumption in favor of equality in a form such as the following: "Differences in treatment of persons need to be justified."[14] The most favored situation for this sort of assumption is one in which there is one person (or group) treating everyone, a person (or group) having *no* right or entitlement to bestow the particular treatment as they wish or even whim. But if I go to one movie theater rather than to another adjacent to it, need I justify my different treatment of the two theater owners? Isn't it enough that I felt like going to one of them? That differences in treatment need to be justified *does* fit contemporary *governments*. Here there is a centralized process treating all, with no entitlement to bestow treatment according to whim. The major portion of distribution in a free society does not, however, come through the actions of the government, nor does failure to overturn the results of the localized individual exchanges constitute "state action." When there is no *one* doing the treating, and all are entitled to bestow their holdings as they wish, it is not clear why the maxim that differences in treatment must be justified should be thought to have extensive application. Why must differences between persons be justified? Why think that we must change, or remedy, or compensate for any inequality which can be changed, remedied, or compensated for? Perhaps here is where social cooperation enters in: though there is no presumption of equality (in, say, primary goods, or things people care about) among all persons, perhaps there is one among persons cooperating together. But it is difficult to see an argument for this; surely not all persons who cooperate together explicitly agree to this presumption as one of the terms of their mutual cooperation. And its acceptance would provide an unfortunate incentive for well-off persons to refuse to cooperate with, or to allow any of their number to cooperate with, some distant people who are less well off than any among them. For entering into such social cooperation, beneficial to those less well off, would seriously worsen the position of the well-off group by creating relations of presumptive equality between themselves and the worse-off group. . . .

Collective Assets

Rawls' view seems to be that everyone has some entitlement or claim on the totality of natural assets (viewed as a pool), with no one having differential claims. The distribution of natural abilities is viewed as a "collective asset."

We see then that the difference principle represents, in effect, an agreement to regard the distribution of natural talents as a common asset and to share in the benefits of this distribution whatever it turns out to be. Those who have been favored by nature, whoever they are, may gain from their good fortune only on terms that improve the situation of those who have lost out. . . . No one deserves his greater natural capacity nor merits a more favorable starting place in society. But it does not follow that one should eliminate these distinctions. There is another way to deal with them. The basic structure can be arranged so that these contingencies work for the good of the least fortunate.[15]

People will differ in how they view regarding natural talents as a common asset. Some will complain, echoing Rawls against utilitarianism,[16] that this "does not take seriously the distinction between persons"; and they will wonder whether any reconstruction of Kant that treats people's abilities and talents as resources for others can be adequate. "The two principles of justice . . . rule out even the tendency to regard men as means to one another's welfare."[17] Only if one presses *very* hard on the distinction between men and their talents, assets, abilities, and special traits. Whether any coherent conception of a person remains when the distinction is so pressed is an open question. Why we, thick with particular traits, should be cheered that (only) the thus purified men within us are not regarded as means is also unclear.

People's talents and abilities *are* an asset to a free community; others in the community benefit from their presence and are better off because they are there rather than elsewhere or nowhere. (Otherwise they wouldn't choose to deal with them.) Life, over time, is not a constant-sum game, wherein if greater ability or effort leads to some getting more, that means that others must lose. In a free society, people's talents do benefit others, and not only themselves. Is it the extraction of even more benefit to others that is supposed to justify treating people's natural assets as a collective resource? What justifies this extraction?

No one deserves his greater natural capacity nor merits a more favorable starting place in society. But it does not follow that one should eliminate these distinctions. There is another way to deal with them. The basic structure can be arranged so that these contingencies work for the good of the least fortunate.[18]

And if there weren't "another way to deal with them?" would it then follow that one should eliminate these distinctions? What exactly would be contemplated in the case of natural assets? If people's assets and talents *couldn't* be harnessed to serve others, would something be done to remove these exceptional assets and talents, or to forbid them from being exercised for the person's own benefit or that of someone else he chose, even though this limitation wouldn't improve the absolute position of those somehow unable to harness the talents and abilities of others for their own benefit? Is it so implausible to claim that envy underlies this conception of justice, forming part of its root notion? . . .

We have used our entitlement conception of justice in holdings to probe Rawls' theory, sharpening our understanding of what the entitlement conception involves by bringing it to bear upon an alternative conception of distributive justice, one that is deep and elegant. Also, I believe, we have probed deep-lying inadequacies in Rawls' theory. I am mindful of Rawls' reiterated point that a theory cannot be evaluated by focusing upon a single feature or part of it; instead the whole theory must be assessed (the reader will not know how whole a theory can be until he has read all of Rawls' book), and a perfect theory is not to be expected. However we have examined an important part of Rawls' theory, and its crucial underlying assumptions. I am as well aware as anyone of how sketchy my discussion of the entitlement conception of justice in holdings has been. But I no more believe we need to have formulated a complete alternative theory in order to reject Rawls' undeniably great advance over utilitarianism, than Rawls needed a complete alternative theory before he could reject utilitarianism. What more does one need or can one have, in order to begin progressing toward a better theory, than a sketch of a plausible alternative view, which from its very different perspective highlights the inadequacies of the best existing well-worked-out theory? Here, as in so many things, we learn from Rawls.

NOTES

1. F. A. Hayek, *The Constitution of Liberty* (Chicago: University of Chicago Press, 1960), p. 87.
2. Further details which this statement should include are contained in my essay "Coercion," in *Philosophy, Science, and Method*, ed. S. Morgenbesser, P. Suppes, and M. White (New York: St. Martin, 1969).
3. I discuss overriding and its moral traces in "Moral Complications and Moral Structures," *Natural Law Forum*, 1968, pp. 1–50.
4. Rawls, *A Theory of Justice*, p.4.
5. Rawls, *Theory of Justice*, p. 12. (See p. 14 in this volume.)
6. Rawls, *Theory of Justice*, pp. 14–15. (See p. 16 in this volume.)
7. Rawls, *Theory of Justice*, sect. 16, especially p. 98.
8. Rawls, *Theory of Justice*, p. 103. (See p. 34 in this volume.)
9. Some years ago, Hayek argued (*The Constitution of Liberty*, Chap. 3) that a free capitalist society, over time, raises the position of those worst off more than any alternative institutional structure; to use present terminology, he argued that *it* best satisfies the end-state principle of justice formulated by the difference principle.
10. Rawls, *Theory of Justice*, p. 72. (See p. 29 in this volume.) Rawls goes on to discuss what he calls a liberal interpretation of his two principles of justice, which is designed to eliminate the influence of social contingencies, but which "intuitively, still appears defective . . . (for) it still permits the distribution of wealth and income to be determined by the natural distribution of abilities and talents . . . distributive shares are decided by the outcome of the natural lottery; and this outcome is arbitrary from a moral perspective. There is no more reason to permit the distribution of income and wealth to be settled by the distribution of natural assets than by historical and social fortune" (pp. 73–74). (See p. 30 in this volume.)
11. Rawls, *Theory of Justice*, p. 104. (See p. 35 in this volume.)
12. Rawls, *Theory of Justice*, pp. 311–312.
13. Rawls, *Theory of Justice*, p. 15. (See p. 16 in this volume.)
14. "No reason need be given for . . . an equal distribution of benefits—for that is 'natural'—self-evidently right and just, and needs no justification, since it is in some sense conceived as being self-justified. . . . The assumption is that equality needs no

reasons, only inequality does so; that uniformity, regularity, similarity, symmetry, . . . need not be specially accounted for, whereas differences, unsystematic behavior, changes in conduct, need explanation and, as a rule, justification. If I have a cake and there are ten persons among whom I wish to divide it, then if I give exactly one-tenth to each, this will not, at any rate automatically, call for justification; whereas if I depart from this principle of equal division I am expected to produce a special reason. It is some sense of this, however latent, that makes equality an idea which has never seemed intrinsically eccentric. . . ." Isaiah Berlin, "Equality," reprinted in Frederick A. Olafson, ed. *Justice and Social Policy* (Englewood Cliffs, N.J.: Prentice Hall, 1961), p. 131. To pursue the analogy with mechanics further, note that it is a substantive theoretical position which specifies a particular state or situation as one which requires no explanation whereas deviations from it are to be explained in terms of external forces. See Ernest Nagel's discussion of D'Alembert's attempt to provide an *a priori* argument for Newton's first law of motion. *The Structure of Science* (New York: Harcourt, Brace, and World, 1961), pp. 175–177.

15. Rawls, *Theory of Justice*, p. 102. (See p. 33 in this volume.)
16. Rawls, *Theory of Justice*, p. 27. (See p. 44 in this volume.)
17. Rawls, *Theory of Justice*, p.183.
18. Rawls, *Theory of Justice*, p.102. (See p. 33 in this volume.)

UTILITARIANISM

Although every philosophy has its precursors, utilitarianism received its classic formulation by Jeremy Bentham in the early nineteenth century and was developed further by John Stuart Mill. Both were English legal and social reformers, as well as philosophers. Bentham, in particular, was concerned with applying the utilitarian principle "promote the greatest happiness of the greatest number" to legislation, and today utilitarianism remains an underlying assumption of many political programs, as well as one of the most important moral and political philosophies.

According to utilitarianism, the rightness or wrongness of actions is determined by the goodness or badness of their consequences—not just for the actor, but for all affected. Bentham was a philosophical hedonist and held that pleasure was the only good. Subsequent utilitarians have frequently disagreed with this, but most utilitarians today would equate goodness with happiness (or, alternatively, with satisfied desire). The principle of utility constitutes the only moral standard; considerations of justice, for example, have no moral weight independent of the goodness or badness of the consequences of an action. Thus, Bentham viewed talk of a social contract or state of nature as purely "fictitious" and of natural rights as "nonsense on stilts." For utilitarians the right (or just or best) distribution of economic goods will be that which results in the most happiness for society as a whole.

Among the most important contemporary descendants of Bentham and Mill are J. J. C. Smart and R. M. Hare. Each subscribes to a version of the utilitarian principle, although very different methods are used to justify that conclusion.

For Smart acceptance of the principle of utility depends on whether or not—and to what extent—we feel a "sentiment of generalized benevolence." By this is meant a desire or wish for the well-being and happiness of other persons. To the extent that this general attitude is present and overrides otner feelings we may have, we will be inclined toward utilitarianism. Smart believes that the moral views which one accepts rest ultimately on emotional preferences and sentiment and so no normative system—including utilitarianism—can be *proved*. Instead, his concern in what follows is to explain what a utilitarian would say about economic justice and to do so in such a way that others will find the utilitarian view acceptable and attractive. He also criticizes alternative positions, showing that each is inconsistent with a desire for the well-being of others and so to that extent unacceptable. Throughout his essay Smart appeals to our natural feelings of benevolence as a basis for choosing between the principle of utility and its rivals.

R. M. Hare argues to a similar conclusion by a very different route. Hare, as we have seen before, views skeptically the appeal to moral intuitions or attitudes, to which most moral philosophers have recourse in their arguments. These attitudes reflect to a large extent simply those values and beliefs which happened to be instilled in us by our society and family when we were young. Hare desires a more secure foundation on which to base our moral claims.

He begins by considering the function of ethical language, which is, he argues, to prescribe or commend a certain type of behavior and to do so universally, that is, for everyone in similar circumstances. Thus, the moral claim "You ought to aid the poor" expresses both (1) a recommendation that you behave a certain way, and (2) the idea that anyone in similar circumstances ought also to give aid. Not all prescriptions are universal, however. For example, "Eat your peas" does not logically commit the speaker to saying that everybody should eat peas! All of this can be seen by considering only the formal or metaethical aspects of moral language.

Intuitively, the idea behind Hare's metaethical analysis of moral language is this: If a person makes a moral judgment—for example, says that a theft is wrong—then he must be willing to say that similar thefts are wrong also. Thus, it won't do for a person to condemn someone's taking his property but to fail to condemn his own theft under similar circumstances. The logic of moral language commits its user to this "universal prescriptivism." To fail to do so is to use the words *right* and *wrong* incorrectly. To claim, "It's wrong for you to do that, but not for me," if we are both performing an action of the same type, is a misuse of language, a kind of inconsistency.

Hare further holds that these logical characteristics of language provide the basis for utilitarianism. In *Freedom and Reason* he writes that as we "endeavor to find lines of conduct which we can prescribe universally in a given situation . . . we find ourselves bound to give equal weight to the desires of all parties (the foundation of distributive justice); and this in turn leads to such views as that we should seek to maximize satisfactions." This is because, in deciding which conduct can be universally prescribed, we should imagine ourselves successively in the position of each affected party. Having done this, a moral agent will be inclined to prescribe that act which would do the most good for the most people—which is what utilitarianism recommends.

In his essay, "Justice and Equality," Hare again begins by looking to the formal properties of ethical reasoning. He discusses three "levels" of moral thinking (metaethical, intuitive, and critical) and distinguishes several senses of "justice." He argues that both Rawls and he treat distributive justice (who gets what goods?) and retributive justice (who gets punished or rewarded?) as analogous problems. Rawls would appeal to the procedure of the original position while Hare himself uses "universalizability" and the idea of occupying "successive positions" to achieve similar results in determining how punishment is to be distributed.

Next Hare considers the ways in which the requirements of formal justice are able to help resolve the problems of economic distribution. His formal procedure (with its utilitarian implications), together with certain plausible factual assumptions, requires, he argues, a generally egalitarian distribution of goods. Taking slavery as an example, Hare elaborates the egalitarian consequences of his view and concludes with a discussion of methodology, relativism, intuition, and related issues.

J. J. C. Smart

Distributive Justice and Utilitarianism

INTRODUCTION

In this paper I shall not be concerned with the defense of utilitarianism against other types of ethical theory. Indeed I hold that questions of ultimate ethical principle are not susceptible of proof, though something can be done to render them more acceptable by presenting them in a clear light and by clearing up certain confusions which (for some people) may get in the way of their acceptance. Ultimately the utilitarian appeals to the sentiment of generalized benevolence, and speaks to others who feel this sentiment too and for whom it is an over-riding feeling. (This does not mean that he will always act from this over-riding feeling. There can be backsliding and action may result from more particular feelings, just as an egoist may go against his own interests, and may regret this.) I shall be concerned here merely to investigate certain consequences of utilitarianism, as they relate to questions of distributive justice. The type of utilitarianism with which I am concerned is act utilitarianism, which is in its normative aspects much the same as the type of utilitarianism which was put forward by Henry Sidgwick, though I differ from Sidgwick over questions of moral epistemology and of the semantics of ethical language.

THE PLACE OF JUSTICE IN UTILITARIAN THEORY

The concept of justice as a *fundamental* ethical concept is really quite foreign to utilitarianism. A utilitarian would compromise his utilitarianism if he allowed principles of justice which might conflict with the maximization of happiness (or more generally of goodness, should he be an 'ideal' utilitarian). He is concerned with the maximization of happiness and not with the distribution of it. Nevertheless he may well deduce from his ethical principle that certain ways of distributing the means to happiness (e.g. money, food, housing) are more conducive to the general good than are others. He will be interested in justice in so far as it is a political or legal or quasi-legal concept. He will consider whether the legal institutions and customary sanctions which operate in particular societies are more or less conducive to the utilitarian end than are other possible institutions and customs. Even if the society consisted entirely of utilitarians (and of course no actual societies have thus consisted) it might still be important to have legal and customary sanctions relating to distribution of goods, because utilitarians might be tempted to backslide and favour non-optimific distributions, perhaps because of bias in their own favour. They might be helped to act in a more nearly utilitarian way because of the presence of these sanctions.

As a utilitarian, therefore, I do not allow the concept of justice as a fundamental moral concept, but I am nevertheless interested in justice in a subordinate way, as a *means* to the utilitarian end. Thus even though I hold that it does not matter in what way happiness is distributed among different persons, provided that the total amount of happiness is maximized, I do of course hold that it can be of vital importance that the *means* to happiness should be distributed in some ways and not in others. Suppose that I have the choice of two alternative actions as follows: I can either give $500 to each of two needy men, Smith and Campbell, or else give $1000 to Smith and nothing to Campbell. It is of course likely to produce the greatest happiness if I divide the money equally. For this reason utilitarianism can often emerge as a theory with egalitarian consequences. If it does so this is because of the empirical situation, and not because of any moral commitment to egalitarianism as such. Consider, for example, another empirical situation in which the $500 was replaced by a half-dose of a life saving drug, in which case the utilitarian would advocate giving two half doses to Smith or Campbell and none to the other. Indeed if Smith and Campbell each possessed a half dose it would be right to take one of the half doses and give it to the other. (I am assuming that a whole dose would preserve life and that a half dose would not. I am also assuming a simplified situation: in some possible situations, especially in a society of non-utilitarians, the wide social ramifications of taking a half dose from Smith and giving it to Campbell might conceivably outweigh the good results of saving Campbell's life.) However, it is probable that in most situations the equal distribution of the means to happiness will be the right utilitarian action, even though the utilitarian has no ultimate moral commitment to egalitarianism. If a utilitarian is given the choice of two actions, one of which will give 2 units of happiness to Smith and 2 to Campbell and the other of which will give 1 unit of happiness to Smith and 9 to Campbell, he will choose the latter course.[1] It may also be that I have the choice between two alternative actions, one of which gives -1 unit of happiness to Smith and $+9$ units to Campbell, and the other of which gives $+2$ to Smith and $+2$ to Campbell. As a utilitarian I will choose the former course, and here I will be in conflict with John Rawls' theory, whose maximin principle would rule out making Smith worse off.

UTILITARIANISM AND RAWLS' THEORY

Rawls deduces his ethical principles from the contract which would be made by a group of rational egoists in an 'original position' in which they thought behind a 'veil of ignorance,' so that they would not know who they were or even what generation they belonged to. Reasoning behind this veil of ignorance, they would apply the maximin principle. John Harsanyi earlier used the notion of a contract in such a position of ignorance, but used not the maximin principle but the principle of maximizing expected utility.[2] Harsanyi's method leads to a form of rule utilitarianism. I see no great merit in this roundabout approach to ethics *via* a contrary to fact supposition, which involves the tricky notion of a social contract and which thus appears already to presuppose a moral position. The approach seems also too Hobbesian: it is anthropologically incorrect to suppose that we are all originally little egoists. I prefer to base ethics on a principle of generalized benevolence, to which some of those with whom I discuss ethics may immediately respond. Possibly it might show something interesting about our common moral notions if it could be proved that they follow from what would be contracted by rational egoists in an 'original position,' but as a utilitarian I am more concerned to advocate a normative theory which might replace our common moral notions than I am to explain these notions. Though some form of utilitarianism might be deducible (as by Harsanyi) from a contract or original position theory, I do not think that it either ought to be or need be defended in this sort of way.

Be that as it may, it is clear that utilitarian views about distribution of happiness do differ from Rawls' view. I have made a distinction between justice as a moral concept and justice as a legal or quasi-legal concept. The utilitarian has no room for the former, but he can have strong views about the latter, though *what* these views are will depend on empirical considerations. Thus whether he will prefer a political theory which advocates a completely socialist state, or whether he will prefer one which advocates a minimal state (as Robert Nozick's book does[3]), or whether again he will advocate something between the two, is something which depends on the facts of economics, sociology, and so on. As someone not expert in these fields I have no desire to dogmatize on these empirical matters. (My own private non-expert opinion is that probably neither extreme leads to maximization of happiness, though I have a liking for rather more socialism than exists in Australia or U.S.A. at present.) As a utilitarian my approach to political theory has to be tentative and empirical. Not believing in moral rights as such I can not deduce theories about the best political arrangements by making deductions (as Nozick does) from propositions which purport to be about such basic rights.

Rawls deduces two principles of justice.[4] The first of these is that 'each person is to have an equal right to the most extensive basic liberty compatible with a similar liberty for others,' and the second one is that 'social and economic inequalities are to be arranged so that they are both (a) reasonably expected to be to everyone's advantage, and (b) attached to positions and offices open to all.' Though a utilitarian could (on empirical grounds) be very much in sympathy with both of these principles, he could not accept them as universal rules. Suppose that a society which had no danger of nuclear war could be achieved only by reducing the liberty of one percent of the world's population. Might it not be right to bring about such a state of affairs if it were in one's power? Indeed might it not be right greatly to reduce the liberty of 100% of the world's population if such a desirable outcome could be achieved? Perhaps the present genera- tion would be pretty miserable and would hanker for their lost liberties. However we must also think about the countless future generations which might exist and be happy provided that mankind can avoid exterminating itself, and we must also think of all the pain, misery and genetic damage which would be brought about by nuclear war even if this did not lead to the total extermination of mankind.

Suppose that this loss of freedom prevented a war so devastating that the whole process of evolution on this planet would come to an end. At the cost of the loss of freedom, instead of the war and the end of evolution there might occur an evolutionary process which was not only long lived but also beneficial: in millions of years there might be creatures descended from *homo sapiens* which had vastly increased talents and capac- ity for happiness. At least such considerations show that Rawls' first princi- ple is far from obvious to the utilitarian, though in certain mundane contexts he might accede to it as a useful approximation. Indeed I do not believe that restriction of liberty, in our present society, could have benefi- cial results in helping to prevent nuclear war, though a case could be made for certain restrictions on the liberty of all present members of society so as to enable the government to prevent nuclear blackmail by gangs of terrorists.

Perhaps in the past considerable restrictions on the personal liber- ties of a large proportion of citizens may have been justifiable on utilitar- ian grounds. In view of the glories of Athens and its contributions to civilization it is possible that the Athenian slave society was justifiable. In one part of his paper, "Nature and Soundness of the Contract and Coher- ence Arguments,"[5] David Lyons has judiciously discussed the question of whether in certain circumstances a utilitarian would condone slavery. He says that it would be unlikely that a utilitarian could condone slavery as it has existed in modern times. However he considers the possibility that less objectionable forms of slavery or near slavery have existed. The less objec- tionable these may have been, the more likely it is that utilitarianism would have condoned them. Lyons remarks that our judgments about the relative advantages of different societies must be very tentative because we do not know enough about human history to say what were the social alternatives at any juncture.[6]

Similar reflections naturally occur in connection with Rawls' second principle. Oligarchic societies, such as that of eighteenth century Britain, may well have been in fact better governed than they would have been if posts of responsibility had been available to all. Certainly to resolve this question we should have to go deeply into empirical investigations of the historical facts. (To prevent misunderstanding, I do think that in our present society utilitarianism would imply adherence to Rawls' second prin- ciple as a general rule.)

A utilitarian is concerned with maximizing total happiness (or goodness, if he is an ideal utilitarian). Rawls largely concerns himself with certain 'primary goods', as he calls them. These include 'rights and liberties, powers and opportunities, income and wealth.'[7] A utilitarian would regard these as mere means to the ultimate good. Nevertheless if he is proposing new laws or changes to social institutions the utilitarian will have to concern himself in practice with the distribution of these 'primary goods' (as Bentham did).[8] But if as an approximation we neglect this distinction, which may be justifiable to the extent that there is a correlation between happiness and the level of these 'primary goods,' we may say that according to Rawls an action is right only if it is to the benefit of the least advantaged person. A utilitarian will hold that a redistribution of the means to happiness is right if it maximizes the general happiness, even though some persons, even the least advantaged ones, are made worse off. A position which is intermediate between the utilitarian position and Rawls' position would be one which held that one ought to maximize some sort of trade off between total happiness and distribution of happiness. Such a position would imply that sometimes we should redistribute in such a way as to make some persons, even the least advantaged ones, worse off, but this would happen less often than it would according to the classical utilitarian theory.

UTILITARIANISM AND SACRIFICE OF INTERESTS

Now though I do not believe that ultimate moral principles are capable of proof or disproof, I wonder whether this disagreement about whether we should ever sacrifice some persons' interests for the sake of the total interest may be connected with different views which philosophers have about human personality. Are we concerned simply to produce the greatest net happiness, or is it independently important that we should take account of *whose* happiness a given quantum of happiness should be? The non-utilitarian will hold that the distinction between Smith on the one hand and Campbell on the other hand is different in an ethically important way from the distinction between two different temporal segments of the same man, say Smith throughout his twenties and Smith throughout his forties. (The non-utilitarian generally feels no puzzlement about the rightness of the twenty-five year old Smith sacrificing himself for the sake of the forty-five year old Smith.) I find it hard to see what the morally relevant difference would be. It is true that we do in fact feel a special concern for future temporal segments of ourselves, perhaps because we are most of the time planning for these future temporal segments. However, sometimes we plan for the welfare of temporal segments of other people, and the man who plans martyrdom, for example, is certainly not planning for any future temporal segment of himself (at least if he does not believe in immortality). Since the utilitarian principle is an expression of the sentiment of generalized benevolence, the utilitarian sees no relevant different between the happiness of one person and the happiness of another.

I have suggested that those who see the matter differently may have a strong metaphysical concept of personality. In the context of modern scientific psychology the notion of a person tends to dissolve into a welter of talk in terms of neurophysiology, cybernetics and information theory. Sidgwick may have been similarly sceptical about our ordinary notions of personality. Using an earlier philosophical idiom he remarks (as a *tu quoque* to the Egoist who asks why he should sacrifice his own present happiness for the happiness of another) that one might equally ask why one should sacrifice a present pleasure for a greater one in the future. He points out that if one accepted Hume's theory of the mind, according to which the mind is just a cluster of feelings, sensations, and images, one might ask why one part of the series of feelings which contribute to the mind should feel concern for another part.[9]

Returning from this speculative excursion, let us simply note that according to classical utilitarianism it can be right to diminish the happiness of Smith in order to bring about a more than compensating increase of the happiness of Campbell. What matters is simply the maximization of happiness, and distribution of happiness is irrelevant. Sidgwick himself qualified this uncompromising stand in a minor way when he introduced a principle of equal distribution which would come into play when each of two alternative actions would produce the same amount of total happiness, each greater than that which would be produced by any other alternative action. Of course there must be an almost zero probability that two alternative actions would produce *exactly* the same total happiness, but as Sidgwick points out, it may be quite common *that as far as we know* the two alternatives would produce equal total happiness. Sidgwick introduces his principle of equal distribution in order to break this sort of tie,[10] and he claims that the principle is implicit in Bentham's somewhat obscure formula 'Everybody to count for one, and nobody for more than one.' Actually, if Sidgwick's principle is needed only to break ties (but why not toss a coin?) then it merely postpones the problem. It would lead us to prefer giving 3 units of happiness to Smith plus 3 to Campbell to giving 2 to Smith plus 4 to Campbell. We could still have a tie between giving 2 units to Smith and 4 to Campbell, on the one hand, and giving 4 units to Smith and 2 to Campbell, on the other hand.

It is not clear to me that in proposing this supplementary principle of distribution Sidgwick is being quite consistent. Suppose that alternative A maximizes happiness and also that B is the alternative action which comes nearest to A in producing happiness, producing only slightly less. Suppose also that A would distribute happiness rather unequally and that B would distribute happiness quite equally. Nevertheless because A produces more happiness Sidgwick would say that A should be done. Since, given a suitable example, the difference between the amounts of happiness produced can be supposed as small as one pleases, it appears that Sidgwick gives equal distribution a vanishingly small value compared with that which he gives to maximization. In fact, according to usual mathematical theories such a vanishingly small value could be no other than zero, and so instead of applying his principle of distribution in order to break ties Sidgwick could surely just as well have tossed a coin. The only way for him to avoid this conclusion, I think, would have been for him to say that the value of equal distribution is non-zero but infinitesimal.[11] However, it does seem to be an odd ethical position that one should give an *infinitesimal* value to equal distribution. It seems more plausible to reject Sidgwick's supplementary principle altogether (as I am inclined to do) or else to try to work out a theory in which equality of distribution comes into the calculation of consequences in all cases, and not just in order to break ties. According to the second alternative, we should be concerned with maximizing some sort of compromise between total happiness and equal distribution of it. Such a theory might make more concessions to common sense notions of distributive justice than classical utilitarianism does.

One proposal for compromising between maximization of happiness and distribution of it is given by Nicholas Rescher in his book *Distributive Justice*.[12] (Rescher modifies utilitarianism in other ways too, but I shall not be concerned with these here.) Rescher's proposal is not for a compromise between *total* happiness and distribution but between *average* happiness and distribution, though an analogous account would hold for the case of total happiness. Rescher proposes that we should maximize an *effective average*, which is the average happiness less half the standard deviation from it. Lawrence H. Powers has argued that Rescher's definition of an effective average leads to unacceptable consequences, and has suggested replacing Rescher's definition by a new one, according to which the effective average is the average happiness less half the average deviation.[13] He gives an example which shows that Rescher's criterion could forbid a change which made everybody better off (a Pareto improvement). Powers claims that his modified criterion does not have bad consequences of this sort. Some philosophers may find this sort of compromise between utilitarianism and egalitarianism more palatable than classical utilitarianism. However, I shall now return to the consideration of distributive justice as it relates to the classical utilitarian position.

SAVINGS FOR FUTURE GENERATIONS AND FOR OTHER COUNTRIES

In thinking about distributive justice we commonly think about the problem of distributing happiness between members of a set of contemporary individuals. However this is to oversimplify the situation with which the utilitarian should be concerned. The consequences of his actions stretch indefinitely into the future, and the happiness to be maximized is that of all sentient beings, whatever their positions in space and time.[14] It is in the context of future generations that the question of whether we should maximize *average* happiness or whether we should maximize *total* happiness becomes particularly relevant. Like Sidgwick[15] I am inclined to advocate the latter type of utilitarianism. In thinking about this issue it is useful once more to compare the question of the happiness of different temporal segments of one person with the question of the happiness of a number of distinct persons. If we think that it is better to have 50 happy years of life than it is to have 20 happy years, then we should also think that it is better to have 50 happy people than to have 20 happy people, and this not just because the 50 happy people would raise the average happiness of the total population of the universe more than the 20 happy people would. (Even if the total population of the universe were 50 or 20, as the case may be, the universe with 50 happy people would be better than the universe with 20.) My argument here is of course meant to be persuasive rather than logically compelling. I suppose that a proponent of average utility could consistently reply that 50 happy years of life are intrinsically no better than 20 such years, though we may prefer a man to live the longer life because of extrinsic considerations, for example the sorrow of a widow with small children to bring up and no husband to help her.

As a utilitarian I hold that we should think of future generations no less than we should think of members of our own generation. Distance in time is no more pertinent to utilitarian considerations than is distance in space. Just as we would not conduct a bomb test on a distant island without considering the possibility that the island contained inhabitants, so also we ought to consider the effects of our actions on our remote or unknown descendants or possible descendants. I have heard it argued that the two cases are not parallel: what inhabitants are now on the island does not depend on our present actions, but who our descendants are does depend in part on our present actions. I cannot see myself why this should be a morally relevant difference. Suppose that one action would cause an island to have in the next generation a population of 1000 whereas an alternative action would cause the island to have a population of 2000 and that the question of the larger or smaller population has no significant effect on the rest of the world. Then as a utilitarian I want to prefer causing the larger population to exist, though a proponent of maximizing average utility would be indifferent between the two cases. Some philosophers might say that we have no duties towards merely possible people. If we opt for the population of 1000 then these 1000 will be actual and we will have duties towards them, but the remainder of the possible population of 2000 would not be actual and would not have rights. However such an argument should not be accepted by a utilitarian, who should not have the notion of 'duty' as a fundamental concept of his system.[16]

Anyway, let us take it that we are concerned here with utilitarianism as a theory of maximizing *total* happiness (not *average* happiness). Let us consider the question of the distribution of happiness and of the means to happiness between different generations. Just as in the case of distribution between contemporaries, utilitarianism is indifferent to various patterns of distribution of total happiness provided that the total is the same. (However the theory will not be indifferent in this sort of way to questions of the distribution of the *means* to happiness.) We must ask what sacrifices we should make now for the sake of the greater happiness of our descendants. Not so long ago it seemed that the fruits of science and technology were bringing the human species towards a golden age. (Unfortunately we have tended to forget the deleterious effect of modern technology—e.g., factory farms—on animal happiness.[17] People are nowadays more sceptical about a future golden age: they point to problems of overpopulation.

environmental pollution, the danger of nuclear war, possible accidents in genetic engineering, and so on. But let us consider what would be the right policy about savings for future generations, assuming that future generations would be happier than ours. In 'future generations' I would want to include 'future generations of non-humans' too, but I shall neglect this point in comparing utilitarianism with Rawls' theory. It indeed is a defect in the contractual theory that it neglects the sufferings of animals: the veil of ignorance prevents us from knowing who we are, i.e. which human being, but it does not, I think, prevent us from knowing that we are at least human. Now if future generations are going to be happier than our generation, it would seem to follow from Rawls' difference principle that we should make no savings for future generations. If we did we should be disadvantaging the worse off for the benefit of the better off. Rawls escapes this consequence by what seems to be an *ad hoc* modification of his original theory: he modifies the egoistic inclinations of people in his 'original position' by allowing them some altruistic feelings, namely feelings for the welfare of their children and grandchildren.

Utilitarianism might seem to imply an opposite conclusion. Instead of implying zero savings (as Rawls' theory could if it did not have the above mentioned modification) utilitarianism would seem to require what many people would regard as an unacceptably high amount of savings. In a discussion of F. P. Ramsey's pioneering paper 'A Mathematical Theory of Saving,'[18] John C. Harsanyi has pointed out[19] that on certain plausible assumptions about the relation between increments of wealth to increments of happiness (assumptions about utility functions), Ramsey's argument might well imply that the present generation should save more than half of their national incomes. However, Harsanyi has argued that utility functions applicable to the present generation do not properly relate savings to future felicity. New technological discoveries may well make present capital investments of little use in the future. For this reason, as well as others which I shall not go into here, Harsanyi has argued that optimal savings would be less than might at first have been supposed on the basis of Ramsey's argument.

Nevertheless it may well be that utilitarian considerations imply that savings for future generations should be much greater than many people think. The less we think that a golden age is coming the stronger these reasons will be. Very much expense and effort need to be made, for example, to show that radio-active waste materials do not harm our remote descendants, or failing that, we must forgo the use of nuclear reactors for generating power. Similarly with respect to the rich countries in relation to the third world, the wasteful technologies, certain fishing areas, and so on, for the benefit of the poorer ones. The fact that such savings or renunciations that are enjoined by utilitarian considerations may well come to far more than would be politically acceptable is no criticism of utilitarianism: it is a reflection of the fact that people are usually more swayed by self-interest than they ought to be. Of course utilitarianism is a theory for individual decision making, and prevailing political attitudes constitute part of the empirical facts about the world with which, like it or not, a utilitarian decision maker will have to contend. Some actions which would be right if they were generally imitated would be merely Quixotic if there were no prospect of such imitation. For example when there was a proposal to raise the salaries of Australian professors, some friends of mine wrote letters to the newspapers saying that it would be better to use this amount of taxpayers' money to increase the number of junior faculty members. When this idea did not catch on, there was obviously no point in their refusing (as individuals) the proposed salary increases. (I neglect the fact here that there would have been great administrative difficulties in putting such individual decisions into effect.) Though utilitarianism is *in theory* not egalitarian, because it does not protect the interests of the worst off people in the way that Rawls' theory does, it is possible that there might be situations in which Rawls' constraint of not making the worst off even more badly off would force Rawls into a decision which would lead to a greater difference between rich and poor than would utilitarian theory. This is because removal of the constraint might, at the cost of making a very few of the worst off members of society still worse off, bring about a more general levelling off on the whole. (Here we must of course make allowance for the fact that if we are concerned with the redistribution of the *means* to happiness, taking what people have may produce more unhappiness than not giving it to them in the first place.) To take a rather fanciful example, suggested to me by some remarks of Harsanyi's,[20] suppose that society spent astronomical sums on very badly off mentally defective people, thus making them able to perform some simple tasks which would otherwise be beyond them, and that this vast expenditure for the mentally defective prevented ordinary health care for the ordinary poor but not handicapped people. On the above supposition utilitarianism would suggest a redistribution of resources *from* the mentally defective *to* better health care for the generality of the poor. This would seem to be forbidden by Rawls' difference principle. Whether in any actual situations Rawls' theory or utilitarian theory would lead to the greater egalitarianism in practice depends on many empirical considerations, and I would not like to pronounce on this matter.

UTILITARIANISM AND NOZICK'S THEORY

General adherence to Robert Nozick's theory (in his *Anarchy, State, and Utopia*) would be compatible with the existence of very great inequality indeed. This is because the whole theory is based quite explicitly on the notion of *rights*: in the very first sentence of the preface of his book we read 'Individuals have rights. . . .' The utilitarian would demur here. A utilitarian legislator might tax the rich in order to give aid to the poor, but a Nozickian legislator would not do so. A utilitarian legislator might impose a heavy tax on inherited wealth, whereas Nozick would allow the relatively fortunate to become even more fortunate, provided that they did not infringe the *rights* of the less fortunate. The utilitarian legislator would hope to increase the total happiness by equalizing things a bit. How far he should go in this direction would depend on empirical considerations. He would not want to equalize things too much if this led to too much weakening of the incentive to work, for example. Of course according to Nozick's system there would be no reason why members of society should not set up a utilitarian utopia, and voluntarily equalize their wealth, and also give wealth to poorer communities outside. However it is questionable whether such isolated utopias could survive in a modern environment, but if they did survive, the conformity of the behaviour of their members to utilitarian theory, rather than the conformity to Nozick's theory, would be what would commend their societies to me.

SUMMARY

In this article I have explained that the notion of justice is not a fundamental notion in utilitarianism, but that utilitarians will characteristically have certain views about such things as the distribution of wealth, savings for the benefit of future generations and for the third world countries and other practical matters. Utilitarianism differs from John Rawls' theory in that it is ready to contemplate some sacrifice to certain individuals (or classes of individuals) for the sake of the greater good of all, and in particular may allow certain limitations of personal freedom which would be ruled out by Rawls' theory. *In practice*, however, the general tendency of utilitarianism may well be towards an egalitarian form of society.

NOTES

1. There are of course difficult problems about the assignment of cardinal utilities to states of mind, but for the purposes of this paper I am assuming that we can intelligibly talk, as utilitarians do, about units of happiness.
2. John C. Harsanyi, 'Cardinal Utility in Welfare Economics and the Theory of Risk-Taking', *Journal of Political Economy*, 61 (1953), 434–435, and 'Cardinal Welfare, Individualistic Ethics, and Interpersonal Comparisons of Utility', ibid., 63 (1955), 309–321. Harasanyi has discussed Rawls' use of the maximin principle and has defended the principle of maximizing expected utility instead, in a paper 'Can the Maximin Principle Serve as a Basis for Morality? A Critique of John Rawls's Theory', *The American Political Science Review*, 69 (1975), 594–606. These articles have been reprinted in John C. Harsanyi, *Essays on Ethics, Social Behavior, and Scientific Explanation* (Dordrecht, Holland: D. Reidel, 1976).
3. Robert Nozick, *Anarchy, State, and Utopia* (Oxford: Blackwell, 1975).
4. Rawls, *A Theory of Justice* (Cambridge, Mass.: Harvard University Press, 1971), p. 60.
5. In Norman Daniels (ed.), *Reading Rawls* (Oxford: Blackwell, 1975), pp. 141–167. See pp.148–149.
6. Lyons, op. cit., p. 149, near top.
7. Rawls, op. cit., p. 62.
8. On this point see Brian Barry, *The Liberal Theory of Justice* (London: Oxford University Press, 1973), p. 55.
9. See Sidgwick, *Methods of Ethics*, 7th Ed. (Chicago: University of Chicago Press, 1962), pp.418–419.
10. Ibid., pp. 416–417.
11. Of course during the nineteenth century the notion of an infinitesimal fell into disrepute among mathematicians, for very good reasons, but it has recently been

made mathematically respectable by Abraham Robinson. See Abraham Robinson, *Non-Standard Analysis* (Amsterdam: North-Holland, 1970). A simple account of Robinson's idea can be found in an article by Martin Davis and Reuben Hersh, 'Non-Standard Analysis', *Scientific American*, June 1972, pp. 78–86.

12. Nicholas Rescher, *Distributive Justice* (Indianapolis: The Bobbs-Merrill Company, 1966). See pp. 31–41.

13. Lawrence H. Powers, 'A More Effective Average: A Note on Distributive Justice', *Philosophical Studies*, 21 (1970), 74–78.

14. There is a question as to whether Jeremy Bentham himself thought in this universalistic way or whether the interests with which he was concerned were restricted in various ways. See David Lyons 'Was Bentham a Utilitarian?', in *Reason and Reality, Royal Institute of Philosophy Lectures*, Vol. 5, 1970–1971 (London: MacMillan, 1972), pp. 196–221.

15. For Sidgwick's remarks on the question of average happiness *versus* total happiness see *Methods of Ethics*, 7th Ed., pp. 414–416.

16. An interesting discussion of the problem of future generations is to be found in Jan Narveson, 'Utilitarianism and New Generations', *Mind*, 76 (1967), 62–72. Narveson is a utilitarian, though his view differs somewhat from my own form of utilitarianism, and his conclusions about future generations are opposed to mine. On p. 63 Narveson says 'Whenever one has a duty, it *must* be possible to say on whose account the duty arises—i.e. *whose* happiness is in question'. I want to deny this statement: I think that I ought to maximize happiness, and I can work out the best ways of achieving this end without knowing *who* are the people who will be happy or miserable. This is why I expect that Narveson's notion of 'duty' differs from my notion of 'ought' and that his notion is perhaps even related to the correlative and non-utilitarian notion of a right. But I am not clear about this and I could easily have misunderstood Narveson's notion of 'duty'.

17. On this matter see Peter Singer's important book, *Animal Liberation* (New York: Random House, 1975).

18. *Economic Journal*, 38 (1928), 543–559.

19. 'Can the Maximin Principle Serve as a Basis for Morality? A Critique of John Rawls' Theory', loc. cit.

20. Ibid.

R. M. Hare
Justice and Equality

THE SENSES OF 'JUST'

There are several reasons why a philosopher of my persuasion should wish to write about justice. The first is the general one that ethical theory ought to be applied to practical issues, both for the sake of improving the theory and for any light it may shed on the practical issues, of which many of the most important involve questions of justice. This is shown by the frequency with which appeals are made to justice and fairness and related ideals when people are arguing about political or economic questions (about wages for example, or about schools policy or about relations between races or sexes). If we do not know what 'just' and 'fair' mean (and it looks as if we do not) and therefore do not know what would settle questions involving these concepts, then we are unlikely to be able to sort out these very difficult moral problems. I have also a particular interest in the topic: I hold a view about moral reasoning which has at least strong affinities with utilitarianism;[1] and there is commonly thought to be some kind of antagonism between justice and utility or, as it is sometimes called, expediency. I have therefore a special need to sort these questions out.

We must start by distinguishing between different kinds of justice, or between different senses or uses of the word 'just' (the distinction between these different ways of putting the matter need not now concern us). In distinguishing between different kinds of justice we shall have to make crucial use of a distinction between different levels of moral thinking which I have explained at length in other places.[2] It is perhaps simplest to distinguish three levels of thought, one ethical or meta-ethical and two moral or normative-ethical. At the meta-ethical level we try to establish the meanings of the moral words, and thus the formal properties of the moral concepts, including their logical properties. Without knowing these a theory of normative moral reasoning cannot begin. Then there are two levels of (normative) moral thinking which have often been in various ways distinguished. I have myself in the past called them 'level 2' and 'level 1'; but for ease of remembering I now think it best to give them names, and propose to call level 2 the *critical* level and level 1 the *intuitive* level. At the intuitive level we make use of *prima facie* moral principles of a fairly simple general sort, and do not question them but merely apply them to cases

© R. M. Hare, 1978. An earlier version of this paper appeared in Polish in *Etyka* (Warsaw).

which we encounter. This level of thinking cannot be (as intuitionists commonly suppose) self-sustaining; there is a need for a critical level of thinking by which we select the *prima facie* principles for use at the intuitive level, settle conflicts between them, and give to the whole system of them a justification which intuition by itself can never provide. It will be one of the objects of this paper to distinguish those kinds of justice whose place is at the intuitive level and which are embodied in *prima facie* principles from those kinds which have a role in critical and indeed in meta-ethical thinking.

The principal result of meta-ethical enquiry in this field is to isolate a sense or kind of justice which has come to be known as 'formal justice'. Formal justice is a property of all moral principles (which is why Professor Rawls heads his chapter on this subject not 'Formal constraints of the concept of *just*' but 'Formal constraints of the concept of *right*',[3] and why his disciple David Richards is able to make a good attempt to found the whole of morality, and not merely a theory of justice, on a similar hypothetical-contract basis).[4] Formal justice is simply another name for the formal requirement of universality in moral principles on which, as I have explained in detail elsewhere,[5] golden-rule arguments are based. From the formal, logical properties of the moral words, and in particular from the logical prohibition of individual references in moral principles, it is possible to derive formal canons of moral argument, such as the rule that we are not allowed to discriminate morally between individuals unless there is some qualitative difference between them which is the ground for the discrimination; and the rule that the equal interests of different individuals have equal moral weight. Formal justice consists simply in the observance of these canons in our moral arguments; it is widely thought that this observance by itself is not enough to secure justice in some more substantial sense. As we shall see, one is not offending against the first rule if one says that extra privileges should be given to people just because they have white skins; and one is not offending against either rule if one says that one should take a cent from everybody and give it to the man with the biggest nose, provided that he benefits as much in total as they lose. The question is, How do we get from formal to substantial justice?

This question arises because there are various kinds of material or substantial justice whose content cannot be established directly by appeal to the uses of moral words or the formal properties of moral concepts (we shall see later how much can be done indirectly by appeal to these formal properties *in conjunction with* other premises or postulates or presuppositions). There is a number of different kinds of substantial justice, and we can hardly do better than begin with Aristotle's classification of them,[6] since it is largely responsible for the different senses which the word 'just' still has in common use. This is a case where it is impossible to appeal to common use, at any rate of the word 'just' (the word 'fair' is better) in order to settle philosophical disputes, because the common use is itself the product of past philosophical theories. The expressions 'distributive' and 'retributive' justice go back to Aristotle,[7] and the word 'just' itself occupies the place (or places) that it does in our language largely because of its place in earlier philosophical discussions.

Aristotle first separated off a generic sense of the Greek word commonly translated 'just', a sense which had been used a lot by Plato: the sense in which justice is the whole of virtue in so far as it concerns our relations with other people.[8] The last qualification reminds us that this is not the most generic sense possible. Theognis had already used it to include the whole of virtue, full stop.[9] These very generic senses of the word, as applied to men and acts, have survived into modern English to confuse philosophers. One of the sources of confusion is that, in the less generic sense of 'just' to be discussed in most of this paper, the judgment that an act would be unjust is sometimes fairly easily overridden by other moral considerations ('unjust', we may say, 'but right as an act of mercy, or unjust, but right because necessary in order to avert an appalling calamity'). It is much more difficult for judgments that an act is required by justice in the generic sense, in which 'unjust' is almost equivalent to 'not right', to be overridden in this way.

Adherents of the *'fiat justitia ruat caelum'*[10] school seldom make clear whether, when they say 'Let justice be done though the heavens fall', they are using a more or less generic sense of 'justice'; and they thus take advantage of its non-overridability in the more generic sense in order to claim unchallengeable sanctity for judgments made using one of the less generic senses. It must be right to do the just thing (whatever that may be) in the sense (if there still is one in English) in which 'just' *means* 'right'. In this sense, if it were right to cause the heavens to fall, and therefore just in the most generic sense, it would of course be right. But we might have to take into account, in deciding whether it would be right, the fact that the heavens would fall (that causing the heavens to fall would be one of the things we were doing if we did the action in question). On the other hand, if it were merely the just act in one of the less generic senses, we might hold that, though just, it was not right, because it would not be right to cause the heavens to fall merely in order to secure justice in this more limited sense; perhaps some concession to mercy, or even to common sense, would be in order.

This is an application of the 'split-level' structure of moral thinking sketched above. One of the theses I wish to maintain is that principles of justice in these less generic senses are all *prima facie* principles and therefore overridable. I shall later be giving a utilitarian account of justice which finds a place, at the intuitive level, for these *prima facie* principles of justice. At this level they have great importance and utility, but it is in accordance with utilitarianism, as indeed with common sense, to claim that they can on unusual occasions be overridden. Having said this, however, it is most important to stress that this does *not* involve conceding the overridability of either the generic kind of justice, which has its place at the critical level, or of formal justice, which operates at the meta-ethical level. These are preserved intact, and therefore defenders of the sanctity of justice ought to be content, since these are the core of justice as of morality. We may call to mind here Aristotle's[11] remarks about the 'better justice' or 'equity' which is required in order to rectify the crudities, giving rise to unacceptable results in particular cases, of a justice whose principles are, as they have to be, couched in general (i.e. simple) terms. The lawgiver who, according to Aristotle, 'would have' given a special prescription if he had been present at this particular case, and to whose prescription we must try to conform if we can, corresponds to the critical moral thinker, who operates under the constraints of formal justice and whose principles are not limited to simple general rules but can be specific enough to cover the peculiarities of unusual cases.

RETRIBUTIVE AND DISTRIBUTIVE JUSTICE

After speaking briefly of generic justice, Aristotle goes on[12] to distinguish two main kinds of justice in the narrower or more particular sense in which it means 'fairness'. He calls these retributive and distributive justice. They have their place, respectively, in the fixing of penalties and rewards for bad and good actions, and in the distribution of goods and the opposite between the possible recipients. One of the most important questions is whether these two sorts of justice are reducible to a single sort. Rawls, for example, thinks that they are, and so do I. By using the expression 'justice as fairness', he implies that all justice can be reduced to kinds of distributive justice, which itself is founded on procedural justice (i.e. on the adoption of fair procedures) in distribution.[13]

We may (without attempting complete accuracy in exposition) explain how Rawls might effect this reduction as follows. The parties in his 'original position' are prevented by his 'veil of ignorance' from knowing what their own positions are in the world in which they are to live; so they are unable when adopting principles of justice to tailor them to suit their own individual interests. Impartiality (a very important constituent, at least, of justice) is thus secured. Therefore the principles which govern *both* the distribution of wealth and power and other good things *and* the assignment of rewards and penalties (and indeed all other matters which have to be regulated by principles of justice) will be impartial as between individuals, and in this sense just. In this way Rawls in effect reduces the justice of acts of retribution to justice in distributing between the affected parties the good and bad effects of a system of retributions, and reduces this distributive justice in turn to the adoption of a just procedure for selecting the system of retributions to be used.

This can be illustrated by considering the case of a criminal facing a judge (a case which has been thought to give trouble to me too, though I dealt with it adequately, on the lines which I am about to repeat here, in my book *Freedom and Reason*).[14] A Rawlsian judge, when sentencing the criminal, could defend himself against the charge of injustice or unfairness by saying that he was faithfully observing the principles of justice which would be adopted in the original position, whose conditions are procedurally fair. What these principles would be requires, no doubt, a great deal of discussion, in the course of which I might find myself in disagreement with Rawls. But my own view on how the judge should justify his action is, in its formal properties, very like his. On my view likewise, the judge can say that, when he asks himself what universal principles he is prepared to adopt for situations exactly like the one he is in, and considers examples of such logically possible situations in which *he* occupies, successively, the positions of judge, and of criminal, and of all those who are affected by the administration and enforcement of the law under which he is sentencing the criminal, including, of course, potential victims of possible future crimes—he can say that when he asks himself this, he has no hesitation in accepting the principle which bids him impose such and such a sentence in accordance with the law.

I am assuming that the judge is justifying himself at the critical level. If he were content with justifying himself at the intuitive level, his task would be easier, because, we hope, he, like most of us, has intuitions about the proper administration of justice in the courts, embodying *prima facie* principles of a sort whose inculcation in judges and in the rest of us has a high social utility. I say this while recognizing that *some* judges have intuitions about these matters which have a high social disutility. The question of what intuitions judges ought to have about retributive justice is a matter for *critical* moral thinking.

On both Rawls' view and mine retributive justice has thus been reduced to distributive; on Rawls' view the principles of justice adopted are those which *distribute* fairly between those affected the good and the evil consequences of having or not having certain enforced criminal laws; on my own view likewise it is the impartiality secured by the requirement to universalize one's prescriptions which makes the judge say what he says, and here too it is an impartiality in distributing good and evil consequences between the affected parties. For the judge to let off the rapist would not be *fair* to all those who would be raped if the law were not enforced. I conclude that retributive justice can be reduced to distributive, and that therefore we shall have done what is required of us if we can give an adequate account of the latter.

What is common to Rawls' method and my own is the recognition that to get solutions to particular questions about what is just or unjust, we have to have a way of selecting principles of justice to answer such questions, and that to ask them in default of such principles is senseless. And we both recognize that the method for selecting the principles has to be founded on what he calls 'the formal constraints of the concept of right'. This measure of agreement can extend to the method of selecting principles of distributive justice as well as retributive. Neither Rawls nor I need be put off our stride by an objector who says that we have not addressed ourselves to the question of what acts are just, but have divagated on to the quite different question of how to select principles of justice. The point is that the first question cannot be answered without answering the second. Most of the apparently intractable conflicts about justice and rights that plague the world have been generated by taking certain answers to the first question as obvious and requiring no argument. We shall resolve these conflicts only by asking what arguments are available for the principles by which questions about the justice of individual acts are to be answered. In short, we need to ascend from intuitive to critical thinking; as I have argued in my review of his book, Rawls is to be reproached with not _completing_ the ascent.[15]

Nozick, however, seems hardly to have begun it.[16] Neither Rawls nor I have anything to fear from him, so long as we stick to the formal part of our systems which we in effect share. When it comes to the application of this formal method to produce substantial principles of justice, I might find myself in disagreement with Rawls, because he relies much too much on his own intuitions which are open to question. Nozick's intuitions differ from Rawls', and sometimes differ from, sometimes agree with mine. This sort of question is simply not to be settled by appeal to intuitions, and it is time that the whole controversy ascended to a more serious, critical level. At this level, the answer which both Rawls and I should give to Nozick is that whatever sort of principles of justice we are after, whether structural principles, as Rawls thinks, or historical principles, as Nozick maintains, they have to be supported by critical thinking, of which Nozick seems hardly to see the necessity. This point is quite independent of the structural-historical disagreement.

For example, if Nozick thinks that it is just for people to retain whatever property they have acquired by voluntary exchange which benefited all parties, starting from a position of equality but perhaps ending up with a position of gross inequality, and if Rawls, by contrast, thinks that such inequality should be rectified in order to make the position of the least advantaged in society as good as possible, how are we to decide between them? Not by intuition, because there seems to be a deadlock between their intuitions. Rawls has a procedure, which _need_ not appeal to intuition, for justifying distributions; this would give him the game, if he were to base the procedure on firm logical grounds, and if he followed it correctly. Actually he does not so base it, and mixes up so many intuitions in the argument that the conclusions he reaches are not such as the procedure really justifies. But Nozick has no procedure at all: only a variety of considerations of different sorts, all in the end based on intuition. Sometimes he seems to be telling us what arrangements in society would be arrived at if bargaining took place in accordance with games-theory between mutually disinterested parties; sometimes what arrangements would maximize the welfare of members of society; and sometimes what arrangements would strike them as fair. He does not often warn us when he is switching from one of these grounds to another; and he does little to convince us by argument that the arrangements so selected would be in accordance with justice. He hopes that we will think what he thinks; but Rawls at least thinks otherwise.

FORMAL JUSTICE AND SUBSTANTIAL EQUALITY

How then do we get from formal to substantial justice? We have had an example of how this is done in the sphere of retributive justice; but how is this method to be extended to cover distributive justice as a whole, and its relation, if any, to equality in distribution? The difficulty of using formal justice in order to establish principles of substantial justice can indeed be illustrated very well by asking whether, and in what sense, justice demands equality in distribution. The complaint is often made that a certain distribution is unfair or unjust because unequal; so it looks, at least, as if the substantial principle that goods ought to be distributed equally in default of reasons to the contrary forms part of some people's conception of justice. Yet, it is argued, this substantial principle cannot be established simply on the basis of the formal notions we have mentioned. The following kind of schematic example is often adduced: consider two possible distributions of a given finite stock of goods, in one of which the goods are distributed equally, and in the other of which a few of the recipients have nearly all the goods, and the rest have what little remains. It is claimed with some plausibility that the second distribution is unfair, and the first fair. But it might also be claimed that impartiality and formal justice alone will not establish that we ought to distribute the goods equally.

There are two reasons which might be given for this second claim, the first of them a bad one, the other more cogent. The bad reason rests on an underestimate of the powers of golden-rule arguments. It is objected, for example, that people with white skins, if they claimed privileges in distribution purely on the ground of skin-colour, would not be offending against the formal principle of impartiality or universalizability, because no individual reference need enter into the principle to which they are appealing. Thus the principle that blacks ought to be subservient to whites is impartial as between *individuals*; any individual whatever who has the bad luck to find himself with a black skin or the good luck to find himself with a white skin is impartially placed by the principle in the appropriate social rank. This move receives a brief answer in my *Freedom and Reason*,[17] and a much fuller one in a forthcoming paper.[18] If the whites are faced with the decision, not merely of whether to frame this principle, but of whether to prescribe its adoption universally in all cases, including hypothetical ones in which their own skins turn black, they will at once reject it.

The other, more cogent-sounding argument is often used as an argument against utilitarians by those who think that justice has a lot to do with equality. It could also, at first sight, be used as an argument against the adequacy of formal justice or impartiality as a basis for distributive justice. That the argument could be leveled against both these methods is no accident; as I have tried to show elsewhere,[19] utilitarianism of a certain sort is the embodiment of—the method of moral reasoning which fulfils in practice—the requirement of universalizability or formal justice. Having shown that neither of these methods can produce a direct justification for equal distribution, I shall then show that both can produce indirect justifications, which depend, not on a priori reasoning alone, but on likely assumptions about what the world and the people in it are like.

The argument is this. Formal impartiality only requires us to treat everybody's interest as of equal weight. Imagine, then, a situation in which utilities are equally distributed. (There is a complication here which we can for the moment avoid by choosing a suitable example. Shortly I shall be mentioning the so-called principle of diminishing marginal utility, and shall indeed be making important use of it. But for now let us take a case in which it does not operate, so that we can, for ease of illustration, treat money as a linear measure of utility.) Suppose that we can vary the equal distribution that we started with by taking a dollar each away from everybody in the town, and that the loss of purchasing power is so small that they hardly notice it, and therefore the utility enjoyed by each is not much diminished. However, when we give the resulting large sum to one man, he is able to buy himself a holiday in Acapulco, which gives him so much pleasure that his access of utility is equal to the sum of the small losses suffered by all the others. Many would say that this redistribution was unfair. But we were, in the required sense, being impartial between the equal interests of all the parties; we were treating an equal access or loss of utility to any party as of equal value or disvalue. For, on our suppositions, the taking away of a dollar from one of the unfortunate parties deprived him of just as much utility as the addition of that dollar gave to the fortunate one. But if we are completely impartial, we have to regard *who has* that dollar or that access of utility as irrelevant. So there will be nothing to choose, from an impartial point of view, between our original equal distribution and our later highly unequal one, in which everybody else is deprived of a cent in order to give one person a holiday in Acapulco. And that is why people say that formal impartiality alone is not enough to secure social justice, nor even to secure impartiality itself in some more substantial sense.

What is needed, in the opinion of these people, is some principle which says that it is unjust to give a person more when he already has more than the others—some sort of egalitarian principle. Egalitarian principles are only one possible kind of principles of distributive justice; and it is so far an open question whether they are to be preferred to alternative inegalitarian principles. It is fairly clear as a matter of history that different principles of justice have been accepted in different societies. As Aristotle says, 'everybody agrees that the just distribution is one in accordance with desert of some kind; but they do not call desert the same thing, but the democrats say it is being a free citizen, the oligarchs being rich, others good lineage, and the aristocrats virtue'.[20] It is not difficult to think of some societies in which it would be thought unjust for one man to have privileges not possessed by all men, and of others in which it would be thought unjust for a slave to have privileges which a free man would take for granted, or for a commoner to have the sort of house which a nobleman could aspire to. Even Aristotle's democrats did not think that slaves, but only citizens, had equal rights; and Plato complains of democracy that it 'bestows equality of a sort on equals and unequals alike'.[21] We have to ask, therefore, whether there are any reasons for preferring one of these attitudes to another.

At this point some philosophers will be ready to step in with their intuitions, and tell us that some distributions or ways of achieving distributions are *obviously* more just than others, or that *everyone will agree on reflection* that they are. These philosophers appeal to our intuitions or prejudices in support of the most widely divergent methods or patterns of distribution. But this is a way of arguing which should be abjured by anybody who wishes to have rational grounds for his moral judgments. Intuitions prove nothing; general consensus proves nothing; both have been used to support conclusions which *our* intuitions and our consensus may well find outrageous. We want arguments, and in this field seldom get them.

However, it is too early to despair of finding some. The utilitarian, and the formalist like me, still have some moves to make. I am supposing that we have already made the major move suggested above, and have ruled out discrimination on grounds of skin colour and the like, in so far as such discrimination could not be accepted by all for cases where they were the ones discriminated against. I am supposing that our society has absorbed this move, and contains no racists, sexists or in general discriminators, but does still contain economic men who do not think it wrong, in pursuit of Nozickian economic liberty, to get what they can, even if the resulting distribution is grotesquely unequal. Has the egalitarian any moves to make against them, and are they moves which can be supported by appeal to formal justice, in conjunction with the empirical facts?

TWO ARGUMENTS FOR EQUAL DISTRIBUTION

He has two. The first is based on that good old prop of egalitarian policies, the diminishing marginal utility, within the ranges that matter, of money and of nearly all goods. Almost always, if money or goods are taken away from someone who has a lot of them already, and given to someone who has little, total utility is increased, other things being equal. As we shall see, they hardly ever are equal; but the principle is all right. Its ground is that the poor man will get more utility out of what he is given than the rich man from whom it is taken would have got. A millionaire minds less about the gain or loss of a dollar than I do, and I than a pauper.

It must be noted that this is not an *a priori* principle. It is an empirical fact (if it is) that people are so disposed. The most important thing I have to say in this paper is that when we are, as we now are, trying to establish *prima facie* principles of distributive justice, it is enough if they can be justified in the world as it actually is, among people as they actually are. It is a wholly illegitimate argument against formalists or utilitarians that states of society or of the people in it could be *conceived of* in which gross inequalities could be justified by formal or utilitarian arguments. We are seeking principles for practical use in the world as it is. The same applies when we ask what qualifications are required to the principles.

Diminishing marginal utility is the firmest support for policies of progressive taxation of the rich and other egalitarian measures. However, as I said above, other things are seldom equal, and there are severe empirical, practical restraints on the equality that can sensibly be imposed by governments. To mention just a few of these hackneyed other things: the removal of incentives to effort may diminish the total stock of goods to be divided up; abrupt confiscation or even very steep progressive taxation may antagonize the victims so much that a whole class turns from a useful element in society to a hostile and dangerous one; or, even if that does not happen, it may merely become demoralized and either lose all enterprise and readiness to take business risks, or else just emigrate if it can. Perhaps one main cause of what is called the English sickness is the alienation of the middle class. It is an empirical question, just when egalitarian measures get to the stage of having these effects: and serious political argument on this subject should concentrate on such empirical questions, instead of indulging in the rhetoric of equal (or for that matter of unequal) rights. Rights are the offspring of *prima facie*, intuitive principles, and I have nothing against them; but the question is, What *prima facie* principles ought we to adopt? What intuitions ought we to have? On these questions the rhetoric of rights sheds no light whatever, any more than do appeals to intuition (i.e. to prejudice, i.e. to the *prima facie* principles, good or bad, which our upbringings happen to have implanted in us). The worth of intuitions is to be known by their fruits; as in the case of the principles to be followed by judges in administering the law, the best principles are those with the highest acceptance-utility, i.e. those whose general accept-ance maximizes the furtherance of the interests, in sum, of all the affected parties, treating all those interests as of equal weight, i.e. impartially, i.e. with formal justice.

We have seen that, given the empirical assumption of diminishing marginal utility, such a method provides a justification for moderately egalitarian policies. The justification is strengthened by a second move that the egalitarian can make. This is to point out that inequality itself has a tendency to produce envy, which is a disagreeable state of mind and leads people to do disagreeable things. It makes no difference to the argument whether the envy is a good or a bad quality, nor whether it is justified or unjustified—any more than it makes a difference whether the alienation of the middle class which I mentioned above is to be condemned or excused. These states of mind are facts, and moral judgments have to be made in the light of the facts as they are. We have to take account of the actual state of the world and of the people in it. We can very easily think of societies which are highly unequal, but in which the more fortu-nate members have contrived to find some real or metaphorical opium or some Platonic noble lie[22] to keep the people quiet, so that the people feel no envy of privileges which we should consider outrageous. Imagine, for example, a society consisting of happy slave-owners and of happy slaves, all of whom know their places and do not have ideas above their station. Since there is *ex hypothesi* no envy, this source of disutility does not exist, and the whole argument from envy collapses.

It is salutary to remember this. It may make us stop looking for purely formal, *a priori* reasons for demanding equality, and look instead at the actual conditions which obtain in particular societies. To make the investigation more concrete, albeit oversimplified, let us ask what would have to be the case before we ought to be ready to push this happy slave-owning society into a revolution—peaceful or violent—which would turn the slaves into free and moderately equal wage-earners. I shall be able only to sketch my answer to this question, without doing nearly enough to justify it.

ARGUMENTS FOR AND AGAINST EGALITARIAN REVOLUTIONS

First of all, as with all moral questions, we should have to ask what would be the actual consequences of what we were doing—which is the same as to ask what we should be *doing*, so that accusations of 'consequentialism'[23] need not be taken very seriously. Suppose, to simplify matters outrageously, that we can actually predict the consequences of the revolution and what will happen during its course. We can then consider two societies (one actual and one possible) and a possible process of transition from one to the other. And we have to ask whether the transition from one to the other will, all in all, promote the interests of all those affected more than to stay as they are, or rather, to develop as they would develop if the revolution did not occur. The question can be divided into questions about the process of transition and questions about the relative merits of the actual society (including its probable subsequent 'natural' development) and the possible society which would be produced by the revolution.

We have supposed that the slaves in the existing society feel no envy, and that therefore the disutility of envy cannot be used as an argument for change. If there *were* envy, as in actual cases is probable, this argument *could* be employed; but let us see what can be done without it. We have the fact that there is gross inequality in the actual society and much greater equality in the possible one. The principle of diminishing marginal utility will therefore support the change, provided that its effects are not outweighed by a reduction in total utility resulting from the change and the way it comes about. But we have to be sure that this condition is fulfilled. Suppose, for example, that the actual society is a happy bucolic one and is likely to remain so, but that the transition to the possible society initiates the growth of an industrial economy in which everybody has to engage in a rat-race and is far less happy. We might in that case pronounce the actual society better. In general it is not self-evident that the access of what is called wealth makes people happier, although they nearly always think that it will.

Let us suppose, however, that we are satisfied that the people in the possible society will be better off all round than in the actual. There is also the point that there will be more generations to enjoy the new regime than suffer in the transition from the old. At least, this is what revolutionaries often say; and we have set them at liberty to say it by assuming, contrary to what is likely to be the case, that the future state of society is predictable. In actual fact, revolutions usually produce states of society very different from, and in most cases worse than, what their authors expected—which does not always stop them being better than what went before, once things have settled down. However, let us waive these difficulties and suppose that the future state of society can be predicted, and that it is markedly better than the existing state, because a greater equality of distribution has, owing to diminishing marginal utility, resulted in greater total utility.

Let us also suppose that the more enterprising economic structure which results leads to increased production without causing a rat-race. There will then be more wealth to go round and the revolution will have additional justification. Other benefits of the same general kind may also be adduced; and what is perhaps the greatest benefit of all, namely liberty itself. That people like having this is an empirical fact; it may not be a fact universally, but it is at least *likely* that by freeing slaves we shall *pro tanto* promote their interests. Philosophers who ask for *a priori* arguments for liberty or equality often talk as if empirical facts like this were totally irrelevant to the question. Genuine egalitarians and liberals ought to abjure the aid of these philosophers, because they have taken away the main ground for such views, namely the fact that people are as they are.

The arguments so far adduced support the call for a revolution. They will have to be balanced against the disutilities which will probably be caused by the process of transition. If heads roll, that is contrary to the interests of their owners; and no doubt the economy will be disrupted at least temporarily, and the new rulers, whoever they are, may infringe liberty just as much as the old, and possibly in an even more arbitrary manner. Few revolutions are pleasant while they are going on. But if the revolution can be more or less smooth or even peaceful, it may well be that (given the arguments already adduced about the desirability of the future society thereby achieved) revolution can have a utilitarian justification, and therefore a justification on grounds of formal impartiality between people's interests. But it is likely to be better for all if the same changes can be achieved less abruptly by an evolutionary process, and those who try to persuade us that this is not so are often merely giving way to impatience and showing a curious indifference to the interests of those for whom they purport to be concerned.

The argument in favour of change from a slave-owning society to a wage-earning one has been extremely superficial, and has served only to illustrate the lines on which a utilitarian or a formalist might argue. If we considered instead the transition from a capitalist society to a socialist one, the same forms of argument would have to be employed, but might not yield the same result. Even if the introduction of a fully socialist economy would promote greater equality, or more equal liberties (and I can see no reason for supposing this, but rather the reverse; for socialism tends to produce very great inequalities of *power*), it needs to be argued what the consequences would be, and then an assessment has to be made of the relative benefits and harms accruing from leaving matters alone and from having various sorts of bloody or bloodless change. Here again the rhetoric of rights will provide nothing but inflammatory material for agitators on both sides. It is designed to lead to, not to resolve, conflicts.

REMARKS ABOUT METHODS

But we must now leave this argument and attend to a methodological point which has become pressing. We have not, in the last few pages, been arguing about what state of society would be just, but about what state of society would best promote the interests of its members. All the arguments have been utilitarian. Where then does justice come in? It is likely to come into the propaganda of revolutionaries, as I have already hinted. But so far as I can see it has no direct bearing on the question of what would be the better society. It has, however, an important indirect bearing which I shall now try to explain. Our *prima facie* moral principles and intuitions are, as I have already said, the products of our upbringings; and it is a very important question *what* principles and intuitions it is best to bring up people to have. I have been arguing on the assumption that this question is to be decided by looking at the consequences for society, and the effects on the interests of people in society, of inculcating different principles. We are looking for the set of principles with the highest acceptance-utility.

   Will these include principles of justice? The answer is obviously 'Yes', if we think that society and the people in it are better off with *some* principles of justice than without any. A 'land without justice' (to use the title of Milovan Djilas' book)[24] is almost bound to be an unhappy one. But what are the principles to be? Are we, for example, to inculcate the principle that it is just for people to perform the duties of their station and not envy those of higher social rank? Or the principle that all inequalities of any sort are unjust and ought to be removed? For my part, I would think that neither of these principles has a very high acceptance-utility. It may be that the principle with the highest acceptance-utility is one which makes just reward vary (but not immoderately) with desert, and assesses desert according to service to the interests of one's fellow-men. It would have to be supplemented by a principle securing equality of opportunity. But it is a partly empirical question what principles would have the highest acceptance-utility, and in any case beyond the scope of this paper. If some such principle is adopted and inculcated, people will *call* breaches of it unjust. Will they *be* unjust? Only in the sense that they will be contrary to a *prima facie* principle of distributive justice which we ought to adopt (not because it is itself a just principle, but because it is the best principle). The only sense that can be given to the question of whether it is a just principle (apart from the purely circular or tautological question of whether the principle obeys itself), is by asking whether the procedure by which we have selected the principle satisfies the logical requirements of critical moral thinking, i.e. is *formally* just. We might add that the adoption of such a formally just procedure and of the principles it selects is just in the *generic* sense mentioned at the beginning of this paper: it is the right thing to do; we morally ought to do it. The reason is that critical thinking, because it follows the requirements of formal justice based on the logical properties of the moral concepts, especially 'ought' and 'right', can therefore not fail, if pursued correctly in the light of the empirical facts, to lead to principles of justice which are in accord with morality. But because the requirements are all formal, they do not by themselves determine the content of the principles of justice. We have to do the thinking.

What principles of justice are best to try to inculcate will depend on the circumstances of particular societies, and especially on psychological facts about their members. One of these facts is their readiness to accept the principles themselves. There might be a principle of justice which it would be highly desirable to inculcate, but which we have no chance of successfully inculcating. The best principles for a society to *have* are, as I said, those with the highest acceptance-utility. But the best principles to *try to inculcate* will not necessarily be these, if these are impossible to inculcate. Imagine that in our happy slave-society both slaves and slave-owners are obstinately conservative and know their places, and that the attempt to get the slaves to have revolutionary or egalitarian thoughts will result only in a very few of them becoming discontented, and probably going to the gallows as a result, and the vast majority merely becoming unsettled and therefore more unhappy. Then we ought not to try to inculcate such an egalitarian principle. On the other hand, if, as is much more likely, the principle stood a good chance of catching on, and the revolution was likely to be as advantageous as we have supposed, then we ought. The difference lies in the dispositions of the inhabitants. I am not saying that the probability of being accepted is the same thing as acceptance-utility; only that the rationality of trying to inculcate a principle (like the rationality of trying to do anything else) varies with the likelihood of success. In this sense the advisability of trying to inculcate principles of justice (though not their merit) is relative to the states of mind of those who, it is hoped, will hold them.

It is important to be clear about the extent to which what I am advocating is a kind of relativism. It is certainly not relativistic in any strong sense. Relativism is the doctrine that the truth of some moral statement depends on whether people accept it. A typical example would be the thesis that if in a certain society people think that they ought to get their male children circumcised, then they ought to get them circumcised, full stop. Needless to say, I am not supporting any such doctrine, which is usually the result of confusion, and against which there are well-known arguments. It is, however, nearly always the case that among the facts relevant to a moral decision are facts about people's thoughts or dispositions. For example, if I am wondering whether I ought to take my wife for a holiday in Acapulco, it is relevant to ask whether she would like it. What I have been saying is to be assimilated to this last example. If we take as given certain dispositions in the members of society (namely dispositions not to accept a certain principle of justice however hard we work at propagating it) then we have to decide whether, in the light of these facts, we ought to propagate it. What principles of justice we ought to propagate will vary with the probable effects of propagating them. The answer to this 'ought'-question is not relative to what we, who are asking it, think about the matter; it is to be arrived at by moral thought on the basis of the facts of the situation. But among these facts are facts about the dispositions of people in the society in question.

The moral I wish to draw from the whole argument is that ethical reasoning *can* provide us with a way of conducting political arguments about justice and rights rationally and with hope of agreement; that such rational arguments have to rest on an understanding of the concepts being used, *and* of the facts of our actual situation. The key question is 'What principles of justice, what attitudes towards the distribution of goods, what ascriptions of rights, are such that their acceptance is in the general interest?' I advocate the asking of this question as a substitute for one which is much more commonly asked, namely 'What rights do I have?' For people who ask this latter question will, being human, nearly always answer that they have just those rights, whatever they are, which will promote a distribution of goods which is in the interest of their own social group. The rhetoric of rights, which is engendered by this question, is a recipe for class war, and civil war. In pursuit of these rights, people will, because they have convinced themselves that justice demands it, inflict almost any harms on the rest of society and on themselves. To live at peace, we need principles such as critical thinking can provide, based on formal justice and on the facts of the actual world in which we have to live. It is possible for all to practise this critical thinking in cooperation, if only they would learn how; for all share the same moral concepts with the same logic, if they could but understand them and follow it.

NOTES

1. See my 'Ethical Theory and Utilitarianism' (*ETU*) in *Contemporary British Philosophy 4*, ed. H. D. Lewis (London, 1976).
2. See, e.g., my 'Principles', *Ar. Soc.* 72 (1972/3), 'Rules of War and Moral Reasoning', *Ph. and Pub. Aff.* 1 (1972) and *ETU*.
3. Rawls, J., *A Theory of Justice* (Cambridge, Mass., 1971), p. 130.
4. Richards, D. A. J., *A Theory of Reasons for Action* (Oxford, 1971).
5. See my *Freedom and Reason*, pt. II (Oxford, 1963) and *ETU*.
6. *Nicomachean Ethics*, bk. V.
7. ib. 1130 b 31, 1131 b 25.
8. ib. 1130 a 8.
9. Theognis 147; also attr. to Phocylides by Aristotle, ib. 1129 b 27.
10. The earliest version of this tag is attr. by the *Oxford Dictionary of Quotations* to the Emperor Ferdinand I (1503–64).
11. ib. 1137 b 8.
12. ib. 1130 a 14 ff.
13. *A Theory of Justice*, p. 136.
14. Pp. 115–7, 124.
15. *Ph. Q.* 23 (1973), repr. in *Reading Rawls*, ed. N. Daniels (Oxford, 1975).
16. Nozick, R., *Anarchy, State, and Utopia* (New York, 1974).
17. Pp. 106f.
18. 'Relevance', in a volume in honour of R. Brandt, W. Frankena and C. Stevenson, eds. A. Goldman and J. Kim (Reidel, forthcoming).
19. See note 2 above.
20. ib. 1131 a 25.
21. *Republic* 558 c.
22. ib. 414 b.
23. See, e.g., Anscombe, G. E. M., 'Modern Moral Philosophy', *Philosophy* 33 (1958) and Williams, B. A. O., in Smart, J. J. C. and Williams, B. A. O., *Utilitarianism: For and Against* (Cambridge, Eng., 1973), p. 82.
24. Djilas, M., *Land without Justice* (London, 1958).

PART II
Criticisms and Alternatives

MERIT AND CONTRIBUTION

Some philosophers would argue that the three approaches presented in Part I are seriously flawed, since none of them recommends that economic goods be distributed according to how much is deserved. For all three theories desert is at best a derivative—not a primary—element. Rawls, for example, argues that once we know that the economic structure (tax policy, welfare programs, employment opportunity) is just, then people can be said to deserve whatever they get *within that structure*. Thus desert is a secondary notion, determined by the justice of the social institutions. Nozick, on the other hand, intentionally employs the notion of "entitlement" rather than "desert." On his free market view individuals may come to have just titles to material goods, but he does not wish to say that they merit what they so receive. Similarly, desert does not play a central role for utilitarians, whose sole concern is to maximize society's happiness. Still it may seem that it is a weakness in each theory that desert is omitted. What, after all, could possibly be more just than to give people exactly what they deserve?

But how can desert be measured? What precisely does it mean? Three conceptions of desert come to mind immediately. First, one might hold that a person's *ability* should determine how much he or she is allowed to have. Second, the amount of *effort* or work that is put forth might be thought the best principle of distribution. Third, the amount one deserves could be determined by the *contribution* a person has made. The idea here is that a person should be rewarded according to how much of the total economic product he or she managed to produce.

However plausible each of these criteria might seem under some circumstances, each is open to serious objections. Abilities to do certain types of work or to perform a job well are often endowments with which one is born or are due to the environment in which one is raised. But if this is so, how can ability be a fair ground for distributing economic goods? In any event, ability alone would not suffice because a talented but lazy worker would not be thought very deserving.

The criterion of effort would remedy this last defect, but anyone using this measure of desert is immediately confronted with the difficult problem of comparison and measurement. The number of hours spent is clearly inadequate, since different jobs require different amounts of effort in a given period of time. Even if we could compare effort where physical labor is involved, how would an hour of construction work be compared with teaching medicine or with singing? One might also question the fairness of using effort as a guide to desert. It is frequently true that people with greater abilities tend to be more motivated and so work harder. Thus, effort itself turns out to be, to some extent, a function of natural abilities, which are not themselves deserved.

Similar problems arise for contribution. Here again measurement poses a difficulty. It might seem that allowing the market to determine economic benefits would be to distribute according to the criterion of contribution because market price indicates the worth to others of what is being offered for sale, and worth to others is fairly close to a measure of contribution. Still, a person might make a contribution of great significance, but one whose market worth is unrecognized at the time. More generally, certain contributions which are of the greatest benefit to society as a whole may not be the kinds of things which the market itself can reward. Imagine a person who does great service to his or her community during an emergency or whose life is devoted to serving the poor. Yet measuring one's contribution to society in this broader sense would be difficult. A second problem is suggested by the fact that what one is able to contribute and whether or not one is able to make a really important contribution would seem to depend upon all sorts of fortuitous circumstances, which are morally irrelevant. At the very least, equality of opportunity would have to be required if contribution were to be a fair distributive criterion, but even this might not suffice. Those with a favorable family upbringing and a natural industriousness would be better suited to contribute, and lady luck would place only certain individuals in the right place at the right time to make a key contribution.

Acknowledging the limitations of the market and the arbitrariness of circumstance, one might argue that distribution should be based simply on a person's overall *moral* worth. Once effort and contribution are rejected as indicators of what a person deserves, however, it is unclear how moral worth is to be ascertained. Perhaps the criterion of moral worth would be appropriate for a small religious community where there is consensus on the relevant moral standard, but its general applicability is doubtful. Further, one might well wonder why the intrinsic moral worth of a person should be rewarded economically. Virtue, some have thought, is its own reward.

Despite these difficulties, desert still seems relevant to justice. Must not justice at least take some account of what people merit? Must it not at least inquire into what individuals have done in the past? The contributors in this section believe that these questions need to be taken seriously. So our original problem remains, and desert, in one or other of the previously mentioned senses, is discussed in the following essays.

In the first of these, James Rachels analyzes carefully the relation between justice and desert, and argues for desert (as measured by work completed) as a basis for distribution. Focusing on the specific moral problem of reverse discrimination, he contends that because of the importance of work for determining desert, it is often true that less qualified members of minorities may deserve a job or admission to a school over a better qualified white male.

Ordinary people agree that desert is relevant to the question of what constitutes just income, but deciding when economic income is deserved is not easy. In his essay, Joel Feinberg discusses several ways of interpreting economic desert and argues that economic income can be spoken of as "deserved" only insofar as it is compensation. Unpleasant, onerous, and hazardous jobs deserve extra economic compensation as do those that involve heavier responsibilities and longer apprenticeships.

Norman Daniels, in his discussion of meritocracy, carefully distinguishes between those principles that govern job placement and those that govern economic reward. Productivity may justify a meritocratic approach to job placement, but it leaves open what rewards different jobs should bring. Daniels sides with Rawls and against Nozick in maintaining that we should attempt to moderate the extent to which morally arbitrary differences among people determine their social rewards. Finally, David Schweickart examines and rebuts the common view that the profit that the owners of capital receive is justified because of their contribution to the process of production.

James Rachels
What People Deserve

James Rachels argues that justice requires (among other things) that people be treated as they deserve to be treated. Treating people as they deserve to be treated is part of treating them as autonomous beings responsible for their own conduct. Rachels also contends that the basis of all desert is a person's own past actions. We may deserve things by working for them, but not simply by being naturally intelligent or talented or lucky. Applying these considerations to the issue of reverse discrimination, Rachels contends that such policies are not unjust insofar as they neutralize undeserved advantages that whites would otherwise enjoy.

I shall discuss the concept of desert, and argue that what people deserve always depends on their own past actions. In order to illustrate the practical consequences of my analysis, I will consider its application to the problem of reverse discrimination.

THE RELATION BETWEEN JUSTICE AND DESERT

It is an important point of logic that if a value-judgment is true, there must be good reasons in support of it. Suppose you are told that you ought to do a certain action, or that so-and-so is a good man. You may ask *why* you ought to do it, or *why* he is a good man, and if no reasons can be given, you may reject those judgments as arbitrary. Claims of justice have this in common with other value-judgments; an action or social policy is just, or unjust, only if there is some reason why it is so. The attempt to decide questions of justice is, therefore, largely a matter of assessing the reasons that can be offered in support of the competing judgments.

Judgments of justice may be distinguished from other sorts of value-judgments by the kinds of reasons that are relevant to supporting them. The fact that an action would make someone unhappy may be a reason why that action *ought not* be done, but it is not a reason why the action would be *unjust*. On the other hand, the fact that an action would violate someone's rights is a reason why the act would be unjust. Questions of justice are narrower than questions of what should be done, in this sense: Any reason why an act would be unjust is also a reason why it should not be done; but not every reason why an act should not be done is a reason for thinking it unjust.

The fact that people are, or are not, treated as they deserve to be treated is one kind of reason why an action or social policy may be just or unjust. I say "one kind of reason" because there are also other sorts of reasons relevant to supporting claims of justice. Besides requiring that people be treated as they deserve, justice may also require that people's rights be respected, which is different, and, as Nozick emphasizes, historical backgrounds may also be relevant to determining justice. A complete theory of justice would provide, among other things, an exhaustive account of the different kinds of reasons relevant to supporting such judgments. I will not attempt to construct a complete theory; instead, I will only sketch that part of the theory having to do with desert. As a preliminary, I want to cite two instances from recent philosophical writing on justice in which the neglect of desert, as one consideration among others, has caused difficulty.

(a) The problem of reverse discrimination is one aspect of the more general problem of distributive justice, having to do with justice in the distribution of jobs and educational opportunities. Black people, women, and members of other groups have often been denied access to jobs and educational opportunities. It is easy enough to say that this is wrong, but it is not so easy to say exactly what should now be done about it. Some believe it is enough that we simply stop discriminating against them. Others think we ought to go further and give such persons preferential treatment, at least temporarily, in order to help rectify the past injustices. And in many cases this is already being done. The problem is whether this sort of preferential treatment is itself unjust to the whites, males, or others who are disadvantaged by it.

The term "distributive justice" is commonly used by philosophers, but as Nozick points out, it can be misleading.[1] It suggests that there is a central supply of things which some authority has to dole out; but for most goods, there is no such supply and no such authority. Goods are produced by diverse individuals and groups who then have rights with respect to them, and the "distribution" of holdings at any particular time will depend, at least in part, on the voluntary exchanges and agreements those people have made. Jobs, for example, do not come from some great stockpile, to be handed out by a master "distributor" who may or may not follow principles of "justice." Jobs are created by the independent decisions of countless business people, who are entitled, within some limits of course, to operate their own businesses according to their own judgments. In a free society those people get to choose with whom they will make what sorts of agreements, and this means, among other things, that they get to choose who is hired from among the various job applicants.

These observations suggest an argument in defense of reverse discrimination: If private business people have a right to hire whomever they please, don't they have a right to hire blacks and women in preference to others? In her paper on "Preferential Hiring" Judith Jarvis Thomson[2] advances an argument based on exactly this idea. The argument begins with this principle:

> No perfect stranger has a right to be given a benefit which is yours to dispose of; no perfect stranger even has a right to be given an equal chance at getting a benefit which is yours to dispose of.[3]

Since many jobs are benefits which private employers have a right to dispose of, those employers violate no one's rights in hiring whomever they wish. If they choose to hire blacks, or women, rather than other applicants, they have a perfect right to do so. Therefore, she concludes, "there is no problem about preferential hiring," at least in the case of private businesses.

Thomson's principle is plausible. If something is *yours*, then no one else has a right to it—at least, no perfect stranger who walks in off the street wanting it. Suppose you have a book which you don't need and decide to give away as a gift. Smith and Jones both want it, and you decide to give it to Smith. Is Jones entitled to complain? Apparently not, since *he* had no claim on it in the first place. If it was your book, you were entitled to give it to whomever you chose; you violated no right of Jones in giving it to Smith. Why shouldn't the same be true of jobs? If you start a business, on your own, why shouldn't you be free to hire whomever you please to work with you? You violate no one's rights in hiring whomever you please, since no one had a right to be hired by you in the first place.

This is an important and powerful argument because it calls attention to a fact that is often overlooked, that people do not naturally have claims of right to jobs and other benefits which are privately produced. However, the argument also depends on another assumption which is false, namely, the assumption that people are treated unjustly *only if* their rights are violated. In fact, a person may be treated unjustly even though no right of his is violated, because he is not treated as he deserves to be treated. Suppose one applicant for a job has worked very hard to qualify himself for it; he has gone to night-school, at great personal sacrifice, to learn the business, and so on. Another applicant could have done all that, but chose not to; instead, he has frittered away his time and done nothing to prepare himself. In addition, the first applicant has worked hard at every previous job he has held, making a good record for himself, whereas the second is a notorious loafer—and it's his own fault; he has no good excuse. Now it may be true that neither applicant has a *right* to the job, in the sense that the employer has the right to give the job to whomever he pleases. However, the first man is clearly more deserving, and if the employer is concerned to treat job applicants fairly he will not hire the second man over the first.

(*b*) Now let me return briefly to Nozick.[4] In Part II of *Anarchy, State, and Utopia* he defends capitalism, not merely as efficient or workable, but as the only moral economic system, because it is the only such system which respects individual rights. Under capitalism people's holdings are determined by the voluntary exchanges (of services and work as well as goods) they make with others. Their right to liberty requires that they be allowed to make such exchanges, provided that they violate no one else's rights in doing so. Having acquired their holdings by such exchanges, they have a right to them; so it violates their rights for the government (or anyone else) to seize their property and give it to others. It is impermissible, therefore, for governments to tax some citizens in order to provide benefits for others.

The obvious objection is that such an arrangement could produce a disastrously unfair distribution of goods. Some lucky entrepreneurs could become enormously rich, while other equally deserving people are poor, and orphans starve. In reply Nozick contends that even if unmodified capitalism did lead to such a distribution, that would not necessarily be unjust. The justice of a distribution, he says, can be determined only by considering the historical process which led to it. We cannot tell whether a distribution is just simply by checking whether it conforms to some nonhistorical pattern, for example the pattern of everyone having equal shares, or everyone having what he or she needs. To show this Nozick gives a now-famous argument starring the basketball player Wilt Chamberlain. First, he says, suppose the goods in a society are distributed according to some pattern which you think just. Call this distribution D_1. Since you regard D_1 as a just distribution, you will agree that under it each person has a right to the holdings in his or her possession. Now suppose a million of these people each decide to give Wilt Chamberlain twenty-five cents to watch him play basketball. Chamberlain becomes rich, and the original pattern is upset. But if the original distribution was just, mustn't we admit that the new distribution (D_2) is also just?

> Each of these persons *chose* to give twenty-five cents of their money to Chamberlain. They could have spent it on going to the movies, or on candy bars, or on copies of *Dissent* magazine, or of *Monthly Review*. But they all, at least one million of them, converged on giving it to Wilt Chamberlain in exchange for watching him play basketball. If D_1 was a just distribution, and people voluntarily moved from it to D_2, transferring parts of their shares they were given under D_1 (what was it for if not to do something with?), isn't D_2 also just? . . . Can anyone else complain on grounds of justice? . . . After someone transfers something to Wilt Chamberlain, third parties *still* have their legitimate shares; *their* shares are not changed.[5]

The main argument here seems to depend on the principle that *If D_1 is a just distribution, and D_2 arises from D_1 by a process in which no one's rights are violated, then D_2 is also just.* Now Nozick is surely right that the historical process which produces a situation is one of the things that must be taken into account in deciding whether it is just. But that need not be the only relevant consideration. The historical process *and* other considerations, such as desert, must be weighed together to determine what is just. Therefore, it would not follow that a distribution is just *simply* because it is the result of a certain process, even a process in which no one's rights are violated. So this argument cannot answer adequately the complaint against unmodified capitalism.

To make the point less abstract, consider the justice of inherited wealth. A common complaint about inherited wealth is that some people gain fortunes which they have done nothing to deserve, while others, of equal merit, have nothing. This seems unjust on the face of it. Nozick points out that if the testators legitimately own their property—if it is *theirs*—then they have a right to give it to others as a gift. (The holdings of third parties will not be changed, etc.) Bequests are gifts; therefore property owners have a right to pass on their property to their heirs. This is fair enough, but at most it shows only that there is more than one consideration to be taken into account here. That some people have more than others, without deserving it, counts against the justice of the distribution. That they came by their holdings in a certain way may count in favor of the justice of the same distribution. It should come as no surprise that in deciding questions of justice competing claims must often be weighed against one another, for that is the way it usually is in ethics.

DESERT AND PAST ACTIONS

Deserts may be positive or negative, that is, a person may deserve to be treated well or badly; and they may be general or specific, that is, a person may deserve to be treated in a generally good or bad way, or he may deserve some specific kind of good or bad treatment. An example may make the latter distinction clear. Suppose a woman has always been kind and generous with others. As a general way of dealing with her, she deserves that others be kind and generous in return. Here we need not specify any *particular* act of kindness to say what she deserves, although of course treating her kindly will involve some particular act or other. What she deserves is that people treat her decently in *whatever* situation might arise. By way of contrast, think of someone who has worked hard to earn promotion in his job. He may deserve, *specifically*, to be promoted.

I wish to argue that the basis of all desert is a person's own past actions. In the case of negative desert, this is generally conceded. In order for a person to deserve punishment, for example, he must have *done something* to deserve it. Moreover, he must have done it "voluntarily," in Aristotle's sense, without any excuse such as ignorance, mistake, or coercion. In allowing these excuses and others like them, the law attempts to restrict punishment to cases in which it is deserved.

But not every negative desert involves punishment, strictly speaking. They may involve more informal responses to other people's misconduct. Suppose Adams and Brown work at the same factory. One morning Adams' car breaks down and he calls Brown to ask for a ride to work. Brown refuses, not for any good reason, but simply because he won't be bothered. Later, Brown finds himself in the same fix: his car won't start, and he can't get to work; so he calls Adams to ask for a lift. Now if Adams is a kind and forgiving person, he may grant Brown's request. And perhaps we all ought to be kind and forgiving. However, if Adams does choose to help Brown, he will be treating Brown better than Brown deserves. Brown deserves to be left in the lurch. Here I am not arguing that we ought to treat people as they deserve—although I do think there are reasons for so treating people, which I will mention presently—here I am only describing what the concept of desert involves. What Brown *deserves*, as opposed to what kindness or any other value might decree, is to be treated as well, *or as badly*, as he himself chooses to treat others.

If I am right, then the familiar lament "What did I do to deserve this?," asked by a victim of misfortune, is more than a mournful cliché. If there is no satisfactory answer, then in fact one does *not* deserve the misfortune. And since there is always a presumption against treating people badly, if a person does not deserve bad treatment it is likely to be wrong to treat him in that way. On the other side, in the case of positive deserts, we may notice a corresponding connection between the concept of desert and the idea of *earning* one's way, which also supports my thesis.

To elaborate an example I used earlier, think of an employer who has to decide which of two employees to give a promotion. One has worked very hard for the company for several years. He has always been willing to do more than his share of work; he has put in a lot of overtime when no one else would; and so on. The other has always done the least he could get by with, never taking on any extra work or otherwise exerting himself beyond the necessary minimum. Clearly, if the choice is between these two candidates, it is the first who deserves the promotion. It is important to notice that this conclusion does not depend on any estimate of how the two candidates are likely to perform in the future. Even if the second candidate were to reform, so that he would work just as hard (and well) in the new position as the first candidate, the first is still more deserving. What one deserves depends on what one has done, not on what one will do.

Of course there may be any number of reasons for not giving the promotion to the most deserving candidate: perhaps it is a family business, and the second candidate is the boss's son, and he will be advanced simply because of who he is. But that does not make him the most deserving candidate; it only means that the promotion is to be awarded on grounds other than desert. Again, the boss might decide to give the position to the second candidate because he is extraordinarily smart and talented, and the boss thinks for that reason he will do a better job (he has promised to work harder in the future). This is again to award the job on grounds other than desert, for no one deserves anything *simply* in virtue of superior intelligence and natural abilities. As Rawls emphasizes, a person no more deserves to be intelligent or talented than he deserves to be the boss's son—or, than he deserves to be born white in a society prejudiced against nonwhites. These things are all matters of chance, at least as far as the lucky individual himself is concerned.

Three questions naturally arise concerning this view. First, aren't there bases of desert *other than* a person's past actions, and if not, why not? Second, if a person may not deserve things in virtue of being naturally talented or intelligent or fortunate in some other way, how can he deserve things by working for them? After all, isn't it merely a matter of luck that one person grows up to be industrious—perhaps as the result of a rigorous upbringing by his parents—while another person is not encouraged, and ends up lazy for reasons beyond his control? And finally, even if I am right about the basis of desert, what reason is there actually to treat people according to their deserts? Why should desert matter? I will take up these questions in order. The answers, as we shall see, are interrelated.

(*a*) In his important article "Justice and Personal Desert" Joel Feinberg says that "If a person is deserving of some sort of treatment, he must, necessarily, be so in virtue of *some possessed characteristic* or prior activity."[6] Among the characteristics that may be the basis of desert he includes abilities, skills, physical attributes, and so on. In a tennis game, for example, the most skillful player deserves to win, and in a beauty contest the prettiest or most handsome deserves to win.

Does the most skillful player deserve to win an athletic competition? It seems a natural enough thing to say. But suppose the less skilled player has worked very hard, for weeks, to prepare himself for the match. He has practiced nine hours a day, left off drinking, and kept to a strict regimen. Meanwhile, his opponent, who is a "natural athlete," has partied, stayed drunk, and done nothing in the way of training. *But he is still the most skilled*, and as a result can probably beat the other guy anyway. Does he *deserve* to win the game, simply because he is better endowed by nature? Does he *deserve* the acclaim and benefits which go with winning? Of course, skills are themselves usually the product of past efforts. People must work to sharpen and develop their natural abilities; therefore, when we think of the most skillful as the most deserving, it may be because we think of them as having worked hardest. (Ted Williams practiced hitting more than anyone else on the Red Sox.) But sometimes that assumption is not true.

Do the prettiest and most handsome deserve to win beauty contests? Again, it seems a natural enough thing to say. There is no doubt that the *correct* decision for the judges of such a competition to make is to award the prize to the best-looking. But this may have little to do with the contestants' deserts. Suppose a judge were to base his decision on desert; we might imagine him reasoning like this: "Miss Montana isn't the prettiest, but after all, she's done her best with what nature provided. She's studied the use of make-up, had her teeth and nose fixed, and spent hours practicing walking down runways in high-heeled shoes. That smile didn't just happen; she had to learn it by spending hours before a mirror. Miss Alabama, on the other hand, is prettier, but she just entered the contest on a lark—walked in, put on a bathing suit, and here she is. Her make-up isn't even very good." If all this seems ridiculous, it is because the point of such contests is *not* to separate the more deserving from the less (and maybe because beauty contests are themselves a little ridiculous, too). The criterion is beauty, not desert, and the two have little to do with one another. The same goes for athletic games: the purpose is to see who is the best player, or at least who is able to defeat all the others, and not to discover who is the most deserving competitor.

There is a reason why past actions are the only bases of desert. A fair amount of our dealings with other people involves holding them responsible, formally or informally, for one thing or another. It is unfair to hold people responsible for things over which they have no control. People have no control over their native endowments—over how smart, or athletic, or beautiful they naturally are—and so we may not hold them responsible for those things. They are, however, in control of (at least some of) their own actions, and so they may rightly be held responsible for the situations they create, or allow to exist, by their voluntary behavior. But those are the *only* things for which they may rightly be held responsible. The concept of desert serves to signify the ways of treating people that are appropriate responses to them, *given that* they are responsible for those actions or states of affairs. That is the role played by desert in our moral vocabulary. And, as ordinary-language philosophers used to like to say, if there weren't such a term, we'd have to invent one. Thus the explanation of why past actions are the only bases of desert connects with the fact that *if* people were never responsible for their own conduct—if hard determinism were true—no one would ever deserve anything, good or bad.

(*b*) According to the view I am defending, we may deserve things by working for them, but not simply by being naturally intelligent or talented or lucky in some other way. Now it may be thought that this view is inconsistent, because whether someone is willing to work is just another matter of luck, in much the same way that intelligence and talent are matters of luck. Rawls takes this position when he says:

> Perhaps some will think that the person with greater natural endowments deserves those assets and the superior character that made their development possible. Because he is more worthy in this sense, he deserves the greater advantages that he could achieve with them. This view, however, is surely incorrect. It seems to be one of the fixed points of our considered judgments that no one deserves his place in the distribution of native endowments, any more than one deserves one's initial starting place in society. The assertion that a man deserves the superior character that enables him to make the effort to cultivate his abilities is equally problematic; for his character depends in large part upon fortunate family and social circumstances for which he can claim no credit. The notion of desert seems not to apply to these cases.[7]

So if a person does not deserve anything on account of his intelligence or natural abilities, how can he deserve anything on account of his industriousness? Isn't willingness to work just another matter of luck?

The first thing to notice here is that people do not deserve things on account of their *willingness* to work, but only on account of their actually having worked. The candidate for promotion does not deserve it because he has been willing to work hard in his old job, or because he is willing to work hard in the new job. Rather he deserves the promotion because he actually *has* worked hard. Therefore it is no objection to the view I am defending to say that willingness to work is a character trait that one does not merit. For, on this view, the basis of desert is not a character trait of any kind, not even industriousness. The basis of desert is a person's past actions.

Now it may be that some people have been so psychologically devastated by a combination of poor native endowment and unfortunate family and social circumstances that they no longer have the capacity for making anything of their lives. If one of these people has a job, for example, and doesn't work very hard at it, it's no use blaming him because, as we would say, he just hasn't got it in him to do any better. On the other hand, there are those in whom the capacity for effort has not been extinguished. Among these, some choose to work hard, and others, who *could* so choose, do not. It is true of everyone in this latter class that he is *able*, as Rawls puts it, "to strive conscientiously." The explanation of why some strive, while others don't, has to do with their own choices. When I say that those who work hard are more deserving of success, promotions, etc., than those who don't, I have in mind comparisons made among people in this latter class, in whom the capacity for effort has not been extinguished.[8]

There is an important formal difference between industriousness, considered as a lucky asset, and other lucky assets such as intelligence. For only by exercising this asset—i.e., by working—can one utilize his other assets, and achieve anything with them. Intelligence alone produces nothing; intelligence plus work can produce something. And the same relation holds between industriousness and every other natural talent or asset. Thus "willingness to work," if it is a lucky asset, is a sort of super-asset which enables one's other assets to be utilized. Working is simply the way one uses whatever else one has. This point may help to explain why the concept of desert is tied to work in a way in which it is not tied to intelligence or talents. And at the same time it may also provide a rationale for the following distinction: if a person displays intelligence and talent in his work, and earns a certain benefit by it, then he deserves the benefit *not* because of the intelligence or talent shown, but only on account of the work done.

(*c*) Finally, we must ask why people ought to be treated according to their deserts. Why should desert matter? In one way, it is an odd question. The reason why the conscientious employee ought to be promoted is precisely that he has earned the promotion by working for it. That is a full and sufficient justification for promoting him, which does not require supplementation of any sort. If we want to know why he should be treated in that way, that is the answer. It is not easy to see what else, by way of justification, is required.

Nevertheless, something more may be said. Treating people as they deserve is one way of treating them as autonomous beings, responsible for their own conduct. A person who is punished for his misdeeds is *held responsible* for them in a concrete way. He is not treated as a mindless automaton, whose defective performances must be "corrected," or whose good performance promoted, but as a responsible agent whose actions merit approval or resentment.[9] The recognition of deserts is bound up with this way of regarding people. Moreover, treating people as they deserve *increases* their control over their own lives and fortunes, for it allows people to determine, through their own actions, how others will respond to them. It can be argued on grounds of kindness that people should not always be treated as they deserve, when they deserve ill. But this should not be taken to imply that deserts count for nothing. They can count for something, and still be overridden in some cases. To deny categorically that desert matters would not only excuse the malefactors; it would leave all of us impotent to earn the good treatment and other benefits which others have to bestow, and thus would deprive us of the ability to control our own destinies as social beings.

REVERSE DISCRIMINATION

Is it right to give preferential treatment to blacks, women, or members of other groups who have been discriminated against in the past? I will approach this issue by considering the deserts of the individuals involved. "Reverse Discrimination" is not a particularly good label for the practices in question because the word "discrimination" has come to have such unsavory connotations. Given the way that word is now used, to ask whether reverse *discrimination* is justified already prejudices the question in favor of a negative answer. But in other ways the term is apt: the most distinctive thing about reverse discrimination is that it *reverses* past patterns, so that those who have been discriminated against are now given preferential treatment. At any rate, the label is now part of our common vocabulary, so I will stay with it.

The following example incorporates the essential elements of reverse discrimination. The admissions committee of a certain law school assesses the qualifications of applicants by assigning numerical values to their college grades, letters of recommendation, and test scores, according to some acceptable formula. (The better the grades, etc., the higher the numerical values assigned.) From past experience the committee judges that a combined score of 600 is necessary for a student to have a reasonable chance of succeeding in the school's program. Thus in order to be minimally qualified for admission an applicant must score at least 600. However, because there are more qualified applicants than places available, many who score over 600 are nevertheless rejected.

Against this background two students, one black and one white, apply for admission. The black student's credentials are rated at 700, and the white student's credentials are rated at 720. So although both exceed the minimum requirement by a comfortable margin, the white student's qualifications are somewhat better. But the white applicant is rejected and the black applicant is accepted. The officials of the school explain that this decision is part of a policy designed to bring more blacks into the legal profession. The scores of the white applicants are generally higher than those of the blacks; so, some blacks with lower scores must be admitted in order to have a fair number of black students in the entering class.

I should point out that this example is patterned after an actual case. In 1971 a student named Marco DeFunis applied for admission to the University of Washington Law School, and was rejected. He then learned that one-fourth of those accepted were minority-group students with academic records inferior to his own. The law school conceded that DeFunis had been passed over to make room for the minority students, and De-Funis brought suit charging that his rights had been violated. A lower court ruled in his favor; the Supreme Court of the state of Washington reversed this decision. The United States Supreme Court heard the case, but then declined to rule on the substance since the specific issue involved—DeFunis' admission to the University of Washington Law School—had become a moot point. DeFunis had been enrolled in the School when he filed suit, and by the time the case reached the highest court he had already graduated! So the example is not merely a philosopher's invention.

Now a number of arguments can be given in support of the law school's policy, and other policies like it. Black people have been, and still are, the victims of racist discrimination. One result is that they are poorly represented in the professions. In order to remedy this it is not enough that we simply stop discriminating against them. For, so long as there are not enough "role models" available—i.e., black people visibly successful in the professions, whom young blacks can recognize as models to emulate—young blacks cannot be expected to aspire to the professions and prepare for careers in the way that young whites do. It is a vicious cycle: while there are relatively few black lawyers, relatively few young blacks will take seriously the possibility of becoming lawyers, and so they will not be prepared for law school. But if relatively few young blacks are well-prepared for law school, and admissions committees hold them to the same high standards as the white applicants, there will be relatively few black lawyers. Law school admissions committees may try to help set things right, and break this cycle, by temporarily giving preferential treatment to black applicants.

Moreover, although many people now recognize that racist discrimination is wrong, prejudice against blacks is still widespread. One aspect of the problem is that a disproportionate number of blacks are still poor and hold only menial jobs, while the most prestigious jobs are occupied mostly by whites. So long as this is so, it will be easy for the white majority to continue with their old stereotyped ideas about black people. But if there were more black people holding prestigious jobs, it would be much more difficult to sustain the old prejudices. So in the long run law school admissions policies favoring black applicants will help reduce racism throughout the society.

I believe these arguments, and others like them, show that policies of reverse discrimination can be socially useful, although this is certainly a debatable point. For one thing, the resentment of those who disapprove of such policies will diminish their net utility. For another, less qualified persons will not perform as well in the positions they attain. However, I will not discuss these issues any further. I will concentrate instead on the more fundamental question of whether policies of reverse discrimination are unjust. After all, the rejected white student may concede the utility of such policies and nevertheless still complain that he has been treated unjustly. He may point out that he has been turned down simply because of his race. If he had been black, and had had exactly the same qualifications, he would have been accepted. This, he may argue, is equally as unjust as discriminating against black people on account of their race. Moreover, he can argue that, even if black people have been mistreated, he was not responsible for it, and so it is unfair to penalize him for it now. These are impressive arguments and, if they cannot be answered, the rightness of reverse discrimination will remain in doubt regardless of its utility.

I will argue that whether the white applicant has been treated unjustly depends on *why* he has better credentials than the black, that is, it depends on what accounts for the 20-point difference in their qualifications. Suppose, for example, that his higher qualifications are due entirely to the fact that he has worked harder. Suppose the two applicants are equally intelligent, and have had the same opportunities. But the black student has spent a lot of time enjoying himself, going to the movies, and so forth, while the white student has passed by such pleasures to devote himself to his studies. If *this* is what accounts for the difference in their qualifications, then it seems that the white applicant really has been treated unjustly. For he has earned his superior qualifications; he deserves to be admitted ahead of the black student because he has worked harder for it.

But now suppose a different explanation is given as to why the white student has ended up with a 20-point advantage in qualifications. Suppose the applicants are equally intelligent *and* they have worked equally hard. However, the black student has had to contend with obstacles which his white competitor has not had to face. For example, his early education was at the hands of ill-trained teachers in crowded, inadequate schools, so that by the time he reached college he was far behind the other students and despite his best efforts he never quite caught up. If *this* is what accounts for the difference in qualifications, things look very different. For now the white student has not earned his superior qualifications. He has done nothing to deserve them. His record is, of course, the result of things he's done, just as the black student's record is the result of things the black student has done. But the fact that he has a *better* record than the black student is not due to anything he has done. That difference is due only to his good luck in having been born into a more advantaged social position. Surely he cannot deserve to be admitted into law school ahead of the black simply because of *that*.

Now in fact black people in the United States have been, and are, systematically discriminated against, and it is reasonable to believe that this mistreatment does make a difference to black people's ability to compete with whites for such goods as law school admission. Therefore, at least some actual cases probably do correspond to the description of my example. Some white students have better qualifications for law school only because they have not had to contend with the obstacles faced by their black competitors. If so, their better qualifications do not automatically entitle them to prior admission.

Thus it is not the fact that the applicant is black that matters. What is important is that, as a result of past discriminatory practices, he has been unfairly handicapped in trying to achieve the sort of academic standing required for admission. If he has a claim to "preferential" treatment now, it is for *that* reason.

It follows that, even though a system of reverse discrimination might involve injustice for some whites, in many cases no injustice will be done. In fact, the reverse is true: If no such system is employed—if, for example, law school admissions are granted purely on the basis of "qualifications"—*that* may involve injustice for the disadvantaged who have been unfairly handicapped in the competition for qualifications.

It also follows that the most common arguments against reverse discrimination are not valid. The white student in our example cannot complain that he is being rejected simply because he is white. The effect of the policy is only to *neutralize an advantage* that he has had because he is white, and that is very different.[10] Nor will it do any good for the white to complain that, while blacks may have suffered unjust hardships, *he* is not responsible for it and so should not be penalized for it. The white applicant is not being penalized, or being made to pay reparations, for the wrongs that have been done to blacks. He is simply not being allowed to *profit* from the fact that those wrongs were done, by now besting the black in a competition that is "fair" only if we ignore the obstacles which one competitor, but not the other, has had to face.

NOTES

1. Robert Nozick, *Anarchy, State, and Utopia* (New York: Basic Books, 1974), pp. 149–150.
2. Judith Jarvis Thomson, "Preferential Hiring," *Philosophy and Public Affairs*, vol. 2, no. 4 (Summer 1973), pp. 364–384.
3. Ibid., p. 369.
4. The following is from my review of *Anarchy, State, and Utopia* in *Philosophia*, vol. 7 (1977).
5. Nozick, p. 161.
6. Joel Feinberg, *Doing and Deserving* (Princeton: Princeton University Press, 1970), p. 58 (italics added).
7. John Rawls, *A Theory of Justice* (Cambridge, Mass.: Harvard University Press, 1971), pp. 103–104.
8. What I am resisting—and what I think Rawls' view leads us towards—is a kind of determinism that would make all moral evaluation of persons meaningless. On this tendency in Rawls, see Nozick, pp. 213–214.
9. This point is elaborated by Herbert Morris in his illuminating paper "Persons and Punishment," *The Monist*, vol. 52 (1968), pp. 475–501.
10. Cf. George Sher, "Justifying Reverse Discrimination in Employment," *Philosophy and Public Affairs*, vol. 4, no. 2 (Winter 1975), pp. 159–170. Sher also argues that "reverse discrimination is justified insofar as it neutralizes competitive disadvantages caused by past privations" (p. 165). I have learned a lot from Sher's paper.

Joel Feinberg

Economic Income as Deserved

Although economists rarely speak of desert, philosophers and ordinary people debate such questions as whether doctors earn more than they deserve or whether teachers receive less than they deserve. In this selection from his book Doing and Deserving, *Joel Feinberg explores the connection between economic income and desert. He argues that income can be seen as deserved only to the extent that it is compensation and that higher incomes are deserved only when they compensate an individual for some greater burden or need.*

Economists rarely speak of desert but both ordinary people and philosophers do, and whether such talk is well advised or not, it does seem to make sense. Some affirm and some deny, for example, that doctors get more or teachers less than they deserve. The problem of interpreting such claims, as in the case of honorable offices, is complicated by the variety of ways in which occupational income is conceived and the consequent concurrence of conflicting criteria.

Suppose we interpret professional income as a prize. This way of viewing the matter is superficially plausible as long as some classes get more than others. The competition is for shares of the national wealth; a whole series of awards from first prize on down are given; and the rules of the contest are the laws of the market supplemented by the criminal code. One immediate consequence of this picture is that, if there is a sense of "desert" in which it means "entitlement," then in that sense everyone deserves what he gets. Providing you obey the rules, the market alone— that is, the social demand for your services—determines what and how much you are entitled to. This is trivially true—this great conservative principle—much as it is true in baseball that the team scoring the most runs wins the game (is entitled to a trophy), or in politics that the candidate who receives the most electoral votes is entitled to the presidency.

Supposing our economic life to be primarily a competition for prizes, what are we to regard as the basis of the competition, the skill or other estimable trait singled out by the rule makers for special treatment and honor? Is it simply craftiness and avarice? Surely not, for even the defenders of the status quo deny that craftiness is a desert basis. No defender of the medical profession, for example, argues that doctors deserve their "prize" because of superior craftiness. But what, then, is the ground for the competition which brings all classes and professions to-

Reprinted from Joel Feinberg, *Doing and Deserving.* © 1970 by Princeton University Press. Reprinted by permission of Princeton University Press.

gether in the same arena? I can think of no one single skill (apart from commercial canniness) in respect to which all members of all professions are in explicit competition, or any one game at which we all play. The competitive model is likely to appeal only to certain businessmen engaged in a kind of running commercial poker game, and recent events indicate that it fits ill even that limited sector of our national life.

It is more plausible to interpret professional income as reward or compensation. The reward model is not, however, without its difficulties. So long as it is a finite pie we are splitting, we cannot reward some with larger slices without punishing others by giving them smaller portions. But, that complication aside, there can be no doubt that persons often do construe larger-than-average incomes either as social recognition of excellence or achievement or else as symbolic expressions of gratitude for unusual services rendered or for contributions made to the general welfare. The argument is not that society or any of its representatives has authorized such rewards or even consented to them, but only that the basis of desert for such rewards does exist in the actual achievements or contributions of the wealthier classes. The argument, of course, often goes the other way: the rich, it is said, are rewarded beyond all desert. In any case, the concept of professional income as social reward seems deeply rooted in our ordinary thinking.

That it makes any contribution to clarity in our ordinary thinking is much less obvious. Persons in certain professions, it is alleged, have contributed more than most to our general welfare and therefore deserve tangible expressions of public gratitude, namely, higher incomes in proportion to their contributions. But the persons who have contributed or are members of classes which have contributed most conspicuously to the public weal—the innovators, reformers, political leaders, artists, and scientists—are not the ones obviously getting or demanding the most conspicuous rewards. This observation suggests that it is contributions to our economic welfare, to our "standard of living," rather than the quality of our life that are said to deserve reward—and perhaps rightly so. After all, contributions to our true and ultimate good are essentially contestable and impossible to measure; and, besides, there may appear to be a fittingness in reserving economic rewards for economic contributions. But more puzzling difficulties remain. It is, first of all, difficult enough to determine how large a share of our national economic wealth is created by each individual or each class;[1] yet even if that is possible in principle, it is still necessary to make out a case for the type of contribution which deserves gratitude. It may, after all, turn out that sharp traders and shrewd investors create the most wealth, and we are not generally inclined to feel grateful for contributions to our welfare that are the accidental consequences of another person's self-interested pursuit of wealth. We could, of course, require that rewards go not simply to those who contribute the most, but to those who contribute from public-spirited or disinterested motives—activities which would "naturally" evoke gratitude. But then the reward would function only to encourage the very type of motive that would disqualify its possessor from reward, and would thus be self-defeating.

Not all rewards express gratitude, however; some express recognition of the excellence or achievement that is their desert basis. A. C. Ewing even speaks with respect (but not complete agreement) of a "retributive theory of reward" according to which it is an end in itself that the virtuous be rewarded. "It is not merely that we think the good ought to be happy," says Ewing, "but that we think they ought to be recognized or manifested [elsewhere he says "approved of" and "appreciated"] as good, and the most impressive form of recognition is by bestowal of the means to happiness [i.e., money]."[2] Ewing himself points out, though, that moral virtue is rarely proposed seriously as a desert basis for economic rewards. And, indeed, there is something repugnant in paying a man for being virtuous.[3] Economic benefits seem to be a highly inappropriate vehicle of recognition partly because they tend to render the recipient suspect and to tarnish the disinterested altruism essential to moral worth. "Rewards for virtue as such could only rightly be given to people who were not virtuous for the sake of the reward and did not need the reward to make them so."[4]

Actually, it is *ability*, not moral virtue, which is commonly held to be a desert basis for economic rewards. It is often said, for example, that doctors, lawyers, engineers, and high executives, simply to perform their functions, need far more talent and skill than most other people, and in virtue of this superior talent they deserve higher income as a kind of public recognition of their superiority. Ability is a desert basis, of course, for various kinds of *prizes* and for *grades*; and when it issues in great achievements, it often calls for and receives public recognition in the form of such *rewards* as testimonial dinners, citations, knighthoods, and other honors. But, again, distributing wages, profits, and salaries to whole classes of people as symbols of the recognition of superior talent seems inappropriate and, indeed, repugnant; for that would be to interpret the principle "Better people deserve better things" in a manner wholly inconsistent with democratic and liberal ideas. That able people are *ipso facto* better people in any nontautologous sense is precisely what the traditional equalitarian and Christian teachings deny. Rewards for industry or self-improvement, or for specific achievements that cry out for recognition in the interests of truth, are another matter; and there may be sound utilitarian reasons for rewarding even superior intelligence or skill. But it is no more self-evident to me that superior intelligence or skill per se *deserves* reward than that great height or physical strength does.[5]

It is much more plausible, I think, to construe income, in part, as *compensation* and to speak of desert in this connection. Collecting garbage is an extremely disagreeable and onerous (not to say malodorous) job which must be done by someone. Garbage collectors do, as a matter of fact, get rather more pay than other workers of comparable skill; and the reason they do no doubt is that greater inducements are needed to draw men into such work. But surely that is not the only reason why garbage collectors should be paid more. It can also be argued that, insofar as the garbage collector's plight is no fault of his own, but only due to his bad luck, lack of skill, or want of opportunity, he *deserves* more money to make up for his unpleasant circumstances.

The same point can be made about extra-hazardous work, and is well made by Benn and Peters:

> Admittedly, some men lack the job-getting qualities, and are forced to take the jobs that no one else wants. But lack of skill or personal charm may not be good enough reasons why a man should suffer the hazards of silicosis or a broken neck. It may be, then, that if such jobs must be done, they ought to carry compensatory benefits.[6]

Not only unpleasant and hazardous work but also terribly responsible positions and functions requiring extensive preliminary training deserve compensation. Here is the real basis for the claim that the executive and the physician *deserve* higher incomes: not that their superior abilities deserve rewards, but rather that their heavier loads of responsibility and worry and (for doctors) their longer period of impoverished apprenticeship *deserve compensation*.

The principle that unpleasant, onerous, and hazardous jobs deserve economic compensation, unlike the claim that superior ability deserves economic reward, is an equalitarian one, for it says only that deprivations for which there is no good reason should be compensated to the point where the deprived one is again brought back to a position of equality with his fellows. It is not that compensation gives him more than others (considering everything), but only that it allows him to catch up.

This point in turn should help clarify the relation between desert and need. It is only in respect to compensation that need can be a desert basis. A man with a chronically sick wife or child deserves compensation since through no fault of his own he has a greater need than others; and the same is true of the man with a large number of dependents. But need is never a desert basis for any other kind of treatment. In fact, in respect to most other modes of treatment, desert is *contrasted* with need. Who should get the prize—the contestant who deserves it or the one with the greatest need for it? Should the student who (as he says) "needs an A to get into law school" be given the grade he needs or the grade he deserves? Some people, we are told by psychiarists, "need" punishment even when they don't deserve it, and the man who has the greatest need for the sheriff's reward is not always the man, even in Hollywood westerns, who has done most to apprehend the wanted desperado. It is only compensation that is deserved by need, and then only when the need is blameless.

If I am right and economic income cannot plausibly be construed as prizes or rewards, and can be spoken of as "deserved" only insofar as it is compensation, then a startling result follows. To say that income ideally ought to be distributed only according to desert is to say that, in respect to all social benefits, all men should ideally be equal. Some, of course, should receive more money than others to compensate them for greater burdens or greater needs, but ideally the compensatory sum should be just sufficient to bring the overall balance of their benefits up to the level of their fellows'.

What follows, though, from this brief discussion of economic benefits is not that wealth ought to be distributed equally with adjustments made only for needs and burdens, but rather that there are important considerations relevant to this question which have *nothing to do with desert.* Unequal incomes tend to promote industry and ambition and also to encourage socially valuable activities and the development of socially important skills and techniques. The incentive of financial gain might very well make possible the creation of so much wealth that even the smaller shares would be greater than the equally shared portions of the smaller equalitarian pie. Desert is essentially a nonutilitarian concept, one which can and often does come into head-on conflict with utility; and there is no *a priori* reason for giving it automatic priority over all other values. Desert is one very important kind of ethical consideration, but it is not the only one.

NOTES

1. Cf. L. T. Hobhouse, *The Elements of Social Justice* (London: George Allen & Unwin, 1949), Ch. 8.
2. *The Morality of Punishment*, 128.
3. Cf. S. I. Benn and R. S. Peters: "there are some sorts of 'worth' for which rewards in terms of income seem inappropriate. Great courage in battle is recognized by medals, not by increased pay." *Social Principles and the Democratic State*, 139.
4. Op.cit., 132. Ewing adds that "the danger is much worse than it is with punishment. . . . For a man formerly given to crime to abstain, even from merely prudential motives, is a step upwards, but for a man who previously did good actions irrespective of reward to come to do them for the sake of the reward is decidedly a step downwards."
5. Ewing (op. cit., 137) claims that all kinds of value (not simply moral value) deserve recognition and approval. For that reason, ability is a desert basis; it *is* a "value" and is to be acknowledged as such or "appreciated." Similarly, punishment is an expression of our recognition of the evil character of an act "vividly impressed" on the criminal. Why, then, doesn't Ewing find ineptitude, inability, and unintelligence, all "disvalues" or "demerits," desert bases for *punishment?*
6. Op. cit., 140. The authors' point that workers do not deserve to be penalized for lack of skill or charm is the counterpart of my point that no one deserves to be rewarded simply for his superior skill or charm.

Norman Daniels
Meritocracy

Norman Daniels discusses what he calls "meritocracies," that is, societies in which one's abilities give one grounds for claiming to deserve a certain job. A defense of meritocracy, he contends, really rests on productivity—that is, on the social desirability of finding the most productive pattern of job assignments. The question of whether one is entitled to a certain job is distinct from the question of what economic reward should be provided by that job, and different types of meritocracy are possible depending on the schedule of benefits and burdens that they attach to different jobs. Unlike Nozick, Daniels contends that our natural characteristics and assets should not be used as a basis for distributing major economic rewards, even if those characteristics are used as a basis for distributing jobs.

Sometimes a person has abilities and interests which enable him or her to perform a given job, position, or office—hereafter, I will just say "job"—better than other available persons. In what sense do such abilities and interests constitute a basis for claiming the more capable person merits the job? Does the fact that someone possesses special abilities and interests which are needed for the superior performance of jobs of considerable social importance and prestige constitute a basis for claiming the person deserves or merits greater rewards for the job? I want to explore some of the issues associated with these questions, but I will do so by analyzing the notion of a meritocracy, a social order built around a particular notion of merit. My hope is that examination of such a hypothetical social order will allow me to assess the broader implications of this particular notion of merit for a theory of distributive justice. Though my model for the meritocracies I consider derives from Michael Young's satire about a world-wide technocratic society in which all assignments of jobs and rewards are organized on a merit basis,[1] I am not concerned with the details of his construction, except for his construal of merit as *ability plus effort.*

A MERITOCRATIC JOB PLACEMENT PRINCIPLE

I take a meritocracy to be a society whose basic institutions are governed by a partial theory of distributive justice consisting of principles of the following three types:

1. A principle of job placement that awards jobs to individuals on the basis of merit;

154

2. A principle specifying the conditions of opportunity under which the job placement principle is applied;
3. A principle specifying reward schedules (salary, benefits, etc.) for jobs.

It is obvious that such principles constitute only a partial theory of distributive justice: they say nothing, for example, about liberty or its distribution, nor about many other questions. But I will concentrate on just this much here since most meritocrats do. I will argue that there is a preferred principle for job placement and one for opportunity and that most meritocrats would agree to them. But, meritocrats will still vary widely on reward principles. My schema allows us to separate problems common to what meritocrats generally share from problems that arise from reward schedules.

Most meritocrats share certain empirical assumptions which give rise to a principle of job placement. First, they assume that different jobs require different sets of human abilities and different personality traits, including motivation, if they are to be performed with maximum competency. Certain skills, whether mental or motor, are more critical for some jobs than others. Second, they assume that people differ in the abilities and personality traits they possess. Some people possess more developed motor skills, some more developed mental skills, than others. Usually, this second assumption is not couched solely in terms of actual skills possessed. Rather, it is assumed people differ in their natively determined capacity to develop a given level of a certain skill. Often the ambiguous word "ability" does double duty here, hedging bets between claims about inequalities of skills and claims about inequalities of capacity. In any case, most meritocrats believe that it is obvious that people differ in levels of skill and that it is at least probable that they differ in the capacity to acquire levels of skills.[2]

Meritocrats infer from these two assumptions that some arrays of assignments of individuals to jobs will be more productive than others. That is, if we take care to match people with the jobs they are best able to perform, then we will have produced a relatively productive array of job assignments. Actually, we are unlikely to find just one particular array of job assignments that is more productive than any other. Rather, it seems likely that there are a number of equally productive arrays of job assignments for any group of jobs and individuals.

A warning is needed about the notion of productivity. It must be accepted as an intuitively applicable notion for a wide range of jobs, positions, or offices for which no standard measurement of productivity exists. For such jobs, economists often take market-determined wage levels to indicate average productivity levels. But, such a device is not satisfactory for many reasons. So I will assume we can meaningfully talk about the productivity of doctors, teachers, lawyers, hairdressers, and so on, even though no single quantitative measure seems acceptable. Meritocrats and non-meritocrats alike operate with intuitively acceptable, if imprecise, notions of competent or productive job performance.

The principle I believe would be preferred for job placement makes use of the idea of equally productive patterns of job assignments. This says that job assignments should be made by selecting the most productive array of job assignments; if that is not possible (because some jobs are already held), then select the next most productive array of job assignments, and so on.[3] Such a Productivity Principle seems desirable because, in the absence of arguments showing that justice or other considerations of right demand some other array than a maximally productive one, there is good reason to seek productivity in social arrangements. I want to leave it an open question how a meritocrat would respond to a claim that justice demanded—as compensation for past services or past injuries—that someone not selected by the Productivity Principle nevertheless be given a particular job. Some such claims would seem to be weighty enough to justify overriding the presumption in favor of productivity considerations. But more on this point shortly.

If the Productivity Principle is adopted, then the notion of individual merit enters the picture in the following, restricted way. An individual may claim to merit one job more than another job, or to merit one job more than another person does, if and only if his occupying that job is an assignment that is part of the assignments selected by the Productivity Principle. The claim of merit or relative merit is dependent for its basis on the rationale for the Principle. The merit does not derive from having the abilities themselves, but only from the fact that abilities can play a certain social role. We focus on the relevant abilities because of their utility, not because there is something intrinsically meritorious about having them. It should be quite clear by now that the particular notion of merit I am concerned with here should not be confused with the more general concept of desert; also it should not be confused with certain ordinary uses of "merit" which are similar to the broader notion of desert. I am concerned with merit as it plays a role in the types of meritocracies I am analyzing.

IMPLICATIONS OF THE PRODUCTIVITY PRINCIPLE

To see why the Productivity Principle is the preferred principle, consider the following case.[4] Jack and Jill both wants jobs A and B and each much prefers A to B. Jill can do either A or B better than Jack. But the situation S in which Jill performs B and Jack A is more productive than Jack doing B and Jill A (S'). The Productivity Principle selects S, not S', because it is attuned to macro, not micro, productivity considerations. It says "select people for jobs so that *overall* job performance is maximized."

It might be felt that the "real" meritocrat would balk at such a macro principle. The "real" meritocrat, it might be argued, is one who thinks a person should get a job if he or she is the best available person for *that* job. We might formulate such a view as the micro-productivity principle that, for any job J, we should select the applicant who can most productively perform J from among those desiring J more than any other job. The micro principle would select S', not S.

I think that, given the rationale for treating job-related abilities as the basis for merit claims in the first place, namely that it is socially desirable to enhance productivity where possible, the macro principle seems preferable. There is something anomalous about basing a merit claim, given our restricted notion of merit, on claims about micro-productivity considerations while at the same time ignoring macro-productivity considerations. We seem to need an explanation why macro considerations should not overrule the micro ones. Alternatively, we might try to divorce the merit claim from all productivity considerations, but this approach makes it completely mysterious why job-related abilities are made the basis of merit in the first place.[5]

I suppose one reason some may think the micro-merit principle is preferable to the Productivity Principle is that it seems *unfair* to Jill that she gets the job she prefers less even though she can do the job Jack gets better than he can. But what is the sense of unfairness here based on? After all, under this arrangement, Jack has the job he prefers more and overall productivity is enhanced. And, if Jill had her way, Jack would not have his, and macroproductivity would suffer as well. It is important to note as well that B is a job Jill wants, though not as much as she wants A. The Productivity Principle does not force people into jobs they do not want at all.

I believe the sense of unfairness here derives from particular, ines-sential features of our economic system. In many hiring or job-placement situations in our society, we make no effort to calculate macroproductivity from job assignments. We assume that macroproductivity is always directly proportional to microproductivity. So, in most hiring that is done on a merit basis (and of course much is not), we tend to use the micro principle. From the micro point of view of such an habitual practice, it does look like the macro Productivity Principle makes Jill pay a price we ordinarily might not make her pay.

But if this explanation does *account for* the sense of unfairness some feel, it does not justify it in a relevant way. Our task is not just to describe the intuitions we have, influenced as they are by existing eco-nomic arrangements. Rather, where we have some reason to think the intuitions are just a by-product of existing institutions, and where our task is to find principles to establish institutions we think more just than exist-ing ones, then we may be forced to modify or abandon some of our habitual intuitions. If the Productivity Principle appears on theoretical grounds to be a more plausible principle governing the institution of job placement, then our favoritism for micro considerations may seem unjusti-fiable. Moreover, if an individual's sense of fairness were molded by insti-tutions which took macroproductivity into account, not just micro productivity, then our data on unfairness might disappear. If Jill (and others) knew the macro Productivity Principle and not the micro principle were determining job placement, no legitimate expectations of hers (or ours) would be unsatisfied by the selection of her for B rather than A.

What I have been trying to show is the appropriateness of using the macro Productivity Principle rather than the alternative micro princi-ple, given the rationale for worrying about job-related abilities in the first place, namely their overall connection to productivity. For purposes of my exposition, however, I do not need to rule out some version of the micro principle wherever it is construed as a rough, practical guide to the application of the macro principle. That is, given societies (like ours) in which there is no provision for a more scientific method of calculating maximally productive job arrays, in which most hiring or placement for positions is on a job-by-job basis, then the micro principle may be the best rule of thumb. Such a compromise in practice is not, however, a compromise with the rationale behind the Productivity Principle. It is important to note, however, that the Productivity Principle seems to presuppose a more sophisticated theory of productivity measurement and may also commit us to more elaborate, centralized hiring than the micro principle. Since my task here is to analyze where a particular notion of merit leads us, I need not evaluate these last considerations to determine the ultimate desirability of the macro Productivity Principle or the micro principle.

In any case, keeping in mind the compromise just proposed, I will assume that meritocrats can agree on the macro Productivity Principle. But it must be clear what this assumption implies: an individual merits a job if his or her placement on that job is part of the most productive array of job assignments. Such a derivation of a merit claim to a job does not presuppose that any kind of desert claim is present other than one derived from productivity considerations. Our obligation to honor a merit claim so derived is only as strong as the *prima facie* obligation to satisfy productivity considerations.

Some may feel that this truncated notion of merit that emerges must be an incorrect one because it omits any appeal to a stronger notion of desert. They are inclined to assert that if Jill has the greater ability, then Jill *deserves* the job. But the force of my argument is to leave us wondering whether there is a plausible basis for such a desert claim at all, given that our selection of certain abilities as relevant for job placement was based on their connection to productivity.[6]

It is worth a brief digression to mention two implications of my analysis for the problem of preferential hiring. Some people object to preferential hiring on the grounds (not necessarily the most convincing ones) that not choosing the most competent candidate, as judged by test scores or other professional criteria, is a violation of that person's presumptive rights. But, if merit claims to jobs are derived from the Productivity Principle, then macro-productivity claims may, as a matter of empirical fact, override the micro-based claims of the most competent applicant. For example, a better mix of race and sex in such professional positions as the law, teaching, or medicine might well pay dividends in terms of services rendered to those who would not otherwise get them, inspiration to long-suppressed motivation, the overcoming of race and sex stereotypes which are counterproductive in other ways, and so on. But the proponent of affirmative action should beware that the appeal to the Productivity Principle does not backfire: suppose productivity is reduced because of sexist or racist opposition to what otherwise would be a meritocratic placement. Then the Productivity Principle might play a conservative role, capitulating to existing biases.

This result leads me to a more important result of my analysis of merit. Whether my claim to merit a particular job more than another does is dependent on an appeal to the Productivity Principle or to a micro principle, it nevertheless is justified only by efficiency considerations. If consideration of right or justice demands we override efficiency considerations—to satisfy a concern for equality, to compensate for past injuries, or to reward for past service—then we are not faced with a case of pitting claims of right against other claims of right. Rather, we pit productivity against considerations of justice. And many will feel less concerned about such a compromise of productivity than they would if a claim to merit a job were really a claim of right, a claim of justice.[7]

MERIT AND REWARD

I would like to return now to discuss the remaining types of principles meritocrats share. Although there may be some exceptions, I believe that most meritocrats would view fair, rather than just formal, equality of opportunity as the appropriate precondition for application of the Productivity Principle. Formal equality of opportunity obtains when there are no legal or quasi-legal barriers to people's having equal access (based on merit) to positions and offices or to the means (education and training) needed to qualify one for access to such jobs. Fair equality of opportunity requires not only that negative legal or quasi-legal constraints on equality of opportunity be eliminated, but also that positive steps be taken to provide equality of access—and the means to achieve such equality of access—to those with inferior initial competitive positions resulting from family background or other biological or social accidents.

If we make the empirical assumption that conditions of fair opportunity maximize the availability of human abilities which would otherwise be wasted under conditions of merely formal opportunity, then considerations of productivity alone carry us some way toward the preference for fair opportunity. Of course, efficiency considerations alone may *not* always point to fair rather than formal opportunity. If there were a tremendous superfluity of abilities available just as a result of formal opportunity, then more might have to be invested through fair opportunity measures to produce increases in the maximally productive class of job assignments than is justified by the size of those increases. Similarly, if early, arbitrary selection of some individuals for special training for certain jobs were maximally efficient, other non-utilitarian arguments might be needed before fair opportunity would be preferred. Rawls, for example, does not rest his argument for fair opportunity on grounds of efficiency alone. Rather, he argues that people will feel they do not have fair access to the centrally important social good of self-realization if formal, rather than fair, opportunity is instituted.[8] In any case, I will assume that meritocrats generally treat fair, not formal, opportunity as the precondition for applying the Productivity Principle. Little in my argument hangs on this assumption.

Thus far I have said nothing about the rewards and burdens that accompany different jobs. The Productivity Principle, as I have presented it, is defined without reference to any particular schedule of rewards and burdens. So far, although an individual may claim to merit a job when his having it satisfies the principle, there is no sense given to his meriting any particular set of rewards or burdens. I have deliberately dissociated the meritocratic basis for job assignment from the process of determining the schedule of benefits and burdens associated with different jobs or positions.[9]

I think it is possible for meritocrats to differ on the reward schedules they join to the system structured by the Productivity Principle and fair equality of opportunity. Consider the following eight meritocracies which differ only in their reward schedules:

1. Status quo meritocracy: the reward schedule for jobs mirrors those inequalities in rewards and burdens which characterize the U.S. status quo.
2. Unbridled meritocracy: the reward schedule allows whatever rewards those who end up with positions of power and prestige can acquire for themselves. (Status quo and unbridled meritocracies may be identical.)
3. Desert meritocracy: the reward schedule allows rewards proportional to the contribution of the jobs (but not constrained by efficiency considerations as in (5)); alternatively, the desert basis might have nothing to do with productivity—it might be moral worthiness, for example.
4. Nationalist meritocracy: inequalities in rewards act to advance the national interest.
5. Utilitarian meritocracy: the reward schedule allows inequalities which act to maximize average or total utility.
6. Maximin meritocracy: the reward schedule allows inequalities which act to maximize the index of primary social goods of those who are worst off.
7. Strict egalitarian meritocracy: no inequalities in reward are allowed.
8. Socialist meritocracy: the reward schedule allows no inequalities in the satisfaction of (basic?) needs.

My list allows for meritocracies which no one may actually have supported. And, for the sake of brevity, it may not mention your favorite meritocracy. But the main point should be clear, namely, I do not consider it an essential feature of a meritocracy that efficiency is the sole principle governing selection of reward schedules, but I do believe that an appeal to productivity in job assignment is always involved in meritocracy through the Productivity Principle.

I believe a number of qualifying remarks are in order. First, unless certain empirical conditions obtain, meritocracy may prove to be a theory which does not determine which job assignments are to be made. If application of the Productivity Principle is effectively to determine job placement, then the number of equally productive patterns of job assignments is going to have to be fairly small. I am inclined to believe, however, that this number will be quite large under real conditions of fair equality of opportunity. With adequate education and training, most people might competently perform almost any job, or at least a very large range of jobs. Second, the Productivity Principle presupposes that we have very good ways of predicting which abilities and personality traits will lead to successful, i.e., productive, performance of a given job. But many of our current efforts in those directions are woefully inadequate.[10]

A final, most important qualification. My analysis might seem to imply that we know how to apply the Productivity Principle independently of fixing a reward schedule. But such independence is unlikely. Different reward schedules would presumably affect the motivations of individuals contemplating entering certain jobs. Just this point is at the heart of Rawls' view that material incentives will be necessary if we are to procure the greatest talent possible for certain burdensome jobs. So it seems we cannot determine the class of maximally productive job assignments, which we need for application of the Productivity Principle, until we know something of the reward structure. But this fact does not alter my main point: we can distinguish the Productivity Principle from reward principles, and what all meritocrats share is appeal to the Productivity Principle and fair equality of opportunity, however else they may differ in their use of reward schedules.[11]

If we keep our attention on the shared features of meritocracy, we can see why many varied theorists have found something attractive in it. Indeed, insisting that job placement be meritocratic under conditions of fair equality of opportunity leads to serious criticism of existing institutions. But these shared principles always operate against a background determined by the reward schedule. And in our society, the reward schedule is rarely itself the target of challenge by meritocrats. But, meritocracy becomes controversial when we begin to see the consequences of meritocratic job placement operating in a context of certain reward schedules.

IS MERITOCRACY UNFAIR?

My concern here, which may disappoint some, is not to debate the merits of different reward schedules in order to arrive at a comprehensive theory of distributive justice. Rather, I want to concentrate on a particular problem raised for certain reward schedules just because they operate in conjunction with the Productivity Principle. The meritocracies I listed earlier offer three types of reward schedules. Type One meritocracies (status quo, unbridled, desert [according to contribution], nationalist, and utilitarian) allow for significant inequalities in rewards with no constraints to protect those with the worst jobs. Type Two meritocracies either allow no significant inequalities (egalitarian) or allow inequalities not based on the social functions of the jobs but rather on the needs or other deserts of the job holder (socialist and some desert meritocracies). Type Three meritocracies allow for inequalities but attempt to constrain them in ways that act to benefit those whose abilities tend to lead to low reward jobs (maximin). Meritocracies of the first type are open to a criticism that Type Two, and possibly Type Three, meritocracies avoid.

If a reward schedule allows significant inequalities of reward to be associated with different jobs, as in Type One meritocracies, then the fortuitous possession of certain natural abilities and traits may also make one the beneficiary of significant social rewards as well. Rawls calls the constellation of genetic and environmental contingencies that determine one's natural abilities and character traits a "natural lottery." Type One, unlike Type Two, meritocracies, reward a desirable payoff in the natural lottery with a second payoff. Many find such a double payoff intuitively unfair. Just as it seems unfair to many that social accidents of birth—being born rich—lead to multiple payoffs, so too it seems unfair that natural accidents of birth and upbringing can lead to such important social consequences.

The basis for the intuition about unfairness is that the operation of the natural lottery is morally arbitrary. The basis for selecting an assignment of natural assets, such as natural abilities, talents, and personality traits, to one person rather than another has nothing to do with any conceivable basis for desert. Rather, it is rooted in biological and psychological contingencies. The core idea seems to be that the person *did* nothing to deserve or earn his natural assets. But is this idea accurate? Are our job-related abilities and talents never assets we did anything to deserve? Robert Nozick argues that people do choose to develop some of their natural assets as opposed to others. Moreover, if this choice results in the possession of more valuable assets, then some desert claim to those assets derives from the act of choice.[12] This objection has force to it: we do not want to view the final product of all development of our abilities and personality traits as completely determined by causal chains we have no responsibility for.

I think Nozick's objection can be circumvented provided we make certain, perhaps overly strong, empirical assumptions. We might reply to Nozick that, although we deserve some credit for some actions that develop our natural assets, nevertheless we are still only developing potentialities constrained by the natural lottery. Whatever credit we deserve is only a thin overlay on a substantial base of arbitrary lottery results. Even our range of choice is limited by the lottery. I cannot effectively choose to develop natural assets I do not have. To the extent, then, that our marketable assets are significantly determined, even if not completely determined, by the natural lottery, they are not assets we have in any way earned or which we deserve. Notice, however, that this reply to Nozick on behalf of Rawls itself depends on an important and powerful empirical assumption, one which Nozick's objection also does not challenge. It assumes that our developed assets *are* in general largely determined by causal sequences that are rooted in biological and psychological causes beyond the individual's control. Just how much truth there is to this assumption cannot be determined here.

Part of the problem here comes from the fact that the same people who view the natural lottery as a morally arbitrary basis for the distribution of some social goods, like rewards, nevertheless still treat it as an acceptable basis for distributing other social goods, the jobs themselves. All the meritocrats I have been considering are committed to the view that job placement, though it depends on a morally arbitrary distribution of natural assets, is nevertheless morally acceptable. Rawls, for example, most vigorously pursues the charge that the distribution of natural assets is morally arbitrary and should not determine the distribution of other social rewards. Yet I believe his principles of justice are meritocratic. He explicitly shares with my other meritocrats provisions for fair equality of opportunity. And he implicitly shares with them the view that abilities which determine job performance should be the basis for placing people in jobs even though the distribution of these abilities is, at least significantly, dependent on the natural lottery. Let us take a closer look at Rawls' argument.

In Sections 12, 13 and 17 of *A Theory of Justice* Rawls offers an *intuitive* argument in favor of a preferred interpretation for the principle of justice that says inequalities should work to "everyone's advantage" and that offices should be "open to all." He argues that "open to all" should be defined by a principle of fair, not just formal, equality of opportunity. Fair, but not formal, equality of opportunity requires that basic institutions are arranged to compensate for inequities of social position. Such social contingencies, Rawls insists, are morally arbitrary and should not determine further distributions of social goods. But even if we modify a free market distributional system—presumably a model of the principle of efficiency—by incorporating fair equality of opportunity, and even if the resulting system

> works to perfection in eliminating the influence of social contingencies, it still permits the distribution of wealth and income to be determined by the natural distribution of abilities and talents. Within the limits allowed by the background arrangements, distributive shares are decided by the outcome of the natural lottery and this outcome is arbitrary from a moral perspective. There is no more reason to permit the distribution of income and wealth to be settled by the distribution of natural assets than by historical and social fortune.[13]

Accordingly, in order to avoid the moral arbitrariness present in a system in which "to everyone's advantage" is defined by the principle of efficiency, we should instead interpret "to everyone's advantage" as determined by the difference principle. The difference principle specifies that differences or inequalities in social goods are allowable only if they act to maximize the interests of the worst-off members of society.

It might seem tempting to infer, from the sequence of points in Rawls' intuitive argument, that the move from the principle of efficiency to the difference principle will avoid or *nullify* the moral arbitrariness involved in the natural lottery. But such an inference is clearly too strong. The natural lottery still determines, under conditions of fair opportunity, access to jobs. Though it is not explicit in Rawls, I believe he is committed to something like my Productivity Principle of efficient job placement. But since the difference principle is compatible with significant inequalities attaching to jobs,[14] the natural lottery will still play a role in determining access to a double payoff—or a double loss for natural losers—however much it is constrained by the interests of the worst off.

A better way to construe Rawls' argument is that the difference principle ameliorates or *moderates* as much as possible the effects of allowing morally arbitrary differences among people to determine access to other social rewards. Because the meritocratic principles still operate in a context of inequalities of reward, Rawls does not avoid tainting his system with the same kind of moral arbitrariness he found under the principle of efficiency. But there is less of a taint:

> The difference principle represents, in effect, an agreement to regard the distribution of natural talents as a common asset and to share in the benefits of this distribution whatever it turns out to be. Those who have been favored by nature, whoever they are, may gain from their good fortune only on terms that improve the situation of those who have lost out. . . . No one deserves his greater natural capacity nor merits a more favorable starting place in society. But it does not follow that one should eliminate these distinctions. There is another way to deal with them. The basic structure can be arranged so that these contingencies work for the good of the least fortunate.[15]

So Rawls' intuitive argument for the difference principle is based centrally on the contention that moral arbitrariness in the distribution of social goods should be reduced to an acceptable minimum. This intuitive argument, it should be noted,[16] is not an argument usable in the original position itself, where appeal to prior moral intuitions is ruled out.

MUST WE AVOID MORALLY ARBITRARY DISTRIBUTIONS?

Rawls' argument from the need to minimize moral arbitrariness in distributions to the selection of the difference principle over the principle of efficiency is not without challenge. Nozick, in Chapter 7 of *Anarchy, State, and Utopia*, is very much interested in showing that there is no such obligation to avoid distributions of social goods that are in any significant way determined by the operation of the natural lottery. He wants to show that we are under no general moral obligation to *nullify* the effects of the natural lottery because an entitlement system like this, using a free market as a distribution mechanism, might well result over time in distributions of holdings causally influenced by the distribution of natural assets. It is not that Nozick wants to establish a distributional principle, "distribute according to the results of the lottery" or "distribute according to merit." He does not. Rather he wants to rebut the presumption he thinks is present in Rawls that we must nullify the effects of the lottery.

Unfortunately, I think Nozick's strategy to rebut the argument from moral arbitrariness cannot establish what he wants. His strategy seems to be to argue that there is no good argument Rawls has which both (a) shows that *nullification* of moral arbitrariness is desirable, and which (b) leaves Rawls' own principles of justice free of moral arbitrariness. But Nozick's argument turns completely on asserting that Rawls is committed to *nullifying* completely the effects of the lottery, not just to *moderating* its effects. *If* Rawls were committed (1) to eliminating all effects of the natural lottery, *and* (2) to allowing significant inequalities in reward, *and* (3) to meritocratic job placement, then he would be in the bind Nozick describes. But, as we have seen, Rawls is only committed to reducing as much as he can the effects of the morally arbitrary lottery. If Rawls is right that the difference principle accomplishes this moderation, then Nozick has not undercut Rawls' argument.[17]

Despite Nozick's objections, then, I think we are led to the view that it is morally desirable either to moderate or to nullify the effects of the natural lottery by not allowing them to be used as the basis for distributing other significant social rewards, even if they may be used as a basis for distributing jobs. Of course, accepting this conclusion depends on accepting the strong empirical assumptions I isolated earlier. Nevertheless, Type One meritocracies, those with reward schedules that allow significant inequalities unconstrained by a concern to redress inequalities in the natural lottery, are open to the objection that they ramify moral arbitrariness. Type Two, and if Rawls is right, Type Three meritocracies may avoid this special objection.

I think the merit of my earlier schema is now better revealed. It allows us to see that the type of merit claim I allowed to be derived from productivity considerations need not commit one to the charge of moral arbitrariness many have felt endemic to meritocracies. The price for avoiding the charge, however, is to insist on egalitarian—or fairly egalitarian—reward schedules. Unfortunately, most proponents of meritocracy have often hidden their infatuation for highly inegalitarian reward schedules behind their praise of meritocratic job placement, blurring the distinction I have insisted on between principles governing job placement and principles governing reward. The meritocrat who advocates meritocratic job placement as just reform may only be replacing one unjust arrangement with another if he fails to worry about the interaction of job placement and reward principles.[18]

NOTES

1. Cf. Michael Young, *Rise of the Meritocracy* (London: Thames and Hudson, 1958). I am not concerned with certain classical meritocracies, that is, with certain views of aristocracy according to which social class was thought to be constitutive of differences in merit and positions were conferred accordingly. Perhaps such meritocracies are just as much concerned with "productivity" as are modern meritocracies, only their social goals differ significantly.
2. Some meritocrats assume (cf. Richard Herrnstein, *IQ in the Meritocracy* [Boston: Atlantic, Little Brown, 1973]) that there is some one scale of capacity differences, usually taken to be IQ, which suffices to rank-order people for job eligibility across the whole spectrum of jobs. I do not think such a uniquely hierarchical view is presupposed by the meritocratic core principles I describe. For critical discussion of IQ as a basis for such a scale, see my "IQ, Heritability, and Human Nature," Proceedings PSA 1974 in *Boston Studies in the Philosophy of Science* XXXII (Dordrecht: Reidel, 1976), pp. 143–180; see also J. Cronin, N. Daniels et al., "Race, Class & Intelli-

gence," *International Journal of Mental Health*, vol. 3, no. 4 (1975), pp. 46–132; see also N. J. Block and G. Dworkin, *The IQ Controversy* (New York: Pantheon, 1976), and S. Bowles and H. Gintis, *Schooling in Capitalist America* (New York: Basic, 1976).

3. Strictly speaking, we do not know there is only one array that is most productive. Instead, we should assume there are a number of equally "most productive" arrays (technically, an "equivalence class" of maximally productive arrays). The Productivity Principle tells us to select any one from among those "most productive" arrays, though for the sake of simplicity of expression, I ignore this complication in the text.

4. John Troyer urged me to consider the implications of this case.

5. Yet another alternative, which I am not concerned to refute here, is that personal traits or achievements other than those related to job competency should be the basis for desert or merit claims for job placement.

6. One possibility is the view that such desert claims derive from a purported "right to self-fulfillment": Jill has a right to be maximally self-fulfilled and exercising her best abilities in a suitable job is necessary for such self-fulfillment. It is worth noting, however, the lack of any uniform connection between a person's sense of fulfillment and the exercise of his best abilities. I may be more fulfilled not doing what I am best at, even more fulfilled than someone better at doing the same job. Further discussion of self-fulfillment, or other ways of trying to rescue and found a stronger notion of desert, would take me too far afield.

7. My argument above does not take into account the role of expectations in actual situations. One could argue (cf. Alan Goldman, "Affirmative Action," *Philosophy and Public Affairs*, vol. 5, no. 2 [Winter, 1976], p. 191) that people who claim a right to a given job on the basis of their better qualifications are doing so because they have been led to form specific expectations about how society distributes social goods, like desirable positions. When institutions standardly lead to certain expectations, and indeed are expected to lead people to form them, and then society "changes the rules of the game," then some sort of compact or contract may be violated. But such an argument from expectations can become woefully conservative if it turns out that the principles governing those institutions and the expectations they generate are not acceptable principles of justice.

   Two further objections are worth noting. First, suppose that Rawlsian contractors would agree (as I think they implicitly do) to adopt meritocratic job placement principles and would do so on the basis of productivity considerations. Then the productivity principle would give rise to entitlements even though it is based on such considerations. I have no quarrel with this objection provided the contractors lexically order the Productivity Principle *below* appropriate compensatory and retributive principles that may specify more important entitlement claims to jobs. Second, it might be argued that certain recipients of services or products, say students or patients, have a right to the highest quality service or product possible. This right might then correlate with a social duty to give the job to the most competent applicant. This duty then gives rise to entitlement claims by the most competent. If such an objection can be supported by a sound argument, it might well force important qualification of the Productivity Principle, perhaps even driving us to use the micro principle instead.

8. John Rawls, *A Theory of Justice*, Harvard, 1971, p. 84.

9. Thomas Nagel makes a related point when he says,

   Certain abilities may be relevant to filling a job from the point of view of efficiency, but not from the point of view of justice, because they provide no indication that one deserves the rewards that go with holding that job. The qualities, experience, and attainments that make success in a certain position likely do not in themselves merit the rewards that happen to attach to occupancy of that position in a competitive economy.

   Cf. "Equal Treatment and Compensatory Discrimination," *Philosophy and Public Affairs*, vol. 2, no. 4 (Summer 1973), p. 352.

10. See note 2.

11. Three further objections might be raised here. John Troyer has suggested the first one: Why would someone who rejects productivity considerations in his reward schedule, adopting instead a strong desert-based reward schedule, subscribe to the Productivity Principle? The answer is, I think, that people might consistently want to know that their rewards will be based on, say, moral worthiness or industriousness and still believe that access to jobs should be determined by merit, as earlier defined, because it is important to secure proper job performance. A second objection is that not all the principles of reward I have described can be readily construed as governing a society's basic institutions or structure, as Rawls would have it. This objection has weight to it, but how much depends on how clear the notion of "basic structure" is. For worries about the clarity of the notion of structure, see Hugo Adam Bedau's "Social Justice and Social Institutions," *Midwest Studies in Philosophy*, vol. III (February 1978).
    Finally, my analysis of meritocracy seems to allow too many types of theories in under that name. For example, Rawls explicitly argues that his Second Principle does not lead to a Young-type meritocracy because natural abilities are viewed as social, not just individual assets, and inequalities act to help the worst-off members of the society. But my saddling Rawls with the label "meritocrat" does not, on my schema, imply he is committed to any of the undesirable features of the meritocracy he attacked. At the same time, the label captures the fact that he shares with other meritocrats certain common principles.
12. R. Nozick, *Anarchy, State and Utopia* (New York: Basic, 1974), p. 214.
13. Rawls, *Theory*, pp. 73–74.
14. Rawls argues, however, that under conditions of fair equality of opportunity there will be a "tendency to equality" since talents will be more plentiful. Therefore, people will not be able to demand high levels of "incentives" (high transfer income and economic rent) before they would take certain jobs. Cf. Section 18.
15. Rawls, *Theory*, pp. 101–102.
16. Robert Nozick discusses this point in *Anarchy, State, and Utopia*, p. 215.
17. Nozick reconstructs four possible arguments Rawls might have intended. Argument (C) is the one closest to what Rawls might have meant. But Rawls would agree only to a weaker premise (1) than the one Nozick attributes to him. Nozick's argument (G) couched in terms of entitlements rather than deserts, also fails to counter Rawls since its crucial premises (2) and (3) beg the question about whether we are entitled to whatever "flows from" our natural assets.
18. This paper grew out of remarks I made as commentator on Alan Soble's "Meritocracy and Rawls' Second Principle" presented at the Western Division APA Meetings, New Orleans, April 1976. I have benefited from discussion with Hugo Bedau and from comments by John Troyer as well as from critical discussion following presentations of versions of this paper at Brown, Calgary, Tufts, and the Pacific Division APA Meetings. A different version of this paper appears in *Philosophy and Public Affairs*, vol. 7, no. 2 (Spring 1978).

David Schweickart

Capitalism, Contribution, and Sacrifice

Capitalists are widely thought to deserve their wealth because the profits they receive reflect their contribution to production. This contribution might be understood, David Schweickart suggests, in three different ways: as the marginal product of capital, as the entrepreneurial activity of the capitalist, or as the capitalist's willingness to wait (that is, to postpone gratification). He examines each of these and argues that none of them justifies property income because each fails to identify some morally relevant way in which capitalists can be seen as contributing to production.

CAPITALIST CONTRIBUTION AS THE MARGINAL PRODUCT OF CAPITAL

John Bates Clark was an early exponent of the claim that capitalist distribution accords with the ethical standard of productive contribution, that capitalism is just because it returns to each individual the value he produces. "The indictment that hangs over society," he writes, "is that of 'exploited labor'." But the charge, he avows, is false, for it can be shown that "the natural effect of competition is . . . to give to each producer the amount of wealth that he specifically brings into existence."[1] Friedrich von Hayek agrees. He sees the fundamental issue to be "whether it is desirable that people should enjoy advantages in proportion to the benefits which their fellows derive from their activity or whether the distribution of advantages should be based on other men's views of their merit." The first alternative, he insists, is that of a free (capitalist) society.[2] Nozick takes exception to Hayek, citing "inheritance, gifts for arbitrary reasons and charity" as countervailing considerations, but he concurs that "distribution according to benefit *is* a major patterned strand in a free capitalist society."[3]

But is it? That is what we will investigate in this and the next section of this chapter. Specifically, we wish to inquire whether property income—income derived from the ownership of means of production—can be legitimized by the canon that "justice consists in the treatment of people according to their actual productive contribution to their group."[4]

According to Milton Friedman and virtually all other neoclassical economists, the essential principle of capitalist distribution is "to each according to what he and the instruments he owns produces."[5] Since it is characteristic of capitalism that those who own means of production are often distinct from those who operate them, this claim presupposes that one can quantitatively distinguish the contribution of the instrument from that of the operator. Marx provided one answer. The value of the instrument is simply passed on to the final product, while new value is created by living labor. If a $100 machine produces 1000 items during its normal lifetime, it contributes ten cents to the value of each item. And since the machine itself is the product of labor, even that ten cents is ultimately traceable to labor. This answer is unacceptable to the neoclassical tradition, which much prefers Clark's alternative.

The modern, textbook version of Clark's solution begins with a concept, adds a couple of definitions, and then adroitly invokes a mathematical theorem (a simple theorem, but perhaps the most ideologically significant in history). The basic concept is that of a *production function*, a technical function that specifies for a given technology the maximum productive output for each and every combination of relevant technical inputs. Suppose, for example, that corn is the joint product of labor and land, each unit of everything being homogeneous in quality. The production function can be represented as $z = P(x, y)$, where z is the maximum number of bushels of corn that can be produced by x laborers working y acres of land using the prevailing technology. Now the question is, what are the distinct contributions of labor and land?

The key to the answer is the notion of *marginal product*. The marginal product of a particular technical input is defined to be the extra output resulting from the addition of *one extra unit* of that input while holding all other inputs constant. For example, the marginal product of labor, given ten laborers and five acres of land, is the difference between what eleven and ten laborers would produce on those five acres. . . . The output of x laborers working y acres of land is equal to the sum of two quantities, the first being the marginal product of labor multiplied by the number of laborers, the second being the marginal product of land multiplied by the number of acres. That is what Euler's Theorem says, when given an economic interpretation. Thus if we *define* the contribution of each laborer to be the marginal product of labor (i.e., $P_x(x, y)$), and the contribution of each acre to be the marginal product of land (i.e., $P_y(x, y)$), then the total contribution of labor, $(P_x(x, y))x$, plus the total contribution of land, $(P_y(x, y))y$ is precisely equal to the total output, $P(x, y)$. We thus have a "natural" division of the total output into the contribution of labor and the contribution of land, computed from purely technical information. No reference has been made to private property, wage-labor, or the market.

Equipped with a systems-neutral definition of contribution, the neoclassical economist can now ask whether or not capitalism distributes its total output accordingly. The answer is a reassuring "not always." Adam Smith's distrust of monopoly is vindicated: monopolies distort distributon. However, in a state of "perfect competition," where uniform goods and services command uniform prices, and where no monopolistic collusions exist, the distribution resulting from each individual striving to maximize her own well-being will be precisely that proposed by Euler's Theorem. In a society of x equally skilled laborers and y acres of uniformly fertile land, the wage rate (per worker) will be $P_x(x, y)$ and the ground rent (per acre) will be $P_y(x, y)$. With sufficient assumptions, this can be rigorously demonstrated.[6]

These results are nontrivial—but what exactly has been proved? Has it been established that perfectly competitive capitalism distributes in accordance with the canon of contribution? Is it true that each person receives in proportion to what he produces? Clark himself has no doubts:

> If each productive factor is paid according to the amount of its product, then each man gets what he himself produces. If he works, he gets what he creates by working; if he also provides capital, he gets what his capital produces, and if further, he renders services by coordinating labor and capital, he gets the product that can be traced separately to that function. Only in one of these three ways can a man produce anything. If he receives all that he brings into existence through any of these three functions, he receives all that he creates at all.[7]

For Clark this conclusion has enormous ethical and political import:

> The welfare of the laboring class depends on whether they get much or little; but their attitude toward other classes—and therefore the stability of society—depends chiefly on the question whether the amount they get, be it large or small, is what they produce. If they create a small amount of wealth and get the whole of it, they may not seek to revolutionize society; but if it were to appear that they produce an ample amount and get only a part of it, many of them would become revolutionists and all would have the right to do so.[8]

In fact Clark has not shown that perfectly competitive capitalism distributes according to contribution, not if "contribution" is to be taken to mean what it means in the ethical canon. Clark has shown that there exists a partition of the total product which can be defined independently of the market mechanism, and that "well-behaved" capitalism distributes according to this partition. That is no mean accomplishment—but it remains to be argued that this notion of contribution is *ethically* appropriate.

To decide this question, let us consider Clark's analysis more closely. Why is a laborer said to receive exactly what he has produced? The neoclassical answer: if he ceases to work, the total product will decline by precisely the value of his wage. . . . Does it follow that if two workers quit together, the total output will decline by the sum of their wages? Not at all—the total product will decline by more than that. The wage *each* worker receives under conditions of perfect competition is the marginal product of the *last* laborer. Moreover, the neoclassical argument presumes a *declining* marginal productivity; that is, the marginal product of the tenth laborer is less than that of the ninth, that of the ninth less than that of the eighth, etc. This decline is not due to declining skills, since all laborers are presumed equally skilled, but to a diminishing-returns assumption. It is presumed that x + 1 laborers on a fixed piece of land (for x sufficiently large) will produce more than x laborers, but that the average production of each will be slightly less. . . .

Because of declining marginal productivity, the total contribution of labor is less than the total product; the difference is precisely the contribution of the land—and hence of the landowner.

What exactly is this latter contribution? Mathematically, it is the marginal product of the y'th acre of land multiplied by the number of acres. But what is its physical significance? It is not the quantity of corn that would have been produced on the land without any laborers, nor is it the amount that could have been produced had the landlords themselves tilled the soil. Nor does it bear any relation to that portion of the social product that must be saved for seed, or plowed back in to replenish fertility. In physical terms, the marginal product of the land is simply the amount by which production would decline if one acre were taken out of cultivation. It does not reflect any *productive activity* whatsoever on the part of the landowner. *It does not, therefore, reflect her productive contribution.*

Let me repeat this argument in a slightly different form, to highlight how the neoclassical terminology obscures the important issue. Clark claims that a person can create wealth in one of three ways: by working, by providing capital, and by coordinating labor and capital. If we regard "coordinating labor and capital" as a managerial activity directly related to the productive process, then both working and coordinating labor and capital are productive activities in a perfectly straightforward sense: should laborers and managers cease their mental and physical work, the production of wealth would likewise cease. The economy would grind to a halt.

"Providing capital," however, is something quite different. In Clark's perfectly competitive world, technology is fixed and risks are nonexistent. "Providing capital" means nothing more than "allowing it to be used." But the act of granting permission can scarcely be considered a productive activity. If laborers ceased to labor, production would cease in any society. But if owners ceased to grant permission, production would cease *only if* their ownership claims were enforced. If they ceased to grant permission because their *authority* over the means of production was no longer recognized, then production need not be affected at all. (If the government nationalized the means of production and charged workers a use-tax, we wouldn't say, would we, that the government was being rewarded for productive activity?) But if providing capital is not a productive activity (at least not within a static neoclassical model), then income derived from this function can hardly be justified as being proportional to one's productive contribution to the group. . . .

In fairness to contemporary neoclassical economists, it should be noted that not many who think seriously about such things accept the ethical dimension of Clark's analysis. H. G. Johnson is typical in this respect:

The positive theory that factors derive their incomes from their contributions to the productive process should be sharply distinguished from the question of whether the owners of the factors are ethically entitled to own them, or whether their returns would be different if ownership or preferences were different.[9]

Johnson thus distances himself from Clark's ethical claim—but *not*, it should be noted, for reasons I have put forth. To the contrary, Johnson's remark implicitly rejects my argument; it is not so neutral as it might appear. It well represents, in fact, the tendency of neoclassical analysis to mislead ethical thought.

Johnson states, contrary to my assertion, that providing capital *is* a productive activity. He doesn't say that exactly; what he does say is incoherent: "Factors derive their incomes from their contributions." But "factors," e.g., land, labor and capital, do not receive income; owners of factors do. So the statement must mean "owners of factors derive their incomes from their contributions to the productive process." The *ethical* issue, therefore, must be (for Johnson) whether owners are entitled to their productive contributions. In other words, the neoclassical formulation, "factors derive income from productive contributions," shifts one's ethical attention to the ethical canon itself—should one receive according to contribution?— and away from an examination of the nature of that peculiar "productive activity" of providing capital. . . .

At the risk of repetition, let me summarize my discontent with neoclassicism. The problem in justifying capitalist distribution is not the suitability or nonsuitability of the ethical canon of contribution, a problem economists are content to leave to philosophers and politicians. The problem with a contribution defense is the notion that providing capital is a productive activity. It is this issue that the neoclassical model obscures. For in conceiving of output as the joint product of "productive factors," and in defining the respective "contributions" of each in such a way as to yield a "natural" division of the product into these respective contributions, what could seem more natural than to call the contribution of the factor the contribution of the owner—particularly when it is precisely that "contribution" which the free market returns to each owner? And if each owner "contributes" to the final product, what could seem more natural than to regard her as engaging in productive activity? What could be more natural?—and yet a sleight of-hand (no doubt unwittingly) has been performed. For when the "contribution" of the factor is shifted to the owner, a technically-defined, ethically-neutral concept suddenly takes on an ethical dimension, since "contribution" when applied to human beings normally has such a dimension. If I contribute to a collective project, don't I deserve a share of the reward? If I engage in a productive activity, don't I deserve a share of the product? If words were being used in their ordinary sense, we would say yes to both these questions. Only when we look closely at the neoclassical definition of contribution do we realize that when this sense is employed, the answer to the first question is "Not necessarily" and to the second—when asked by a landowner or capitalist—"But you haven't!"

The marginal product definition of contribution is thus not only inadequate to the task of showing that capitalist distribution accords with the ethical canon of contribution; it is highly misleading in any ethical context. It provides a criterion for judging the assertion, " 'X' percent of the product was the contribution of labor; 'Y' percent, of capital, and so on," but it does so at the cost of severing the "contribution" of a factor owner from anything but a legal relation to the factor itself. In a technologically-fixed, perfectly-competitive world capitalists qua capitalists take no risks, do not innovate, do not sacrifice, do not engage in anything that could be called a productive activity. The abstraction from individual activity that allows one to define the contribution of a factor in a precise mathematical manner also removes from consideration any reason one might give for claiming that the "contribution" of the factor is, in any ethically relevant sense, the contribution of the owner. If one is to defend capitalism, one must either redefine "capitalist contribution" or abandon the contribution canon as its justification. However mathematically elegant marginal product theory may be, it fails as the basis for an ethical argument.

CAPITALIST CONTRIBUTION AS ENTREPRENEURIAL ACTIVITY

The marginalist definition of contribution fails to agree with ordinary ethical usage because it abstracts completely from all characteristic activities of property owners. An alternative definition is suggested by Joseph Schumpeter's well-known critique of the neoclassical, static-equilibrium model we have just considered:

> The essential point to grasp is that in dealing with capitalism we are dealing with an evolutionary process. It may seem strange that anyone can fail to see so obvious a fact which moreover was long ago emphasized by Karl Marx. Yet that fragmentary analysis which yields the bulk of our propositions about the functioning of modern capitalism persistently neglects it. . . .
> The fundamental impulse that sets and keeps the capitalist engine in motion comes from new consumer goods, the new markets, the new forms of industrial organization that capitalist enterprise creates.[10]

If it is true as Schumpeter and Marx propose, that the fundamental feature of capitalism is its dynamism, then it would seem more appropriate in determining the respective contribution of laborers and capitalists to compare society at different points in time than to assume a given production function (with a fixed technology) at a given point in time. Insofar as a particular increase in output *over time* can be attributed to the activities of a capitalist, perhaps we can define his contribution to be that increase. A simple model illustrates this definition. Suppose a capitalist-landowner employs ten people to grow corn. Working in the usual fashion these workers could produce, let us say, 1500 bushels of corn. But suppose our capitalist-landowner reorganizes production, innovates, with the result that his workers can now produce 2000 bushels. The extra 500 bushels, by our new definition, is the capitalist's contribution. . . .

This concept of contribution seems both unambiguous and straightforwardly ethical. The contribution of the capitalist is linked to a specific productive activity, namely, innovation. But a complication arises if we continue our analysis into the second year. The process just described can now repeat itself with one important difference: no *new* innovation is necessary for a two thousand bushel harvest. The blueprint for the plow, the reorganization scheme, in short, the technology, is now in existence. Suppose the laborers work the second year as they did in the first, and another two thousand bushel harvest is recorded. *Who*, we must ask, contributed this two thousand bushels? In a sense the capitalist has contributed five hundred, since the increase, measured from the original basepoint, is five hundred and is due to his innovation. But if we take the basepoint to be the preceding year, then there has been no increase, a conclusion consistent with our assumption that the capitalist introduced no *new* innovation. Which sense of capitalist contribution do we intend when we define it to be the increase in production which can be attributed to his activities?

The second sense surely cannot be intended, for it depends on a completely arbitrary specification of a time interval. To measure the increase from the preceding year might seem natural in the case of corn, which has an annual growing season, but it seems hardly so natural in the case of steel production or shoe-making. We might just as well specify two years or ten, or six months or six weeks. There is no "natural" time interval beyond which the contribution ceases to be that of the capitalist and becomes that of his workers. (The lifetime of the innovator might seem tempting, particularly to advocates of confiscatory inheritance taxes, but that won't do. It would violate our language to define the quantitative contribution of an innovation in terms of the longevity of the innovator. If Edison had lived ten years longer in an advanced state of senility, we cannot say, can we, that his contribution would have been greater?)

On the other hand, if we do not specify a limit, we have a definition of contribution which entails that certain contributions are perpetual while others are only transitory. The capitalist and his laborers both expend mental and physical energy during the first year, and each makes a "contribution." However, the contribution of the capitalist continues into the next year and into the next. If he innovates anew, he will be entitled (by the canon of contribution) to the increase brought on by his new innovation as well, but his original contribution never ceases. The contribution of a laborer, by contrast, ends with his labor. . . .

In all capitalist societies there are institutions that reward an individual irrespective of her present activity. An accumulation of money, however acquired, may be invested as an individual sees fit. She may put it in a savings account, or buy government or corporate bonds, and collect interest indefinitely. He may purchase stocks and receive annual dividends.

Such income is quite independent of any original innovation (if there was any) to which the original accumulation is traceable. Of course the reward is not eternal as a matter of logical necessity; we live after all in a contingent world. But the reward is not tied either legally or in practice to the continued performance of any productive activity. As John Kenneth Galbraith observes:

> No grant of feudal privilege has ever equalled, for effortless return, that of the grandparent who bought and endowed his descendants with a thousand shares of General Motors or General Electric. The beneficiaries of this foresight have become and remain rich by no exercise or intelligence beyond the decision to do nothing, embracing as it did the decision not to sell.[11]

. . . It is tempting to say that the capitalist *supplies the money*; she *provides the capital*. This is certainly her distinctive "service" qua capitalist. But we are back to the problem encountered in the neoclassical argument. And our conclusion is the same. *Providing capital is no more a productive activity in a dynamic setting than in a static one.*

Let us dwell on this point, for it is as significant to our culture as it is counterintuitive. Objections scream to be heard. Isn't capital vital to growth? Isn't supplying it a productive endeavor nonpareil? Do not all countries, especially underdeveloped ones, strain mightily to acquire capital? Do they not offer investment incentives and tax credits to attract it? Such policies are not irrational, are they?

. . . What is "capital"? Marx says it is a social relation, but few contemporary economists think in such terms. Capital, for most, is one of two things—or rather both at once: physical things (equipment and material) and money for investment. Now of course capital, as existing material means of production, is crucial to production. Without means of production, nothing can be produced. But "providing" this sort of capital—an existing material thing—is simply "allowing it to be used," the *non*-productive activity analyzed in the last section.

Capital as investment funds would seem to be another matter. Investment funds generate growth, do they not? Isn't that an axiom of economic theory? Let us think for a moment. Consider a person with a chest full of cash, eager to invest. How he acquired it need not concern us. We want to understand how his disposal of it will increase production. To produce something there must be brought together equipment, raw materials and laborers. Let our investor loan his money to an entrepreneur who purchases these necessaries. The laborers are set to work with the machinery on the raw materials, and soon goods are produced. It is all quite simple.

But notice, this case is also a matter of granting permission. The workers, raw material, and machinery already exist. The workers might have begun production themselves (perhaps at the instigation of an enterprising comrade)—except that property rights intervened. "Providing capital" is simply a means by which certain property rights are transferred from one set of owners to another, the latter then granting permission that things be used.

But what if the machinery were not already in existence? Suppose our entrepreneur used her borrowed capital to place an order. Wouldn't that bring a machine into being? Yes—but she (or the workers) could have placed that order without borrowing money. In either case human beings exist who could produce the desired machine. Would they do so? With borrowed money the entrepreneur can pay them in advance, or on delivery. But if the machinist to whom our entrepreneur advances a sum can buy food with it, then that food already exists. So the farmer, say, *could* advance that food. And the things the farmer would buy already exist, so they could be advanced. The farmers, machinists, and laborers (including entrepreneurial laborers) are all necessary for production and for growth—but not people to "provide capital." (We are not concerned here with questions of motivation and incentive. How best to motivate people to interact in socially desirable ways is a matter for comparative analysis; that will come later. Here I am simply arguing that a class of people who "provide capital" are not necessary for production.)

Two arguments are sometimes better than one. Let us look at the matter from another angle. Suppose, instead of relying on our friend with the chest full of money, the government simply rolled its presses to produce the same quantity of crisp bills, and *gave* them to our entrepreneur. Exactly the same production would result. But would we want to call the printing of money a productive activity? That might be very dangerous usage, tempting officials to believe that rolling the presses longer and longer would miraculously generate wealth. It is equally dangerous—at least to clear thinking about the ethical issues—to speak of providing capital as a productive activity. . . .

Questions concerning efficiency, innovativeness or risk are totally irrelevant to our present concern, namely, whether capitalism can be ethically justified on the grounds that individuals receive in proportion to their productive contribution to society. Such a justification requires that we identify a productive activity engaged in exclusively by capitalists that merits not merely a reward but a perpetual reward. This we have not been able to do. Innovative activity seemed the best candidate, but this "entrepreneurial" definition has not survived analysis. The only distinctive activity of a capitalist is providing capital, and that, I have argued, is not productive at all.

The neoclassical definition of contribution considered in the first section fails for lack of ethical content; the entrepreneurial definition of this section fails not for that reason but because the class of entrepreneurs is not at all coextensive with the class of capitalists. Such a coexistence might once have been (roughly) the case, but it is not so today. Nor is there anything in the structure of capitalism to keep the classes from diverging. Indeed, the capitalist entrepreneur as Schumpeter himself observes, declines in functional importance as capitalism develops. . . .

INTEREST AS A REWARD FOR WAITING

The basic problem in trying to justify capitalism by an appeal to contribution is the impossibility of identifying an activity (or set of activities) engaged in by all and only capitalists which can be called (preserving the ethical connotations of the word) "contribution." It is true that some capitalists innovate, reorganize, manage, but it is also true that many do not. This fact (if not its ethical implications) is readily acknowledged by most economists; it is reflected, for example, in their distinction between interest and profit. Interest (in the neoclassical camp) is the return to capital, the reward for owning a productive asset. Profit is the residual accruing to the entrepreneur after wage, rental, and interest bills have been paid; it is his reward for risk and innovative achievement. Samuelson's definition exemplifies this distinction:

> The market rate of interest is that percentage of return per year which has to be paid on any safe loan of money, which has to be yielded on any safe bond or other security, and which has to be earned on the value of any capital asset (such as a machine, a hotel building, a patent right) in any competitive market where there are no risks or where all the risk factors have already been taken care of by special premium payments to protect against any risks.[12]

The basic problem in justifying capitalism is precisely this element: interest, a return that requires neither risk nor entrepreneurial activity on the part of the recipient. If interest cannot be justified by productive contribution, what can be its justification? Alfred Marshall, the enormously influential British pre-Keynesian, responds with an alternative neoclassical answer: interest is the *reward for waiting*. Like Clark, Marshall confronts the Marxian critique:

> It is not true that the spinning of yarn in a factory, after allowance has been made for the wear and tear of the machinery, is the product of the labor of the operatives. It is the product of their labor, together with that of the employer and subordinate managers, and of the capital employed; and that capital itself is the product of labor and waiting. If we admit it is the product of labor alone, and not of labor and waiting, we can no doubt be compelled by an inexorable logic to admit that there is no justification of interest, the reward of waiting; for the conclusion is implied in the premises. . . .
>   To put the same thing in other words, if it be true that the postponement of gratification involves *in general* a sacrifice on the part of him who postpones, just as additional effort does on the part of him who labors, and if it be true that this postponement enables man to use methods of production of which the first cost is great but by which the aggregate of enjoyment is increased, as certainly as it could be by an increase of labor, then it cannot be true that the value of the thing depends simply on the amount of labor spent on it. Every attempt to establish this premise has necessarily assumed implicitly that the service performed by capital is a

'free good,' rendered without sacrifice, and therefore needing no interest as a reward for its continuance.[13]

. . . Marshall has introduced a new element into the neoclassical story; his appeal is not to productive contribution, but to *sacrifice*. A different ethical canon has been invoked. . . .

Any demonstration that capitalist distribution accords with the ethical canon of sacrifice must involve three steps: first, a specification of the nature of each person's sacrifice; second, an identification of some standard for quantitative interpersonal comparisons; third, a demonstration that capitalism (in general) distributes according to the sacrifice so defined. (A complete argument would also require a justification of the canon itself and a proof that the defined sacrifice is appropriate to the canon, but these steps will not concern us. The argument fails before it gets that far.)

The first step seems straightforward enough, at least in the case of workers. All sacrifice their leisure; many also undergo mental and physical discomfort. As for capitalists, Marshall answers that they *wait*, i.e., they postpone gratification; when a person has to choose between consuming at once and deferring consumption, she normally finds it painful to postpone gratification, and this pain is not fully compensated by later consumption of an equal amount.

The second step of the argument involves comparison. Marshall asserts that the sacrifice of deferred consumption leads to an increase in the aggregate enjoyment, an increase which could have also been effected by additional labor. Now of course we cannot *define* the quantity of postponement-sacrifice to be the quantity of increase, for that would reduce a seeming appeal to sacrifice to a disguised (and confused) appeal to contribution. On the other hand, if it could be shown to be an *empirical fact* that (in general) the pain and discomfort of deferred gratification is proportional to the increase effected by that sacrifice, then the argument would be in much better shape. We would have, in fact, an ethically relevant link (such as we were unable to discover in the appeals to contribution) between the owner of a productive asset and the asset's effect on production.

It is precisely this link that Marshall attempts to forge. His method is to bring the neoclassical categories to bear on *interest rates*. These rates, according to Marshall, are determined by the "money market," which brings entrepreneurs in search of capital face to face with households tempted to save. The market is in equilibrium when interest rates are such as to call forth exactly as much savings as entrepreneurs are desirous of borrowing. If the market is in equilibrium at 6 percent say, this indicates that savers require a 6 percent premium as a reward for deferred gratification, while at the same time entrepreneurs expect to be able to increase productivity enough with the money they borrow to pay this premium and still have sufficient excess to reward themselves for risk and entrepreneurial skills. Thus the connection between pain and productivity.

Common sense suggests that something is amiss here. Analysis reveals some difficulties. Even if we assume the general validity of the neoclassical account of interest-rate formation, the argument does not show that capitalism rewards in accordance with sacrifice. In fact the neoclassical account *demonstrates* that it does not. The 6 percent premium is not what the average saver or savers "in general" require as an inducement to save; it is what the *most reluctant* saver requires, the saver at the margin. It is the premium required to entice the last few dollars from the last few households to bring total savings into line with total investments. Unless it were the case that nobody would save without a 6 percent compensation (scarcely a plausible assumption nor one compatible with the neoclassical worldview), some people would have saved at 4 percent though presumably fewer, some at 2 percent, etc. These people, according to the neoclassical tale, have evaluated their pain of deferred gratification at less than 6 percent, and so are being *over*-compensated by the market. Indeed, for some it is extremely convenient that there are social institutions that will pay for the use of accumulated wealth. Beyond a certain point personal consumption might prove difficult and alternative arrangements expensive (storage facilities and guards would need to be employed). One's "pain of abstinence" in such cases might well be negative; one would pay *not* to consume. One's "pain," that is, is pleasure. Now plainly a system which rewards pleasure—or which rewards generally in excess of a saver's pain—cannot be justified by the canon of sacrifice.

An alternative, more straightforward critique of Marshall's argument is to deny that his paradigm applies to reality. The plausibility of Marshall's analysis, with its "in general" clause, rests on the assumption that the typical saving unit is a small or medium income household; for such a household "waiting" might plausibly involve pain comparable to a laborer's discomfort. But in contemporary capitalist societies such households are not the typical savers; the bulk of the interest payments do not go to them. As Simon Kuznets has noted, "according to all recent studies, only the upper income groups save; the total savings of groups below the top decile are fairly close to zero."[14]

But if the significant savers are not the small or medium income households but the wealthy, then the plausibility of comparing the "sacrifice" of postponement with the sacrifice of labor evaporates. . . .

Of course, if a society wishes to *increase* its stock of capital goods, it may have to postpone some gratification. If we assume full employment of people and resources (which we must, since we are assuming maximal production), then a capital-goods increase requires a shifting of a part of the workforce (and/or machinery and raw materials) from the consumer-goods sector to the capital-goods sector. This shift will allow the "aggregate enjoyment" to be increased at a later date, as the increased output of capital goods makes its way to the consumer-goods sector, but in the meantime actual consumption must be cut back from what is technically possible. Society must "wait," but its waiting will pay a social dividend. This is the valid core of Marshall's doctrine.

It is significant—and surprising—to notice that this concept of waiting has nothing whatsoever to do with saving—not if by "saving" we mean the setting aside a portion of the total output. Many societies (and individuals) save in this sense. Grain reserves are maintained; cans of tomatoes are stored in the basement. . . . Saving in this sense has no connection with bringing means of production into being—or rather, it has a negative effect: the more the workforce must produce emergency reserves, the less it can produce means of production *or* goods for current consumption.

Now of course in *some* societies a different sort of saving occurs. Not things are saved but money. And the money is not stashed in a mattress but put in a bank—which then loans it out again. It is *this* sort of saving Nozick and the neoclassicals have in mind when they see "saving" as "bringing means of production into being." Again, the formulation is unfortunate, for it suggests that the act of saving (or is it the non-act of not consuming?) is some sort of universal, wealth-creating, productive activity. It is not. I have already argued that "providing capital" is not a productive activity. . . . When an individual (in a market society) saves his money rather than spends it, his "act" of deferment reduces aggregate demand. A signal is sent (in the form of unsold consumer goods) for the market to contract. He "votes" for less production. If that money is placed in a bank, and if an investor then borrows it, and if she then spends it, a counter-signal is given. Since the investor's expenditures are likely to be (at least in part) for capital goods, the net effect of the two signals is to shift workers from the consumer-goods sector of the economy to the capital-goods sector. Thus a societal decision to "wait" is registered.

There are various complications that could be added to the above scenario, but we will not pursue them here. The important point to be made is that the institutional arrangements which allow investment funds to be generated by private monetary savings are better regarded as part of the global *decision-making* apparatus of society than as part of its *productive* apparatus. The act of saving is no more an act of production than purchasing a commodity or voting to increase governmental spending. The complex institutional arrangements covered by the concept "saving" are but one set among many for arriving at decisions regarding deferment of social consumption and a rechanneling of workers. Workers can be ordered or enticed, by investors, voters, or authoritarian figures, from one sector of the economy to another. Investment funds can be generated by private savings, by taxation, or by printing presses. Which of these (or other) methods is optimal is a matter we will consider in detail later. . . . We must avoid simplistic assumptions about the causal links between saving, societal deferment of consumption, and the production of capital goods.

NOTES

1. John Bates Clark, *The Distribution of Wealth* (New York: Kelley and Millman, 1956), pp. 4–5. (This work was originally published in 1899.)
2. Friedrich A. Hayek, *The Constitution of Liberty* (London: Routledge and Kegan Paul, 1960). p. 94.
3. Nozick, *Anarchy, State, and Utopia*, p. 158.

4. Nicholas Rescher, *Distributive Justice* (Indianapolis: Bobbs-Merrill, 1966), p. 78. This canon is called variously the canon of "productivity," "social contribution," "productive contribution," or simply "contribution."

5. Milton Friedman, *Capitalism and Freedom* (Chicago: University of Chicago Press, 1962), p. 161. This is the *essential* principle. Contemporary neoclassical distribution theory has added many refinements that need not concern us here.

6. Cf. Jan Pen, *Income Distribution: Facts, Theories, Policies* (New York: Praeger, 1971), pp. 76–87. Essentially the argument is this: wages will be at least as high as the marginal product of the last laborer, for if they were lower, each landowner would try to entice laborers away from his neighbors; wages will not be any higher than that, for that would involve paying the last person more than he yields.

7. Clark, *Distribution of Wealth*, p. 7.

8. Ibid., p.4.

9. Harry G. Johnson, *The Theory of Income Distribution* (London: Gray-Mills, 1973), p. 37.

10. Joseph Schumpeter, *Capitalism, Socialism and Democracy* (New York: Harper Torchbooks, 1962), p. 83. Schumpeter himself does not advance the ethical argument we are about to consider. Like so many of his colleagues, he eschews ethics for "science." He is, however, the foremost exponent of the view that the entrepreneur is the cornerstone of capitalism, the view associated with the ethical argument of this section.

11. John Kenneth Galbraith, *The New Industrial State* (Boston: Houghton Mifflin, 1967), p. 394.

12. Paul Samuelson, *Economics*, 9th ed. (New York: McGraw-Hill, 1973), p. 599.

13. Alfred Marshall, *Principles of Economics*, 8th ed. (New York: Macmillan, 1948), p. 587.

14. Simon Kuznets, *Economic Growth and Structure* (New York: W. W. Norton, 1965), p. 263.

PROPERTY
AND THE MARKET

The "Market" refers to the exchange of products, to the buying and selling of goods, between individual persons or enterprises. The market is the spiritual center of any laissez-faire economic system, since there is no overall social planning. Where the market is free, individual initiative and decision shape the content of production and the distribution of economic goods. Commerce is unregulated, and individuals exchange as they please without any government assistance or restriction. Libertarians, as we have seen, defend the pure capitalism of the laissez-faire model as an answer to the problem of distributive justice. This contention is the focus of the contributors to this section.

Defenders of the free market from Adam Smith to Milton Friedman have always pointed to the productive efficiency of capitalism. Not only does it have record accomplishments to its credit, they argue, but if it were really given full rein—if the market were truly unfettered by government restrictions—then its productive fruits would be even more bountiful. True, wealth is not distributed equally, but to a large extent this only reflects individual differences in taste, ambition, and perseverance. Moreover, not only do free-market initiative and enterprise produce abundance, but wealth will spread to all: Profits are available to encourage the wealthy to invest in enterprises that are efficient and productive, thus benefiting the less well-off. Leaving the economic realm to the free choices of individuals provides incentive to innovation, development, and (thus) progress while still protecting liberty. All people are free to work on what or for whom they wish. Free enterprise also serves the demands of consumers more responsively and flexibly than can any rival system. Customers get what they want, and this economic democracy is matched by the general freedom promoted by a laissez-faire system.

The economic systems in the United States and other Western countries, as the defenders of laissez faire are first to point out, are a far cry from this free market ideal. The government actively intervenes in the marketplace: A minimum wage is set, individuals and companies are taxed, the interest rate is decreed, union monopolies are supported, profits are monitored, and corporate activities from hiring to marketing are policed and regulated. By a variety of economic devices like tax policy, the state attempts to direct economic growth, as well as to set its pace. Such efforts may be motivated in part by the political philosophy of contemporary liberalism, which has as an ideal ensuring equality of opportunity and the material well-being of the citizenry. But equally important, government interference in the marketplace results from a critique of laissez-faire economic theory that won wide-spread support in the 1930s. Recently, however, there has been renewed debate over the efficiency of the market and the impact of governmental attempts to regulate it. In the first essay of this section, Allen Buchanan surveys the range of arguments for and against the notion that free markets are efficient.

As seen earlier in this book, a second defense of an unregulated market system comes today from libertarians who defend it, not necessarily as the most efficient vehicle for human happiness, but rather as a matter of principle. Robert Nozick's statement of this case, in particular, has engendered extensive controversy. In response to his arguments, philosophers have been forced to reconsider assumptions many of them had taken for granted and to examine even more carefully the concept of rights, the nature of property, and the dynamics and moral implications of a market system. The remaining essays of this section reflect this reexamination.

In "Rights and the Market" Peter Singer attacks the libertarian view of rights as too narrow and argues that the market is not neutral but can, in fact, violate people's rights. He maintains that any plausible theory of rights must permit some social and economic planning. Libertarians, of course, see such planning as an unjust interference with individual liberty. In "Robert Nozick and Wilt Chamberlain: How Patterns Preserve Liberty," G. A. Cohen defends socialism against this criticism. Socialism, Cohen contends, can be seen as an effort to expand the freedom of the majority, which capitalism now erodes.

The final essay of this section connects the discussion of rights, property, and the market to the issue of third-world starvation and global justice. In "Global Justice, Capitalism, and the Third World," Kai Nielsen focuses on the economic dynamics that have often set the stage for famine in the Third World. He maintains that justice calls for a global economic redistribution.

Allen Buchanan

Efficiency Arguments For and Against the Market

Libertarians defend the free market because, they claim, it respects people's rights to acquire and transfer what they legitimately own. Other advocates of the market claim that market-oriented economies produce and distribute goods more efficiently than centralizied economies. Critics of the market, however, contend that reliance on markets can have a range of untoward consequences including overproduction of goods at the expense of leisure, high unemployment, and failure to provide public goods. In the following essay Allen Buchanan assesses these claims.

EFFICIENCY ARGUMENTS *FOR* THE MARKET

The Ideal Market   The case for the market on grounds of efficiency rests on two main claims: (1) a theoretical statement that exchanges in the ideal market reach an equilibrium state that is Pareto Optimal* . . . , and (2) the assumption that actual (nonideal) markets, or feasible modifications of actual markets, sufficiently approximate the efficiency of the ideal market to make them preferable to nonmarket arrangements. We must begin, then, with a description of the conditions that define the ideal market and that ensure that exchanges result in a Pareto Optimal equilibrium state.

1. Full information is available about the performance and quality of goods and services and the costs of all alternative ways of producing them, and the cost of this information is zero.
2. Costs of enforcing contracts and property rights are zero, and property rights, including rights to the means of production, are established and stable.
3. Individuals are rational in this sense: their preferences are organized in a transitive ordering (such that if an individual prefers A to B and B to C, he also prefers A to C) and they are capable of selecting appropriate means toward their ends.
4. (a) Transaction costs are zero (transaction costs include costs of bringing goods and services together for exchange, and costs of reaching agreements for exchange, for example, costs of formulating mutually acceptable

From Allen Buchanan, "Efficiency Arguments For and Against the Market," in *Ethics, Efficiency, and the Market*, Rowan and Allanheld, 1985.

*Pareto optimality refers to situations in which nobody can be made better-off without making somebody else worse-off.—Eds.

contracts, and costs of information about potential offers to buy and sell) *or* (b) there is perfect competition (that is, no buyer or seller can influence prices by his own independent actions and there is complete freedom to enter and exit the market) and no externalities are present. (An externality is a "neighborhood" or "third-party" effect of a market exchange: an effect on some one's well-being which is not taken into account in the market exchange. Those neighborhood effects which are beneficial are called external economies or positive externalities; those which are detrimental are called external diseconomies or negative externalities. An example of a positive externality is the pleasant view I enjoy of my neighbor's flower garden. The exchange between my neighbor and his landscaper took into account only the costs and benefits to the parties to the exchange, not the benefits to me. An example of a negative externality is a chemical producer's discharge of noxious gases into the air: the cost of breathing bad air is not taken into account in the bargain that is struck between the chemical producer and the customer who buys his product.)

5. Products offered in the market are undifferentiated—buyers cannot distinguish between the products offered by various sellers, and vice versa.

Pareto Optimal outcomes are guaranteed only if all of these conditions are satisfied. When they are satisfied, production and exchanges will occur until an equilibrium state is reached which is such that no one could be made better off without someone being made worse off.[1]

Since the immensely strong conditions that define the ideal market are never met in actual markets, the case for the market on grounds of efficiency depends on the extent to which actual markets do approximate or can be modified to approximate, the ideal market.

The Diachronic Efficiencies of the Market The preceding way of understanding the efficiency of the ideal market, by focusing only on the exchange of existing goods and services, overlooks what may be called the diachronic efficiencies of the market. The latter are efficiencies that result from competition over time. Competition among producers reduces costs of production, since producers who fail to develop and utilize less-costly methods of production are replaced by those who do. Competition among entrepreneurs reduces transaction costs, because the entrepreneur who can match buyers with sellers with the least expenditure of his own resources can charge less for his services and capture a larger share of the market. Finally, the need for information on the part of producers, consumers, and entrepreneurs creates a market for information. In each of these respects, competition in nonideal markets generates incentives for behavior that tends toward the more perfect satisfaction of the conditions of the ideal market, in particular, zero transaction costs, full information, and zero information costs.

Some celebrants of the market, especially F. A. Hayek, have emphasized not only that competition in nonideal markets tends toward more perfect fulfillment of the conditions of the ideal market by efficiently producing and distributing new information, but also that there is a more basic sense in which markets utilize information efficiently.[2] In the market enormous amounts of complex information are utilized in the emergence and adjustments of prices over time, and yet it is not necessary that all of this information, or even a minuscule fraction of it, be possessed by any individual or group for the system to tend toward efficient outcomes. The market thus enables individuals and groups to economize on information.

Hayek's point can best be appreciated if we contrast the information requirements of decentralized allocations production and distribution in the market with the information requirements of attempts to organize a large-scale economy through centralized planning without the aid of markets. Consider, for the purposes of simplicity, only the amount and complexity of information that would have to be gathered and successfully integrated in order to make even a rather limited decision to allocate social resources among alternative lines of production. In order to make a reasonable choice among different proposals for allocating resources across existing and possible lines of production, the individual planner (or planning group) must be able to estimate reliably the costs of producing X amount of good G, relative to Y amount of good H, and so forth for all of the types of goods under consideration. To make such estimates it is necessary for the individual (or group) to integrate a staggering amount of information concerning the least-costly method of production for each producing unit (for example, each physical plant) in each line of production (for example, manufacturing vehicles for public transportation). And even if all of this information were available to each planner and even if each planner were able to integrate it successfully in a cost schedule for all of the goods under consideration at any given time, constant revision would be necessary, since the least-costly method of production for any existing or possible product can change with developments in technology, organizational techniques, and discoveries or depletions of minerals and other raw materials.

All of this, however, is a vast simplification. So far we have proceeded as if information about costs of production were not dependent upon information about individuals' preferences. If the planner's selection of an allocation proposal is to take into account the preferences of the individuals for whom the goods are being produced, he must know what those preferences are—which goods each individual wants, in what amounts, and at what cost in foregone opportunities for enjoying other goods or other goods in larger quantities that might have been produced. The problem of information is profoundly exacerbated once the diachronic dimension is recognized: individual preferences change over time.

In comparison, the information required of participants in the market is minimal. The information a successful consumer or producer or entrepreneur must possess is quite narrow. For example, a producer of tables needs to know if he can expect to sell a certain number of tables at a certain price; he need not know how many tables the economy as a whole should produce, or what the ratio should be of tables relative to automobiles. The same competitive forces that give rise to specialization in the production of goods and sevices also produce specialization in the gathering and using of information. Or, perhaps more accurately, specialization in the gathering and utilization of information is just one aspect of specialization in economic roles in the market. In the case of the entrepreneur this is most obvious, since there is a sense in which information (about possible matches between buyers and sellers) is his only business. But in every case exchangers in the market are specialists in limited, concrete information of various sorts.[3] The market, then, can be viewed as a device for efficiently coordinating the actions of many individuals through specialization in the gathering and use of information.

So far we have contrasted the information requirements of the ideal market and economic planning only from a *cognitive* standpoint, but the case for the market on grounds of efficiency in gathering and utilizing information is strengthened if we also focus on the *motivational* aspects of that process. Those who argue for the market on grounds of informational efficiency can contend not only that their system makes more realistic demands on the individual's cognitive abilities, but also that it makes more realistic demands on individual motivation. The same simple motivational assumptions that explain the tendency toward efficient exchanges in general also explain why it is that the individual will be sufficiently motivated to gather, integrate and apply the limited information he needs. Since the individual will bear the costs of failing to gather and utilize needed information, each has an incentive to be well-informed. Those who reject the argument for the market on grounds of informational efficiency must show not only that planners would have the cognitive ability to gather, integrate and apply vast amounts of complex, constantly changing information; they must also provide a theory of motivation to show that the individuals in question would have sufficient incentives to do what they are cognitively equipped to do.

The Productive Efficiency of the Market   Finally, proponents of the market tout its productive efficiency: it enables a society to maximize overall outputs relative to initial overall inputs. While exchange in the ideal market ensures that an economic pie of a given size will be distributed in a Pareto Optimal fashion, competition—by placing resources in the hands of producers who most closely approximate the least-costly methods of production—increases the size of the economic pie.

Some of the earliest advocates of the market, such as Adam Smith and Bernard Mandeville, suggest that the general argument for the market on grounds of productive efficiency can be applied to the particular case of what they regard as a scarce productive resource: altruistic behavior. Their point is that the market does not rely upon altruistic behavior in satisfying human needs and preferences and that in this sense it economizes on the "expenditure" of altruism. There are several assumptions behind this argument. One is that the scarcity of altruistic behavior is a fact about human nature, or as Hume put it, that men are generally only capable of "limited altruism" directed toward a small circle of family and friends. If in fact the sentiment of altruism is by nature severely limited, and tends to lose its practical effectiveness as we attempt to extend it to more distant individuals, then a system that organizes large numbers of individuals without depending upon altruism will not only avoid futile attempts to rely upon altruism to do what it cannot do; it will also "free up" our limited resources of altruism for their proper function: the effective expression of concern for those with whom we are most closely associated. In this sense, then, the market system uses altruism more efficiently than alternative systems, just as attaching a button with a thread is a more efficient use of that thread than attempting to use it to hoist a boulder.[4]

Critics of the market, whether they be romantic conservatives who pine for the alleged altruism of premarket communities or Marxian socialists who predict a widening of altruism in postcapitalist society, challenge this empirical assumption. They argue that the limited altruism which Hume and Smith took for an unalterable feature of the human condition is in fact a transient characteristic of human beings in market society. They conclude that the fact that the market system does not require lavish expenditures of the scarce resource of altruism is hardly an argument for the market system if it produced the "shortage" of altruism in the first place.

EFFICIENCY ARGUMENTS *AGAINST* THE MARKET: MAJOR SOURCES OF INEFFICIENCY

The most obvious challenges to the market on grounds of efficiency are attempts to show that actual market processes fail to satisfy important conditions of the ideal market. Inefficiencies result from (a) high transaction costs, (b) lack of information on the part of producers and consumers, (c) monopolistic tendencies, (d) the presence of externalities, (e) the existence of barriers to successful voluntary collective action to secure certain goods which the market cannot provide (public goods), (f) lack of congruence between the satisfaction of the individual's preferences as they are revealed in the market and the individual's well-being, and (g) unemployment.

High Transaction Costs Actual markets tend toward Pareto Optimal outcomes only to the extent that transaction costs approximate the zero transaction costs of the ideal market. But transaction costs are never zero in the real world. Buyers and sellers must struggle with various logistical problems, including those involving transportation and communication costs. Strategic behavior (for example, bluffing with lower offers than one is prepared to pay or threatening to withdraw from the bargaining process) are also transaction costs. Further, if the total costs of the legal system as far as it is involved with the drafting, interpretation, and enforcement of contracts is included, transaction costs are enormous. The most that can be said in defense of actual markets here is that competition tends to reduce transaction costs.

Lack of Information A host of psychological, institutional, and technological factors ensure that producers and consumers in actual markets lack information required for Pareto Optimal outcomes. Producers must proceed on the basis of often highly speculative predictions of changing consumer preferences, and even experienced firms may overproduce or underproduce. Producers also often lack information about the methods of production employed by rival firms, either because producers with less-costly methods deliberately keep this information secret, or because it is restricted by patents, or because it is too costly to obtain, or because it is simply overlooked. (The primary information-gathering task is the gathering of information about what sort of information to look for and where to look for it.) Similarly, consumers may lack relevant information about the existence of alternative products or about the quality or performance of products.

Lack of consumer information about medical care is often cited as an example of ignorance as a barrier to efficient outcomes in the market. Defenders of the market reply that consumer ignorance here is largely a result of lack of competition among producers because of licensure laws which limit competition by restricting entry into the market and because of laws and professional codes of ethics which prohibit or discourage advertising. It is extremely difficult, however, to determine to what extent the removal of these sorts of barriers to competition would in fact remedy the deficiency of consumer information, since the technical character of some information may itself be an obstacle to consumers.

While the defender of the market relies upon advertising, broadly construed, and competition to ameliorate deficiencies of information, the critic of the market counters by pointing out that successful advertising often consists at least in part of nonrational appeals which either misrepresent, or omit altogether, relevant information. Further, attempts to ameliorate this problem by monitoring advertising in order to enforce prohibitions against misrepresentation may be extremely costly and relatively ineffective. And even in cases in which there is no misrepresentation, advertising may stimulate demand without conveying information which the individual himself, upon considered judgment, would agree is relevant to the making of a reasonable choice, granted his own stable preferences.

Monopolistic Tendencies Monopolistic tendencies exist when some exchanger can unilaterally influence prices. We have already seen several circumstances which make this possible: restrictions on entry into markets due to licensure, prohibitions against advertising, and trade secrets. Monopolistic tendencies may also result, of course, from government support (as in the case of legal prohibitions against the delivery of first-class mail by anyone other than the U.S. Post Office) or from collusion among firms to fix prices or drive out competitors or by some combination of government support and collusion. In principle, at least, so-called natural monopolies can arise and persist without government support if some firms happen to enjoy unique access to certain raw materials or if economies of scale make it difficult for new firms to survive long enough to amass sufficient capital to produce competitively.

There is, however, considerable dispute as to whether "natural" and collusive monopolies pose a serious threat to efficiency in the absence of government support. It can be argued that both "natural" and collusive monopolies are inherently unstable and tend to break down eventually through competition. Advocates of the market often infer, then, that government-supported monopoly is the only serious threat to efficiency in the long run. They then go on to draw the *additional* conclusion that monopolistic inefficiencies are not a serious objection to the market because they arise only when the market is not allowed to operate freely. This last conclusion, however, is a gross non sequitur. Even if monopolies would vanish or be of little consequence if they were not supported by government, it would follow that the presence of monopolies is not a serious objection to the market on grounds of efficiency *only if* there were good reason to believe that government support for monopolies can *in fact* be eliminated. It would be an error of excessive rationalism to assume that once it is recognized that monopolies reduce overall efficiency, firms and government officials will cease the practice of government support for monopolies. . . .

   Externalities   Critics of the market have been quick to point out the pervasiveness and seriousness of neighborhood effects, or externalities, as a key source of the market's failure to achieve efficient outcomes. Perhaps the most commonly cited contemporary example is the external costs that are imposed on people who breathe air polluted by chemical producers. Such negative externalities can be viewed as inefficiencies of *over-production.* More of the chemical is produced than would be produced if the total costs of production, including the costs to breathers of polluted air, were taken into account in establishing the equilibrium price for the product. Because the cost to the producer of producing the chemical is less than it would be if the costs to third parties were included in his costs, the producer can sell the chemical at a lower price and still make a profit. But since more will be sold at this lower price, more will be produced than would be if the total costs, including detrimental third-party effects, were taken into account.

   Positive externalities (beneficial third-party effects) are also inefficient. Standard examples include the beneficial effects of education and vaccination. It is argued that private exchanges for educational services, at least the more basic ones, generate beneficial effects for those not involved in the exchange. (An educated citizenry is valuable to society at large, not simply to those who purchase educational services or to those who are paid to provide them.) Similarly, if some individuals purchase vaccinations, others who do not will benefit from this exchange because the probability of contracting the disease in question will decrease for everyone, including those who are not vaccinated. Positive externalities, then, can be viewed as inefficiencies of *underproduction:* if the benefits of something can be had without purchasing it, then less of it will be produced (if any of it is produced at all) than would be produced if all the benefits flowing from it were obtainable only through purchase.

Failure to Provide Public Goods Anticipation of positive external-ities can result in the failure to provide *public goods.*[5] There are five fea-tures of public goods which together can result in a failure to provide the good: (a) Action by some or all members of the group is necessary and sufficient to provide the good, but action by one or a few members is not sufficient. (b) The good, if provided, will be available to all, including noncontributors (jointness of supply). (c) There is no way or no practical way to prevent noncontributors from partaking of the good (nonexcluda-bility). (d) The individual's contribution is a cost to that individual. In the case of a *pure* public good, there is an additional feature: (e) One individ-ual's consumption of the good does not diminish the supply of it available to others.

Two related problems can prevent the provision of a good when conditions a–d are satisfied. One, the *free-rider problem* occurs when some or all individuals attempt to take a free ride on the presumed contribu-tions of others to the provision of the good in question. The individual, if rational, will conclude that either enough others will contribute to achieve the good, in which case his contribution (which is a cost to him) would be wasted; or not enough others will contribute to achieve the good, in which case his contribution (which is a cost to him) would again be wasted. Since the individual's contribution is a cost to him, he will, if rational, conclude that regardless of whether or not others contribute, he should not contrib-ute. But if all or a sufficient number of individuals reason thusly, the good will not be provided.

The second barrier to successful collective action is the *assurance problem.* An individual who is willing to contribute if assured that others will contribute, does not intend to take a free ride on the efforts of others. Nevertheless, if he has reason to believe that others will not contribute (perhaps because *they* will attempt to be free-riders), he may decide not to contribute.

Attempts to use strictly voluntary agreements to eliminate either negative externalities, as in the case of chemical pollution, or positive externalities, as in the case of public goods such as national defense or the benefits of having an educated citizenry or of vaccination, can be blocked by the free-rider and assurance problems. For example, if several polluting chemical firms make a purely voluntary, unenforced agreement to limit or eliminate the discharge of air-borne pollutants, each firm will have an incentive for noncompliance: they may not comply, either in order to take a free ride on the compliance of others, or because of lack of assurance that others will comply, or both. While either the free-rider or assurance problems may by itself be sufficient to block collective action, competition ensures that the free-rider problem will be the dominant difficulty. A firm which complies only on the condition of assurance that others will do so will at least avoid being placed at a competitive disadvantage relative to others. But even if a particular firm has assurance that all others will comply it would gain a competitive advantage over others by taking a free ride and not complying. Similarly, a purely voluntary, unenforced agreement to contribute to the provision of national defense or to participate in a vaccination program may also break down either because some attempt to take a free ride and reap an external benefit from the "exchange" among those who do comply or because they are unwilling to comply unless they are assured that others will keep their part of the bargain of exchanging compliance for compliance.

Government may intervene in the market in several ways to attempt to eliminate externalities or to overcome public goods problems.

1. Government officials may attempt to persuade parties who are producing negative externalities such as pollution, to comply voluntarily with an announced program or to conform voluntarily to an announced standard. Such efforts, however, are vulnerable to the assurance and free-rider problems and are unlikely to succeed.

2. Government may simply prohibit the behavior that produces the negative externality (for example, outlaw the manufacture of the polluting substance). This alternative may itself be inefficient if there is no pollution-free way to produce the product and if the product is highly valued.

3. Government may allow the activity that produces the negative externality to continue, but tax the producer either in order to reduce the volume of production by increasing production costs or in order to use the tax-proceeds to compensate those who suffer the ill effects of the activity, or both.

4. Government may set and enforce standards which those engaged in the activity must meet (for example, clean air standards for industrial smoke-stacks).

5. Government may enforce a legal system which allows affected third parties (either individually or in class-actions) to sue for compensation for costs imposed on them by the actions of others.[6]

6. Government may enforce voluntary agreements among individuals or groups.

7. Government may create and enforce private property rights in order to "internalize" externalities or "privatize" public goods—that is, to transform a public good into a collection of privately consumable goods for which the free-rider problem does not arise. For example, if the free-rider problem vitiates voluntary agreements to avoid overgrazing of communal pastures or open range or to limit fur-trapping or lumbering in national forests, government may create private property rights to the resources in question.[7] At least in the case of such replenishable natural resources, private ownership provides individuals with incentives to conserve which are not present in situations in which resources are unowned or communally owned. In many cases, however, externalities cannot be internalized and public goods cannot be privatized because private property rights in the item in question are not feasible. For example, the problem of preventing acid rain (an externality) or of obtaining clean air (a public good) cannot be solved in this way because private property rights in the planet's atmosphere are not feasible.

8. Government itself may become the provider of a public good which the market fails to provide because of the assurance or free-rider problems. Perhaps the most commonly cited example is government provision of city parks, the idea being that since noncontributors could benefit from these pleasant environments they would probably not come about through voluntary contribution schemes or through private market exchanges.

The inability of the market to eliminate externalities and to provide public goods is a serious and pervasive departure from efficiency. However, if this is to serve as a sufficient reason either for attempting to abandon the market altogether or for restricting its scope by government intervention or by supplementing it with government provision of goods and services, additional premises are needed. First, it must be shown that government intervention, government provision of goods and services, or some other alternative to the market, will itself be less costly—that is, will not involve equally great or greater inefficiences than the market.

This crucial assessment becomes more difficult to support once it is understood that governmental intervention may itself produce externalities, and that limiting government intervention may itself be a public good, subject to the free-rider and assurance problems. Government regulation—especially because it is devised and administered by fallible human beings—may hinder innovation, contribute to inflation and unemployment by raising production costs, and endanger civil and political liberties by concentrating too much power in the government. Excessive generosity in the awarding of compensation to those adversely affected by externalities may also contribute to higher prices. Although each individual may recognize that the cumulative effects of singly salutory government interventions in the market may make us all worse off, the individual may nonetheless find it rational to refrain from exercising restraint when it comes to those particular interventions which promise to advance his own goals or those interventions which, considered in isolation, may benefit all. . . .

More radical critics of the market might protest at this point that the need to show that inefficiencies due to government intervention in the market would not equal or exceed the inefficiencies they are designed to eliminate is a serious problem only if one proposes to reform rather than *abolish* the market system. The problem of weighing these government inefficiencies does not arise for more fundamental proposals to replace the market with an alternative system. The fact that intervening in inefficient market processes may produce equally worrisome inefficiencies may be a sign that the whole system should be scrapped, not a vindication of a noninterventionist policy.

If this radical challenge to the market on grounds of efficiency is to have force, however, *the alternative system must be explained in sufficient detail to make efficiency comparisons between it and the market system possible.* The argument would then have to be that the alternative system would provide a closer approximation to the efficiency of the ideal market than the nonideal market system we now have or are likely to have through modifying the current system. . . .

Lack of Congruence Between Individual Well-being and the Satifaction of Preferences Revealed in the Market

[A]nother fundamental condition for efficiency in the ideal competitive market is the assumption that satisfying an individual's preferences, as the latter are revealed in his exchanges in the market, makes him better off. . . . This assumption can be understood either as resting on the claim that 'well-being' simply means satisfaction of revealed preferences or upon the empirical claim that in general the preferences an individual reveals in his market behavior are the most reliable indicator of what will in fact make him better off. As a meaning claim, the assumption must be rejected. It makes perfectly good sense to ask whether satisfying a particular preference in fact makes one better off. One reason why this is so is that, at least in the less than perfect conditions of actual markets, individuals can be and are mistaken about what is most conducive to their own good, either because they are less than perfectly knowledgeable or less than perfectly rational, or both. The empirical version of the assumption is more plausible but far from uncontroversial.

Perhaps the most potentially serious criticism of the empirical version of the assumption and hence of the efficiency argument for the market which relies upon it, is the Marxist objection that the market process itself tends to generate "distorted" preferences whose satisfaction does not promote the individual's well-being.[8] Hence even if the market does a good job of satisfying the preferences people express in it, outcomes will not be efficient according to that formulation of the Pareto Optimality Principle which focuses on well-being.

Here I will consider only one especially serious attempt to fill out this Marxist objection. G.A. Cohen has argued that advanced capitalism produces a lack of congruence between well-being and the satisfaction of preferences expressed in the market because it has a tendency toward expanding output and consumption at the expense of reducing toil.[9] Like Marx, Cohen acknowledges that capitalism greatly increases productivity— that the ratio of outputs to inputs is much greater in capitalism than in premarket modes of production, such as feudalism. Increased productivity provides an opportunity either to reduce toil (roughly unwanted labor activity), while maintaining the same level of output; or to expand output, without reducing toil; or to strike some balance between reduced toil and expanded output.

However, Cohen argues, the same competitive self-interest that results in greater productivity produces a bias toward continual expansion of outputs and toward encouraging (through advertising) continually increasing consumption of what is produced. Now at some point, increased freedom from toil (that is, leisure) is rationally preferable to increased consumption. Advanced capitalism is irrational (or, as an economist would say, inefficient) because it has an inherent tendency to push output and consumption past the optimal trade-off point between leisure and toil.

This argument, however, is far from convincing. First of all, at most it establishes that advanced capitalism has a *tendency* toward irrationality. It does not rule out the possibility that this tendency will be held in check by opposing tendencies.[10] Two obvious opposing tendencies are competition for labor and labor union activity. Labor unions can and do fight for shorter working hours and more pleasant work environments. And, if firms must compete for labor, one way to attract employees is to offer less toilsome work, either by shortening working hours or by making work more intrinsically rewarding. Further, even if firms do not advertise directly for increased leisure . . . nonetheless, advertisements for leisure products and services may indirectly encourage people to increase leisure time if only by leading them to reflect upon whether their current patterns of consumption permit them to take advantage of desirable leisure products and services. For example, if I see an advertisement for golf clubs or for fishing rods which persuasively portrays the pleasures of outdoor sports, I may be prompted to reconsider my decision to take a higher-paying but more time-consuming job which would not permit me to engage in these recreational activities.

Furthermore, it can be argued that even if advanced capitalism has a tendency toward inefficient trade-offs between leisure and toil, this tendency is not unique to capitalism. There is considerable empirical evidence to suggest that Soviet planners continue to expand output at the expense of individual well-being in order to support a massive military establishment both at home and in client countries and in order to compete in a "growth race" with the United States and other nonsocialist countries such as West Germany. . . .

There is, however, a more fundamental incompleteness in the Marxist objection. That objection assumes that well-being is a function of at least two factors, leisure and consumption of goods and services, and then argues that the market system tends to increase consumption at the expense of leisure. Yet even if it can be shown that this tendency will not be checked in capitalism, the result is a telling argument against the market system *only if there is a feasible alternative system which is also highly productive*. In other words, demonstrating that a nonmarket system would not tend to increase toil beyond the optimal leisure/toil trade-off point is not sufficient to establish the superiority of that system unless that system can be shown at least to approach the productivity of the market system. For if the alternative is sufficiently unproductive, the market system may be preferable, on grounds of efficiency, even if the market system fails to achieve the optimal leisure/toil trade-off. . . .

Unemployment Critics of the market are quick to point out that the foregoing list of sources of inefficiency is incomplete because it fails to acknowledge the problem of unemployment. Unemployment, . . . is an instance of aggregative inefficiency—a failure to utilize all available productive resources, in this case labor power.

The simple economic models used to show that the ideal market system will reach a Pareto Optimal equilibrium state disguise the problem insofar as they *assume* full employment. In other words, when it is demonstrated that production and exchange in the ideal market result in a Pareto Optimal equilibrium it is assumed that everyone whose welfare is taken into account in the statement that "no one can be made better off without making someone worse off" is actually participating as an exchanger and/or producer in the system.

There are two ways to understand the charge that unemployment is a serious inefficiency of the market system. The less radical, but nonetheless important interpretation is that even if the ideal market system would reach an equilibrium in which there is full employment (of all who wish to work), imperfect, real world market systems suffer from grave inefficiencies due to unemployment. The second, more radical interpretation of the charge is that even in the ideal market system there is no guarantee that there will be full employment at equilibrium. . . .

On the second, more radical interpretation, the objection is that even in a perfectly competitive market the equilibrium state need not be a state of full employment. So even if departures from perfect competition just mentioned could be eliminated, unemployment might still exist.

The mere possibility that a perfectly competitive market equilibrium could coexist with unemployment is not, of course, a telling objection. However, once the reasons for concluding that this possibility exists are understood, the objection can be stated much more strongly as the charge that *there is no reason to believe that full employment will be achieved at equilibrium*, even in a perfectly competitive market.

The radical version of the unemployment objection can best be understood as a criticism of the traditional neoclassical economists' argument to show that even if unemployment did occur at some point, a perfectly competitive system would automatically move to a full-employment equilibrium state, without any need for government intervention. The neoclassical argument, in its simplest form, is as follows. Suppose that at present there is some unemployment. If there is free competition for jobs, then (since the supply of labor relative to the demand for it is high), the price of labor, that is, wages, will decrease. As wages decrease, production costs decrease. In attempting to maximize profits, firms act so as to make the marginal cost of their products (the cost of producing one additional unit of the product) equal to the price of the product. In order to equalize marginal costs and price, firms expand production. But expanding production requires hiring more workers. Therefore unemployment is reduced.

Marx and other early critics of capitalism pointed out a problem which this argument overlooks: the problem of *decreasing aggregate demand*, that is, the total demand for what is produced in the economy. Firms will not expand production if they notice that the additional output is not being bought by consumers. But if wages are sufficiently low and if a large enough portion of the consuming public pays for its consumption through wages, then aggregate demand will be insufficient, expansion of production will not occur, additional workers will not be hired, and unemployment will persist.

The neoclassicists had a reply which seemed to rule out the possibility that expansion would be blocked by deficient aggregate demand. Relying upon the work of the eighteenth-century economist J. B. Say, they noted that since at market equilibrium every good produced generates an equivalent value of income, a shortfall of aggregate demand could not exist at equilibrium. So far as unemployment results from insufficient aggregate demand, then, the market system, if left to function freely, would eventually eliminate unemployment.

This last argument contains a hidden assumption which was challenged by John Maynard Keynes in *The General Theory of Employment, Interest, and Money*. Keynes argued that even if every good produced generates income of equivalent value, the proportion of income saved relative to the proportion invested may vary. But continued expansion of production (and hence the reduction of unemployment) depends upon the proportion of income devoted to investment. Unless enough of the income from what is produced is "plowed back" into production, not enough expansion will occur to overcome the problem of insufficient aggregate demand and unemployment will continue to exist. Keynes concluded that there is no reason to believe that precisely the correct relationship between savings and investment will be achieved at equilibrium to ensure full employment. His proposed *solution* to the problem of unemployment (which should be carefully distinguished from his critique of the neoclassical view) is government intervention in the form of fiscal and monetary policies to stimulate aggregate demand. Though Keynes was concerned with the problem of unemployment in real world market systems, it is important to emphasize that his criticism of the neoclassical argument for full-employment market equilibrium does not depend upon the assumption that real world market systems are not perfectly competitive. . . .

NOTES

1. Any standard microeconomic textbook provides an explanation of why the general equilibrium of production and exchange in the ideal market is Pareto Optimal. The usual, and perhaps the most illuminating method of explanation employs a graphic representation which combines the Edgeworth Box and indifference curves. . . .
2. F. A. Hayek, *The Constitution of Liberty*, pp. 54–70; Hayek, *Individualism and the Economic Order*, pp. 119–208.
3. J. Gray, "F. A. Hayek and the Rebirth of Classical Liberalism," p. 32.
4. B. Mandeville, *Fable of the Bees: Or Private Vices, Public Benefits;* and A. Smith, *The Wealth of Nations*, p. 14.
5. For three of the most influential treatments of the problem of providing public goods, see J. M. Buchanan, *The Demand and Supply of Public Goods*; G. Hardin, "The Tragedy of the Commons," *Science* (December 13, 1968); and M. Olson, *The Logic of Collective Action*.
6. A clear presentation of economic analyses of principles of compensation is found in J. G. Murphy and J. L. Coleman, *The Philosophy of Law: An Introduction to Jurisprudence*, chapter 5. See also M. Kuperberg and C. Beitz, eds., *Law, Economics, and Philosophy: A Critical Introduction with Application to the Law of Torts*.
7. H. Demsetz, "Toward a Theory of Property Rights," pp. 347–59.
8. A. E. Buchanan, *Marx and Justice: The Radical Critique of Liberalism*, pp. 21–35. The author develops an account of the role of the concept of distorted desires in Marx's historical materialist theory of consciousness and in his evaluation of capitalism.
9. G. A. Cohen, "Labor, Leisure, and a Distinctive Contradiction of Advanced Capitalism," in G. Dworkin, G. Bermant, and P. G. Brown, eds., *Markets and Morals*, pp. 107–36.
10. *Morals and Markets*, p. 8.

Peter Singer
Rights and the Market

Peter Singer argues that libertarians hold too narrow a conception of rights: There are positive rights to recipience as well as the negative rights of noninterference favored by libertarians. Singer's main argument, though, is that the market is not a neutral, liberty-maximizing operator. His comparison of blood systems is intended to illustrate that markets can in some cases restrict the options available to individuals and even violate their rights. Further examples are adduced to show that what may be economically rational from the point of view of an individual in the market can be irrational from a collective point of view. Contrary to libertarians, Singer concludes that any plausible moral theory must allow for social and economic planning.

Introduction

How should goods and services be distributed? In theory there is a wide range of possible answers to this question: in accordance with need, utility, merit, effort, contribution to production, seniority, strict equality, competitive examinations, ancestry as determined by a free market, and so on. At some time each of these answers has been endorsed by some thinkers, and each has been put into practice as the basis of distribution of at least some goods and services in some societies. Within limited spheres, each is still used today. This use is often controversial. Should seniority be a ground for promotion, as it frequently is in areas of employment like teaching and the civil service? Should a person be able to inherit great wealth merely because he is the most direct living descendant of a miserly recluse who died without leaving a will? Should university places be allocated strictly in accordance with examination grades? Interesting as such issues are, they tend to be overshadowed by a more fundamental division of opinion: should distribution by and large be left to the workings of a free market, in which individuals trade voluntarily, or should society as a whole, through the agency of the government, seek to distribute goods and services in accordance with some criterion generally regarded as desirable? It is this issue which is at the center of the political division between right and left, and consequently is the subject of dispute between political parties, in most nations which have political parties, as well as between philosophers, who, like Robert Nozick, are clearly aligned with the free market advocates and those who, like John Rawls, support distribution in accordance with a favored criterion of justice.

This essay deals with only one aspect of this basic disagreement, though a central one. Those who favor leaving distribution to the market have used two distinct types of argument. One is utilitarian in character. It asserts that if we leave distribution to the market we shall end up with a better outcome than if we interfere with the market because the market will promote efficient methods of production and exchange, and hence will lead to more people getting what they want than any alternative means of distribution. I shall not discuss this type of argument here. It is obvious that, although difficult to test, the utilitarian argument rests on a factual claim and consequently would have to be given up if non-market modes of distribution could be shown to be compatible with as much or more efficiency in production and exchange as the market. This line of argument is not, therefore, a defense of the market in principle, but rather a defense of the market as a means to an end—the end of maximum satisfaction, or something similar.[1]

Nozick's View

The second line of argument is less vulnerable to empirical criticism, for it does not defend the market as a means to an end. Nozick's position is an extreme instance of this. He rejects altogether the idea that institutions—or actions, for that matter—are ultimately to be judged by the ends they promote. That an institution maximizes happiness and minimizes pain would not, in Nozick's view, be a sufficient reason for recommending the institution. If the institution violates rights, then he would consider the institution unjustifiable, no matter how great its superiority in producing happiness or alleviating pain may be. Nor would other goals, like the maximization of freedom, or even the minimization of violations of rights, suffice to justify an institution which violates rights. Nozick's system takes absolute (or virtually absolute) "side constraints" as primary, and hence is structurally distinct from any "maximizing" view.[2]

Nozick therefore defends distribution through the market on the grounds that this method does not violate rights, whereas alternatives such as government distribution in accordance with, say, need do. For, Nozick would say, market distribution is distribution in accordance with the voluntary decisions of individuals to buy or sell goods and services, while government distribution in accordance with need will, in practice, involve the government in taking resources from some individuals, usually by taxation, to give to others, irrespective of whether those from whom the resources are taken wish to give to those in need. Nozick sees the voluntary nature of each of the many individual exchanges which together make up the market system as proof that the market does not violate rights, and the coercion by the government of those from whom resources are taken as proof that government distribution does violate rights.

Empirical investigation of how the market distributes goods and services will not refute this second type of defense of the market. Nozick acknowledges that any distribution at all can result from the market. Some may trade shrewdly and make great fortunes; others may gamble recklessly and lose everything. Even if everyone worked equally hard and traded equally wisely, fortune would favor some and ruin others. So far as justice is concerned this is all, in Nozick's view, irrelevant: any distribution, no matter how unequal, is just, if it has arisen from an originally just position through transfers which do not violate rights. This defense of the market is a philosophical argument. So far as its application to the real world is concerned it might be met by arguing—as Marxists have frequently argued—that the "free market" is a figment of the imagination of bourgeois economists, that all actual markets fall under the dominant influence of a few monopolists, and so do not allow consumers or producers to choose freely after all. Let us take Nozick's argument on a more theoretical level, however, and consider what philosophical objections can be brought against it. One strong philosophical objection is to the moral stance on which it is based. I have elsewhere suggested that the grounds Nozick offers for rejecting utilitarianism are inadequate, and that the utilitarian theory of distribution is preferable to Nozick's own view.[3] But it is also worth considering if such defenses of the market can be shown to be unsatisfactory even within the terms of a moral theory which takes the prohibition of violations of rights as prior to the maximization of utility, and on the assumption that a free market would not be distorted by monopolistic practices.

The first point to be made is that it is only if we accept a very narrow conception of the nature of rights that the market has any chance at all of being shown to be necessarily superior to other systems of distribution in avoiding violations of rights. To see this, consider, for instance, the right to life. It is commonly said that we have a right to life that comprises, not merely a right not to be killed by attackers, but also a right to food if we are starving while others have plenty, and a right to a minimal level of medical care if the society in which we live can afford to provide it. If a society allows people to die from starvation when there is more than enough food to go around, or to die from diseases because they are too poor or too ignorant to obtain a simple and inexpensive injection, we would not consider that society to be one in which the right to life is greatly respected. The right to life, in other words, is widely seen as a right of *recipience*, as well as a right against interference.[4] Another important and frequently claimed right of recipience is the right to education. Clearly, if there are such rights, the market will not necessarily protect them; if it does protect them at a particular time in a particular society, it does so only accidentally, since the market is not structured to produce any particular distribution. A planned distribution, financed by taxation, on the other hand, could aim directly at protecting such rights, and could thereby protect them more effectively.

Nozick recognizes that his position requires a narrow interpretation of rights. With reference to someone who argues, as he himself does, that the state should not interfere in distribution, he says that the position

> will be a consistent one if his conception of rights holds that your being *forced* to contribute to another's welfare violates your rights, whereas someone else's not providing you with things you need greatly, including things essential to the protection of your rights, does not *itself* violate your rights.[5]

Oddly, while Nozick is aware of the importance of this conception of rights to his general position, he provides no argument for it. Instead, he appears to take it as a natural consequence of his starting point, which is Locke's state of nature. If we start, as Hobbes, and following him Locke, do, with independent individuals in a state of nature, we may be led naturally enough to a conception of rights in which so long as each leaves the other alone, no rights are violated. This line of reasoning seems to go: "If I do not make you any worse off than you would have been if I had never come into contact with you, then I do not violate your rights, for I might quite properly have maintained my independent existence if I had wished to do so." But why should we start with such an unhistorical, abstract, and ultimately inexplicable idea as an independent individual? It is now well known that our ancestors were social beings long before they were human beings, and could not have become human beings, with the abilities and capacities of human beings, had they not been social beings first.

Admittedly, Nozick does not present his picture of the state of nature as an historical account of how the state actually arose. He says: "We learn much by seeing how the state could have arisen, even if it didn't arise that way."[6] But if we know that, human nature being what it is, the state could *not* have arisen that way, maybe we don't learn so much. On the mistakenly individualistic aspect of Locke's view of society, however, enough has been said by others and there is no need for repetition here. It is surprising that Nozick should ignore this extensive literature and accept Locke's starting point without providing any reply to these damaging criticisms.[7]

If we reject the idea of independent individuals and start with people living together in a community, it is by no means obvious that rights must be restricted to rights against interference. When people live together, they may be born into, grow up with, and live in, a web of rights and obligations which include obligations to help others in need, and rights to be helped oneself when in need.[8] It is reasonable to suppose that such altruistic practices are the very foundation of our moral concepts.

It is also worth noting that Nozick's conception of rights cannot be supported by appeal to the only other ethical tradition on which Nozick draws, that of Kant. Nozick defends his ethic of 'side constraints' rather than goals as a reflection of "the underlying Kantian principle that individuals are ends and not merely means; they may not be sacrificed or used for the achieving of other ends without their consent."[9]

The Kantian principle to which Nozick refers, however, cannot bear the gloss Nozick places on it. Any undergraduate who has studied Kant's famous (notorious?) four examples of the application of the categorical imperative knows that Kant thinks we have an obligation to help others in distress. Elsewhere he describes charity as "an act of duty imposed upon us by the rights of others and the debt we owe to them." Only if "none of us drew to himself a greater share of the world's wealth than his neighbour" would this debt and the consequent rights and duties not exist.[10]

It can, indeed, well be argued that rational beings have rights of recipience precisely *because* they are ends in themselves, and that to refuse a starving person the food he needs to survive is to fail to treat him with the respect due to a being that is an end in itself. Nor does it follow from the fact that people are autonomous, in the Kantian sense in which autonomy of the will is opposed to heteronomy of the will, that it is always wrong to force a person to do what he does not do voluntarily.[11]

An Example: A Market in Blood

The distinction between "civil society" conceived as Locke and Nozick conceive it, as an association of fully-formed independent human beings, and the alternative conception of a community bound together by moral ties which affect the nature of the human beings who grow up in it, has been illustrated in a recent empirical study which is directly relevant to the choice between market and non-market modes of distributing goods: *The Gift Relationship* by R. M. Titmuss.[12] This work is worth examining in some detail, because it presents a rare opportunity to compare, not in theory but in the real world, the operation of market and non-market modes of distribution. Thereby it enables us to observe how rights and freedoms are affected by the two systems of distribution. We shall see that the question is a much more subtle and complex one than libertarian defenders of the market assume.

The good whose distribution Titmuss studied is blood. In Britain, human blood required for medical purposes is obtained by means far removed from the market. It is neither bought nor sold. It is given voluntarily, and without reward beyond a cup of tea and a biscuit. It is available to anyone who needs it without charge and without obligation. Donors gain no preference over non-donors; but since enough blood is available for all, they need no preference. Nor does the donor have any hope of a return favor from the recipient. Although the gift is in one way a very intimate one—the blood that now flows in the donor's veins will soon flow in those of the recipient—the donor will never know whom he or she has helped. It is a gift from one stranger to another. The system is as close to a perfect example of institutionalized generosity as can be imagined.

By contrast, in the United States, only about 7 percent of the blood obtained for medical purposes comes from similar voluntary donations. Around 40 percent is given to avoid having to pay for blood received, or to build up credit so that blood will be available without charge if needed. Approximately half of the blood and plasma obtained in America is bought and sold on a strictly commercial basis, like any other commodity.

Which of these contrasting systems of blood collection violates rights, and which does not? One obvious point is that if we accept that there is a right of recipience to a level of medical care consonant with the community's resources, then the British system provides for this right, while a pure market system would not. It is only the intervention of the state which can guarantee that everyone who needs blood will receive it. Under a market system those needing large quantities of blood have to be extremely wealthy to survive. Hemophiliacs, for example, may require treatment with large quantities of blood plasma twenty or thirty times a year. In the United States each such treatment costs around $2250. Not surprisingly, the private health insurance market considers hemophiliacs "bad risks" and will not insure them. In Britain hemophiliacs receive the blood they need free of charge.[13] If hemophiliacs have a right to life, which goes beyond the right not to be killed, the market cannot protect this right.

Titmuss's study also reveals some more subtle ways in which the market may violate rights, including rights which are not rights of recipience. It does this in two ways. First, it provides an example of how individual actions which appear harmless can contribute to the restriction of the freedom of others. Second, it shows that one cannot assume without a great deal of argument about the nature of rights, that the state acts neutrally when it allows people to trade without restriction. I shall take this second point first. Supporters of laissez faire overlook the extent to which one's conception of a "neutral" position is affected by one's view about what rights people have. If we ask: "Under which system does the individual have the right to choose whether to give or to sell his blood?" the answer must be that this right is recognized only when there is a commercial system as well as a voluntary one. This aspect of the situation is the basis of the claim made by many advocates of the market, that the market simply allows people to sell what is theirs if they so desire—providing they can find buyers—and thus grants a right to sell without in any way impairing the right of anyone else to give away his or her property if he or she prefers to do so.[14] Why, these supporters of the market ask, should we prohibit the selling of blood? Is it not a flagrant infringement of people's freedom to prevent them doing something which harms no one and is, literally, their own business?

This approach overlooks the fact that the existence of a market in goods or services changes the way in which these goods or services are perceived in the community. On the basis of statistical data, as well as the results of a questionnaire Titmuss carried out on blood donors in Britain, Titmuss has shown that the existence of a commercial system discourages voluntary donors.[15] This is not because those who would otherwise have made voluntary donations choose to sell their blood—donors and sellers come from, in the main, different sections of the population—but because the fact that blood is available as a commodity, to be bought and sold, affects the nature of the gift that is made when blood is given.

If blood is a commodity with a price, to give blood means merely to save someone money. Blood has a cash value of a certain number of dollars, and the importance of the gift will vary with the wealth of the recipient. If blood cannot be bought, however, the gift's value depends upon the need of the recipient. Often, it will be worth life itself. Under these circumstances blood becomes a very special kind of gift, and giving it means providing for strangers, without hope of reward, something they cannot buy and without which they may die. The gift relates strangers in a manner that is not possible when blood is a commodity.

This may sound like a philosopher's abstraction, far removed from the thoughts of ordinary people. On the contrary, it is an idea spontaneously expressed by British donors in response to Titmuss's questionnaire. As one woman, a machine operator, wrote in reply to the question why she first decided to become a blood donor:

> You can't get blood from supermarkets and chain stores. People themselves must come forward; sick people can't get out of bed to ask you for a pint to save their life, so I came forward in hopes to help somebody who needs blood.[16]

The implication of this answer, and others like it, is that even if the formal right to give blood can coexist with commercial blood banks, the respondent's action would have lost much of its significance to her, and the blood would probably not have been given at all. When blood is a commodity, and can be purchased if it is not given, altruism becomes unnecessary, and so loosens the bonds that can otherwise exist between strangers in a community. The existence of a market in blood does not threaten the formal right to give blood: but it does away with the right to give blood which cannot be bought, has no cash value, and must be given freely if it is to be obtained at all. If there is such a right, it is incompatible with the right to sell blood, and we cannot avoid violating one of these rights when we grant the other.

Is there really a right to give something that is outside the sphere of the market? Supporters of the market will no doubt deny the existence of any such right. They might argue against it on the grounds that any such right would be one that can be violated by two individuals trading, and trading seems to be a private act between consenting parties. (Compare Nozick's dictum: "The socialist society would have to forbid capitalist acts between consenting adults.") Acts which make commodities of things which were not previously commodities are not, however, purely private acts, for they have an impact on society as a whole,

If we do not now take the commercialization of a previously noncommercial process very seriously, it is because we have grown used to almost everything being commercialized. We are still, perhaps, vaguely uneasy when we see the few remaining non-commercial areas of our lives disappearing: when sport becomes a means of earning a living, instead of an activity entered into for its intrinsic qualities; when once-independent publishing houses, now swallowed by giant corporations, begin ruthlessly pruning the less profitable types of work from their lists; and when, as is now beginning to happen, a market develops in organs for transplantation.[17] But our unease is stilled by the belief that these developments are "inevitable" and that they bring gains as well as losses. The continuing commercialization of our lives is, however, no more inevitable than the American Supersonic Transport, and as Titmuss has convincingly shown in the case of blood, the alleged gains of commercialization are often illusory, and where not illusory, outweighed by the losses.[18]

Nozick's political theory itself represents the ultimate triumph of commercialization, for in his theory rights themselves become commodities with a price. Nozick often writes as if he holds that it is always wrong to violate someone's rights. In fact, however, he holds nothing of the kind: he holds that it is always wrong to violate someone's rights *unless* you compensate them for the violation. The distinction is crucial. If Nozick never allowed violations of rights with compensation, life in a world governed by his conception of rights would become impossible. One could not even move around without first obtaining the permission of the owners of the land one wished to cross—and one might well not be able to obtain this permission without moving on to the land first in order to locate the owner. Nozick recognizes the necessity of allowing violations of rights with compensation (Ch. 4, especially pp. 71–84) but he does not realize that implicit in allowing these violations is the assumption that rights have some monetary or at least barter value. For what can compensation be except money or the bartering of goods and services? But what if there is no monetary or other compensation that I am willing to accept in exchange for the violation of my rights? This is not an implausible assumption. Someone who has enough to feed and clothe himself may well prize solitude, quiet, or clean air above all compensation. So to violate rights, with an intention to compensate, may be an unconditional violation of rights—for in any given instance no adequate compensation may be possible. Hence Nozick's theory does not really protect rights at all. It can only be thought to do so if one assumes that every right has its price.

What must be borne in mind about the process of commercialization is that whether an act constitutes an interference in the lives of others cannot be decided independently of the nature of the society in which the act takes place, and the significance of existing social practices in the lives of the individuals who make up that society. Advocates of the market commonly claim, as Nozick does, that "the market is neutral between persons' desires" and merely "reflects and transmits widely scattered information via prices and coordinates persons' activities."[19] In fact, however, the market is not neutral. It affects the way in which goods and services are perceived, and it affects, as Titmuss has shown, how people act. If a prohibition on the buying and selling of a particular "commodity" interferes with those who wish to buy or sell it, the making of something into a commodity is also a form of interference with those for whom the fact that the good or service was not previously a commodity is significant. Whether we should recognize a right to buy and sell anything that is one's own, or whether, instead, we should recognize the conflicting rights of people to retain certain goods and services outside the influence of the commercial sphere is therefore not a question that can be decided by adhering to strictures about avoiding interference or remaining neutral between people's desires; it can properly be decided only if we take into consideration how recognition of these rights affects people, not only directly but also indirectly, through its effect on society as a whole.

These broader issues are entirely overlooked by most defenders of the market, who pay attention to the forms of freedom and ignore its substance. They regard every law extending the range of choices formally open to people as an increase in their freedom, and every law diminishing this range of choice as a decrease in their freedom; whether the choice is a real or attractive one is irrelevant. Nor is any consideration given to the long-range consequences of a large number of individual choices, each of which may be rational from the point of view of the interests of each individual at the time of making the choice, although the cumulative effects may be disastrous for everyone. Titmuss's study suggests that the decision to sell one's blood could be in this category.

Individual Rationality and Collective Irrationality

Other examples of this phenomenon of individual rationality and collective irrationality are now well known. If public transport is poor, it is in my interest to travel to work by car, for the car will get me there faster and more comfortably, and the marginal increase my additional vehicle makes to pollution, traffic jams and the depletion of oil reserves does not materially affect me. If everyone has this same choice of transportation and makes the same rationally self-interested decision, however, the result is a dangerous level of air pollution, choked roads and swift exhaustion of oil reserves, none of which anyone wants. It would therefore be in all our interests if steps were taken to improve public transport; but once a pattern of private transport has set in, public transport can only be economically viable if people are deterred from using their own vehicles. Hence restrictions on the use of cars may well be in everyone's interest.

Suppose that in the above situation a law is enacted prohibiting the use of private vehicles in a defined inner city area. In one sense the range of choice of transport open to people has been reduced; but on the other hand a new choice now opens up—the choice of using a fast and frequent public transport system at a moderate cost. Most reasonable people, given the choice between, say, an hour's crawl along congested, exhaust-filled roads and 20 minutes' comfortable ride on a bus or train, would have little hesitation in choosing the latter. Let us assume that for economic reasons the possibility of choosing the quick and comfortable ride on public transport would not have existed if private transport had not been restricted. Nevertheless, because the choice of driving oneself to work has been eliminated by a deliberate human act, the defenders of laissez faire will regard this restriction as an interference with freedom; and they will not accept that the nonexistence of the option of efficient public transport, if private transport is not restricted, is a comparable interference with freedom, the removal of which compensates for the restriction of private transport. They will argue that it is circumstances, not deliberate human acts, which preclude the coexistence of efficient public transport and the unrestricted use of private vehicles. In the view of laissez-faire theorists—and some other philosophers as well—freedom is not restricted, and rights are not infringed, by "circumstances," but only by deliberate human acts.[20] This position makes, in my view, an untenable moral distinction between an overt act and the omission of an act. If we can act to alter circumstances but decide not to do so, then we must take responsibility for our omission, just as we must take responsibility for our overt act.[21] Therefore circumstances which it is within our power to alter may limit our freedom as much as deliberate human acts.

Turning back now to the subject of a market in human blood we can see that here too profound social consequences, though of a more subtle kind, can arise from the cumulative effect of many seemingly insignificant decisions. We know that altruistic behavior by some can foster further altruistic acts in others.[22] Titmuss has suggested that a society which has and encourages institutions in which some members of society freely render important services to other members of the society, including others with whom they are not acquainted, whose identity they may never know, and from whom they can expect no reward, tends to differ in other important aspects from a society in which people are not expected or encouraged to perform services for strangers except for a direct, and usually monetary, reward. The difference is related to the different views of the state held by philosophers like Hobbes and Locke, on the one hand, and Rousseau, Hegel and Marx on the other. For Hobbes and Locke, as we have seen, the state is composed of people who join and remain in society for the advantage they get out of it. The state then becomes an association of self-interested individuals, which exists because, and as long as, all or most of its members find it useful and profitable. Rousseau and his successors, on the other hand, see the state more as a community which, in addition to merely providing opportunities for material gains, gives meaning to the individual's existence and inevitably has a formative influence on the nature of the people who grow up in it. Through this influence human beings become social beings, and see the interests of the community and of other members of it as a part of their own interests. While for Hobbes and Locke the state can do no more than paper over the ultimately irresolvable difference between the interests of its members, providing at best a superficial, temporary harmony which is always liable to break down, for Rousseau, Hegel and Marx a good society creates a genuine, deep-seated harmony because it actually resolves the differences between the interests of its members.[23]

The phenomenon of cumulative irrationality of individually rational choices, and the still more fundamental point that the nature of human beings is influenced by the institutions of the society in which they live, both point in the same direction: the need to recognize the rights of members of a society to act collectively to control their lives and to determine the nature of the society in which they live. Even if the distinction between laws which interfere with others (like laws prohibiting the sale of blood, or the driving of cars in a prescribed area) from laws which purportedly do not so interfere (like laws allowing people to sell their blood, or drive their cars to work) can be rescued from the objections I have offered, I would still argue that if a majority of the members of a society should decide that unless they interfere with the actions of others the lives of most members of society will become significantly worse—as in the examples we have been discussing—then the majority have a right to interfere. (This does not justify unlimited interference. The extent and

nature of the interference that is permissible would vary with the seriousness of the harm that it is intended to avert; but this topic is too large to
discuss here.[24])

It might be said that to allow the majority a right to interfere is
dangerous, in that it sacrifices the individual to the collective, and leads
straight to a totalitarian dictatorship of the majority. There is, however, no
reason why the right I would allow the majority should lead to totalitarianism. It is quite compatible with many valid anti-totalitarian arguments,
including utilitarian arguments against totalitarianism, and most of the
arguments for individual liberty advanced by John Stuart Mill in *On Liberty*. These arguments are sufficient to rebut the claims of totalitarians. If,
despite this, it is claimed that we need to uphold the absolute inviolability
of individual rights because any other position, while not itself supporting
totalitarianism, is always likely to be distorted by those seeking to establish
a totalitarian state, then the appropriate reply is that it is fallacious to
object to a principle because one objects to the actions of those who distort
the principle for their own ends. If it is only through distortion that the
principle lends support to totalitarianism, then it is to the distortion, and
not to the principle itself, that objections should be made.[25]

In contrast to the dangers of granting a right to the majority to
interfere with individual members of the society, which exist only if this
principle is distorted or added to in objectionable ways, the dangers of the
opposite position are real enough and are truly entailed by the position
itself. The effect of the doctrine that our freedom is not diminished and
our rights are not violated by circumstances—including the cumulative
effect of individual choices, each of which would be quite harmless on its
own—is to tie our hands against effective action in situations which
threaten the survival of our species. Pollution, overpopulation, economic
depression, the breakdown of social cohesion—all of these may be brought
about by millions of separate acts, each one falling within what is normally
perceived as the sphere of individual rights.

Nozick and other defenders of individual rights may assert that the
moral status of rights does not depend on the consequences of not violating them; but if they leave people with no legitimate means of controlling
the course their society is to take, with no legitimate means, even, of
steering away from looming disaster, then they have not succeeded in
providing a plausible theory of rights.

Nozick might reply that what my argument shows is that these
individual actions do violate rights after all, and his theory of rights can
therefore cope with them by the usual procedures for violations of rights,
namely prohibition or compensation. In the case of pollution, Nozick does
outline a scheme for enforcing the payment of compensation to those
whose *property* is damaged by pollution, but he concedes that his discussion
is incomplete in that it does not cover the pollution of unowned things
like the sky or the sea.[26] Perhaps we can imagine how Nozick would extend
his view to handle those cases, but I at least cannot see any way in which it
could deal satisfactorily with, for instance, overpopulation. The claim that
having children violates the rights of others would be difficult to reconcile

with other elements of Nozick's view of rights. Yet by comparison with the problem of overpopulation, the pollution problems Nozick thinks he can cope with are only symptoms, not causes, of the real problem. Nozick might, I suppose, take a hard line and say that when it comes to the crunch, evolutionary forces will take care of the population problem, and only the fittest will survive. Any moral theory that reaches this conclusion reveals its inadequacy more convincingly than I could ever hope to do.

Conclusions

There are, then, three main conclusions which have emerged from this discussion of the effects of markets on rights. First, the view that the market necessarily respects rights, while government systems of distribution involving coercion do not, requires a peculiarly narrow conception of rights which lacks justification once its basis in an individualistic theory of the "state of nature" is rejected. Second, it is incorrect to hold that the state acts neutrally by allowing markets to operate without restriction in any commodity. A market can interfere with people, and may reasonably be said to violate their rights. To draw a line between interference and non-interference is a far more complex task than advocates of the unrestricted market generally assume. Third, and finally, on any plausible theory of rights, some social and economic planning must be permissible. Individuals cannot have an absolute right to buy and sell without interference, any more than they can have an absolute right to pollute or to populate without interference. To grant individuals these rights is to make social planning impossible, and hence to deny to the "individuals" who make up that society the right to control their own lives.[27]

NOTES

1. I discuss the utilitarian argument for the market, in respect of the provision of health care, in "Freedoms and Utilities in the Distribution of Health Care" in R. Veatch and R. Branson (eds.), *Ethics and Health Policy* (Ballinger, Cambridge, Mass., 1976).
2. *Anarchy, State, and Utopia*, pp. 28–33. My hesitation about the degree of absoluteness is prompted by the final paragraph of the footnote commencing on p. 29, in which Nozick refrains from stating whether his side-constraints may be violated to avoid catastrophic moral horror. If he were to say that they may be, he would need to show how this thin end of the utilitarian wedge can be accommodated while resistance to other utilitarian considerations is maintained. Since I cannot predict how Nozick would overcome this difficulty I shall henceforth ignore the possibility that his side-constraints may not be quite absolute.
3. See my review of *Anarchy, State, and Utopia* in *The New York Review of Books*, March 6, 1975; and see also J. J. C. Smart's essay in this volume, pp. 106–117.
4. I take the term "right of recipience" from H. J. McCloskey, "Rights—Some Conceptual Issues," *Australasian Journal of Philosophy*, vol. 54 (1976), p. 103.
5. *Anarchy, State, and Utopia*, p. 30.
6. Ibid., p. 9.
7. The political philosophies of Hegel, Marx and their successors are built upon the rejection of Locke's individualist starting point. The classic, though characteristically

obscure, reference in Hegel is Paragraph 258 of *The Philosophy of Right*. Marx makes the general point on several occasions. The following example is from the *Economic and Philosophical Manuscripts of 1844*:

> Above all we must avoid postulating "Society" again as an abstraction *vis-à-vis* the individual. The individual *is the social being*. (trans. Martin Milligan, International Publishers, New York, 1964, pp. 137–138).

A more recent and more fully argued philosophical critique of the individualism of Hobbes and Locke is to be found in C. B. Macpherson's *The Political Theory of Possessive Individualism* (Clarendon Press, Oxford, 1962). Further discussion of the literature on individualism can be found in Steven Lukes, *Individualism* (Blackwells, Oxford, 1973). For a dramatic introduction to the factual material bearing on the social nature of our ancestors, see Robert Ardrey, *The Social Contract* (Collins, London, 1970). Ardrey himself is unreliable, but his bibliography and references are useful.

8. It seems likely that our moral concepts have developed out of those altruistic practices. See, for instance, Edward O. Wilson *Sociobiology: The New Synthesis* (Belknap Press, Cambridge, Mass., 1975) and Richard Brandt, "The Psychology of Benevolence and Its Implications for Philosophy," *Journal of Philosophy*, LXXIII (1976), pp. 429–453.
9. *Anarchy, State, and Utopia*, pp. 30–31.
10. See the *Groundwork of the Metaphysics of Morals*, trans. H. J. Paton under the title *The Moral Law* (Hutchinson, London, 1948), p. 86, and *Lectures on Ethics*, trans. L. Infield (Harper, New York, 1963), pp. 194, 236.
11. I am indebted to H. J. McCloskey for these points about Kant, although Alan H. Goldman makes a similar point in "The Entitlement Theory of Distributive Justice," *Journal of Philosophy*, LXXIII, pp. 823–835 (Dec. 2, 1976).
12. Allen & Unwin, London, 1970. The substance of the following paragraphs is taken from the article cited in Note 1, above, and also appeared in "Altruism and Commerce: A Defense of Titmuss against Arrow," *Philosophy and Public Affairs*, 2 (1973), pp. 312–320.
13. *The Gift Relationship*, pp. 206–207. The price quoted is a 1966 figure, and has no doubt risen considerably.
14. Cf. Kenneth Arrow, "Gifts and Exchanges." *Philosophy and Public Affairs*, 1 (1972), p. 350.
15. *The Gift Relationship*, passim. For a summary of the evidence see "Altruism and Commerce: A Defense of Titmuss against Arrow," pp. 314–315.
16. *The Gift Relationship*, p. 277. Spelling and punctuation have been corrected.
17. Amitai Etzioni, *Genetic Fix* (Harper & Row, New York, 1973), p. 137; *Wall Street Journal*, Dec. 16, 1975.
18. *The Gift Relationship*, especially chapters 8 & 9. Again, I am indebted to H. J. McCloskey for bringing the significance of Nozick's use of compensation to my attention.
19. *Anarchy, State, and Utopia*, pp. 163–164.
20. For instance, F. A. Hayek: " 'Freedom' refers solely to a relation of men to other men, and the only infringement on it is coercion by men." (*The Constitution of Liberty*, Routledge & Kegan Paul, London, 1960, p. 12) and for a similar view, Isaiah Berlin, "Two Concepts of Liberty" in *Four Essays on Liberty*, p. 122. The discussion on pp. 237–238 of *Anarchy, State and Utopia* indicates that Nozick, though primarily concerned with rights rather than freedom, also holds that my rights are not infringed if the collective result of a series of legitimate individual actions by others is a drastic curtailment of my freedom of action. On this question see the discussion by Thomas Scanlon in "Nozick on Rights, Liberty and Property," *Philosophy and Public Affairs*, vol. 5, no. 1 (Fall 1976), especially pp. 14–15. Scanlon writes:

> It is the connection with justification that makes plausible Nozick's restriction of attention to limitations on alternatives that are brought about by human action. Even though acts of nature may limit our alternatives, they are not subject to demands for justification. But individual human acts are not the only things

subject to such demands; we are also concerned with social institutions that make it possible for agents to do what they do.

Scanlon is right to point out that social institutions need to be justified, but he lets Nozick off too lightly in respect to acts of nature. When acts of nature are preventable, the omission of human acts that would have prevented them may require justification.

21. See Michael Tooley, "Abortion and Infanticide," *Philosophy and Public Affairs*, 2 (1972), especially p. 50 ff; James Rachels, "Active and Passive Euthanasia," *New England Journal of Medicine*, 292 (1975), pp. 78–80.
22. Derek Wright, *The Psychology of Moral Behaviour* (Penguin, London, 1971), pp. 133–139.
23. One does not, of course, have to accept in their entirety the views of any of these philosophers in order to accept the central point that the structure of a society influences the nature of those who are members of it, and that given that this influence will occur, it is better that it be directed toward a community of interests than toward a conflict of interests.
24. I have touched upon it—though in a different context—in *Democracy and Disobedience* (Clarendon Press, Oxford, 1973), especially pp. 64–72.
25. Much of the argument against the positive concept of liberty in Berlin's "Two Concepts of Liberty" commits this fallacy.
26. *Anarchy, State, and Utopia*, pp. 79–81.
27. H. J. McCloskey, J. J. C. Smart, C. L. Ten and Robert Young made useful criticisms of an earlier version of this article.

G. A. Cohen

Robert Nozick and Wilt Chamberlain: How Patterns Preserve Liberty

As illustrated by Nozick's famous Wilt Chamberlain parable, libertarians argue that a socialist (or any patterned) principle of justice must be rejected as incompatible with liberty. In examining the Chamberlain example, G. A. Cohen challenges Nozick's conception of justice, arguing that he has yet to prove his case against socialism. Further, Cohen denies that socialism is infeasible or that it would involve, as libertarians claim, an unacceptable interference with liberty. Socialists restrict some liberties in order to expand our freedom generally. Libertarians cannot complain about this because capitalism itself erodes the liberty of a large class of people.

Let us now suppose that I have sold the product of my own labour for money, and have used the money to hire a labourer, i.e., I have bought somebody else's labour-power. Having taken advantage of this labour-power of another, I turn out to be the owner of value which is considerably higher than the value I spent on its purchase. This, *from one point of view*, is very just, because it has already been recognized, after all, that I can use what I have secured by exchange as is best and most advantageous to myself . . .[1]

Persons, who under a vicious order of things have obtained a competent share of social enjoyments, are never in want of arguments to justify to the eye of reason such a state of society; for what may not admit of apology when exhibited in but *one point of view*? If the same individuals were tomorrow required to cast anew the lots assigning them a place in society, they would find many things to object to.[2]

Robert Nozick occupies the point of view Plekhanov describes, and his *Anarchy, State, and Utopia* is in large measure an ingenious elaboration of the argument for capitalism Plekhanov adumbrates. The capitalism Nozick advocates is more pure than the one we know today. It lacks taxation for social welfare, and it permits degrees of inequality far greater than most apologists for contemporary bourgeois society would now countenance.

An earlier version of this article appeared in *Erkenntnis* 11 (1977), pp. 5–23. D. Reidel Publishing Company, Dordrecht-Holland. Reprinted by permission.

This paper is only indirectly a critique of Nozick's defense of capitalism. Its immediate aim is to refute Nozick's major argument against a rival of capitalism, socialism. The refutation vindicates socialism against that argument, but no one opposed to socialism on other grounds should expect to be converted by this paper.

Nozick's case against socialism can be taken in two ways. He proposes a definition of justice in terms of liberty, and on that basis he argues that what socialists[3] consider just is not in fact just. But even if his definition of justice is wrong, so that the basis of his critique, taken in this first way, is faulty, he still has a claim against socialism, namely that, however *just* it may be, it is incompatible with *liberty*. Even if Nozick is mistaken about what justice is, he might still be right that the cost in loss of liberty imposed by what socialists regard as just is intolerably high. (Hence the title of the section of the book on which we shall focus: 'How Liberty Upsets Patterns'—patterns being distributions answering to, for example, a socialist principle of justice). So it is not enough, in defending socialism against Nozick, to prove that he has not shown it is unjust. It must also be proved that he has not shown that it is opposed to liberty.

A full definition of socialism is not required for our purposes. All we need suppose is that a socialist society upholds some principle of equality in the distribution of benefits enjoyed and burdens borne by its members. The principle need not be specified further, for Nozick's argument is against the institution of *any* such principle. Let us now imagine that such an egalitarian principle is instituted, and that it leads to a distribution of goods and bads which, following Nozick, we call D1. Then Nozick reasons by example that D1 can be maintained only at the price of tyranny and injustice. The example concerns the best basketball player in the imagined society.[4]

> . . . suppose that Wilt Chamberlain is greatly in demand by basketball teams, being a great gate attraction . . . He signs the following sort of contract with a team: In each home game, twenty-five cents from the price of each ticket of admission goes to him . . . The season starts, and people cheerfully attend his team's games; they buy their tickets, each time droping a separate twenty-five cents of their admission price into a special box with Chamberlain's name on it. They are excited about seeing him play; it is worth the total admission price to them. Let us suppose that in one season one million persons attend his home games, and Wilt Chamberlain winds up with $250,000, a much larger sum than the average income. . . . Is he entitled to this income? Is this new distribution D2, unjust? If so, why? There is *no* question about whether each of the people was entitled to the control over the resources they held in D1; because that was the distribution . . . that (for the purposes of argument) we assumed was acceptable. Each of these persons *chose* to give twenty-five cents of their money to Chamberlain. They could have spent it on going to the movies, or on candy bars, or on copies of *Dissent* magazine, or of *Monthy Review*. But they all, at least one million of them, converged on giving it to Wilt Chamberlain in exchange for watching him play basketball. If D1 was a just distribution, and people voluntarily moved from it to D2, transferring parts of their shares they were given under D1 (what was it for if not to do something with?), isn't D2 also just? If the people were

entitled to dispose of the resources to which they were entitled (under D1), didn't this include their being entitled to give it to, or exchange it with, Wilt Chamberlain? Can anyone else complain on grounds of justice? Each other person already has his legitimate share under D1. Under D1, there is nothing that anyone has that anyone else has a claim of justice against. After someone transfers something to Wilt Chamberlain, third parties *still* have their legitimate shares; *their* shares are not changed. By what process could such a transfer among two persons give rise to a legitimate claim of distributive justice on a portion of what was transferred, by a third party who had no claim of justice on any holding of the others *before* the transfer?

According to Nozick

(1) Whatever arises from a just situation by just steps is itself just. (p. 151)

Steps are just if they are free of injustice, and they are free of injustice if they are fully voluntary on the part of all legitimately concerned persons. Hence

(2) Whatever arises from a just situation as a result of fully voluntary transactions on the part of all legitimately concerned persons is itself just.

So convinced is Nozick that (2) is true that he thinks it must be accepted by people attached to a doctrine of justice which in other respects differs from his own. That is why he feels able to employ (2) in the Chamberlain parable, despite having granted, for the sake of argument, the justice of an initial situation patterned by an egalitarian principle.

Even if (2) is true, it does not follow that pattern D1 can be maintained only at the price of injustice, for people might simply *fail* to use their liberty in a pattern-subverting manner. But that is not an interesting possibility. A more interesting one is that they deliberately *refuse* to use their liberty subversively. Reasons for refusing will be adduced shortly. But is (2) true? Does liberty always preserve justice?

A standard way of testing the claim would be to look for states of affairs which would be accounted unjust but which might be generated by the route (2) approves. Perhaps, the strongest counterexample of this form would be slavery. We then say: voluntary self-enslavement is possible, slavery is unjust, therefore (2) is false. But whatever may be the merits of that argument, we know that Nozick is not moved by it. For he thinks there is no injustice in slavery to the extent that it arises out of the approved processes.

Though Nozick consistently endorses slavery of appropriate genesis, there is a restriction, derived from (2) itself, on the kind of slavery he accepts. (2) does not allow slave status to be inherited by offspring of the self-enslaved, for then a concerned party's situation would be decided for him, independently of his will. "Some things individuals may choose for themselves no one may choose for another" (p. 331). Let us remember this when we come to scrutinize the Wilt Chamberlain transaction, for widespread contracting of the kind which occurs in the parable might have the effect of seriously modifying, for the worse, the situation of members of future generations.

Should we say that in Nozick's conception of justice a slave society need be no less just than one where people are free? That would be a tendentious formulation. For Nozick can claim that rational persons in an initially just situation are unlikely to contract into slavery, except, indeed, where circumstances are so special that it would be wrong to forbid them to do so. This diminishes the danger that (2) can be used to stamp approval on morally repellent social arrangements.

I attribute some such response to Nozick on the basis, *inter alia* of this passage:

> . . . it must be granted that were people's reasons for transferring some of their holdings to others always irrational or arbitrary, we would find this *disturbing* . . . We feel more comfortable upholding the justice of an entitlement system if most of the transfers under it are done for reasons. This does not mean necessarily that all deserve what holdings they receive. It means only that there is a purpose or point to someone's transferring a holding to one person rather than to another; that usually we can see what the transferrer *thinks* he's gaining, what cause he *thinks* he's serving, what goals he *thinks* he's helping to achieve, and so forth. Since in a capitalist society people often transfer holdings to others in accordance with how much they *perceive* these others benefiting them, the fabric constituted by the individual transactions and transfers is largely reasonable and intelligible (p. 159, my emphases).

Accordingly, Nozick emphasizes the motives people have when they pay to watch Chamberlain, instead of stipulating that they do so freely and leaving us to guess why. The example would be less impressive if Chamberlain or his agent had induced in the fans an inordinate taste for basketball, by means which fell short of what Nozick would consider coercive or fraudulent, but which remained unattractive. It is important to the persuasive allure of the example that we should think what the fans are doing not only voluntary but sensible.

So transactions are disturbing (even though they are just?[5]) when we cannot see what the (or some of the) contracting parties think they are gaining by them. But we should surely also be disturbed if though we can see what the agent *thinks* he's gaining, we know that what he *will* gain is not that, but something he thinks less valuable; or that what results is not only the gain he expects but also unforeseen consequences which render negative the net value, according to his preferences and standards, of the transaction. We should not be content if what he *thinks* he is getting is good, but what he actually gets is bad, by his own lights. I shall assume that Nozick would accept this plausible extension of his concession. If he would not, so much the worse for his position.

Hence if we can show that Chamberlain's fans get not only the pleasure of watching him minus twenty-five cents, but also uncontemplated disbenefits of a high order, then even if for Nozick the outcome remains just, it should, even to Nozick, be rather disturbing. We shall need to ask whether we do not find irrationality in the Chamberlain transaction, when we think through, as Nozick's fans do not, the *full* consequences of what they are doing.

But now we can go further. For, in the light of the considerations just reviewed, (2) appears very probably false. Nozick says a transaction is free of injustice if every concerned party agrees to it. Perhaps that is so. But transactional justice, so characterized, is supposed—given an initially just situation—to confer justice on what results from it. (That is why (2) follows from (1)). And that is questionable. Of each person who agrees to a transaction we may ask: *would he have agreed to it had he known what its outcome was to be?* Since the answer may be negative, it is far from evident that transactional justice, as described, transmits justice to its results. Perhaps the effect obtains when the answer is positive. Perhaps, in other words, (3) is true:

> (3) Whatever arises from a just situation as a result of fully voluntary transactions which all transagents would still have agreed to if they had known what the results of so transacting were to be is itself just.

(3) looks plausible, but its power to endorse market-generated states of affairs is, while not nil, very weak. Stronger principles may also be available,[6] but (2), Nozick's principle, is certainly too strong.

A CLOSER LOOK AT CHAMBERLAIN

Let us now apply this critique of Nozick's principles to the parable which is supposed to secure (or reveal) our allegiance to them.

Before describing the Chamberlain transaction, Nozick says: "It is not clear how those holding alternative conceptions of distributive justice can reject the entitlement conception of justice in holdings" (p. 160). There follows the Chamberlain story, where we assume that D1 is just, and are then, supposedly, constrained to admit that D2, into which it is converted, must also be just; an admission, according to Nozick, which is tantamount to accepting the entitlement conception. But how much of it must we accept if we endorse D2 as just? At most that there is *a* role for the entitlement principle. For what the transaction subverts is the original pattern, not the principle governing it, taken as a principle conjoinable with others to form a total theory of just or legitimate holdings. The example, even if successful, does not defeat the initial assumption that D1 is just. Rather, it exploits that assumption to argue that D2, though it breaks D1's pattern, is also just. The story, if sound, impugns not the original distribution, but the *exclusive* rightness of the principle determining it.

Now Nozick is certainly right to this extent, even if we reject the Chamberlain story: there must be *a* role for entitlement in determining acceptable holdings. For unless the just society forbids gifts, it must allow transfers which do not answer to a patterning principle. This is compatible with placing restraints on the scope of gift, and we shall shortly see why it may be justified in doing so. More generally, assigning a certain role to unregulated transactions in the determination of holdings is compatible with using an egalitarian principle to decide the major distribution of goods and to limit, for example by taxation, how much more or less than what he would get under that principle alone a person may come to have in virtue of transactions which escape its writ. I think socialists do well to concede that an egalitarian principle should not be the only guide to the justice of holdings, or, if it is, then justice should not be the only guide to the moral legitimacy of holdings.[7]

Among the reasons for limiting how much an individual may hold, regardless of how he came to hold it, is to prevent him from acquiring, through his holdings, an unacceptable amount of power over others.[8]

Is the Chamberlain transaction really beneficial (or at worst harmless) to everyone with an interest in it? I shall argue that it threatens to generate a situation in which some have unacceptable amounts of power over others.

The fans "are excited about seeing him play; it is worth the total admission price to them." The idea is that they see him play if and only if they pay, and seeing him play is worth more to them than anything else they can get for twenty-five cents. So it *may* be, but this fails to capture everything in the outcome which is relevant. For once Chamberlain has received the payments he is in a very special position of power in what was previously an egalitarian society. The fans' access to resources may now be prejudiced by the disproportionate access Chamberlain's wealth gives him, and the consequent power over others he now has. *For all Nozick says*, the socialist may claim that this is not a bargain informed people in an egalitarian society will be apt to make: they will refrain from so contracting as to upset the equality they prize. They will be especially averse to doing so because the resulting changes would profoundly affect their children. (This may seem an hysterical projection of the effect of the Chamberlain transaction, but I take it we have to consider the upshot of general performance of transactions of that kind, and then the projection is entirely realistic.)

It is easy to think carelessly about the example. How we feel about people like Chamberlain getting a lot of money *as things are* is a poor index of how people would feel in the imagined situation. Among us the ranks of the rich and the powerful exist, and it can be pleasing, given that they do, when a figure like Chamberlain joins them. Who better and more innocently deserves to be among them? But the case before us is a society of equality in danger of corruption. Reflective people would have to consider not only the joy of watching Chamberlain and its immediate money price but also the fact, which socialists say they would deplore, that their society would be set on the road to class division. In presenting the Chamberlain fable Nozick ignores the commitment people may have to living in a society of a particular kind, and the rhetorical power of the illustration depends on that omission. Later—see p. 220 below—Nozick takes up this point, but he says nothing interesting about it.

Nozick tacitly supposes that a person willing to pay twenty-five cents to watch Wilt play is *ipso facto* a person willing to pay *Wilt* twenty-five cents to watch him play. It is no doubt true that in our society people rarely care who gets the money they forgo to obtain goods. But the tacit supposition is false, and the common unconcern is irrational. Nozick exploits our familiarity with this unconcern. Yet a person might welcome a world in which he and a million others watch Wilt play, at a cost of twenty-five cents to each, and consistently disfavour one in which, in addition, Wilt receives a cool quarter million.

So if a citizen of the Dl society joins with others in paying twenty-five cents to Wilt to watch Wilt play, without thinking about the effect on Wilt's power, then the result may be deemed 'disturbing' in the sense of p. 159. Of course a single person's paying a quarter will make no appreciable difference if the rest are already going to do so. But a convention might evolve not to make such payments, or, more simply, there could be a democratically authorized taxation system which maintains wealth differentials within acceptable limits. Whether Wilt would then still play is a further question on which I shall not comment, except to say that anyone who thinks it obvious he would not misunderstands human nature, or basketball, or both.

In defending the justice of the Chamberlain transaction, Nozick glances at the position of persons not directly party to it: "After someone transfers something to Wilt Chamberlain, third parties *still* have their legitimate shares; *their* shares are not changed." This is false, in one relevant sense. For a person's effective share depends on what he can do with what he has, and that depends not only on how much he has but on what others have and on how what others have is distributed. If it is distributed equally among them he will often be better placed than if some have especially large shares. Third parties, including the as yet unborn, therefore have an interest against the contract, which is not catered for. It is roughly the same interest as the fans have in not making it.

Nozick addresses this issue in a footnote:

> Might not a transfer have instrumental effects on a third party, changing his feasible options? (But what if the two parties to a transfer independently had used their holdings in this fashion?) (p. 162)

He promises further treatment of the problem later, and though he does not say where, he presumably means his section on 'Voluntary Exchange,' which we shall examine at the end of this paper. Here I respond to his parenthetical rhetorical question.

First, there are some upshots of transfers of holdings, some effects on the options of the other parties, which will not occur as effects of the unconcerted use of dispersed holdings by individuals, because they could not, or because they would not use them in that way. The Chamberlain fans, acting independently, would probably be unable to buy a set of houses and leave them unoccupied, with speculative intent, but Chamberlain can. Sometimes, though, a set of fans, acting independently, could indeed bring about effects inimical to the legitimate interests of others, of just the kind one fears Chamberlain might cause. But whoever worries about Chamberlain doing so will probably also be concerned about the case where it results from the independent action of many. Nozick's rhetorical question does not provide those who ask the first one with a case where they need to agree with him.

As an argument about *justice*[9] the Chamberlain story is either question-begging or uncompelling. Nozick asks:

> If the people were entitled to dispose of the resources to which they were entitled (under D1), didn't this include their being entitled to give it to, or exchange it with, Wilt Chamberlain? (p. 161)

If this interrogative is intended as a vivid way of asserting the corresponding indicative, then Nozick is telling us that the rights in shares with which they were vested are violated unless they are allowed to contract as described. If so, he begs the question. For it will be clear that their rights are violated only if the entitlement they received was of the absolute Nozickian sort, and this cannot be assumed. Whatever principles underlie D1 will generate restrictions on the use of what is distributed in accordance with them.[10]

The other way of taking the quoted question is not as an assertion but as an appeal. Nozick is then asking us whether we do not agree that any restrictions which would forbid the Chamberlain transaction must be unjustified. So construed the argument is not question-begging, but it is inconclusive. For considerations which might justify restrictions are not canvassed, such as the fact that the contract may generate inordinate power. It is easy to think that what happens afterwards is that Chamberlain eats lots of chocolate, sees lots of movies and buys lots of subscriptions to expensive socialist journals. But, as I have insisted, we must remember the considerable power he can now exercise over others.[11] In general holdings are not only sources of enjoyment but in certain distributions sources of power. Transfers which look unexceptionable come to seem otherwise when we bring into relief the aspect neglected by bourgeois apologetic.

Turning from justice to *liberty*, is it true that a "socialist society would have to forbid capitalist acts between consenting adults" (p. 163)? Socialism perishes if there are too many such acts, but it does not follow that it must forbid them. In traditional socialist doctrine capitalist action wanes not primarily because it is illegal, but because the impulse behind it atrophies, or, less Utopianly, because other impulses become stronger, or because people believe that capitalistic exchange is unfair. *Such expectation rests on a conception of human nature, and so does its denial.* Nozick has a different conception, for which he does not argue, one that fits many 20th century Americans, which is no reason for concluding it is universally true. The people in his state of nature are intelligible only as well socialized products of a market society. In the contrary socialist conception human beings have and may develop further an unqualified (that is, non-'instrumental') desire for community, an unqualified relish of cooperation, and an unqualified aversion to being on either side of a master/servant relationship. No one should assume without argument, or take it on trust from the socialist tradition, that this conception is sound. But *if* it is sound, there will be no need for incessant invigilation against 'capitalist acts', and Nozick does not *argue* that it is unsound. Hence he has not shown that socialism conflicts with freedom, even if his unargued premise that its citizens will want to perform capitalist acts attracts the assent of the majority of his readers.

How much equality would conflict with liberty in given circumstances depends on how much people would value equality in those circumstances. If life in a cooperative commonwealth appeals to them, they do not have to sacrifice liberty to belong to it.

IS SOCIALISM MORALLY PERMISSIBLE?

This banal point relates to the first of Nozick's three 'unrealistic' presuppositions of the moral and practical feasibility of socialism:

(5) "that all will most want to maintain the [socialist] pattern"
(6) "that each can gather enough information about his own actions and the ongoing activities of others to discover which of his actions will upset the pattern"
(7) "that diverse and far-flung persons can coordinate their actions to dovetail into the pattern." (p. 163)

Something like the first presupposition is made by socialists in the light of the idea of human nature which informs their tradition. It is, of course, controversial, but its dismissal as 'unrealistic' contributes nothing to the controversy.

Only something *like* (5) is presupposed, because a socialist need think only that a great majority will have socialist sentiments, not all, especially not in the nascency of socialism. If (5) itself is unrealistic, three possibilities present themselves: very few would lack enthusiasm for socialism; very many would; some intermediate proportion would. What I mean by these magnitudes will emerge immediately.

Consider then the first possibility: there remain a few capitalistically minded persons, meaning by 'a few' that their capitalist acts would not undermine the basic socialist structure. No sane socialist should commit himself to the suppression of capitalist activity on the stated scale. (It might even be desirable to allocate to these capitalists a territory in which they can bargain with and hire one another.)

Suppose, though, that the disposition to perform capitalist acts is strong and widespread, so that 'socialism'[12] is possible only with tyranny. What socialist favours socialism in such circumstances? What socialist denies that there are such circumstances? Certainly Marx insisted it would be folly to attempt an institution of socialism except under the propitious conditions he was confident capitalism would create.[13] A socialist believes propitious conditions are accessible. He need not proclaim the superiority of socialism regardless of circumstances.

Could a socialist society contain an amount of inclination to capitalism of such a size that unless it were coercively checked socialism would be subverted, yet sufficiently small that in socialist judgment socialism, with the required coercion, would still be worthwhile? Marxian socialists believe so, and that does commit them to a prohibition on capitalist acts between consenting adults in certain circumstances, notably those which follow a successful revolution. But why should they flinch from imposing the prohibition? They can defend it by reference to the social good and widened freedom it promotes. Nozick will object that the prohibition violates moral 'side constraints': certain freedoms, for example of contract, ought never to be infringed, whatever the consequences of allowing their exercise may be. We shall look at side constraints in a moment.

But first we must treat presuppositions (6) and (7). Unlike (5), these are red herrings. At most, they are preconditions of realising socialist justice *perfectly*.[14] But justice is not the only virtue of social orders (and it is not even 'the first virtue' of socialism, for most socialists). Even if we identify justice with equality, as socialists, broadly speaking, do, we may tolerate deviations from equality consequent on differential capacity to enjoy the same things, or resulting from the random distribution that arises out of gift, etc. Considerations of privacy, acquired expectations, the moral and economic costs of surveillance, etc. declare against attempting a realization of justice in the high degree that would be possible if (6) and (7) were satisfied. We let justice remain rough, in deference to other values.

Accordingly, socialism tolerates gift-giving, and 'loving behaviour' is not 'forbidden' (p. 167). Gift is possible under a system which limits how much anyone may have and what he may do with it. Relatively well endowed persons will sometimes not be fit recipients of gifts, but we are assuming a socialist psychology whose natural tendency is not to give to him that hath. And the notion that the institutions we are contemplating fetter the expression of love is too multiply bizarre to require comment.

SIDE CONSTRAINTS

Any but the most utopian socialist must be willing under certain conditions to restrict the liberty of some for the sake of others. He thereby flouts what Nozick calls the "moral side constraints" on all human action. Nozick thinks we may never limit one man's freedom in order to enhance the welfare or freedom of very many others, or even of everyone, him included, where we know he will benefit as a result at a future time.[15]

If children are undernourished in our society, we are not allowed to tax millionaires in order to finance a subsidy on the price of milk to poor families, for we would be violating the rights, and the 'dignity' (p. 334) of the millionaires.[16] We cannot appeal that the effective liberty of the

men the children will be would be greatly enhanced at little expense to the
millionaires' freedom, for Nozick forbids any act which restricts freedom:
he does not call for its maximization. (This means that if it were true that
certain exercises of freedom would lead to totalitarianism, Nozick would
still protect them. Market freedom itself would be sacrificed by Nozick if
the only way to preserve it were by limiting it.[17])

If Nozick argues for this position, he does so in the section called
'Why Side Constraints?', which begins as follows:

> Isn't it *irrational* to accept a side constraint C, rather than a view that
> directs minimizing the violations of C? . . . If nonviolation of C is so
> important, shouldn't that be the goal? How can a concern for the non-
> violation of C lead to the refusal to violate C even when this would
> prevent other more extensive violations of C? What is the rationale for
> placing the nonviolation of rights as a side constraint upon action instead
> of including it solely as a goal of one's actions?[18]
>   Side constraints upon action reflect the underlying Kantian principle
> that individuals are ends and not merely means; they may not be sacri-
> ficed or used for the achieving of other ends without their consent. Individ-
> uals are inviolable. (pp. 30–31)

The second paragraph is lame as a response to the questions of the
first, for they obviously reassert themselves: if such sacrifice and violation
is so horrendous, why should we not be concerned to minimize its oc-
currence? There is more appearance of argument[19] at the end of the section:

> Side constraints express the inviolability of other persons. But why may
> not one violate persons for the greater social good? Individually, we each
> sometimes choose to undergo some pain or sacrifice for a greater benefit
> or to avoid a greater harm. . . Why not, *similarly*, hold that some persons
> have to bear some costs that benefit other persons more, for the sake of
> the overall social good? But there is no *social entity* with a good that
> undergoes some sacrifice for its own good. There are only individual
> people, different individual people, with their own individual lives. Using
> one of these people for the benefit of others, uses him and benefits the
> others. Nothing more. What happens is that something is done to him for
> the sake of others. Talk of an overall social good covers this up . . . (pp.
> 32–33)

This passage is hard to construe. In one interpretation what it says
is correct but irrelevant, in the other what it says is relevant but wrong,
and anyone who is impressed has probably failed to spot the ambiguity.
For it is unclear whether Nozick is only arguing *against* one who puts
redistribution across lives on a moral par with a man's sacrificing something for his own greater benefit, or arguing *for* the moral impermissibility
of redistribution. In other words, is Nozick simply rejecting argument *A*,
or is he (also) propounding argument *B*?

A   Since Persons compose a social entity relevantly akin to the
             entity a single person is (*p*),
             redistribution across persons is morally permissible (*q*).
B   Since it is false that *p*, it is false that *q*.

If Nozick is just rejecting A, then I accept what he says, but the side
constraints remain unjustified. Unless we take him as propounding B,
there is no case to answer. And then the answer is that the truth of *p* is not
a necessary condition of the truth of *q*. A redistributor does not have to
believe in a social entity.[20]

Side constraints remain unjustified, and socialists need not apolo-
gise for being willing to restrict freedom in order to expand it.

VOLUNTARY EXCHANGE

We now examine Nozick's section on 'Voluntary Exchange,' which I presumed (see pp. 218) to be his more extended treatment of the problem of
the effect of market transactions on persons not party to them, including
the as yet unborn. He allows that agreed exchanges between A and B may
reduce the options of an absent C, but he implies that they do not thereby
reduce C's freedom. He explicitly says that they do not render involuntary
anything C does. And since what C is forced to do he does involuntarily, if
it follows that, for Nozick, the actions of A and B, though reducing C's
options, do not have the result that C is forced to do something he might
not otherwise have done.

The last claim entails a denial of a thesis central to the socialist
critique of capitalism, which may usefully be expressed in the terms of
Nozick's doctrine of natural rights, without commitment to the truth of the
latter.

For Nozick, every man has a natural right not to work for any
other man. If one is a slave, then, unless one enslaved oneself (see pp. 214
above), one's rights were violated, as they are in slave states, which do not
confer on every one as a matter of civil right the rights he enjoys naturally.
And natural rights would remain violated if the law permitted slaves to
choose for which master they shall labour, as long it forbade them to
withhold their services from all masters whatsoever.

One difference between a capitalist state and a slave state is that
the natural right not to be subordinate in the manner of a slave is a civil
right in liberal capitalism. The law excludes formation of a set of persons
legally obliged to work for other persons. That status being forbidden
everyone is entitled to work for no one. But the power corresponding to
this right[21] is differentially enjoyed. Some *can* live without subordinating
themselves, but most cannot. The latter face a structure generated by a
history of market transactions in which, it is reasonable to say, they are
forced to work for some or other person or group. Their natural rights are
not matched by corresponding effective powers.

This division between the powerful and the powerless with respect to the alienation of labour power is the heart of the socialist objection to capitalism. The rights Nozick says we have by nature we also have civilly under capitalism, but the corresponding power is widely lacking. The lack is softened in contemporary capitalism because of a hard-won institutionalization of a measure of working class power. In Nozick's capitalism that institutionalization, being coercive, would be forbidden, and the lack would be greater.

But Nozick, in the course of his full reply to the problem of 'third parties,' denies that even the most abject proletarian is forced to work for some capitalist or other. Addressing himself to "market exchanges between workers and owners of capital," he invites us to reflect on the situation of a certain Z (so-called because he is at the bottom of the heap in a twenty-six person economy) who is "faced with working [for a capitalist] or starving":

> . . . the choices and actions of all other persons do not add up to providing Z with some other option. (He may have various options about what job to take). Does Z choose to work voluntarily? . . . Z does choose voluntarily if the other individuals A through Y each acted voluntarily and within their rights. . . . A person's choice among differing degrees of unpalatable alternatives is not rendered nonvoluntary by the fact that others voluntarily chose and acted within their rights in a way that did not provide him with a more palatable alternative . . . [Whether other people's option-closing action] makes one's resulting action non-voluntary depends on whether these others had the right to act as they did. (pp. 262, 263–64)

One might think that people of necessity lack the right so to act that someone ends up in Z's position, a view we put forward later. But here we suppose, with Nozick, that all of A through Y acted as impeccably upright marketeers and therefore did nothing wrong. If so, says Nozick, Z is not *forced* to work for a capitalist. If he chooses to, the choice is voluntary.

Nozick is not saying that Z, though forced to work *or* starve, is not forced to *work*, since he may choose to starve. Rather he would deny that Z is forced to work or starve, even though Z has no other alternative, and would accept that Z is indeed forced to work, if contrary to what Nozick holds, he is forced to work or starve. For Nozick believes that if Z is forced to do A or B, and A is the only thing it would be reasonable to do, and Z does A for this reason, then Z is forced to do A.[22]

Nozick holds that (8) Z is forced to choose between working and starving only if human actions caused his alternatives to be restricted in this way, and (9) Z is forced so to choose only if the actions bringing about the restriction on his alternatives were illegitimate. Both claims are false, but we need not discuss (8) here.[23] For we are concerned with choice restriction which Nozick himself attributes to the actions of persons, *viz.*, some or all of A through Y. We need therefore only reject his claim that if someone is forced to do something, then someone acted illegitimately: we need refute statement (9) only. Again:

> Other people's actions may place limits on one's available opportunities.
> Whether this makes one's resulting action non-voluntary depends upon
> whether these others had the right to act as they did. (p. 262)

But there is no such dependence, as the following pair of examples
show.

Suppose farmer F owns a tract of land across which villager V has
a right of way. (To still objections Nozick might otherwise have to this
statement, imagine that V has the right by virtue of a contract between F
and himself). Then if F erects an insurmountable fence around the land, V
is forced to use another route, as Nozick will agree, since F, in erecting the
fence, acted illegitimately. Now consider farmer G, whose similar tract is
regularly traversed by villager W, not as of right, but by dint of G's
tolerant nature. But then G erects an insurmountable fence around his
land for reasons which, all men of good will would agree, justify him in
doing so. According to Nozick, W may not truly say that, like V, he is now
forced to use another route. But the examples, though different, do not so
contrast as to make that statement false. W is no less forced to change his
route than V is. (9) is false even if—what I also deny—(8) is true, and the
thesis that Z is forced to place his labour power at the disposal of some or
other member of the capitalist class is resoundingly sustained.

CONCLUSION

Nozick's claim about Z is so implausible that it may seem puzzling, coming
as it does from an extremely acute thinker.[24] Can it be that he is driven to
it because it occupies a strategic place in his defense of libertarian capitalism? How is libertarian capitalism *libertarian* if it erodes the liberty of a
large class of people?

Still, we can imagine Nozick granting that Z is forced to work for a
capitalist, and attempting to recoup his position as follows: Z is indeed so
forced, but since what brings it about that he is is a sequence of legitimate
transactions, there is no moral case against his being so forced, no injustice
in it. (Cf. (1) and (2), p. 214 above).

This would be less impressive than the original claim. Nozick is in
a stronger position—could he but sustain it—when he holds that capitalism
does not deprive workers of freedom than if he grants the worker is
forced to subordinate himself yet insists that even so his situation, being
justly generated, is, however regrettable, unexceptionable from the standpoint of justice. For the original claim, if true, entitles Nozick to say, given
his other theses, that capitalism is not only a just but also a free society;
while the revised claim makes him say that capitalism is just, but not
entirely free. When Z is accurately described capitalism is less attractive,
whatever we may say about it from the standpoint of justice.

Turning to that standpoint, and bearing Z in mind, what should
we say about Nozick's important thesis (1)? It seems reasonable to add to
the constraints on just acquisition a provision that no one may so acquire

goods that others suffer severe loss of liberty as a result. We might, that is, *accept* thesis (1) but extend the conditions steps must meet to be just, and thus reject capitalism.[25]

Alternatively, we might grant, in concessive spirit, that there is no transactional injustice (no unjust step) in the generation of Z's position, but *reject* (1), and contend that the generative process must be regulated, at the cost of some injustice, to prevent it issuing in very unjust results. Nozick would invoke side constraints against that, but they lack authority (see pp. 221–23 above).

Whatever option we take—and there are others—it should now be clear that 'libertarian' capitalism sacrifices liberty to capitalism, a truth its advocates are able to deny only because they are prepared to abuse the language of freedom.[26]

NOTES

1. George Plekhanov, *The Development of the Monist View of History*, Moscow, 1956, pp. 94–95 (my emphasis). Plekhanov proceeds to associate himself with another point of view, one which is defended in this paper.
2. Jean-Baptiste Say, *A Treatise on Political Economy*, Philadelphia, 1834, p. liii (my emphasis).
3. And others, such as American liberals, but our concern is with the application of the argument to socialism.
4. *Anarchy, State, and Utopia,* New York, 1974, pp. 161–162. All future references to Nozick, except the one in Note 22, are to this book.
5. Nozick does not say that what *disturbs* us undermines the *justice* of the transaction.
6. Some might say this is one of them, but I would disagree:

   (4) Whatever arises from a just situation as a result of fully voluntary transactions whose transagents know in advance the probabilities of all significantly different possible outcomes is itself just.

7. I prefer the second formulation, being persuaded that justice, very roughly, *is* equality. (See Christopher Ake, "Justice as Equality," *Philosophy and Public Affairs,* November, 1975).
8. My near-exclusive emphasis on this consideration in the sequel does not mean I think there are no other important ones.
9. Recall the two ways of taking Nozick, distinguished on p. 213 above.
10. Thomas Nagel diagnoses Nozick as above, and this is his rebuttal of Nozick, so diagnosed. See "Libertarianism Without Foundations," *Yale Law Journal,* November, 1975.
11. Once again—see p. 217 above—this assessment will seem hysterical only if we fail to take the Chamberlain transaction as we must for it to pose a serious challenge, namely as an example of something which occurs regularly, or will occur regularly in the future.
12. I add scare-quotes because socialism, properly defined, is incompatible with tyranny; but, contrary to what some socialists seem to think, that is no argument against those who say that the form of economy socialists favour requires tyranny.
13. According to Marx, no socialist revolution will succeed unless "capitalist production has already developed the productive forces of labour in general to a sufficiently high level" (*Theories of Surplus Value,* Volume II, Moscow, 1968, p. 580), failing which "all the old filthy business would necessarily be reproduced" (*German Ideology,* Moscow, 1964, p. 46) in the aftermath of revolution. See sections (6) and (7) of Chapter VII of my forthcoming *Karl Marx's Theory of History,* Oxford and Princeton, 1978.
14. I say "at most" because even this is probably false. Given the truth of (5), people could

form a Pattern Maintenance Association and appoint experts to watch over and correct the pattern. With popular willingness to do what the experts said, and a properly sophisticated technology for detecting deviations, (6) and (7) would be unnecessary to pattern maintenance without coercion (unless doing what the experts say counts as a way of coordinating action, in which case (7) is required in the above fantasy, but it is easily satisfied).

15. Qualifications imposed on this statement by the "Lockean Proviso" (pp. 174–183) are not relevant here.

16. " 'But isn't justice to be tempered with compassion?' Not by the guns of the state. When private persons choose to transfer resources to help others, this fits within the entitlement conception of justice" (p. 348). "Fits within" is evasive. The choice "fits" because it is a choice, not because of its content. For Nozick there is no more justice in a millionaire's giving a five dollar bill to a starving child than in his using it to light his cigar.

For subtle comments on Nozick's falsely exclusive and exhaustive distinction between compulsory and voluntary donation, see Nagel, *op. cit.*, pp. 145–146.

17. The hypothesised contingency has been actualised. Market freedom is less than it was, partly because, had the bourgeois state not imposed restrictions on it, its survival would have been jeopardized.

18. *Tertium datur,* but let that pass.

19. Note, though, that what Nozick initially contends against is *violating rights to reduce the violation of rights*, whereas in what follows his target is *violating rights to expand social welfare*. He is unconvincing on both counts, but one who agrees with him about "overall social good" could still press the opening questions of the section.

20. For elaboration, see Nagel (*op. cit.*, pp. 142–143), who takes Nozick to be propounding *B*.

21. The concept of a *power which corresponds to a right* is explicated briefly in my "On Some Criticisms of Historical Materialism," *Proceedings of the Aristotelian Society*, Supp. Vol., 1970, pp. 133–135, and at length in Chapter VIII of the book mentioned in Note 13 above. The basic idea: power p corresponds to right r if and only if what X is *de jure* able to do when he has r is what he is *de facto* able to do when he has p.

22. See Nozick, "Coercion," in *Philosophy, Science and Method: Essays in Honour of Ernest Nagel*, New York, 1969, p. 446. I derive the claim formulated above from principle (7) of the "Coercion" essay on the basis of Nozick's commitment to: Z is forced to do A if and only if there is a person P who forces Z to do A. Nozick thinks principle (7) is perhaps only roughly true, but rough truth will do for present purposes.

23. For criticism of (8), see H. Frankfurt, "Coercion and Moral Responsibility," in Honderich (ed.), *Essays on Freedom of Action*, London, 1973, pp. 83–84.

24. Those who have read Nozick will know that this description is not ironical.

25. It is immaterial if this yields what Nozick would call a "gimmicky" reading of (1) (p. 157).

26. I thank Gerald Dworkin, Ted Honderich and Michael Slote for useful comments on a draft of this paper.

Kai Nielsen

Global Justice, Capitalism, and the Third World

Kai Nielsen attempts to situate the problem of third-world starvation and malnutrition within its real-world context, and he sketches the changes in the international food order and in international economic relations that have contributed to famine. Nielsen then explores whether justice requires North–South redistribution. Contrary to those writers who believe that considerations of justice arise only when individuals are engaged in a scheme of mutual cooperation, Nielsen contends that moral reciprocity is sufficient to ground claims of justice. In his view, however, a necessary condition of ending global injustice and inhumanity is the abolition of capitalism.

I

Let us start with some stark empirical realities. Approximately 10,000 people starve every day. There was a severe drought last year (1983) in Africa and about twenty million people, spread through 18 countries, face severe shortages of food: shortages that will in some instances bring on starvation and in others, for very many people, will bring about debilitating malnutrition—a malnutrition that sometimes will permanently and seriously damage them. The Brandt Report of 1980 estimates that 800 million people cannot afford an adequate diet. This means that millions are constantly hungry, that millions suffer from deficiency diseases and from infections that they could resist with a more adequate diet. Approximately fifteen million children die each year from the combined effects of malnutrition and infection. In some areas of the world half the children born will die before their fifth birthday. Life for not a few of us in the industriously developed world is indeed, in various ways, grim. But our level of deprivation hardly begins to approximate to the level of poverty and utter misery that nearly 40% of the people in the Third World face.

As Robert McNamara, who is surely no spokesman for the Left, put it, there are these masses of "severely deprived human beings struggling to survive in a set of squalid and degraded circumstances almost beyond the power of sophisticated imaginations and privileged circumstances to conceive."[1] Human misery is very much concentrated in the southern hemisphere (hereafter "the South") and by any reasonable stand-

Reprinted with permission from the *Journal of Applied Philosophy*, vol. 1, no. 2 (1984).

ard of justice there is a global imbalance of the benefits and burdens of life—the resources available to people—that calls for an extensive redistribution of resources from the industrial countries of the northern hemisphere ("the North") to the South.

This, of course, assumes that there is something properly called global justice and this, in certain quarters, will be resisted as a mirage or as being an incoherent conception. We can properly speak of justice within a society with a common labour market, but we cannot speak of justice for the world community as a whole. We cannot say, some claim, of the world community as a whole that it is just or unjust. Justice is only possible, the claim goes, where there are common bonds of reciprocity. There are no such bonds between a Taude of Highland New Guinea and a farmer in Manitoba. In general there are no such bonds between people at great distances from each other and with no cultural ties, so, given what justice is, we cannot correctly speak of global justice. I think this is a mistaken way of construing things and I shall return to it in a moment.

The call for a massive redistribution of resources also assumes, what Neo-Malthusians will not grant, namely that we can carry this out without still greater harm resulting.[2] Part of the demand for the redistribution of resources is in the redistribution of food and in the resources (including the technology and the technological know-how) to realize agricultural potential. Neo-Malthusians believe that this redistribution, at least for the worst-off parts of the Third World, is suicidal.

It is a moral truism, but for all of that true, that it would be better, if no greater harm would follow from our achieving it, if we had a world in which no one starved and no one suffered from malnutrition. But, some Neo-Malthusians argue, greater harm would in fact follow if starvation were prevented in the really desperate parts of the world, for with the world's extensive population-explosion resulting from improved medicine and the like, the earth, if population growth is not severely checked, will exceed its carrying capacity. An analogy is made with a lifeboat. Suppose the sea is full of desperate swimmers and the only available lifeboat can only take on a certain number. It has, after all, a very definite carrying capacity. If too many are taken on the lifeboat it will swamp and everyone will drown. So the thing is not to go beyond the maximum carrying capacity of the lifeboat.

We are, Neo-Malthusians claim, in a similar position *vis-à-vis* the earth. It is like a lifeboat and if the population goes out of control and gets too large in relation to the carrying capacity of the earth there will be mass starvation and an unsettlement bringing on a suffering vastly exceeding the already terrible suffering that is upon us. Sometimes our choices are between evils and, where this is so, the rational and morally appropriate choice is to choose the lesser evil. It may be true that we may never do evil that good may come, but faced with the choice between two certain evils we should choose the lesser evil. Better four dead than twenty. But, some Neo-Malthusians claim, *vis-à-vis* famine relief, this is just the terrible situation we are in.

Parts of the earth have already, they claim, exceeded their carrying capacity. The population there is too great for the region to yield enough food for its expanding population. Yet it is in the poorer parts of the world that the population continues to swell and, it is terrible but still necessary to recognise, it is the above horrendous situation that we are facing in many parts of the world.

Neo-Malthusians maintain that if we do not check this population explosion in a rather drastic way the whole earth will in time be in the desperate position of the Sahel. Redistributive reform is softhearted and softheaded, encouraging the poor to increase their numbers and with that to increase the sum total of misery in the world.

I shall talk about Neo-Malthusianism first and then, after I have considered the International Food Order, turn to a consideration of whether we have a coherent conception of global justice. Neo-Malthusianism, I shall argue, is a pseudo-realism making dramatics out of a severe and tragic morality of triage when the facts in the case will not rationally warrant such dramatics—will not warrant in these circumstances a morality of triage.

In the first place, while lifeboats have a determinate carrying capacity, we have no clear conception of what this means with respect to the earth. What population density makes for commodious living is very subjective indeed; technological innovations continually improve crop yield and could do so even more adequately if more scientific effort were set in that direction.

Secondly, for the foreseeable future we have plenty of available fertile land and the agricultural potential adequately to feed a very much larger world population than we actually have.[3] Less than half of the available fertile land of the world is being used for any type of food production. In Africa, for example, as everyone knows, there are severe famine conditions and radical underdevelopment, but African agriculture has been declining for the last twenty years.[4] Farmers are paid as little as possible, masses of people have gone into the large urban centres where industrialization is going on. Domestic food production is falling while a lot of food is imported at prices that a very large number of people in the Third World cannot afford to pay. Yet Africa has half the unused farm land in the world. If it were only utilized, Africa could readily feed itself and be a large exporter of food.[5] The principal problem is not overpopulation or even drought but man-made problems, problems on which I will elaborate in a moment when I discuss the Postwar International Food Order.

Thirdly, the land that is used is very frequently used in incredibly inefficient ways. The *latifundia* system in Latin America is a case in point.[6] In Latin America as a whole, and by conservative estimates, landless families form 40% of all farm families. One percent of all farm families control, again by conservative estimates, 50% of all farm land. This landed elite has incredible power in Latin America and they use this power to keep the peasantry poor, disorganized and dependent. The *latifundia* system is an autocratic system, but—and this is what is most relevant for our purposes—it is also a very inefficient system of agricultural production.

The landowner, not infrequently through his farm manager, has firm control over the running of the farm and over the destinies of his farm labourers. The *latifundios* are very large estates and the land on them is underworked. Much of it is used for pasture. Only 4% of all the land in large estates is actually in crops. There is more fallow land, that is land not even used for pasture but held idle, than there is land in crops. If the *latifundia* land were redistributed to peasants and they were allowed to work it intensively and particularly if they formed into peasant cooperatives, the food production would be increased enormously. Again, it isn't the lack of land or the size of the population that is the problem but the way the land is used.

Fourthly, there is the problem of cash crops: crops such as peanuts, strawberries, bananas, mangos, artichokes, and the like. Key farm land, once used by local residents for subsistence farming, is now used for these cash crops, driving subsistence farmers off the best land into increasingly marginal land and, in many instances, forcing them to purchase food at very high prices, prices they often cannot afford to pay. The result has been increasing malnutrition and starvation and impoverishment. Previously in New Guinea most of the tribal peoples had a reasonably adequate diet. Now, with the incursion of the multinationals and the introduction of cash crops, severe malnutrition is rife. The good land is used for cash crops and the farming for local consumption is on the marginal land. Mexican peasants, to take another example, did reasonably well on a staple diet of corn and beans. With the advent of multinational food producers, they became a rural, but typically underemployed, proletariat, in one not atypical instance, planting, harvesting and processing in freezing plants strawberries for export and importing food to replace the staple food they had previously grown themselves.[7] The catch was that the food they purchased was typically less nutritious and was at prices they could hardly afford. Again, in those Mexican communities malnutrition is rife but the principal cause here, just as in New Guinea, is in the socio-economic system and not in droughts or population explosion.

In fine, against Neo-Malthusians, it is not the case that the basic cause of famine is the failure of the food supply relative to the population. Rather the basic cause of famine is poverty and certain economic policies. People who are not poor are not hungry. We look at North-South imbalance and it is plain as anything can be that this is the result of the workings of the world economic system and a clear indicator of that is the food economy. A stark difference between North and South is in the vast malnutrition and starvation which is principally a phenomenon of the South. But these famine conditions result from the working of the economic system in allocating the ability of people to acquire goods.[8] As Amartya Sen has shown for the great Bengal famine of 1943–1944, a famine in which around three million people died, it was not the result of any great crop failure or population explosion.[9] In 1942 there had been an extraordinary harvest but the 1943 crop was only somewhat lower and was in fact higher than the crop of 1941 which was not a famine year. Sen's figures show that the 1943 crop was only 10% less than the average of the five preceding years. Yet 1943 was a famine year of gigantic proportions. Why? The answer lies in people's economic position.[10] People have entitlements to a range of goods that they can acquire. Whether they have such entitlements, whether they can command the goods they need, depends on the workings of the economic system. Given—to take a current (1983) example—the minimum wage in Brazil (something for which approximately 1/3 of the work force labours), if that situation persists, many workers will not have the entitlement to the food they need to survive. In fact, right now a day's wage enables them only to command a kilo of beans. They can, that is, only purchase a kilo of beans for a day's work at the minimum wage. So people in such circumstances, understandably, reasonably and indeed rightly, take considerable risks to loot supermarkets and the like. People starve when their entitlements are not sufficiently large to buy the food necessary to keep them alive. That, to return to Sen's example of the great famine in Bengal, is precisely what happened in Bengal in 1943–44 and is happening again in Brazil and, with greater severity, in a not inconsiderable number of other places.

The food available to people is a matter of income distribution and that, in the capitalist system, is fundamentally rooted in their ability to provide services that people in the economy are willing to pay for. In poorer countries for many people about two-thirds of their total income goes for expenditures on food. Where there is some rapid industrialization newly employed workers are likely, with increased entitlements, to spend more on food. This, under a capitalist system, will force food prices up and it is very likely as a result that the entitlements of very poor agricultural labourers—labourers who own no land and have only their labor power to sell—will fall, until, even with a constant supply of food in their environment, they will no longer be able to purchase food to meet their minimum needs. Where people are on the margin of sustainable life, a famine may be created by such an increase of demand with little or no decline in the food supply.[11] What we need to recognise is that hunger, malnutrition and famine are fundamentally questions of distribution of income and the entitlements to food. And here, of course, we have plainly questions of justice and, I shall argue in Section III, questions of global justice. But in trying to achieve a moral assessment of what should be done in the face of such extensive starvation and malnutrition, Neo-Malthusian accounts are very wide of the mark, principally because of their failure to understand what causes and sustains such misery.

II

In order to make more perspicuous my discussion of global justice and to make even clearer why we should *not* regard the starvation and malnutrition facing the South as a matter of actual food shortages caused by or at least exacerbated by population explosion, I want to do a bit of political sociology and describe—an interpretative description if you like—the rise and fall of the Postwar International Food Order.[12] Since the early 1970s the perception of scarcity and disaster because of that scarcity has been a popular refrain of much of our discussion of the world food economy. But this, as I in effect indicated in the previous section, is more ideology than fact. To understand what is going on, we need to come to understand the political economy of food as it was developed after World War II in the capitalist world. The capitalist world, after the last great war, went from the gold standard to the dollar standard with the United States clearly becoming the preponderant world power. In the 1950s and 1960s, the American State, reflecting plainly the interests of its capitalists, developed a policy of food aid to Third World countries. These were countries which were often trying rapidly to industrialise. This food aid, at one and the same time, provided a lot of cheap food for their new and very inexpensive industrial labour force and a respite for the American farmers with their, relative to the market, overproduction. (We must remember that since the Roosevelt years the farmers had come to be a powerful lobby.) But it should also be noted that this food aid program helped turn self-sufficient agrarian countries into economically dependent countries dependent on food aid. It led to a commodification of food and to placing structurally these Third World countries in the commodity exchange system of the capitalist order.

The easiest way to see how the postwar food order developed and declined is to chart the fate of wheat in the world economy. In the 1950s and 1960s the surplus in wheat in the United States was sustained both for domestic-political reasons and to pull the newly emerging Third World countries firmly into the capitalist orbit. It was an astute way to help make the world safe for the flourishing of capitalism. Cheap food exported and subsidised from America encouraged in Third World countries the growth, in the process of industrialisation, of urban populations. It encouraged, that is, the formation of a proletariat and a lumpen-proletariat from a previously peasant population—a proletariat and a lumpen-proletariat dependent on cheap food sold to them principally as a commodity. A previously self-sufficient agriculture in Third World countries radically declined and ceased to be self-sufficient. Much of the rural population, in a state of impoverishment, as a huge reserve industrial army, was in effect driven into the cities and in tandem with that, as rural production declined, rural life became ever more impoverished.

Though there were in the 1950s and 1960s great hardships for both the new urban workers and the peasants in the countryside, nonetheless the system based on the export of cheap food from America worked in some reasonable fashion until the early 1970s. Then it began to come apart. This International Food Order "encouraged a massive increase in the numbers of people in all countries separated from direct ties to agriculture."[13] In such a situation an increase in grain prices will trigger an increase in scarcity, though the scarcity is not rooted in what "can technically be produced but in what people with constant or declining real monetary incomes can buy."[14] What we had facing us in the 1960s was an "extraordinary growth of urban populations—an aspect of proletarianisation—and agricultural underdevelopment."[15] The capitalist rationale for this activity was plain, food aid was intended to assist capitalist development in the Third World while appeasing the farm lobby in America. The thing was to integrate these Third World societies into the capitalist economic system: a system which was becoming a world system. Cheap foreign wheat facilitated this by facilitating the growth of urban populations, but it also contributed to underemployment and poverty in the countryside in these very same countries. But in the 1970s the International Food Order began to break down. Grain surpluses dwindled, prices rose, food aid was cut back. The food aid program gradually ceased to have a capitalist rationale. What had happened was that the food aid program had in the course of time made commercial markets work. In virtue of its very success, food aid became increasingly superfluous from a capitalist perspective. Some of the urban workers could now afford to buy food under market conditions, though many in the urban centers (those marginally employed or unemployed) had the *need* for the food but in a market system no longer had the *entitlement*. Similar things obtained for rural farm labourers rotting in the countryside where agricultural production had been cut back. The difficulty for Third World countries in continuing to get cheap food was exacerbated by the huge Russian/American grain deals of 1972 and 1973. Consumerism and a meat diet American Style became a goal in the Soviet Union and in Eastern Europe. And even though détente is now a thing of the past, or at least temporarily shelved, the grain sales to the Soviet Union still go on. But food aid to the Third World has almost vanished, the western agricultural sector continues to decline, farmers become fewer, now pitted against consumers, and food prices continue to rise so that the many poor in Third World countries lose their entitlements. Capitalism, of course, needs a workforce that can reproduce itself but with newly developed industrial enterprises in the Third World a little starvation and malnutrition will not hurt, will not affect the efficiency of capitalist production, as long as they have, as they indeed have, a huge labour pool to draw upon. Individual workers can starve as long as there are plenty of replacements. Things like this happened with the industrialisation of the Western World under capitalism in the nineteenth century. It is now being repeated in the Third World in the twentieth century.

III

With this sketch of political sociology before us, we can now return to the topic of global justice. There are some who would maintain that talk of justice can only coherently be applied within particular societies or at best between societies similarly situated and in a condition of mutual cooperation. I want to show why this doctrine is false and why it is quite morally imperative for us to speak of global justice and injustice and to characterise these notions in a perspicuous fashion.

 Those who would argue against extending justice arguments into a North-South context and into the international arena generally, will argue that when we talk about what is to be done here we need to recognise that we are beyond the circumstances of justice. For considerations of justice coherently to arise there must, between the people involved, be (a) a rough equality in the powers and capacities of persons, (b) be a situation where people do cooperate largely on the basis of reciprocal advantage and (c) a situation where all parties are in a condition of moderate scarcity.[16] It is, many have argued, only in such circumstances that issues of justice are at home. Only in such circumstances, the claim goes, can we appeal to principles of justice to adjudicate conflicting claims on moderately scarce goods. For principles of justice to function, there must be enough reciprocity around for people to find some balance of reciprocal advantage. If they cannot find that, they have no basis for regulating their conduct in accordance with the principles of justice.

However, if these really are the circumstances of justice, it looks at least as if we can have no global justice, for the richest nations do not seem to be related to the poorest ones in such a way that the rich nations secure a reciprocal advantage if justice is done. It very likely makes more sense for them to go on cruelly exploiting the poor nations as they have done in the past. There is, in short, in most circumstances at least, little in it for them if they would do, what in circumstances of greater equality, we would uncontroversially say is the just thing to do.

The mistake here, I believe, is in sticking with the existence of a skein of actual cooperative reciprocity as essential for the circumstances of justice. The world is certainly not a cooperative scheme. We do not have in place internationally schemes for mutual support. It is even rather far-fetched, given the class nature of our own societies, to regard discrete societies as cooperative partnerships, but certainly the world is not. We do not have in place there the cooperative reciprocal interdependency which, some say, is essential for justice.

However, this condition for the very possibility of justice is too strong. That this is so can be seen from the following considerations. There is a world-wide network of international trade; poor countries stand to rich countries in complex relations of interdependence, indeed in an interdependency relation that places poor countries in a position of dependence. The rich nations, functioning as instruments for gigantic capitalist enterprises, have dominated and exploited underdeveloped countries using their resources and markets on unfair terms. Between North and South—between rich and poor nations—there are conflicts of interest and competing claims under conditions not so far from moderate scarcity such that conditions giving scope for arguments of justice obtain. In intrastate situations we do not need conditions of actual reciprocity of mutual advantage for issues of justice to be in place. The Australian aborigine population could be too small, too weak, and too marginal to mainstream life in Australia for the non-aboriginal population to gain any advantage from *not* seizing their lands and driving them from them without any compensation. But such an action would not only be plainly wrong it would be grossly unjust. Yet it is quite possible that the non-aboriginal population would stand to gain rather than lose from such an action. Still, that would not make such an action one whit the less unjust. What we need to invoke instead is a *moral reciprocity* not resting on actual schemes of cooperation for mutual advantage but instead on a broadly Kantian conception of moral equality in which justice requires that we all treat each other as equals, namely, we are to treat all people as persons and in doing so treat them as we would reasonably wish to be treated ourselves.[17] In other words, we must, in reasoning justly, be willing to universalise and to engage in role reversal. It does not take much moral imagination for us, if we are relatively privileged members of the so-called First World, to realise that we would not wish to live the marginal existence of many people in the Third World. We would, that is, not wish to starve or have our children starve or to be in one way or another crippled by malnutrition or live, where this could be avoided, without anything like an adequate education or without adequate housing and the like. We would not accept role reversal here. If our feet, that is, were in their shoes, we would not take as morally tolerable, where such conditions could be avoided, such conditions of life for ourselves. But there is no relevant difference here between ourselves and them. If, in such circumstances, we would not will it for ourselves, we cannot will it for them either.

In the light of our conception of the moral equality of people, we could not accept such inequalities as just. Yet it is just such inequalities that the International Food Order, a deliberate policy objective of the United States, acting for the capitalist order, has brought about in the postwar years. Even given Nozickian notions of justice in rectification, it would be correct to say that many people in Third World countries are not being treated justly. However, the injustice of such an order is even more evident if we develop a conception of justice as fair reciprocity. People, through conquest, domination and exploitation, have been made worse off than they were before these relations were brought into place. They had been driven into bargains they would not have made if they had not been driven to the wall. They are plainly being coerced and they are surely not being treated as moral equals.

If we start with an idea of moral reciprocity in which all human beings are treated as equals, we cannot accept the relations that stand between North and South as something that has even the simulacrum of justice. But any tolerably adequate understanding of what morality requires of us will not allow us to accept anything less than a commitment to relations of moral equality. Starting from there we can see that global justice is a plain extension of domestic justice when we remember that in the international arena as well as in the domestic arena we stand (a) in conditions of interdependence, (b) in conditions of moderate scarcity (if we pool our resources) and (c) in conditions where our interests sometimes conflict. Moreover, by any plausible principles of global justice we might enunciate, the relations between North and South are so unjust that extensive redistributions of resources are in order. Whatever critical standards we use to regulate conflicting claims over scarce goods, we cannot, if we have any tolerably good knowledge of the facts in the case and a sense of fairness, but think the present relations are unjust and require rectification. There is not even in the various states of the North a fair access to basic natural and cultural resources, but viewed globally to speak of anything like a fair access to basic natural and cultural resources, where people are being treated as equals, can be nothing but a cruel and rather stupid joke.

If we start from a premise of *moral* equality as the vast majority of social theorists and moral philosophers right across the political spectrum do, from Robert Nozick to G. A. Cohen, we will believe that the interest of everyone matters and matters equally. There is no not believing in that, if we believe in *moral* equality.

For liberal egalitarians, such as Ronald Dworkin, this will involve a commitment to attain, not equality of condition but equality of resources, while for a radical egalitarian it will involve, as well, under conditions of productive abundance, a commitment to try to move as close as we reasonably can to an equality of condition. While rejecting all such egalitarian readings of *moral* equality, Nozick, with most other philosophers and economists on the right, thinks of moral equality as consisting most essentially in protecting individual rights to non-interference. Individuals in a just social order must be protected in their rights peacefully to pursue their own interests without interference from government, Church or anyone else. Even if the kind of redistribution from North to South I am advocating did not bring about financial hari-kari for people in the North, it would still involve an interference with their right peacefully to pursue their own interests where they are not harming anyone. Thus such a redistribution would still be wrong.

There are at least two responses that should be made here. The first is to assert that such capitalist behaviour has in fact harmed people. Sometimes this has been intentional, often not. But in any event, harm has been done. This is a factual issue, but if the factual descriptions I have given are near to the mark, and particularly if I have accurately described the workings of the international food order, the capitalist order centered in the West has indeed harmed, and continues to harm, very deeply many people in the Third World. (I do not mean to imply that it only harms people in the Third World.) But in our historical circumstances this is unnecessary for we could have an economic system whose underlying rationale was production to meet human needs and which was controlled democratically. Moreover, we now have the technical capacity to develop our productive powers so that the needs of people could be met. But the capitalist order has been massively supported in a very large part of the North and a not inconsiderable number of people in the North have been the beneficiaries of a socio-economic order that did so exploit. (Of course, there are others in the North who are just victims of that order.) This being so, even Nozickian notions of justice in rectification would require redistribution between North and South.

However, a second response seems to me more fundamental, less puritanical and less concerned with blaming people. To see best what is at issue we should proceed rather indirectly. We not only have rights to non-interference, we also have rights to fair cooperation and these rights can conflict. A very important liberty is the liberty to be able to guide one's own life in accordance with one's own unmystified preferences. Central to liberty is the capacity and opportunity to make rational choices and to be able to act on those rational choices.[18] This is much broader than to construe liberty as simply the absence of restrictions or interference, though it certainly includes that. What is vital to see here is that liberty will not be adequately protected if we limit our rights to the protection of rights to non-interference. We must also give central weight to the rights of fair cooperation. If the right of all to effective participation in government and, more generally, to effective direction of their lives is to be attained, there must be in place in our social organisations a respect for the right of everyone to fair cooperation. It is, of course, evident that respect for this right is not very widespread in the world. It will not only not be in place where there is subordination and domination, it will also not be effective where there is widespread starvation, malnutrition, exploitation and ignorance. What is unavoidable is that in class-based societies rights to fair cooperation and rights to non-interference will conflict. To move toward correcting the imbalances between North and South, we will have to move to a collective ownership and control of the means of production, for otherwise economic power becomes concentrated in the hands of a few and they will dominate and exploit others. But moving to collective ownership will in turn have the effect of overriding the rights to non-interference of Horatio Alger types who, capitalistically inclined, seek to acquire productive property through hard work and honest bargains. (It is hardly accurate or fair to say that there are no capitalists like that, particularly small capitalists.) In following their entirely peaceful interests—they have no wish to dominate or impoverish anyone—they wish to invest, buy and sell, and own productive property. If we are to protect their rights to non-interference, these activities can hardly be stopped, but if they are allowed to go on, the institutional stage is set, whatever the particular agent's own inclinations may be, for the undermining of rights to fair cooperation. So we have a fundamental clash of rights: rights of non-subordination with rights to non-interference.

To overcome the great disparities between North and South, even to put an end to the conditions of immiseration in the South—starvation, malnutrition, lack of work, extreme poverty—there would have to be significant and varied redistribution from North to South. In doing this we would have to give rather more weight to the rights of fair cooperation than to rights of non-interference. But—and here is what is alleged to be the catch—there is no significant consensus concerning which rights are to be overriding when they conflict.

I think that there would be a consensus if we came to command a clear view of these rights and their relations, along with some other powerful moral considerations and came, as well, to command a clear view of the relevant social realities. Surely people have a right to pursue their interests without interference. But there are interests and interests. (Indeed rights are most paradigmatically linked to our vital interests.) There is, among these interests, our interest in maintaining our bodily and moral integrity.

To require, for example, that a person (say a quite ordinary person), quite against her wishes, donate a kidney to keep someone alive whose value to the society is extensive is, that fact notwithstanding, still an intolerable intrusion on that involuntary donor's bodily integrity; to require a person to give up her religion or political convictions to enhance social harmony or even peace is another intolerable intrusion in that person's life—it simply runs roughshod over her civil liberties. But the interference with the peaceful pursuit of a person's interests that would go with a collective ownership of the means of production would not touch such vital interests. Rather what would be touched is her freedom to buy and sell, to invest and to bequeath *productive* property. But these interests are not nearly as vital as the above type of interests which genuinely are vital for our personal integrity. When the price for overriding those less vital interests is, as it is in the North/South situation, the overcoming of starvation, malnutrition, domination, subordination, great poverty and ignorance (certainly vital interests for any person), there is no serious doubt about in which direction the tradeoffs should go. That there is not a massive consensus about this results, I believe, not from deeply embedded moral differences between people but from disputes or at least from different beliefs about what is in fact the case and about what in fact can come to be the case.[19] Ideological mystification leads us to believe that there is nothing significant that could be done about these matters or nothing that could be done short of impoverishing us all or undermining our civil liberties. But that is just ideological mystification.

IV

So we know that from the moral point of view, justice, or at least humanity, requires an extensive redistribution between North and South. We also know, if we have anything of a sense of *realpolitik*, that nothing like this is going to happen within the present socio-economic order. We can, as I have tried to indicate, know something of what morality requires here but what is far more important to know, and much less obvious, is what are the mechanisms by which this conception of moral requiredness can become a reality in the lives of people so that our societies can be turned around. You may think that what I am about to say is too *parti pris* or perhaps you will even believe it to be vulgar, but it seems to me to be plainly true all that notwithstanding. And, even if it is vulgar, it is better to say something which if true is importantly true than to be evasive out of a sense of nicety or out of fear of saying something obvious.

What I think is plainly true is this: our capitalist masters, in principal control of the consciousness industry, have a plain interest in maintaining something not very different from the present North-South state of affairs.[20] To stabilise things they might, in certain circumstances, where they envisage a threat, favour some minor redistribution of wealth, but it would be very much against their interests, and that of a tiny stratum beholden to them, to make any extensive redistributions—redistributions that would touch their secure power base. Capitalism requires, and indeed can accept, at most a somewhat improved and more efficient version of the present and that, in turn, requires great injustice and inhumanity. It could only marginally improve our lot. A necessary but not a sufficient condition for attaining the end of such global injustice and inhumanity is the shedding of capitalism. As long, that is, as we live in a capitalist system, we are going to have such injustices. At most we might lessen their severity a bit.

If we are morally serious and not ideologically blinkered, we will realise that it is our central social task to get rid of capitalism. But concretely how this is to be done, given capitalist dominance in Western industrial societies, is anything but obvious. (This is exacerbated by the technological sophistication of these societies—by their awesome means of surveillance and control.) However, that the way or the ways are not obvious does not mean, if our efforts are over the long haul, that it cannot be done or that we should settle, as many do, for some reformist tinkering inside bourgeois parameters. We are not going to get justice or even a reign of common humanity that way. Recognising that there are no quick fixes, we need to continue to struggle, without hiding from ourselves the sobering and indeed depressing recognition that things are probably going to get much worse before they get better.

NOTES

1. Robert McNamara as cited by Peter Singer (1979) *Practical Ethics* (London: Cambridge University Press), p. 159.
2. Hardin, Garrett "Lifeboat ethics: the case against helping the poor" and Fletcher, Joseph "Give if it helps but not if it hurts," both in Aiken, William & La Follette, Hugh (Eds) (1977) *World Hunger and Moral Obligation* (Englewood Cliffs, N.J.: Prentice Hall).
3. Friedmann, Harriet (1982) The political economy of food: the rise and fall of the postwar International Food Order, in Burawoy, Michael & Skocpol, Theda (Eds) *Marxist Inquiries* (Chicago: University of Chicago Press), pp. 248–286.
4. Ibid.
5. Ibid.
6. Feder, Ernest (1971) Latifundia and agricultural labour in Latin America, in Shanin, Teodor (Ed.) *Peasants and Peasant Societies* (Harmondsworth: Penguin), pp. 83–102.
7. Moore Lappé, Frances & Collins, Joseph (1977) *Food First: Beyond the myth of scarcity* (Boston: Houghton Mifflin), pp. 256–258, 278–281; Feder, Ernest (1978) *Strawberry Imperialism: An enquiry into the mechanisms of dependency in Mexican agriculture* (The Hague: Institute of Social Studies).
8. Sen, Amartya (1981) *Poverty and Famines: An essay on entitlement and deprivation* (Oxford: Clarendon Press); Arrow, Kenneth J. Why people go hungry, *New York Review of Books*, vol. XXIX, no. 12 (15 July 1982), pp. 24–26.
9. Sen, op. cit., pp. 52–83.
10. Ibid.
11. Ibid., pp. 24–37.
12. My account here is indebted to Harriet Friedman's masterful account of this order. See Friedman, op. cit., pp. 248–286.
13. Ibid., p. 250.
14. Ibid.
15. Ibid., p. 268.

16. Hume, David (1964), in Selby-Brigge, L. A. (Ed.) *A Treatise of Human Nature* (Oxford: Clarendon Press), pp. 485–495; Rawls, John (1971) *A Theory of Justice* (Cambridge, Mass.: Harvard University Press), pp. 126–130; Barry, Brian Circumstances of justice and future generations, in Sikora, R. I. & Barry, Brian (1978) (eds) *Obligations to Future Generations* (Philadelphia: Temple University Press), pp. 204–248.
17. Richards, David A. J. (1982) International distributive justice, in Pennock, Roland J. & Chapman, John W. (Eds) *Nomos*, vol. XXIV (New York: New York University Press), pp. 275–295; Nagel, Thomas (1979) *Mortal Questions* (Cambridge: Cambridge University Press), pp. 111–112.
18. Norman, Richard (1981) Liberty, equality, property, *Aristotelian Society*, Supplementary Volume, LV (1981), pp. 199–202.
19. This is powerfully argued by Andrew Collier in Scientific socialism and the question of socialist values, in Nielsen, Kai & Patten, Steven (eds) (1981) *Marx and Morality* (Guelph, Ontario: Canadian Association for Publishing in Philosophy), pp. 121–154.
20. Enzensberger, Hans Magnus (1974) *The Consciousness Industry* (New York: Seabury Press), pp. 3–25.

LIBERALISM AND COMMUNITY

Since its publication in 1971, John Rawls's *A Theory of Justice* has spawned a stimulating and wide-ranging debate over justice and economic distribution. Designed as an alternative to utilitarianism in political philosophy, Rawls's social contract theory was soon challenged, as we have seen, by Robert Nozick's powerful restatement of the libertarian position. Part I of this volume presented in some detail the complex interplay of these three contrasting approaches to the problem of economic justice. In the years since the first edition of this book, however, an important, rival perspective has arisen in political philosophy. Those associated with it are generally labeled *communitarians*, and in this section we reproduce selections from the writings of three important communitarian theorists—Michael Sandel, Alasdair MacIntyre, and Michael Walzer.

The communitarian perspective cuts across traditional political categories, and the themes and emphases of communitarian writers vary. Among them, only Walzer addresses in any detail the problems of economic distribution that have concerned earlier writers in this volume. What does unite communitarians is their opposition to what they see as the dominant political philosophy of our times, namely, *liberalism*.

Communitarians join with Rawls and Nozick in rejecting utilitarianism, but they see the approaches of Rawls and Nozick as fatally flawed by a kind of abstract and individualistic approach to political philosophy. Communitarians are skeptical about efforts to base a conception of justice on abstract individual rights and on the priority of the right over the good (which they see as common to both Rawls's and Nozick's approach), rather than on a fuller vision of the morally good life. In contrast to utilitarians, communitarians favor a contextualized, historical understanding of the good of persons and of a community. That is, communitarians seek to locate justice not on the basis of a generalized, abstract, and ahistorical notion of human happiness but on the basis of an historically evolved conception of the good of citizens living as members of a particular community.

In the first two selections, communitarians Michael Sandel and Alasdair MacIntyre argue against liberalism. They reject its agnosticism about the good and contend that liberalism rests on mistaken assumptions about the nature of a person. We cannot adequately understand what it is to be a person, much less a good person, without looking to social roles; nor can we hope to arrive at an adequate conception of justice by thinking of the state as a neutral framework of rights. Virtue and desert are, and must be, central to any adequate political philosophy.

Continuing many of Sandel's and MacIntyre's themes, Michael Walzer spells out an alternative to Rawlsian liberalism which, while egalitarian, is not based on utility, social contract, or natural rights. Arguing that each type of social good carries its own criteria of distribution, he considers the importance of community membership and then weighs various criteria for distribution of economic income, hard work, and political power in the workplace. In the following article Marilyn Friedman seeks to place the debate between liberals and communitarians in the context of recent feminist thinking about community.

In the final selection, John Rawls (now one of many interpreters of his own work) describes his own view of the aims and limitations of justice as fairness, thereby answering many of the charges leveled against him by his communitarian critics.

Michael J. Sandel

Morality and the Liberal Ideal

In the following essay, Michael Sandel explores the differences among the "liberal" approaches of Rawls and Nozick, utilitarianism, and his own communitarian perspective. While agreeing that utilitarianism must be rejected, he also argues against rights-based liberalism, claiming it rests on a mistaken conception of an "unencumbered" self that exists prior to its ends and roles. He then considers some of the political disagreements that divide liberals from communitarians.

Liberals often take pride in defending what they oppose—pornography, for example, or unpopular views. They say the state should not impose on its citizens a preferred way of life, but should leave them as free as possible to choose their own values and ends, consistent with a similar liberty for others. This commitment to freedom of choice requires liberals constantly to distinguish between permission and praise, between allowing a practice and endorsing it. It is one thing to allow pornography, they argue, something else to affirm it.

Conservatives sometimes exploit this distinction by ignoring it. They charge that those who would allow abortions favor abortion, that opponents of school prayer oppose prayer, that those who defend the rights of Communists sympathize with their cause. And in a pattern of argument familiar in our politics, liberals reply by invoking higher principles; it is not that they dislike pornography less, but rather that they value toleration, or freedom of choice, or fair procedures more.

But in contemporary debate, the liberal rejoinder seems increasingly fragile, its moral basis increasingly unclear. Why should toleration and freedom of choice prevail when other important values are also at stake? Too often the answer implies some version of moral relativism, the idea that it is wrong to "legislate morality" because all morality is merely subjective. "Who is to say what is literature and what is filth? That is a value judgment, and whose values should decide?"

Relativism usually appears less as a claim than as a question. "Who is to judge?" But it is a question that can also be asked of the values that liberals defend. Toleration and freedom and fairness are values too, and they can hardly be defended by the claim that no values can be defended. So it is a mistake to affirm liberal values by arguing that all values are merely subjective. The relativist defense of liberalism is no defense at all.

What, then, can be the moral basis of the higher principles the liberal invokes? Recent political philosophy has offered two main alternatives—one utilitarian, the other Kantian. The utilitarian view, following John Stuart Mill, defends liberal principles in the name of maximizing the general welfare. The state should not impose on its citizens a preferred way of life, even for their own good, because doing so will reduce the sum of human happiness, at least in the long run; better that people choose for themselves, even if, on occasion, they get it wrong. "The only freedom which deserves the name," writes Mill in *On Liberty*, "is that of pursuing our own good in our own way, so long as we do not attempt to deprive others of theirs, or impede their efforts to obtain it." He adds that his argument does not depend on any notion of abstract right, only on the principle of the greatest good for the greatest number. "I regard utility as the ultimate appeal on all ethical questions; but it must be utility in the largest sense, grounded on the permanent interests of man as a progressive being."

Many objections have been raised against utilitarianism as a general doctrine of moral philosophy. Some have questioned the concept of utility, and the assumption that all human goods are in principle commensurable. Others have objected that by reducing all values to preferences and desires, utilitarians are unable to admit qualitative distinctions of worth, unable to distinguish noble desires from base ones. But most recent debate has focused on whether utilitarianism offers a convincing basis for liberal principles, including respect for individual rights.

In one respect, utilitarianism would seem well suited to liberal purposes. Seeking to maximize overall happiness does not require judging people's values, only aggregating them. And the willingness to aggregate preferences without judging them suggests a tolerant spirit, even a democratic one. When people go to the polls we count their votes, whatever they are.

But the utilitarian calculus is not always as liberal as it first appears. If enough cheering Romans pack the Coliseum to watch the lion devour the Christian, the collective pleasure of the Romans will surely outweigh the pain of the Christian, intense though it be. Or if a big majority abhors a small religion and wants it banned, the balance of preferences will favor suppression, not toleration. Utilitarians sometimes defend individual rights on the grounds that respecting them now will serve utility in the long run. But this calculation is precarious and contingent. It hardly secures the liberal promise not to impose on some the values of others. As the majority will is an inadequate instrument of liberal politics— by itself it fails to secure individual rights—so the utilitarian philosophy is an inadequate foundation for liberal principles.

The case against utilitarianism was made most powerfully by Immanuel Kant. He argued that empirical principles, such as utility, were unfit to serve as basis for the moral law. A wholly instrumental defense of freedom and rights not only leaves rights vulnerable, but fails to respect the inherent dignity of persons. The utilitarian calculus treats people as means to the happiness of others, not as ends in themselves, worthy of respect.

Contemporary liberals extend Kant's argument with the claim that utilitarianism fails to take seriously the distinction between persons. In seeking above all to maximize the general welfare, the utilitarian treats society as a whole as if it were a single person; it conflates our many, diverse desires into a single system of desires. It is indifferent to the distribution of satisfactions among persons, except insofar as this may affect the overall sum. But this fails to respect our plurality and distinctness. It uses some as means to the happiness of all, and so fails to respect each as an end in himself.

In the view of modern-day Kantians, certain rights are so fundamental that even the general welfare cannot override them. As John Rawls writes in his important work, *A Theory of Justice*, "Each person possesses an inviolability founded on justice that even the welfare of society as a whole cannot override. . . . The rights secured by justice are not subject to political bargaining or to the calculus of social interests."

So Kantian liberals need an account of rights that does not depend on utilitarian considerations. More than this, they need an account that does not depend on any particular conception of the good, that does not presuppose the superiority of one way of life over others. Only a justification neutral about ends could preserve the liberal resolve not to favor any particular ends, or to impose on its citizens a preferred way of life. But what sort of justification could this be? How is it possible to affirm certain liberties and rights as fundamental without embracing some vision of the good life, without endorsing some ends over others? It would seem we are back to the relativist predicament—to affirm liberal principles without embracing any particular ends.

The solution proposed by Kantian liberals is to draw a distinction between the "right" and the "good"—between a framework of basic rights and liberties, and the conceptions of the good that people may choose to pursue within the framework. It is one thing for the state to support a fair framework, they argue, something else to affirm some particular ends. For example, it is one thing to defend the right to free speech so that people may be free to form their own opinions and choose their own ends, but something else to support it on the grounds that a life of political discussion is inherently worthier than a life unconcerned with public affairs, or on the grounds that free speech will increase the general welfare. Only the first defense is available in the Kantian view, resting as it does on the ideal of a neutral framework.

Now, the commitment to a framework neutral with respect to ends can be seen as a kind of value—in this sense the Kantian liberal is no relativist—but its value consists precisely in its refusal to affirm a preferred way of life or conception of the good. For Kantian liberals, then, the right is prior to the good, and in two senses. First, individual rights cannot be sacrificed for the sake of the general good; and second, the principles of justice that specify these rights cannot be premised on any particular vision of the good life. What justifies the rights is not that they maximize the general welfare or otherwise promote the good, but rather that they comprise a fair framework within which individuals and groups can choose their own values and ends, consistent with a similar liberty for others.

Of course, proponents of the rights-based ethic notoriously disagree about what rights are fundamental, and about what political arrangements the ideal of the neutral framework requires. Egalitarian liberals support the welfare state, and favor a scheme of civil liberties together with certain social and economic rights—rights to welfare, education, health care, and so on. Libertarian liberals defend the market economy, and claim that redistributive policies violate peoples' rights; they favor a scheme of civil liberties combined with a strict regime of private property rights. But whether egalitarian or libertarian, rights-based liberalism begins with the claim that we are separate, individual persons, each with our own aims, interests, and conceptions of the good; it seeks a framework of rights that will enable us to realize our capacity as free moral agents, consistent with a similar liberty for others.

Within academic philosophy, the last decade or so has seen the ascendance of the rights-based ethic over the utilitarian one, due in large part to the influence of Rawls's *A Theory of Justice*. The legal philosopher H. L. A. Hart recently described the shift from "the old faith that some form of utilitarianism must capture the essence of political morality" to the new faith that "the truth must lie with a doctrine of basic human rights, protecting specific basic liberties and interests of individuals. . . . Whereas not so long ago great energy and much ingenuity of many philosophers were devoted to making some form of utilitarianism work, latterly such energies and ingenuity have been devoted to the articulation of theories of basic rights."

But in philosophy as in life, the new faith becomes the old orthodoxy before long. Even as it has come to prevail over its utilitarian rival, the rights-based ethic has recently faced a growing challenge from a different direction, from a view that gives fuller expression to the claims of citizenship and community than the liberal vision allows. The communitarian critics, unlike modern liberals, make the case for a politics of the common good. Recalling the arguments of Hegel against Kant, they question the liberal claim for the priority of the right over the good, and the picture of the freely choosing individual it embodies. Following Aristotle, they argue that we cannot justify political arrangements without reference to common purposes and ends, and that we cannot conceive of ourselves without reference to our role as citizens, as participants in a common life.

This debate reflects two contrasting pictures of the self. The rights-based ethic, and the conception of the person it embodies, were shaped in large part in the encounter with utilitarianism. Where utilitarians conflate our many desires into a single system of desire, Kantians insist on the separateness of persons. Where the utilitarian self is simply defined as the sum of its desires, the Kantian self is a choosing self, independent of the desires and ends it may have at any moment. As Rawls writes, "The self is prior to the ends which are affirmed by it; even a dominant end must be chosen from among numerous possibilities."

The priority of the self over its ends means I am never defined by my aims and attachments, but always capable of standing back to survey and assess and possibly to revise them. This is what it means to be a free and independent self, capable of choice. And this is the vision of the self that finds expression in the ideal of the state as a neutral framework. On the rights-based ethic, it is precisely because we are essentially separate, independent selves that we need a neutral framework, a framework of rights that refuses to choose among competing purposes and ends. If the self is prior to its ends, then the right must be prior to the good.

Communitarian critics of rights-based liberalism say we cannot conceive ourselves as independent in this way, as bearers of selves wholly detached from our aims and attachments. They say that certain of our roles are partly constitutive of the persons we are—as citizens of a country, or members of a movement, or partisans of a cause. But if we are partly defined by the communities we inhabit, then we must also be implicated in the purposes and ends characteristic of those communities. As Alasdair MacIntyre writes in his book, *After Virtue*, "What is good for me has to be the good for one who inhabits these roles." Open-ended though it be, the story of my life is always embedded in the story of those communities from which I derive my identity—whether family or city, tribe or nation, party or cause. In the communitarian view, these stories make a moral difference, not only a psychological one. They situate us in the world and give our lives their moral particularity.

What is at stake for politics in the debate between unencumbered selves and situated ones? What are the practical differences between a politics of rights and a politics of the common good? On some issues, the two theories may produce different arguments for similar policies. For example, the civil rights movement of the 1960s might be justified by liberals in the name of human dignity and respect for persons, and by communitarians in the name of recognizing the full membership of fellow citizens wrongly excluded from the common life of the nation. And where liberals might support public education in hopes of equipping students to become autonomous individuals, capable of choosing their own ends and pursuing them effectively, communitarians might support public education in hopes of equipping students to become good citizens, capable of contributing meaningfully to public deliberations and pursuits.

On other issues, the two ethics might lead to different policies. Communitarians would be more likely than liberals to allow a town to ban pornographic bookstores, on the grounds that pornography offends its way of life and the values that sustain it. But a politics of civic virtue does not always part company with liberalism in favor of conservative policies. For example, communitarians would be more willing than some rights-oriented liberals to see states enact laws regulating plant closings, to protect their communities from the disruptive effects of capital mobility and sudden industrial change. More generally, where the liberal regards the expansion of individual rights and entitlements as unqualified moral and political progress, the communitarian is troubled by the tendency of liberal programs to displace politics from smaller forms of association to more comprehensive ones. Where libertarian liberals defend the private economy and egalitarian liberals defend the welfare state, communitarians worry about the concentration of power in both the corporate economy and the bureaucratic state, and the erosion of those intermediate forms of community that have at times sustained a more vital public life.

Liberals often argue that a politics of the common good, drawing as it must on particular loyalties, obligations, and traditions, opens the way to prejudice and intolerance. The modern nation-state is not the Athenian polis, they point out; the scale and diversity of modern life have rendered the Aristotelian political ethic nostalgic at best and dangerous at worst. Any attempt to govern by a vision of the good is likely to lead to a slippery slope of totalitarian temptations.

Communitarians reply, rightly in my view, that intolerance flourishes most where forms of life are dislocated, roots unsettled, traditions undone. In our day, the totalitarian impulse has sprung less from the convictions of confidently situated selves than from the confusions of atomized, dislocated, frustrated selves, at sea in a world where common meanings have lost their force. As Hannah Arendt has written, "What makes mass society so difficult to bear is not the number of people involved, or at least not primarily, but the fact that the world between them has lost its power to gather them together, to relate and to separate them." Insofar as our public life has withered, our sense of common involvement diminished, we lie vulnerable to the mass politics of totalitarian solutions. So responds the party of the common good to the party of rights. If the party of the common good is right, our most pressing moral and political project is to revitalize those civic republican possibilities implicit in our tradition but fading in our time.

Alasdair MacIntyre
Virtues, the Unity of Life, and the Liberal Tradition

Elaborating on a number of threads in Michael Sandel's article, Alasdair MacIntyre begins with a discussion of virtue. To understand its meaning, he says, we must understand the notion of a practice, the role of narrative in understanding both action and selfhood, and, finally, the idea of a tradition. The good of society cannot, he claims, be understood independently of a conception of the good of its citizens, and that good requires us to situate them within a narrative and a tradition. Those who (like Rawls and Nozick) would seek to define justice without specifying a concept of virtue and outside of a particular moral and political tradition must inevitably fail, he argues. Given their individualistic premises, they cannot provide a basis for either community or for ideas of desert and virtue. Their disagreement over justice is irresolvable as well as fruitless. In the final section, taken from his most recent book, MacIntyre addresses the claim of liberalism to have found a rationally defensible, ahistorical conception of justice that exists outside any particular tradition. Instead, he argues, liberalism rests on a vision of the individual self and political reason based on preference fulfillment and of society as the outcome of a market-like bargaining process. Justice then becomes a matter, not of substance, but of process and persuasion. Although liberalism initially rejects any overriding theory of the good, it comes to embody just such a theory. Its principles of social justice are themselves the articulation of an historically developed and developing set of social institutions and forms of activity.

VIRTUES AND PRACTICES

[T]here are no less than three stages in the logical development of the concept, which have to be identified in order, if the core conception of a virtue is to be understood, and each of these stages has its own conceptual background. The first stage requires a background account of what I shall call a practice, the second an account of what I have already characterised as the narrative order of a single human life and the third an account a good deal fuller than I have given up to now of what constitutes a moral tradition. Each later stage presupposes the earlier, but not *vice versa.* . . .

      By a 'practice' I am going to mean any coherent and complex form of socially established cooperative human activity through which goods internal to that form of activity are realised in the course of trying to achieve those standards of excellence which are appropriate to, and partially definitive of, that form of activity, with the result that human powers to achieve excellence, and human conceptions of the ends and goods involved, are systematically extended. Tic-tac-toe is not an example of a practice in this sense, nor is throwing a football with skill; but the game of football is, and so is chess. Bricklaying is not a practice; architecture is. Planting turnips is not a practice; farming is. So are the enquiries of physics, chemistry and biology, and so is the work of the historian, and so are painting and music. In the ancient and medieval worlds the creation and sustaining of human communities—of households, cities, nations—is generally taken to be a practice in the sense in which I have defined it. Thus the range of practices is wide: arts, sciences, games, politics in the Aristotelian sense, the making and sustaining of family life, all fall under the concept. But the question of the precise range of practices is not at this stage of the first importance. Instead let me explain some of the key terms involved in my definition, beginning with the notion of goods internal to a practice.

Consider the example of a highly intelligent seven-year-old child whom I wish to teach to play chess, although the child has no particular desire to learn the game. The child does however have a very strong desire for candy and little chance of obtaining it. I therefore tell the child that if the child will play chess with me once a week I will give the child 50¢ worth of candy; moreover I tell the child that I will always play in such a way that it will be difficult, but not impossible, for the child to win and that, if the child wins, the child will receive an extra 50¢ worth of candy. Thus motivated the child plays and plays to win. Notice however that, so long as it is the candy alone which provides the child with a good reason for playing chess, the child has no reason not to cheat and every reason to cheat, provided he or she can do so successfully. But, so we may hope, there will come a time when the child will find in those goods specific to chess, in the achievement of a certain highly particular kind of analytical skill, strategic imagination and competitive intensity, a new set of reasons, reasons now not just for winning on a particular occasion, but for trying to excel in whatever way the game of chess demands. Now if the child cheats, he or she will be defeating not me, but himself or herself.

There are thus two kinds of good possibly to be gained by playing chess. On the one hand there are those goods externally and contingently attached to chess-playing and to other practices by the accidents of social circumstance—in the case of the imaginary child candy, in the case of real adults such goods as prestige, status and money. There are always alternative ways for achieving such goods, and their achievement is never to be had *only* by engaging in some particular kind of practice. On the other hand there are the goods internal to the practice of chess which cannot be had in any way but by playing chess or some other game of that specific kind. We call them internal for two reasons: first, as I have already suggested, because we can only specify them in terms of chess or some other game of that specific kind and by means of examples from such games (otherwise the meagerness of our vocabulary for speaking of such goods forces us into such devices as my own resort to writing of 'a certain highly particular kind of'); and secondly because they can only be identified and recognised by the experience of participating in the practice in question. Those who lack the relevant experience are incompetent thereby as judges of internal goods. . . .

[Take portrait painting as an example.] There is first of all the excellence of the products, both the excellence in performance by the painters and that of each portrait itself. This excellence—the very verb 'excel' suggests it—has to be understood historically. The sequences of development find their point and purpose in a progress towards and beyond a variety of types and modes of excellence. There are of course sequences of decline as well as progress, and progress is rarely to be understood as straightforwardly linear. But it is in participation in the attempts to sustain progress and to respond creatively to moments that the second kind of good internal to the practices of portrait painting is to be found. For what the artist discovers within the pursuit of excellence in portrait painting—and what is true of portrait painting is true of the practice of the fine arts in general—is the good of a certain kind of life. That life may not constitute the whole of life for someone who is a painter by a very long way or it may at least for a period, Gauguin-like, absorb him or her at the expense of almost everything else. But it is the painter's living out of a greater or lesser part of his or her life *as a painter* that is the second kind of good internal to painting. And judgment upon these goods requires at the very least the kind of competence that is only to be acquired either as a painter or as someone willing to learn systematically what the portrait painter has to teach.

A practice involves standards of excellence and obedience to rules as well as the achievement of goods. To enter into a practice is to accept the authority of those standards and the inadequacy of my own performance as judged by them. It is to subject my own attitudes, choices, preferences and tastes to the standards which currently and partially define the practice. Practices of course, as I have just noticed, have a history: games, sciences and arts all have histories. Thus the standards are not themselves immune from criticism, but none the less we cannot be initiated into a practice without accepting the authority of the best standards realised so far. If, on starting to listen to music, I do not accept my own incapacity to judge correctly, I will never learn to hear, let alone to appreciate, Bartok's last quartets. If, on starting to play baseball, I do not accept that others know better than I when to throw a fast ball and when not, I will never learn to appreciate good pitching let alone to pitch. In the realm of practices the authority of both goods and standards operates in such a way as to rule out all subjectivist and emotivist analyses of judgment. De gustibus *est* disputandum. . . .

But what does all or any of this have to do with the concept of the virtues? It turns out that we are now in a position to formulate a first, even if partial and tentative definition of a virtue: *A virtue is an acquired human quality the possession and exercise of which tends to enable us to achieve those goods which are internal to practices and the lack of which effectively prevents us from achieving any such goods*. Later this definition will need amplification and amendment. But as a first approximation to an adequate definition it already illuminates the place of the virtues in human life. For it is not difficult to show for a whole range of key virtues that without them the goods internal to practices are barred to us, but not just barred to us generally, barred in a very particular way.

It belongs to the concept of a practice as I have outlined it—and as we are all familiar with it already in our actual lives, whether we are painters or physicists or quarterbacks or indeed just lovers of good painting or first-rate experiments or a well-thrown pass—that its goods can only be achieved by subordinating ourselves to the best standard so far achieved, and that entails subordinating ourselves within the practice in our relationship to other practitioners. We have to learn to recognise what is due to whom; we have to be prepared to take whatever self-endangering risks are demanded along the way; and we have to listen carefully to what we are told about our own inadequacies and to reply with the same carefulness for the facts. In other words we have to accept as necessary components of any practice with internal goods and standards of excellence the virtues of justice, courage and honesty. For not to accept these, to be willing to cheat as our imagined child was willing to cheat in his or her early days at chess, so far bars us from achieving the standards of excellence or the goods internal to the practice that it renders the practice pointless except as a device for achieving external goods.

We can put the same point in another way. Every practice requires a certain kind of relationship between those who participate in it. Now the virtues are those goods by reference to which, whether we like it or not, we define our relationships to those other people with whom we share the kind of purposes and standards which inform practices. Consider an example of how reference to the virtues has to be made in certain kinds of human relationship.

A, B, C, and D are friends in that sense of friendship which Aristotle takes to be primary: they share in the pursuit of certain goods. In my terms they share in a practice. D dies in obscure circumstances, A discovers how D died and tells the truth about it to B while lying to C. C discovers the lie. What A cannot then intelligibly claim is that he stands in the same relationship of friendship to both B and C. By telling the truth to one and lying to the other he has partially defined a difference in the relationship. Of course it is open to A to explain this difference in a number of ways; perhaps he was trying to spare C pain or perhaps he is simply cheating C. But some difference in the relationship now exists as a result of the lie. For their allegiance to each other in the pursuit of common goods has been put in question.

Just as, so long as we share the standards and purposes characteristic of practices, we define our relationships to each other, whether we acknowledge it or not, by reference to standards of truthfulness and trust, so we define them too by reference to standards of justice and of courage. If A, a professor, gives B and C the grades that their papers deserve, but grades D because he is attracted by D's blue eyes or is repelled by D's dandruff, he has defined his relationship to D differently from his rela-tionship to the other members of the class, whether he wishes it or not. Justice requires that we treat others in respect of merit or desert according to uniform and impersonal standards; to depart from the standards of justice in some particular instance defines our relationship with the rele-vant person as in some way special or distinctive.

The case with courage is a little different. We hold courage to be a virtue because the care and concern for individuals, communities and causes which is so crucial to so much in practices requires the existence of such a virtue. If someone says that he cares for some individual, commu-nity or cause, but is unwilling to risk harm or danger on his, her or its own behalf, he puts in question the genuineness of his care and concern. Courage, the capacity to risk harm or danger to oneself, has its role in human life because of this connection with care and concern. This is not to say that a man cannot genuinely care and also be a coward. It is in part to say that a man who genuinely cares and has not the capacity for risking harm or danger has to define himself, both to himself and to others, as a coward.

I take it then that from the standpoint of those types of relation-ship without which practices cannot be sustained truthfulness, justice and courage—and perhaps some others—are genuine excellences, are virtues in the light of which we have to characterise ourselves and others, what-ever our private moral standpoint or our society's particular codes may be. . . .

I have defined the virtues partly in terms of their place in prac-tices. But surely, it may be suggested, some practices—that is, some coher-ent human activities which answer to the description of what I have called a practice—are evil. So in discussions by some moral philosophers of this type of account of the virtues it has been suggested that torture and sado-masochistic sexual activities might be examples of practices. But how can a disposition be a virtue if it is the kind of disposition which sustains prac-tices and some practices issue in evil? My answer to this objection falls into two parts.

First I want to allow that there *may* be practices—in the sense in which I understand the concept—which simply *are* evil. I am far from convinced that there are, and I do not in fact believe that either torture or sado-masochistic sexuality answer to the description of a practice which my account of the virtues employs. But I do not want to rest my case on this lack of conviction, especially since it is plain that as a matter of contingent fact many types of practice may on particular occasions be productive of evil. For the range of practices includes the arts, the sciences and certain types of intellectual and athletic game. And it is at once obvious that any of these may under certain conditions be a source of evil: the desire to excel and to win can corrupt, a man may be so engrossed by his painting that he neglects his family, what was initially an honourable resort to war can issue in savage cruelty. But what follows from this?

It certainly is not the case that my account entails *either* that we ought to excuse or condone such evils *or* that whatever flows from a virtue is right. I do have to allow that courage sometimes sustains injustice, that loyalty has been known to strengthen a murderous aggressor and that generosity has sometimes weakened the capacity to do good. . . .

Secondly without an overriding conception of the *telos* of a whole human life, conceived as a unity, our conception of certain individual virtues has to remain partial and incomplete. Consider [patience]. . . . The medieval exponents of the virtue of patience claimed that there are certain types of situation in which the virtue of patience requires that I do not ever give up on some person or task, situations in which, as they would have put it, I am required to embody in my attitude to that person or task something of the patient attitude of God towards his creation. But this could only be so if patience served some overriding good, some *telos* which warranted putting other goods in a subordinate place. Thus it turns out that the content of the virtue of patience depends upon how we order various goods in a hierarchy and *a fortiori* on whether we are able rationally so to order these particular goods.

I have suggested so far that unless there is a *telos* which transcends the limited goods of practices by constituting the good of a whole human life, the good of a human life conceived as a unity, it will *both* be the case that a certain subversive arbitrariness will invade the moral life *and* that we shall be unable to specify the context of certain virtues adequately. These two considerations are reinforced by a third: that there is at least one virtue recognised by the tradition which cannot be specified at all except with reference to the wholeness of a human life—the virtue of integrity or constancy. 'Purity of heart,' said Kierkegaard, 'is to will one thing.' This notion of singleness of purpose in a whole life can have no application unless that of a whole life does.

It is clear therefore that my preliminary account of the virtues in terms of practices captures much, but very far from all, of what the Aristotelian tradition taught about the virtues. It is also clear that to give an account that is at once more fully adequate to the tradition and rationally defensible, it is necessary to raise a question to which the Aristotelian tradition presupposed an answer, an answer so widely shared in the premodern world that it never had to be formulated explicitly in any detailed way. This question is: is it rationally justifiable to conceive of each human life as a unity, so that we may try to specify each such life as having its good and so that we may understand the virtues as having their function in enabling an individual to make of his or her life one kind of unity rather than another? . . .

THE UNITY OF LIFE AND THE CONCEPT OF A TRADITION

[I]n defining the particular pre-modern concept of the virtues with which I have been preoccupied, it has become necessary to say something of the concomitant concept of selfhood, a concept of a self whose unity resides in the unity of a narrative which links birth to life to death as narrative beginning to middle to end. . . .

It is a conceptual commonplace, both for philosophers and for ordinary agents, that one and the same segment of human behaviour may be correctly characterised in a number of different ways. To the question 'What is he doing?' the answers may with equal truth and appropriateness be 'Digging', 'Gardening', 'Taking exercise', 'Preparing for winter' or 'Pleasing his wife'. Some of these answers will characterise the agent's intentions, others unintended consequences of his actions, and of these unintended consequences some may be such that the agent is aware of them and others not. What is important to notice immediately is that any answer to the questions of how we are to understand or to explain a given segment of behaviour will presuppose some prior answer to the question of how these different correct answers to the question 'What is he doing?' are related to each other. For if someone's primary intention is to put the garden in order before the winter and it is only incidentally the case that in so doing he is taking exercise and pleasing his wife, we have one type of behaviour to be explained; but if the agent's primary intention is to please his wife by taking exercise, we have quite another type of behaviour to be explained and we will have to look in a different direction for understanding and explanation.

In the first place the episode has been situated in an annual cycle of domestic activity, and the behaviour embodies an intention which presupposes a particular type of household-cum-garden setting with the peculiar narrative history of that setting in which this segment of behaviour now becomes an episode. In the second instance the episode has been situated in the narrative history of a marriage, a very different, even if related, social setting. We cannot, that is to say, characterise behaviour independently of intentions, and we cannot characterise intentions independently of the settings which make those intentions intelligible both to agents themselves and to others.

I use the word 'setting' here as a relatively inclusive term. A social setting may be an institution, it may be what I have called a practice, or it may be a milieu of some other human kind. But it is central to the notion of a setting as I am going to understand it that a setting has a history, a history within which the histories of individual agents not only are, but have to be, situated, just because without the setting and its changes through time the history of the individual agent and his changes through time will be unintelligible. Of course one and the same piece of behaviour may belong to more than one setting. . . .

Consider another equally trivial example of a set of compatibly correct answers to the question 'What is he doing?' 'Writing a sentence'; 'Finishing his book'; 'Contributing to the debate on the theory of action'; 'Trying to get tenure'. Here the intentions can be ordered in terms of the stretch of time to which reference is made. Each of the shorter-term intentions is, and can only be made, intelligible by reference to some longer-term intentions; and the characterization of the behaviour in terms of the longer-term intentions can only be correct if some of the characterisations in terms of shorter-term intentions are also correct. Hence the behaviour is only characterised adequately when we know what the longer and longest-term intentions invoked are and how the shorter-term intentions are related to the longer. Once again we are involved in writing a narrative history. . . .

I am presenting . . . human actions in general as enacted narratives. Narrative is not the work of poets, dramatists and novelists reflecting upon events which had no narrative order before one was imposed by the singer or the writer; narrative form is neither disguise nor decoration. Barbara Hardy has written that 'we dream in narrative, daydream in narrative, remember, anticipate, hope, despair, believe, doubt, plan, revise, criticise, construct, gossip, learn, hate and love by narrative' in arguing the same point (Hardy 1968, p.5).

At the beginning of this chapter I argued that in successfully identifying and understanding what someone else is doing we always move towards placing a particular episode in the context of a set of narrative histories, histories both of the individuals concerned and of the settings in which they act and suffer. It is now becoming clear that we render the actions of others intelligible in this way because action itself has a basically historical character. It is because we all live out narratives in our lives and because we understand our own lives in terms of the narratives that we live out that the form of narrative is appropriate for understanding the actions of others. Stories are lived before they are told—except in the case of fiction. . . .

Now I must emphasize that what the agent is able to do and say intelligibly as an actor is deeply affected by the fact that we are never more (and sometimes less) than the co-authors of our own narratives. Only in fantasy do we live what story we please. In life, as both Aristotle and Engels noted, we are always under certain constraints. We enter upon a stage which we did not design and we find ourselves part of an action that was not of our making. Each of us being a main character in his own drama plays subordinate parts in the dramas of others, and each drama constrains the others. In my drama, perhaps, I am Hamlet or Iago or at least the swineherd who may yet become a prince, but to you I am only A Gentleman or at best Second Murderer, while you are my Polonius or my Gravedigger, but your own hero. Each of our dramas exerts constraints on each other's, making the whole different from the parts, but still dramatic.

It is considerations as complex as these which are involved in making the notion of intelligibility the conceptual connecting link between the notion of action and that of narrative. Once we have understood its importance the claim that the concept of an action is secondary to that of an intelligible action will perhaps appear less bizarre and so too will the claim that the notion of 'an' action, while of the highest practical importance, is always a potentially misleading abstraction. An action is a moment in a possible or actual history or in a number of such histories. The notion of a history is as fundamental a notion as the notion of an action. Each requires the other. . . .

What I have called a history is an enacted dramatic narrative in which the characters are also the authors. . . . The difference between imaginary characters and real ones is not in the narrative form of what they do; it is in the degree of their authorship of that form and of their own deeds. Of course just as they do not begin where they please, they cannot go on exactly as they please either; each character is constrained by the actions of others and by the social settings presupposed in his and their actions, a point forcibly made by Marx in the classical, if not entirely satisfactory account of human life as enacted dramatic narrative, *The Eighteenth Brumaire of Louis Bonaparte*.

I call Marx's account less than satisfactory partly because he wishes to present the narrative of human social life in a way that will be compatible with a view of that life as law-governed and predictable in a particular way. But it is crucial that at any given point in an enacted dramatic narrative we do not know what will happen next. . . .

This unpredictability coexists with a second crucial characteristic of all lived narratives, a certain teleological character. We live out our lives, both individually and in our relationships with each other, in the light of certain conceptions of a possible shared future, a future in which certain possibilities beckon us forward and others repel us, some seem already foreclosed and others perhaps inevitable. There is no present which is not informed by some image of some future and an image of the future which always presents itself in the form of a *telos*—or of a variety of ends or goals—towards which we are either moving or failing to move in the present. Unpredictability and teleology therefore coexist as part of our lives; like characters in a fictional narrative we do not know what will happen next, but none the less our lives have a certain form which projects itself towards our future. Thus the narratives which we live out have both an unpredictable and a partially teleological character. If the narrative of our individual and social lives is to continue intelligibly—and either type of narrative may lapse into unintelligibility—it is always both the case that there are constraints on how the story can continue *and* that within those constraints there are indefinitely many ways that it can continue.

A central thesis then begins to emerge: man is in his actions and practice, as well as in his fictions, essentially a story-telling animal. He is not essentially, but becomes through his history, a teller of stories that aspire to truth. But the key question for men is not about their own authorship; I can only answer the question 'What am I to do?' if I can answer the prior question 'Of what story or stories do I find myself a part?' We enter human society, that is, with one or more imputed characters—roles into which we have been drafted—and we have to learn what they are in order to be able to understand how others respond to us and how our responses to them are apt to be construed. It is through hearing stories about wicked stepmothers, lost children, good but misguided kings, wolves that suckle twin boys, youngest sons who receive no inheritance but must make their own way in the world and eldest sons who waste their inheritance on riotous living and go into exile to live with the swine, that children learn or mislearn both what a child and what a parent is, what the cast of characters may be in the drama into which they have been born and what the ways of the world are. Deprive children of stories and you leave them unscripted, anxious stutterers in their actions as in their words. Hence there is no way to give us an understanding of any society, including our own, except through the stock of stories which constitute its initial dramatic resources. . . .

It is now possible to return to the question from which this enquiry into the nature of human action and identity started: In what does the unity of an individual life consist? The answer is that its unity is the unity of a narrative embodied in a single life. To ask 'What is the good for me?' is to ask how best I might live out that unity and bring it to completion. To ask 'What is the good for man?' is to ask what all answers to the former question must have in common. But now it is important to emphasise that it is the systematic asking of these two questions and the attempt to answer them in deed as well as in word which provide the moral life with its unity. The unity of a human life is the unity of a narrative quest. Quests sometimes fail, are frustrated, abandoned or dissipated into distractions; and human lives may in all these ways also fail. But the only criteria for success or failure in a human life as a whole are the criteria of success or failure in a narrated or to-be-narrated quest. A quest for what?

Two key features of the medieval conception of a quest need to be recalled. The first is that without some at least partly determinate conception of the final *telos* there could not be any beginning to a quest. Some conception of the good for man is required. Whence is such a conception to be drawn? Precisely from those questions which led us to attempt to transcend that limited conception of the virtues which is available in and through practices. It is in looking for a conception of *the* good which will enable us to order other goods, for a conception of *the* good which will enable us to extend our understanding of the purpose and content of the virtues, for a conception of *the* good which will enable us to understand the place of integrity and constancy in life, that we initially define the kind of life which is a quest for the good. But secondly it is clear the medieval conception of a quest is not at all that of a search for something already adequately characterised, as miners search for gold or geologists for oil. It is in the course of the quest and only through encountering and coping with the various particular harms, dangers, temptations and distractions which provide any quest with its episodes and incidents that the goal of the quest is finally to be understood. A quest is always an education both as to the character of that which is sought and in self-knowledge.

The virtues therefore are to be understood as those dispositions which will not only sustain practices and enable us to achieve the goods internal to practices, but which will also sustain us in the relevant kind of quest for the good, by enabling us to overcome the harms, dangers, temptations and distractions which we encounter, and which will furnish us with increasing self-knowledge and increasing knowledge of the good. The catalogue of the virtues will therefore include the virtues required to sustain the kind of households and the kind of political communities in which men and women can seek for the good together and the virtues necessary for philosophical enquiry about the character of the good. We have then arrived at a provisional conclusion about the good life for man: the good life for man is the life spent in seeking for the good life for man, and the virtues necessary for the seeking are those which will enable us to understand what more and what else the good life for man is. We have also completed the second stage in our account of the virtues, by situating them in relation to the good life for man and not only in relation to practices. But our enquiry requires a third stage.

For I am never able to seek for the good or exercise the virtues only *qua* individual. This is partly because what it is to live the good life concretely varies from circumstance to circumstance even when it is one and the same conception of the good life and one and the same set of virtues which are being embodied in a human life. What the good life is for a fifth-century Athenian general will not be the same as what it was for a medieval nun or a seventeenth-century farmer. But it is not just that different individuals live in different social circumstances; it is also that we all approach our own circumstances as bearers of a particular social identity. I am someone's son or daughter, someone else's cousin or uncle; I am a citizen of this or that city, a member of this or that guild or profession; I belong to this clan, that tribe, this nation. Hence what is good for me has to be the good for one who inhabits these roles. As such, I inherit from the past of my family, my city, my tribe, my nation, a variety of debts, inheritances, rightful expectations and obligations. These constitute the given of my life, my moral starting point. This is in part what gives my life its own moral particularity.

This thought is likely to appear alien and even surprising from the standpoint of modern individualism. From the standpoint of individualism I am what I myself choose to be. I can always, if I wish to, put in question what are taken to be the merely contingent social features of my existence. I may biologically be my father's son; but I cannot be held responsible for what he did unless I choose implicitly or explicitly to assume such responsibility. I may legally be a citizen of a certain country; but I cannot be held responsible for what my country does or has done unless I choose implicitly or explicitly to assume such responsibility. Such individualism is expressed by those modern Americans who deny any responsibility for the effects of slavery upon black Americans, saying 'I never owned any slaves'. It is more subtly the standpoint of those other modern Americans who accept a nicely calculated responsibility for such effects measured precisely by the benefits they themselves as individuals have indirectly received from slavery. In both cases 'being an American' is not in itself taken to be part of the moral identity of the individual. And of course there is nothing peculiar to modern Americans in this attitude: the Englishman who says, '*I* never did any wrong to Ireland; why bring up that old history as though it had something to do with *me*?' or the young German who believes that being born after 1945 means that what Nazis did to Jews has no moral relevance to his relationship to his Jewish contemporaries, exhibit the same attitude, that according to which the self is detachable from its social and historical roles and statuses. And the self so detached is . . . a self that can have no history. The contrast with the narrative view of the self is clear. For the story of my life is always embedded in the story of those communities from which I derive my identity. I am born with a past; and to try to cut myself off from that past, in the individualist mode, is to deform my present relationships. The possession of an historical identity and the possession of a social identity coincide. Notice that rebellion against my identity is always one possible mode of expressing it.

Notice also that the fact that the self has to find its moral identity in and through its membership in communities such as those of the family, the neighbourhood, the city and the tribe does not entail that the self has to accept the moral *limitations* of the particularity of those forms of community. Without those moral particularities to begin from there would never be anywhere to begin; but it is in moving forward from such particularity that the search for the good, for the universal, consists. Yet particularity can never be simply left behind or obliterated. The notion of escaping from it into a realm of entirely universal maxims which belong to man as such, whether in its eighteenth-century Kantian form or in the presentation of some modern analytical moral philosophies, is an illusion and an illusion with painful consequences. When men and women identify what are in fact their partial and particular causes too easily and too completely with the cause of some universal principle, they usually behave worse than they would otherwise do.

What I am, therefore, is in key part what I inherit, a specific past that is present to some degree in my present. I find myself part of a history and that is generally to say, whether I like it or not, whether I recognise it or not, one of the bearers of a tradition. It was important when I characterised the concept of a practice to notice that practices always have histories and that at any given moment what a practice is depends on a mode of understanding it which has been transmitted often through many generations. And thus, insofar as the virtues sustain the relationships required for practices, they have to sustain relationships to the past—and to the future—as well as in the present. But the traditions through which particular practices are transmitted and reshaped never exist in isolation from larger social traditions. What constitutes such traditions?

We are apt to be misled here by the ideological uses to which the concept of a tradition has been put by conservative political theorists. Characteristically such theorists have followed Burke in contrasting tradition with reason and the stability of tradition with conflict. Both contrasts obfuscate. For all reasoning takes place within the context of some traditional mode of thought, transcending through criticism and invention the limitations of what had hitherto been reasoned in that tradition; this is as true of modern physics as of medieval logic. Moreover when a tradition is in good order it is always partially constituted by an argument about the goods the pursuit of which gives to that tradition its particular point and purpose.

So when an institution—a university, say, or a farm, or a hospital—is the bearer of a tradition of practice or practices, its common life will be partly, but in a centrally important way, constituted by a continuous argument as to what a university is and ought to be or what good farming is or what good medicine is. Traditions, when vital, embody continuities of conflict. Indeed when a tradition becomes Burkean, it is always dying or dead. . . .

A living tradition then is an historically extended, socially embodied argument, and an argument precisely in part about the goods which constitute that tradition. Within a tradition the pursuit of goods extends through generations, sometimes through many generations. Hence the individual's search for his or her good is generally and characteristically conducted within a context defined by those traditions of which the individual's life is a part, and this is true both of those goods which are internal to practices and of the goods of a single life. Once again the narrative phenomenon of embedding is crucial: the history of a practice in our time is generally and characteristically embedded in and made intelligible in terms of the larger and longer history of the tradition through which the practice in its present form was conveyed to us; the history of each of our own lives is generally and characteristically embedded in and made intelligible in terms of the larger and longer histories of a number of traditions. I have to say 'generally and characteristically' rather than 'always', for traditions decay, disintegrate and disappear. What then sustains and strengthens traditions? What weakens and destroys them?

The answer in key part is: the exercise or the lack of exercise of the relevant virtues. The virtues find their point and purpose not only in sustaining those relationships necessary if the variety of goods internal to practices are to be achieved and not only in sustaining the form of an individual life in which that individual may seek out his or her good as the good of his or her whole life, but also in sustaining those traditions which provide both practices and individual lives with their necessary historical context. Lack of justice, lack of truthfulness, lack of courage, lack of the relevant intellectual virtues—these corrupt traditions, just as they do those institutions and practices which derive their life from the traditions of which they are the contemporary embodiments. To recognise this is of course also to recognise the existence of an additional virtue, one whose importance is perhaps most obvious when it is least present, the virtue of having an adequate sense of the traditions to which one belongs or which confront one. This virtue is not to be confused with any form of conservative antiquarianism. . . . It is rather the case that an adequate sense of tradition manifests itself in a grasp of those future possibilities which the past has made available to the present. Living traditions, just because they continue a not-yet-completed narrative, confront a future whose determinate and determinable character, so far as it possesses any, derives from the past. . . .

JUSTICE AS A VIRTUE: CHANGING CONCEPTIONS

When Aristotle praised justice as the first virtue of political life, he did so in such a way as to suggest that a community which lacks practical agreement on a conception of justice must also lack the necessary basis for political community. But the lack of such a basis must therefore threaten our own society. For the outcome of that history . . . has not only been an inability to agree upon a catalogue of the virtues and an even more fundamental inability to agree upon the relative importance of the virtue concepts within a moral scheme in which notions of rights and of utility also have a key place. It has also been an inability to agree upon the content and character of particular virtues. For since a virtue is now generally

understood as a disposition or sentiment which will produce in us obedience to certain rules, agreement on what the relevant rules are to be is
always a prerequisite for agreement upon the nature and content of a
particular virtue. But this prior agreement in rules is . . . something which
our individualist culture is unable to secure. Nowhere is this more marked
and nowhere are the consequences more threatening than in the case of
justice. Everyday life is pervaded by them and basic controversies cannot
therefore be rationally resolved. Consider one such controversy, endemic
in the politics of the United States today—I present it in the form of a
debate between two ideal-typical characters unimaginatively named 'A' and
'B'.

A, who may own a store or be a police officer or a construction
worker, has struggled to save enough from his earnings to buy a small
house, to send his children to the local college, to pay for some special
type of medical care for his parents. He now finds all of his projects
threatened by rising taxes. He regards this threat to his projects as *unjust*;
he claims to have a right to what he has earned and that nobody else has a
right to take away what he acquired legitimately and to which he has a just
title. He intends to vote for candidates for political office who will defend
his property, his projects *and* his conception of justice.

B, who may be a member of one of the liberal professions, or a
social worker, or someone with inherited wealth, is impressed with the
arbitrariness of the inequalities in the distribution of wealth, income and
opportunity. He is, if anything, even more impressed with the inability of
the poor and the deprived to do very much about their own condition as a
result of inequalities in the distribution of power. He regards both these
types of inequality as *unjust* and as constantly engendering further injustice. He believes more generally that all inequality stands in need of justification and that the only possible justification for inequality is to improve
the condition of the poor and the deprived—by, for example, fostering
economic growth. He draws the conclusion that in present circumstances
redistributive taxation which will finance welfare and the social sciences is
what justice demands. He intends to vote for candidates for political office
who will defend redistributive taxation *and* his conception of justice.

It is clear that in the actual circumstances of our social and political
order A and B are going to disagree about policies and politicians. But
must they so disagree? The answer seems to be that under certain types of
economic condition their disagreement need not manifest itself at the level
of political conflict. If A and B belong to a society where economic resources are such, or are at least believed to be such, that B's public redistributive projects can be carried through at least to a certain point without
threatening A's private life-plan projects, A and B might for some time
vote for the same politicians and policies. Indeed they might even on
occasion be one and the same person. But if it is, or comes to be, the case
that economic circumstances are such that either A's projects must be
sacrificed to B's or *vice versa*, it at once becomes clear that A and B have
views of justice which are not only logically incompatible with each other
but which . . . invoke considerations which are incommensurable with those
advanced by the adversary party. . . .

What I want to argue is threefold: first, that the incompatibility of Rawls's and Nozick's accounts does up to a point genuinely mirror the incompatibility of A's position with B's, and that to this extent at least Rawls and Nozick successfully articulate at the level of moral philosophy the disagreement between such ordinary non-philosophical citizens as A and B; but that Rawls and Nozick also reproduce the very same type of incompatibility and incommensurability at the level of philosophical argument that made A's and B's debate unsettlable at the level of social conflict; and secondly, that there is none the less an element in the position of both A and B which neither Rawls's account nor Nozick's captures, an element which survives from that older classical tradition in which the virtues were central. When we reflect on both these points, a third emerges: namely, that in their conjunction we have an important clue to the social presuppositions which Rawls and Nozick to some degree share.

Rawls makes primary what is in effect a principle of equality with respect to needs. His conception of 'the worst off' sector of the community is a conception of those whose needs are gravest in respect of income, wealth and other goods. Nozick makes primary what is a principle of equality with respect to entitlement. For Rawls how those who are now in grave need come to be in grave need is irrelevant; justice is made into a matter of present patterns of distribution to which the past is irrelevant. For Nozick only evidence about what has been legitimately acquired in the past is relevant; present patterns of distribution in themselves must be irrelevant to *justice* (although not perhaps to kindness or generosity). To say even this much makes it clear how close Rawls is to B and how close Nozick is to A. For A appealed against distributive canons to a justice of entitlement, and B appealed against canons of entitlement to a justice which regards needs. Yet it is also at once clear that Rawls's priorities are not only in a way parallel to that in which B's is incompatible with A's, but also that Rawls's position is incommensurable with Nozick's in a way similarly parallel to that in which B's is incommensurable with A's. For how can a claim that gives priority to equality of needs be rationally weighed against one which gives priority to entitlements? If Rawls were to argue that anyone *behind the veil of ignorance*, who knew neither whether and how his needs would be met nor what his entitlements would be, ought rationally to prefer a principle which respects needs to one which respects entitlements, invoking perhaps principles of rational decision theory to do so, the immediate answer must be not only that *we* are *never* behind such a veil of ignorance, but also that this leaves unimpugned Nozick's premise about inalienable rights. And if Nozick were to argue that any distributive principle, if enforced, could violate a freedom to which everyone of us is entitled—as he does indeed argue—the immediate answer must be that in so interpreting the inviolability of basic rights he begs the question in favour of his own argument and leaves unimpugned Rawls's premises.

None the less there is something important, if negative, which Rawls's account shares with Nozick's. Neither of them make any reference to *desert* in their account of justice, nor could they consistently do so. And yet both A and B did make such a reference—and it is imperative here to notice that 'A' and 'B' are not the names of mere arbitrary constructions of my own; their arguments faithfully reproduce, for example, a good deal of what was actually said in recent fiscal debates in California, New Jersey and elsewhere. What A complains of on his own behalf is not merely that he is entitled to what he has earned, but that he *deserves* it in virtue of his life of hard work; what B complains of on behalf of the poor and deprived is that their poverty and deprivation is *undeserved* and therefore unwarranted. And it seems clear that in the case of the real-life counterparts of A and B it is the reference to desert which makes them feel strongly that what they are complaining about is injustice, rather than some other kind of wrong or harm.

Neither Rawls's account nor Nozick's allows this central place, or indeed any kind of place, for desert in claims about justice and injustice. Rawls (p. 310) allows that common sense views of justice connect it with desert, but argues first that we do not know what anyone deserves until we have already formulated the rules of justice (and hence we cannot base our understanding of justice upon desert), and secondly that when we have formulated the rules of justice it turns out that it is not desert that is in question anyway, but only legitimate expectations. He also argues that to attempt to apply notions of desert would be impracticable—the ghost of Hume walks in his pages at this point.

Nozick is less explicit, but his scheme of justice being based exclusively on entitlements can allow no place for desert. He does at one point discuss the possibility of a principle for the rectification of injustice, but what he writes on that point is so tentative and cryptic that it affords no guidance for amending his general viewpoint. It is in any case clear that for both Nozick and Rawls a society is composed of individuals, each with his or her own interest, who then have to come together and formulate common rules of life. In Nozick's case there is the additional negative constraint of a set of basic rights. In Rawls's case the only constraints are those that a prudent rationality would impose. Individuals are thus in both accounts primary and society secondary, and the identification of individual interests is prior to, and independent of, the construction of any moral or social bonds between them. But we have already seen that the notion of desert is at home only in the context of a community whose primary bond is a shared understanding both of the good for man and of the good of that community and where individuals identify their primary interests with reference to those goods. Rawls explicitly makes it a presupposition of his view that we must expect to disagree with others about what the good life for man is and must therefore exclude any understanding of it that we may have from our formulation of the principles of justice. Only those goods in which everyone, whatever their view of the good life, takes an interest are to be admitted to consideration. In Nozick's argument too, the concept of community required for the notion of desert to have application is simply absent. . . .

[Notice] the shared social presuppositions of Rawls and Nozick. It is, from both standpoints, as though we had been shipwrecked on an uninhabited island with a group of other individuals, each of whom is a stranger to me and to all the others. What have to be worked out are rules which will safeguard each one of us maximally in such a situation. Nozick's premise concerning rights introduces a strong set of constraints; we do know that certain types of interference with each other are absolutely prohibited. But there is a limit to the bonds between us, a limit set by our private and competing interests. This individualistic view has of course . . . a distinguished ancestry: Hobbes, Locke (whose views Nozick treats with great respect), Machiavelli and others. And it contains within itself a certain note of realism about modern society; modern society is indeed often, at least in surface appearance, nothing but a collection of strangers, each pursuing his or her own interests under minimal constraints. We still of course, even in modern society, find it difficult to think of families, colleges and other genuine communities in this way; but even our thinking about those is now invaded to an increasing degree by individualist conceptions, especially in the law courts. Thus Rawls and Nozick articulate with great power a shared view which envisages entry into social life as—at least ideally—the voluntary act of at least potentially rational individuals with prior interests who have to ask the question 'What kind of social contract with others is it reasonable for me to enter into?' Not surprisingly it is a consequence of this that their views exclude any account of human community in which the notion of desert in relation to contributions to the common tasks of that community in pursing shared goods could provide the basis for judgments about virtue and injustice. . . .

LIBERALISM TRANSFORMED INTO A TRADITION

[I]t is of the first importance to remember that the project of founding a form of social order in which individuals could emancipate themselves from the contingency and particularity of tradition by appealing to genuinely universal, tradition-independent norms was and is not only, and not principally, a project of philosophers. It was and is the project of modern liberal, individualist society, and the most cogent reasons that we have for believing that the hope of a tradition-independent rational universality is an illusion derive from the history of that project. For in the course of that history liberalism, which began as an appeal to alleged principles of shared rationality against what was felt to be the tyranny of tradition, has itself been transformed into a tradition whose continuities are partly defined by the interminability of the debate over such principles. An interminability which was from the standpoint of an earlier liberalism a grave defect to be remedied as soon as possible has become, in the eyes of some liberals at least, a kind of virtue.

Initially the liberal claim was to provide a political, legal, and economic framework in which assent to one and the same set of rationally justifiable principles would enable those who espouse widely different and incompatible conceptions of the good life for human beings to live together peaceably within the same society, enjoying the same political status and engaging in the same economic relationships. Every individual is to be equally free to propose and to live by whatever conception of the good he or she pleases, derived from whatever theory or tradition he or she may adhere to, unless that conception of the good involves reshaping the life of the rest of the community in accordance with it. Any conception of the human good according to which, for example, it is the duty of government to educate the members of the community morally, so that they come to live out that conception of the good, may up to a point be held as a private theory by individuals or groups, but any serious attempt to embody it in public life will be proscribed. And this qualification of course entails not only that liberal individualism does indeed have its own broad conception of the good, which it is engaged in imposing politically, legally, socially, and culturally wherever it has the power to do so, but also that in so doing its toleration of rival conceptions of the good in the public arena is severely limited.

What is permitted in that arena is the expression of preferences, either the preferences of individuals or the preferences of groups, the latter being understood as the preferences of the individuals who make up those groups, summed in some way or other. It may well be that in some cases it is some nonliberal theory or conception of the human good which leads individuals to express the preferences that they do. But only in the guise of such expressions of preference are such theories and conceptions allowed to receive expression.

The parallels between this understanding of the relationship of human beings in the social and political realm and the institution of the market, the dominant institution in a liberal economy, are clear. In markets too it is only through the expression of individual preferences that a heterogeneous variety of needs, desires, and goods conceived in one way or another are given a voice. The weight given to an individual preference in the market is a matter of the cost which the individual is able and willing to pay; only so far as an individual has the means to bargain with those who can supply what he or she needs does the individual have an effective voice. So also in the political and social realm it is the ability to bargain that is crucial. The preferences of some are accorded weight by others only insofar as the satisfaction of those preferences will lead to the satisfaction of their own preferences. Only those who have something to give get. The disadvantaged in a liberal society are those without the means to bargain.

Against this background two central features of the liberal system of evaluation become intelligible. The first concerns the way in which the liberal is committed to there being no one overriding good. The recognition of a range of goods is accompanied by a recognition of a range of compartmentalized spheres within each of which some good is pursued: political, economic, familial, artistic, athletic, scientific. So it is within a variety of distinct groups that each individual pursues his or her good, and the preferences which he or she expresses will express this variety of social relationships (see John Rawls 'The Idea of Social Union' chapter 79, [*A Theory of Justice*]).

The liberal norm is characteristically, therefore, one according to which different kinds of evaluation, each independent of the other, are exercised in these different types of social environment. The heterogeneity is such that no overall ordering of goods is possible. And to be educated into the culture of a liberal social order is, therefore, characteristically to become the kind of person to whom it appears normal that a variety of goods should be pursued, each appropriate to its own sphere, with no overall good supplying any overall unity to life. To notice a passage from John Rawls once more: "Human good is heterogeneous because the aims of the self are heterogeneous. Although to subordinate all our aims to one end does not strictly speaking violate the principles of rational choice . . . it still strikes us as irrational or more likely as mad. The self is disfigured. . . ." So Rawls equates the human self with the liberal self in a way which is atypical of the liberal tradition only in its clarity of conception and statement.

The liberal self then is one that moves from sphere to sphere, compartmentalizing its attitudes. The claims of any one sphere to attention or to resources are once again to be determined by the summing of individual preferences and by bargaining. So it is important for all areas of human life and not only for explicitly political and economic transactions that there should be acceptable rules of bargaining. And what each individual and each group has to hope for from these rules is that they should be such as to enable that individual or that group to be as effective as possible in implementing his, her, or their preferences. This kind of effectiveness thus becomes a central value of liberal modernity.

Within this liberal scheme the rules of justice have a distinctive function. The rules of distributive justice are both to set constraints upon the bargaining process, so as to ensure access to it by those otherwise disadvantaged, and to protect individuals so that they may have freedom to express and, within limits, to implement their preferences. The stability of property, for Hume an overriding value, is valued by liberals only insofar as it contributes to that protection and does not exclude the disadvantaged from due consideration. Desert is, except in some of those subordinate associations in which groups pursue particular chosen goods, irrelevant to justice. . . .

For in the liberal public realm individuals understand each other and themselves as each possessing his or her own ordered schedule of preferences. Their actions are understood as designed to implement those preferences, and indeed it is by the way in which individuals act that we are provided with the best evidence as to what their preferences are. Each individual, therefore, in contemplating prospective action has first to ask him or herself the question: What are my wants? And how are they ordered?. . .

Desires of course had always been recognized as motives for action, and someone could always explain his or her action by expressing the desire which had motivated by means of some such expression as 'I want'. Nor was there anything new about it being believed that it is good to satisfy certain desires or that the pleasure in so satisfying them is good. What was new was the transformation of first-person expressions of desire themselves, without further qualification, into statements of a reason for action, into premises for practical reasoning. And this transformation, I want to suggest, is brought about by a restructuring of thought and action in a way which accords with the procedures of the public realms of the market and of liberal individualist politics. In those realms the ultimate data are preferences. These are weighed against each other; how they were arrived at is irrelevant to the weight assigned to them. That people in general have such and such preferences is held to provide by itself a sufficient reason for acting so as to satisfy them. But if this is true in the polity at large, then surely each individual can equally find in his or her own preferences a sufficient reason for his or her acting similarly. And there will be an analogous procedure for weighing our individual desires against one another. . . .

The only *rational* way in which these disagreements could be resolved would be by means of a philosophical enquiry aimed at deciding which out of the conflicting sets of premises, if any, is true. But a liberal order, as we have already seen, is one in which each standpoint may make its claims but can do no more within the framework of the public order, since no overall theory of the human good is to be regarded as justified. Hence at this level debate is necessarily barren; rival appeals to accounts of the human good or of justice necessarily assume a rhetorical form such that it is as assertion and counterassertion, rather than as argument and counterargument, that rival standpoints confront one another. Nonrational persuasion displaces rational argument. Standpoints are construed as the expressions of attitude and feeling and often enough come to be no more than that. The philosophical theorists who had claimed that all evaluative and normative judgments *can* be no more than expressions of attitude and feeling, that all such judgments are emotive, turn out to have told us the truth not about evaluative and normative judgments as such, but about what such judgments become in this kind of increasingly emotivist culture (see chapters II and III of *After Virtue*). . . .

The first level, that of debate about the human good in general, is, as we have already seen, necessarily barren of substantive agreed conclusions in a liberal social order. The second level, that at which preferences are tallied and weighed, presupposes that the procedures and rules which govern such tallying and weighing are themselves the outcome of rational debate of quite another kind, that at which the principles of shared rationality have been identified by philosophical enquiry. It is therefore in some ways unsurprising, in the light of the argument so far, that liberalism requires for its social embodiment continuous philosophical and quasi-philosophical debate about the principles of justice, debate which, for reasons which have already been given, is perpetually inconclusive but nonetheless socially effective in suggesting that if the relevant set of principles has not yet been finally discovered, nonetheless their discovery remains a central goal of the social order.

This third level, once again a level of debate, thus provides a certain kind of sanction for the rules and procedures functioning at the second level. And even if the philosophical theorists of liberal individualism do not and cannot agree upon any precise formulation of the principles of justice, they are by and large agreed on what such principles should be designed to achieve. Just because the principles of justice are to govern the tallying and weighing of preferences, they must provide, so far as is possible, a justification to each individual *qua* individual for tallying and weighing his or her particular preferences in the way that they do. So any inequality in the treatment of individuals *qua* individuals requires justification. Justice is *prima facie* egalitarian. The goods about which it is egalitarian in this way are those which, it is presumed, everyone values: freedom to express and to implement preferences and a share in the means required to make that implementation effective. It is in these two respects that *prima facie* equality is required. But it is just here that argument between liberal theorists begins, argument in which the contributions of the greatest names in the foundation of liberalism, Kant, Jefferson, and Mill, have been continued by such distinguished contemporaries as Hart, Rawls, Gewirth, Nozick, Dworkin, and Ackerman. The continuing inconclusiveness of the debates to which they have contributed is of course also one more tribute to the necessary inconclusiveness of modern academic philosophy.

What has become clear, however, is that gradually less and less importance has been attached to arriving at substantive conclusions and more and more to continuing the debate for its own sake. For the nature of the debate itself and not of its outcome provides underpinning in a variety of ways for the fourth level at which appeals to justice may be heard in a liberal individualist order, that of the rules and procedures of the formal legal system. The function of that system is to enforce an order in which conflict resolution takes place without invoking any overall theory of human good. To achieve this end almost any position taken in the philosophical debates of liberal jurisprudence may on occasion be invoked. And the mark of a liberal order is to refer its conflicts for their resolution, not to those debates, but to the verdicts of its legal system. The lawyers, not the philosophers, are the clergy of liberalism.

Liberalism thus provides a distinctive conception of a just order which is closely integrated with the conception of practical reasoning required by public transactions conducted within the terms set by a liberal polity. The principles which inform such practical reasoning and the theory and practice of justice within such a polity are not neutral with respect to rival and conflicting theories of the human good. Where they are in force they impose a particular conception of the good life, of practical reasoning, and of justice upon those who willingly or unwillingly accept the liberal procedures and the liberal terms of debate. The overriding good of liberalism is no more and no less than the continued sustenance of the liberal social and political order.

Thus liberalism, while initially rejecting the claims of any overriding theory of the good, does in fact come to embody just such a theory. Moreover, liberalism can provide no compelling arguments in favor of its conception of the human good except by appeal to premises which collectively already presuppose that theory. The starting points of liberal theorizing are never neutral as between conceptions of the human good; they are always liberal starting points. And the inconclusiveness of the debates within liberalism as to the fundamental principles of liberal justice (see *After Virtue*, pp. 262–66 above) reinforces the view that liberal theory is best understood, not at all as an attempt to find a rationality independent of tradition, but as itself the articulation of an historically developed and developing set of social institutions and forms of activity, that is, as the voice of a tradition. Like other traditions, liberalism has internal to it its own standards of rational justification. Like other traditions, liberalism has its set of authoritative texts and its disputes over their interpretation. Like other traditions, liberalism expresses itself socially through a particular kind of hierarchy.

For in a society in which preferences, whether in the market or in politics or in private life, are assigned the place which they have in a liberal order, power lies with those who are able to determine what the alternatives are to be between which choices will be available. The consumer, the voter, and the individual in general are accorded the right of expressing their preferences for one or more out of the alternatives which they are offered, but the range of possible alternatives is controlled by an elite, and how they are presented is also so controlled. The ruling elites within liberalism are thus bound to value highly competence in the persuasive presentation of alternatives, that is, in the cosmetic arts. So a certain kind of power is assigned a certain kind of authority. . . .

Michael Walzer
Spheres of Justice

Liberals tend to think of obligations as falling into one of two categories: Some follow from promises or contracts we have voluntarily made; others are universal, like the duty to help somebody in need or to support just institutions. Walzer, in common with other communitarians, stresses a third category of obligations: Those based on membership. Rejecting efforts to seek a general criterion that can be used to distribute all the various forms of goods—such as free exchange, desert, or need—he then argues for a pluralistic understanding of justice that requires that different goods be distributed according to the "inner logic" of each type of good.

Included among the goods he examines in his book are punishment, rewards, love, religious grace, political power and offices. In the selection that follows, however, he discusses distribution of goods that are related to economic justice: Medical care, money and commodities, dirty, degrading work, and power to control the workplace.

COMPLEX EQUALITY

. . . Justice is a human construction, and it is doubtful that it can be made in only one way. At any rate, I shall begin by doubting, and more than doubting, this standard philosophical assumption. The questions posed by the theory of distributive justice admit of a range of answers, and there is room within the range for cultural diversity and political choice. It's not only a matter of implementing some singular principle or set of principles in different historical settings. No one would deny that there is a range of morally permissible implementations. I want to argue for more than this: that the principles of justice are themselves pluralistic in form; that different social goods ought to be distributed for different reasons, in accordance with different procedures, by different agents; and that all these differences derive from different understandings of the social goods themselves—the inevitable product of historical and cultural particularism.

A Theory of Goods

Theories of distributive justice focus on a social process commonly described as if it had this form:

From Michael Walzer, *Spheres of Justice*, Basic Books Inc. (1983). Reprinted by permission. Some footnotes omitted.

People distribute goods to (other) people.

Here, "distribute" means give, allocate, exchange, and so on, and the focus is on the individuals who stand at either end of these actions: not on producers and consumers, but on distributive agents and recipients of goods. We are as always interested in ourselves, but, in this case, in a special and limited version of ourselves, as people who give and take. What is our nature? What are our rights? What do we need, want, deserve? What are we entitled to? What would we accept under ideal conditions? Answers to these questions are turned into distributive principles, which are supposed to control the movement of goods. The goods, defined by abstraction, are taken to be movable in any direction.

But this is too simple an understanding of what actually happens, and it forces us too quickly to make large assertions about human nature and moral agency—assertions unlikely, ever, to command general agreement. I want to propose a more precise and complex description of the central process:

> *People conceive and create goods, which they then distribute among themselves.*

Here, the conception and creation precede and control the distribution. Goods don't just appear in the hands of distributive agents who do with them as they like or give them out in accordance with some general principle.[1] Rather, goods with their meanings—because of their meanings—are the crucial medium of social relations; they come into people's minds before they come into their hands; distributions are patterned in accordance with shared conceptions of what the goods are and what they are for. Distributive agents are constrained by the goods they hold; one might almost say that goods distribute themselves among people.

> Things are in the saddle
> And ride mankind.[2]

But these are always particular things and particular groups of men and women. And, of course, we make the things—even the saddle. I don't want to deny the importance of human agency, only to shift our attention from distribution itself to conception and creation: the naming of the goods, and the giving of meaning, and the collective making. What we need to explain and limit the pluralism of distributive possibilities is a theory of goods. For our immediate purposes, that theory can be summed up in six propositions.

1. All the goods with which distributive justice is concerned are social goods. They are not and they cannot be idiosyncratically valued. I am not sure that there are any other kinds of goods; I mean to leave the question open. Some domestic objects are cherished for private and sentimental reasons, but only in cultures where sentiment regularly attaches to such objects. A beautiful sunset, the smell of new-mown hay, the excitement of an urban vista: these perhaps are privately valued goods, though

they are also, and more obviously, the objects of cultural assessment. Even new inventions are not valued in accordance with the ideas of their inventors; they are subject to a wider process of conception and creation. . . .

2. Men and women take on concrete identities because of the way they conceive and create, and then possess and employ social goods. "The line between what is me and mine," wrote William James, "is very hard to draw."[3] Distributions can not be understood as the acts of men and women who do not yet have particular goods in their minds or in their hands. In fact, people already stand in a relation to a set of goods; they have a history of transactions, not only with one another but also with the moral and material world in which they live. Without such a history, which begins at birth, they wouldn't be men and women in any recognizable sense, and they wouldn't have the first notion of how to go about the business of giving, allocating, and exchanging goods.

3. There is no single set of primary or basic goods conceivable across all moral and material worlds—or, any such set would have to be conceived in terms so abstract that they would be of little use in thinking about particular distributions. Even the range of necessities, if we take into account moral as well as physical necessities, is very wide, and the rank orderings are very different. A single necessary good, and one that is always necessary—food, for example—carries different meanings in different places. Bread is the staff of life, the body of Christ, the symbol of the Sabbath, the means of hospitality, and so on. Conceivably, there is a limited sense in which the first of these is primary, so that if there were twenty people in the world and just enough bread to feed the twenty, the primacy of bread-as-staff-of-life would yield a sufficient distributive principle. But that is the only circumstance in which it would do so; and even there, we can't be sure. If the religious uses of bread were to conflict with its nutritional uses—if the gods demanded that bread be baked and burned rather than eaten—it is by no means clear which use would be primary. How, then, is bread to be incorporated into the universal list? The question is even harder to answer, the conventional answers less plausible, as we pass from necessities to opportunities, powers, reputations, and so on. These can be incorporated only if they are abstracted from every particular meaning—hence, for all practical purposes, rendered meaningless.

4. But it is the meaning of goods that determines their movement. Distributive criteria and arrangements are intrinsic not to the good-in-itself but to the social good. If we understand what it is, what it means to those for whom it is a good, we understand how, by whom, and for what reasons it ought to be distributed. All distributions are just or unjust relative to the social meanings of the goods at stake. This is in obvious ways a principle of legitimation, but it is also a critical principle.* When medieval Christians,

*Aren't social meanings, as Marx said, nothing other than "the ideas of the ruling class," "the dominant material relationships grasped as ideas"?[4] I don't think that they are ever only that or simply that, though the members of the ruling class and the intellectuals they patronize may well be in a position to exploit and distort social meanings in their own interests. When they do that, however, they are likely to encounter resistance, rooted (intellectually) in those same meanings. A people's culture is always a joint, even if it isn't an entirely cooperative,

for example, condemned the sin of simony, they were claiming that the meaning of a particular social good, ecclesiastical office, excluded its sale and purchase. Given the Christian understanding of office, it followed—I am inclined to say, it necessarily followed—that office holders should be chosen for their knowledge and piety and not for their wealth. There are presumably things that money can buy, but not this thing. Similarly, the words *prostitution* and *bribery*, like *simony*, describe the sale and purchase of goods that, given certain understandings of their meaning, ought never to be sold or purchased.

5. Social meanings are historical in character; and so distributions, and just and unjust distributions, change over time. To be sure, certain key goods have what we might think of as characteristic normative structures, reiterated across the lines (but not all the lines) of time and space. It is because of this reiteration that the British philosopher Bernard Williams is able to argue that goods should always be distributed for "relevant reasons"—where relevance seems to connect to essential rather than to social meanings.[5] The idea that offices, for example, should go to qualified candidates—though not the only idea that has been held about offices—is plainly visible in very different societies where simony and nepotism, under different names, have similarly been thought sinful or unjust. (But there has been a wide divergence of views about what sorts of position and place are properly called "offices.") Again, punishment has been widely understood as a negative good that ought to go to people who are judged to deserve it on the basis of a verdict, not of a political decision. (But what constitutes a verdict? Who is to deliver it? How, in short, is justice to be done to accused men and women? About these questions there has been significant disagreement.) These examples invite empirical investigation. There is no merely intuitive or speculative procedure for seizing upon relevant reasons.

6. When meanings are distinct, distributions must be autonomous. Every social good or set of goods constitutes, as it were, a distributive sphere within which only certain criteria and arrangements are appropriate. Money is inappropriate in the sphere of ecclesiastical office; it is an intrusion from another sphere. And piety should make for no advantage in the marketplace, as the marketplace has commonly been understood. Whatever can rightly be sold ought to be sold to pious men and women and also to profane, heretical, and sinful men and women (else no one would do much business). The market is open to all comers; the church is not. In no society, of course, are social meanings entirely distinct. What happens in one distributive sphere affects what happens in the others; we can look, at most, for relative autonomy. But relative autonomy, like social meaning, is a critical principle—indeed, as I shall be arguing throughout this book, a radical principle. It is radical even though it doesn't point to a

production; and it is always a complex production. The common understanding of particular goods incorporates principles, procedures, conceptions of agency, that the rulers would not choose if they were choosing *right now*—and so provides the terms of social criticism. The appeal to what I shall call "internal" principles against the usurpations of powerful men and women is the ordinary form of critical discourse.

single standard against which all distributions are to be measured. There is no single standard. But there are standards (roughly knowable even when they are also controversial) for every social good and every distributive sphere in every particular society; and these standards are often violated, the goods usurped, the spheres invaded, by powerful men and women.

Dominance and Monopoly

In fact, the violations are systematic. Autonomy is a matter of social meaning and shared values, but it is more likely to make for occasional reformation and rebellion than for everyday enforcement. For all the complexity of their distributive arrangements, most societies are organized on what we might think of as a social version of the gold standard: one good or one set of goods is dominant and determinative of value in all the spheres of distribution. And that good or set of goods is commonly monopolized, its value upheld by the strength and cohesion of its owners. I call a good dominant if the individuals who have it, because they have it, can command a wide range of other goods. It is monopolized whenever a single man or woman, a monarch in the world of value—or a group of men and women, oligarchs—successfully hold it against all rivals. . . .

SECURITY AND WELFARE

Membership and Need

Membership is important because of what the members of a political community owe to one another and to no one else, or to no one else in the same degree. And the first thing they owe is the communal provision of security and welfare. This claim might be reversed: communal provision is important because it teaches us the value of membership. If we did not provide for one another, if we recognized no distinction between members and strangers, we would have no reason to form and maintain political communities. "How shall men love their country," Rousseau asked, "if it is nothing more for them than for strangers, and bestows on them only that which it can refuse to none?"[6] Rousseau believed that citizens ought to love their country and therefore that their country ought to give them particular reasons to do so. Membership (like kinship) is a special relation. It's not enough to say, as Edmund Burke did, that "to make us love our country, our country ought to be lovely."[7] The crucial thing is that it be lovely for us—though we always hope that it will be lovely for others (we also love its reflected loveliness).

Political community for the sake of provision, provision for the sake of community: the process works both ways, and that is perhaps its crucial feature. Philosophers and political theorists have been too quick to turn it into a simple calculation. Indeed, we are rationalists of everyday life; we come together, we sign the social contract or reiterate the signing of it, in order to provide for our needs. And we value the contract insofar as those needs are met. But one of our needs is community itself: culture, religion, and politics. It is only under the aegis of these three that all the other things we need become *socially recognized needs*, take on historical and determinate form. The social contract is an agreement to reach decisions together about what goods are necessary to our common life, and then to provide those goods for one another. The signers owe one another more than mutual aid, for that they owe or can owe to anyone. They owe mutual provision of all those things for the sake of which they have separated themselves from mankind as a whole and joined forces in a particular community. *Amour social* is one of those things; but though it is a distributed good—often unevenly distributed—it arises only in the course of other distributions (and of the political choices that the other distributions require). Mutual provision breeds mutuality. So the common life is simultaneously the prerequisite of provision and one of its products.

Men and women come together because they literally cannot live apart. But they can live together in many different ways. Their survival and then their well-being require a common effort: against the wrath of the gods, the hostility of other people, the indifference and malevolence of nature (famine, flood, fire, and disease), the brief transit of a human life. Not army camps alone, as David Hume wrote, but temples, storehouses, irrigation works, and burial grounds are the true mothers of cities.[8] As the list suggests, origins are not singular in character. Cities differ from one another, partly because of the natural environments in which they are built and the immediate dangers their builders encounter, partly because of the conceptions of social goods that the builders hold. They recognize but also create one another's needs and so give a particular shape to what I will call the "sphere of security and welfare." The sphere itself is as old as the oldest human community. Indeed, one might say that the original community is a sphere of security and welfare, a system of communal provision, distorted, no doubt, by gross inequalities of strength and cunning. But the system has, in any case, no natural form. Different experiences and different conceptions lead to different patterns of provision. Though there are some goods that are needed absolutely, there is no good such that once we see it, we know how it stands vis-à-vis all other goods and how much of it we owe to one another. The nature of a need is not self-evident.

Communal provision is both general and particular. It is general whenever public funds are spent so as to benefit all or most of the members without any distribution to individuals. It is particular whenever goods are actually handed over to all or any of the members.* Water, for exam-

---

*I don't mean to reiterate here the technical distinction that economists make between public and private goods. General provision is always public, at least on the less stringent definitions of that term (which specify only that public goods are those that can't be provided to some and not to other members of the community). So are most forms of particular provision, for even goods delivered to individuals generate non-exclusive benefits for the community as a whole. Scholarships to orphans, for example, are private to the orphans, public to the community of citizens within which the orphans will one day work and vote. But public goods of this latter sort, which depend upon prior distributions to particular persons or groups, have been controversial in many societies; and I have designed my categories so as to enable me to examine them closely.

ple, is one of "the bare requirements of civil life," and the building of reservoirs is a form of general provision[9]. But the delivery of water to one rather than to another neighborhood (where, say, the wealthier citizens live) is particular. The securing of the food supply is general; the distribution of food to widows and orphans is particular. Public health is most often general, the care of the sick, most often particular. Sometimes the criteria for general and particular provision will differ radically. The building of temples and the organization of religious services is an example of general provision designed to meet the needs of the community as a whole, but communion with the gods may be allowed only to particularly meritorious members (or it may be sought privately in secret or in nonconformist sects). The system of justice is a general good, meeting common needs; but the actual distribution of rewards and punishments may serve the particular needs of a ruling class, or it may be organized, as we commonly think it should be, to give to individuals what they individually deserve. Simone Weil has argued that, with regard to justice, need operates at both the general and the particular levels, since criminals need to be punished.[10] But that is an idiosyncratic use of the word *need*. More likely, the punishment of criminals is something only the rest of us need. But need does operate both generally and particularly for other goods: health care is an obvious example that I will later consider in some detail.

Despite the inherent forcefulness of the word, needs are elusive. People don't just have needs, they have ideas about their needs; they have priorities, they have degrees of need; and these priorities and degrees are related not only to their human nature but also to their history and culture. Since resources are always scarce, hard choices have to be made. I suspect that these can only be political choices. They are subject to a certain philosophical elucidation, but the idea of need and the commitment to communal provision do not by themselves yield any clear determination of priorities or degrees. Clearly we can't meet, and we don't have to meet, every need to the same degree or any need to the ultimate degree. The ancient Athenians, for example, provided public baths and gymnasiums for the citizens but never provided anything remotely resembling unemployment insurance or social security. They made a choice about how to spend public funds, a choice shaped presumably by their understanding of what the common life required. It would be hard to argue that they made a mistake. I suppose there are notions of need that would yield such a conclusion, but these would not be notions acceptable to—they might not even be comprehensible to—the Athenians themselves.

The question of degree suggests even more clearly the importance of political choice and the irrelevance of any merely philosophical stipulation. Needs are not only elusive; they are also expansive. In the phrase of the contemporary philosopher Charles Fried, needs are voracious; they eat up resources.[11] But it would be wrong to suggest that therefore need cannot be a distributive principle. It is, rather, a principle subject to political limitation; and the limits (within limits) can be arbitrary, fixed by some temporary coalition of interests or majority of voters. Consider the case of physical security in a modern American city. We could provide absolute security, eliminate every source of violence except domestic violence, if we put a street light every ten yards and stationed a policeman every thirty yards throughout the city. But that would be very expensive, and so we settle for something less. How much less can only be decided politically.* One can imagine the sorts of things that would figure in the debates. Above all, I think, there would be a certain understanding—more or less widely shared, controversial only at the margins—of what constitutes "enough" security or of what level of insecurity is simply intolerable. The decision would also be affected by other factors: alternate needs, the state of the economy, the agitation of the policemen's union, and so on. But whatever decision is ultimately reached, for whatever reasons, security is provided because the citizens need it. And because, at some level, they all need it, the criterion of need remains a critical standard (as we shall see) even though it cannot determine priority and degree. . . .

An American Welfare State

What sort of communal provision is appropriate in a society like our own? It's not my purpose here to anticipate the outcomes of demo-cratic debate or to stipulate in detail the extent or the forms of provision. But it can be argued, I think, that the citizens of a modern industrial democracy owe a great deal to one another, and the argument will provide a useful opportunity to test the critical force of the principles I have defended up until now: that every political community must attend to the needs of its members as they collectively understand those needs; that the goods that are distributed must be distributed in proportion to need; and that the distribution must recognize and uphold the underlying equality of membership. These are very general principles; they are meant to apply to a wide range of communities—to any community, in fact, where the mem-bers are each other's equals (before God or the law), or where it can plausibly be said that, however they are treated in fact, they ought to be each other's equals. The principles probably don't apply to a community organized hierarchically, as in traditional India, where the fruits of the harvest are distributed not according to need but according to caste—or rather, as Louis Dumont has written, where "the needs of each are con-ceived to be different, depending on [his] caste." Everyone is guaranteed a share, so Dumont's Indian village is still a welfare state, "a sort of coopera-tive where the main aim is to ensure the subsistence of everyone in accord-ance with his social function," but not a welfare state or a cooperative whose principles we can readily understand.[12] (But Dumont does not tell us how food is supposed to be distributed in time of scarcity. If the subsistence standard is the same for everyone, then we are back in a familiar world.)

Clearly, the three principles apply to the citizens of the United

---

*And should be decided politically: that is what democratic political arrangements are for. Any philosophical effort to stipulate in detail the rights or the entitlements of individuals would radically constrain the scope of democratic decision making. . . .

States; and they have considerable force here because of the affluence of the community and the expansive understanding of individual need. On the other hand, the United States currently maintains one of the shabbier systems of communal provision in the Western world. This is so for a variety of reasons: the community of citizens is loosely organized; various ethnic and religious groups run welfare programs of their own; the ideology of self-reliance and entrepreneural opportunity is widely accepted; and the movements of the left, particularly the labor movement, are relatively weak. Democratic decision making reflects these realities, and there is nothing in principle wrong with that. Nevertheless, the established pattern of provision doesn't measure up to the internal requirements of the sphere of security and welfare, and the common understandings of the citizens point toward a more elaborate pattern. One might also argue that American citizens should work to build a stronger and more intensely experienced political community. But this argument, though it would have distributive consequences, is not, properly speaking, an argument about distributive justice. The question is, What do the citizens owe one another, given the community they actually inhabit?

Consider the example of criminal justice. The actual distribution of punishments is an issue I will take up in a later chapter. But the autonomy of punishment, the certainty that people are being punished for the right reasons (whatever those are), depends upon the distribution of resources within the legal system. If accused men and women are to receive their rightful share of justice, they must first have a rightful share of legal aid. Hence the institution of the public defender and the assigned counsel: just as the hungry must be fed, so the accused must be defended; and they must be defended in proportion to their needs. But no impartial observer of the American legal system today can doubt that the resources necessary to meet this standard are not generally available.[13] The rich and the poor are treated differently in American courts, though it is the public commitment of the courts to treat them the same. The argument for a more generous provision follows from that commitment. If justice is to be provided at all, it must be provided equally for all accused citizens without regard to their wealth (or their race, religion, political partisanship, and so on). I don't mean to underestimate the practical difficulties here; but this, again, is the inner logic of provision, and it makes for an illuminating example of complex equality. For the inner logic of reward and punishment is different, requiring, as I shall argue later, that distributions be proportional to desert and not to need. Punishment is a negative good that ought to be monopolized by those who have acted badly—and who have been found guilty of acting badly (after a resourceful defense).

Legal aid raises no theoretical problems because the institutional structures for providing it already exist, and what is at stake is only the readiness of the community to live up to the logic of its own institutions. I want to turn now to an area where American institutions are relatively underdeveloped, and where communal commitment is problematic, the subject of continuing political debate: the area of medical care. But here the argument for a more extensive provision must move more slowly. It isn't enough to summon up a "right to treatment." I shall have to recount something of the history of medical care as a social good.

The Case of Medical Care Until recent times, the practice of medicine was mostly a matter of free enterprise. Doctors made their diagnosis, gave their advice, healed or didn't heal their patients, for a fee. Perhaps the private character of the economic relationship was connected to the intimate character of the professional relationship. More likely, I think, it had to do with the relative marginality of medicine itself. Doctors could, in fact, do very little for their patients; and the common attitude in the face of disease (as in the face of poverty) was a stoical fatalism. Or, popular remedies were developed that were not much less effective, sometimes more effective, than those prescribed by established physicians. Folk medicine sometimes produced a kind of communal provision at the local level, but it was equally likely to generate new practitioners, charging fees in their turn. Faith healing followed a similar pattern.

Leaving these two aside, we can say that the distribution of medical care has historically rested in the hands of the medical profession, a guild of physicians that dates at least from the time of Hippocrates in the fifth century B.C. The guild has functioned to exclude unconventional practitioners and to regulate the number of physicians in any given community. A genuinely free market has never been in the interest of its members. But it is in the interest of the members to sell their services to individual patients; and thus, by and large, the well-to-do have been well cared for (in accordance with the current understanding of good care) and the poor hardly cared for at all. In a few urban communities in the medieval Jewish communities, for example—medical services were more widely available. But they were virtually unknown for most people most of the time. Doctors were the servants of the rich, often attached to noble houses and royal courts. With regard to this practical outcome, however, the profession has always had a collective bad conscience. For the distributive logic of the practice of medicine seems to be this: that care should be proportionate to illness and not to wealth. Hence, there have always been doctors, like those honored in ancient Greece, who served the poor on the side, as it were, even while they earned their living from paying patients. Most doctors, present in an emergency, still feel bound to help the victim without regard to his material status. It is a matter of professional Good Samaritanism that the call "Is there a doctor in the house?" should not go unanswered if there is a doctor to answer it. In ordinary times, however, there was little call for medical help, largely because there was little faith in its actual helpfulness. And so the bad conscience of the profession was not echoed by any political demand for the replacement of free enterprise by communal provision.

In Europe during the Middle Ages, the cure of souls was public, the cure of bodies private. Today, in most European countries, the situation is reversed. The reversal is best explained in terms of a major shift in the common understanding of souls and bodies: we have lost confidence in the cure of souls, and we have come increasingly to believe, even to be obsessed with, the cure of bodies. . . . Among modern citizens, longevity is a socially recognized need; and increasingly every effort is made to see that it is widely and equally distributed, that every citizen has an equal chance at a long and healthy life: hence doctors and hospitals in every district, regular check-ups, health education for the young, compulsory vaccination, and so on.

Parallel to the shift in attitudes, and following naturally from it, was a shift in institutions: from the church to the clinic and the hospital. But the shift has been gradual: a slow development of communal interest in medical care, a slow erosion of interest in religious care. The first major form of medical provision came in the area of prevention, not of treatment, probably because the former involved no interference with the prerogatives of the guild of physicians. But the beginnings of provision in the area of treatment were roughly simultaneous with the great public health campaigns of the late nineteenth century, and the two undoubtedly reflect the same sensitivity to questions of physical survival. The licensing of physicians, the establishment of state medical schools and urban clinics, the filtering of tax money into the great voluntary hospitals: these measures involved, perhaps, only marginal interference with the profession—some of them, in fact, reinforced its guildlike character; but they already represent an important public commitment. Indeed, they represent a commitment that ultimately can be fulfilled only by turning physicians, or some substantial number of them, into public physicians (as a smaller number once turned themselves into court physicians) and by abolishing or constraining the market in medical care. But before I defend that transformation, I want to stress the unavoidability of the commitment from which it follows.

What has happened in the modern world is simply that disease itself, even when it is endemic rather than epidemic, has come to be seen as a plague. And since the plague can be dealt with, it *must* be dealt with. People will not endure what they no longer believe they have to endure. Dealing with tuberculosis, cancer, or heart failure, however, requires a common effort. Medical research is expensive, and the treatment of many particular diseases lies far beyond the resources of ordinary citizens. So the community must step in, and any democratic community will in fact step in, more or less vigorously, more or less effectively, depending on the outcome of particular political battles. Thus, the role of the American government (or governments, for much of the activity is at the state and local levels): subsidizing research, training doctors, providing hospitals and equipment, regulating voluntary insurance schemes, underwriting the treatment of the very old. All this represents "the contrivance of human wisdom to provide for human wants." And all that is required to make it morally necessary is the development of a "want" so widely and deeply felt that it can plausibly be said that it is the want not of this or that person alone but of the community generally—a "human want" even though culturally shaped and stressed.*

***

*Arguing against Bernard Williams's claim that the only proper criterion for the distribution of medical care is medical need,[14] Robert Nozick asks why it doesn't then follow "that the

But once communal provision begins, it is subject to further moral constraints: it must provide what is "wanted" equally to all the members of the community; and it must do so in ways that respect their membership. Now, even the pattern of medical provision in the United States, though it stops far short of a national health service, is intended to provide minimally decent care to all who need it. Once public funds are committed, public officials can hardly intend anything less. At the same time, however, no political decision has yet been made to challenge directly the system of free enterprise in medical care. And so long as that system exists, wealth will be dominant in (this part of) the sphere of security and welfare; individuals will be cared for in proportion to their ability to pay and not to their need for care. In fact, the situation is more complex than that formula suggests, for communal provision already encroaches upon the free market, and the very sick and the very old sometimes receive exactly the treatment they should receive. But it is clear that poverty remains a significant bar to adequate and consistent treatment. Perhaps the most telling statistic about contemporary American medicine is the correlation of visits to doctors and hospitals with social class rather than with degree or incidence of illness. Middle- and upper-class Americans are considerably more likely to have a private physician and to see him often, and considerably less likely to be seriously ill, than are their poorer fellow citizens. Were medical care a luxury, these discrepancies would not matter much; but as soon as medical care becomes a socially recognized need, and as soon as the community invests in its provision, they matter a great deal. For then deprivation is a double loss—to one's health and to one's social standing. Doctors and hospitals have become such massively important features of contemporary life that to be cut off from the help they provide is not only dangerous but also degrading.

But any fully developed system of medical provision will require the constraint of the guild of physicians. Indeed, this is more generally true: the provision of security and welfare requires the constraint of those men and women who had previously controlled the goods in question and sold them on the market (assuming, what is by no means always true, that the market predates communal provision). For what we do when we declare this or that good to be a needed good is to block or constrain its free exchange. We also block any other distributive procedure that doesn't attend to need—popular election, meritocratic competition, personal or familial preference, and so on. But the market is, at least in the United States today, the chief rival of the sphere of security and welfare; and it is most importantly the market that is pre-empted by the welfare state.

---

only proper criterion for the distribution of barbering services is barbering need?"[15] Perhaps it does follow if one attends only to the "internal goal" of the activity, conceived in universal terms. But it doesn't follow if one attends to the social meaning of the activity, the place of the good it distributes in the life of a particular group of people. One can conceive of a society in which haircuts took on such central cultural significance that communal provision would be morally required, but it is something more than an interesting fact that no such society has ever existed. I have been helped in thinking about these issues by an article of Thomas Scanlon's; I adopt here his "conventionalist" alternative.[16]

Needed goods cannot be left to the whim, or distributed in the interest, of some powerful group of owners or practitioners.

Most often, ownership is abolished, and practitioners are effectively conscripted or, at least, "signed up" in the public service. They serve for the sake of the social need and not, or not simply, for their own sakes: thus, priests for the sake of eternal life, soldiers for the sake of national defense, public school teachers for the sake of their pupils' education. Priests act wrongly if they sell salvation; soldiers, if they set up as mercenaries; teachers, if they cater to the children of the wealthy. Sometimes the conscription is only partial, as when lawyers are required to be officers of the court, serving the cause of justice even while they also serve their clients and themselves. Sometimes the conscription is occasional and temporary, as when lawyers are required to act as "assigned counsels" for defendants unable to pay. In these cases, a special effort is made to respect the personal character of the lawyer-client relationship. I would look for a similar effort in any fully developed national health service. But I see no reason to respect the doctor's market freedom. Needed goods are not commodities. Or, more precisely, they can be bought and sold only insofar as they are available above and beyond whatever level of provision is fixed by democratic decision making (and only insofar as the buying and selling doesn't distort distributions below that level).

It might be argued, however, that the refusal thus far to finance a national health service constitutes a political decision by the American people about the level of communal care (and about the relative importance of other goods): a minimal standard for everyone—namely, the standard of the urban clinics; and free enterprise beyond that. That would seem to me an inadequate standard, but it would not necessarily be an unjust decision. It is not, however, the decision the American people have made. The common appreciation of the importance of medical care has carried them well beyond that. In fact, federal, state, and local governments now subsidize different levels of care for different classes of citizens. This might be all right, too, if the classification were connected to the purposes of the care—if, for example, soldiers and defense workers were given special treatment in time of war. But the poor, the middle class, and the rich make an indefensible triage. So long as communal funds are spent, as they currently are, to finance research, build hospitals, and pay the fees of doctors in private practice, the services that these expenditures underwrite must be equally available to all citizens.

This, then, is the argument for an expanded American welfare state. It follows from the three principles with which I began, and it suggests that the tendency of those principles is to free security and welfare from the prevailing patterns of dominance. Though a variety of institutional arrangements is possible, the three principles would seem to favor provision in kind; they suggest an important argument against current proposals to distribute money instead of education, legal aid, or medical care. The negative income tax, for example, is a plan to increase the purchasing power of the poor—a modified version of simple equality. This plan would not, however, abolish the dominance of wealth in the sphere of need. Short of a radical equalization, men and women with greater purchasing power could still, and surely would, bid up the price of needed services. So the community would be investing, though now only indirectly, in individual welfare but without fitting provision to the shape of need. Even with equal incomes, health care delivered through the market would not be responsive to need; nor would the market provide adequately for medical research. This is not an argument against the negative income tax, however, for it may be the case that money itself, in a market economy, is one of the things that people need. And then it too, perhaps, should be provided in kind.

I want to stress again that no *a priori* stipulation of what needs ought to be recognized is possible; nor is there any *a priori* way of determining appropriate levels of provision. Our attitudes toward medical care have a history; they have been different; they will be different again. The forms of communal provision have changed in the past and will continue to change. But they don't change automatically as attitudes change. The old order has its clients; there is a lethargy in institutions as in individuals. Moreover, popular attitudes are rarely so clear as they are in the case of medical care. So change is always a matter of political argument, organization, and struggle. All that the philosopher can do is to describe the basic structure of the arguments and the constraints they entail. Hence the three principles, which can be summed up in a revised version of Marx's famous maxim: From each according to his ability (or his resources); to each according to his socially recognized needs. This, I think, is the deepest meaning of the social contract. It only remains to work out the details—but in everyday life, the details are everything. . . .

MONEY AND COMMODITIES

Blocked Exchanges

Let me try to suggest the full set of blocked exchanges in the United States today. I will rely in part on the first chapter of Arthur Okun's *Equality and Efficiency*, where Okun draws a line between the sphere of money and what he calls "the domain of rights."[17] Rights, of course, are proof against sale and purchase, and Okun revealingly recasts the Bill of Rights as a series of blocked exchanges. But it's not only rights that stand outside the cash nexus. Whenever we ban the use of money, we do indeed establish a right—namely, that this particular good be distributed in some other way. But we must argue about the meaning of the good before we can say anything more about its rightful distribution. . . . Blocked exchanges set limits on the dominance of wealth.

1. Human beings cannot be bought and sold. The sale of slaves, even of oneself as a slave, is ruled out. This is an example of what Okun calls "prohibitions on exchanges born of desperation."[18] There are many such prohibitions; but the others merely regulate the labor market, and I will list them separately. This one establishes what is and is not marketable: not persons or the liberty of persons, but only their labor power and the things they make. (Animals are marketable because we conceive them to be without personality, even though liberty is undoubtedly a value for some of

them.) Personal liberty is not, however, proof against conscription or imprisonment; it is proof only against sale and purchase.

2. Political power and influence cannot be bought and sold. Citizens cannot sell their votes or officials their decisions. Bribery is an illegal transaction. It hasn't always been so; in many cultures gifts from clients and suitors are a normal part of the remuneration of office holders. But here the gift relationship will only work—that is, fit into a set of more or less coherent meanings—when "office" hasn't fully emerged as an autonomous good, and when the line between public and private is hazy and indistinct. It won't work in a republic, which draws the line sharply: Athens, for example, had an extraordinary set of rules designed to repress bribery; the more offices the citizens shared, the more elaborate the rules became.

3. Criminal justice is not for sale. It is not only that judges and juries cannot be bribed, but that the services of defense attorneys are a matter of communal provision—a necessary form of welfare given the adversary system.

4. Freedom of speech, press, religion, assembly: none of these require money payments; none of them are available at auction; they are simply guaranteed to every citizen. It's often said that the exercise of these freedoms costs money, but that's not strictly speaking the case: talk and worship are cheap; so is the meeting of citizens; so is publication in many of its forms. Quick access to large audiences is expensive, but that is another matter, not of freedom itself but of influence and power.

5. Marriage and procreation rights are not for sale. Citizens are limited to one spouse and cannot purchase a license for polygamy. And if limits are ever set on the number of children we can have, I assume that these won't take the form [of] licenses to give birth that can be traded on the market.

6. The right to leave the political community is not for sale. The modern state has, to be sure, an investment in every citizen, and it might legitimately require that some part of that investment be repaid, in work or money, before permitting emigration. The Soviet Union has adopted a policy of this sort, chiefly as a mechanism to bar emigration altogether. Used differently, it seems fair enough, even if it then has differential effects on successful and unsuccessful citizens. But the citizens can claim, in their turn, that they never sought the health care and education that they received (as children, say) and owe nothing in return. That claim underestimates the benefits of citizenship, but nicely captures its consensual character. And so it is best to let them go, once they have fulfilled those obligations-in-kind (military service) that are fulfilled in any case by young men and women who aren't yet fully consenting citizens. No one can buy his way out of these.

7. And so, again, exemptions from military service, from jury duty, and from any other form of communally imposed work cannot be sold by the government or bought by citizens—for reasons I have already given.

8. Political offices cannot be bought; to buy them would be a kind of simony, for the political community is like a church in this sense, that its

services matter a great deal to its members and wealth is no adequate sign of a capacity to deliver those services. Nor can professional standing be bought, insofar as this is regulated by the community, for doctors and lawyers are our secular priests; we need to be sure about their qualifications.

9. Basic welfare services like police protection or primary and secondary schooling are purchasable only at the margins. A minimum is guaranteed to every citizen and doesn't have to be paid for by individuals. If policemen dun shopkeepers for protection money, they are acting like gangsters, not like policemen. But shopkeepers can hire security guards and nightwatchmen for the sake of a higher level of protection than the political community is willing to pay for. Similarly, parents can hire private tutors for their children or send them to private schools. The market in services is subject to restraint only if it distorts the character, or lowers the value, of communal provision. (I should also note that some goods are partially provided, hence partially insulated from market control. The mechanism here is not the blocked but the subsidized exchange—as in the case of college and university education, many cultural activities, travel generally, and so on.)

10. Desperate exchanges, "trades of last resort," are barred, though the meaning of desperation is always open to dispute. The eight-hour day, minimum wage laws, health and safety regulations: all these set a floor, establish basic standards, below which workers cannot bid against one another for employment. Jobs can be auctioned off, but only within these limits. This is a restraint of market liberty for the sake of some communal conception of personal liberty, a reassertion, at lower levels of loss, of the ban on slavery.

11. Prizes and honors of many sorts, public and private, are not available for purchase. The Congressional Medal of Honor cannot be bought, nor can the Pulitzer Prize or the Most Valuable Player Award, or even the trophy given by a local Chamber of Commerce to the "businessman of the year." Celebrity is certainly for sale, though the price can be high, but a good name is not. Prestige, esteem, and status stand somewhere between these two. Money is implicated in their distribution; but even in our own society, it is only sometimes determinative.

12. Divine grace cannot be bought—and not only because God doesn't need the money. His servants and deputies often do need it. Still, the sale of indulgences is commonly thought to require reform, if not Reformation.

13. Love and friendship cannot be bought, not on our common understanding of what these two mean. Of course, one can buy all sorts of things—clothing, automobiles, gourmet foods, and so on—that make one a better candidate for love and friendship or more self-confident in the pursuit of lovers and friends. Advertisers commonly play on these possibilities, and they are real enough.

. . . But the direct purchase is blocked, not in the law but more deeply, in our shared morality and sensibility. Men and women marry for money, but this is not a "marriage of true minds." Sex is for sale, but the sale does not make for "a meaningful relationship." People who believe that sexual intercourse is morally tied to love and marriage are likely to favor a ban on prostitution—just as, in other cultures, people who believed that intercourse was a sacred ritual would have deplored the behavior of priestesses who tried to make a little money on the side. Sex can be sold only when it is understood in terms of pleasure and not exclusively in terms of married love or religious worship.

14. Finally, a long series of criminal sales are ruled out. Murder, Inc., cannot sell its services; blackmail is illegal; heroin cannot be sold, nor can stolen goods, or goods fraudulently described, or adulterated milk, or information thought vital to the security of the state. And arguments go on about unsafe cars, guns, inflammable shirts, drugs with uncertain side effects, and so on. All these are useful illustrations of the fact that the sphere of money and commodities is subject to continuous redefinition.

I think that this is an exhaustive list, though it is possible that I have omitted some crucial category. In any case, the list is long enough to suggest that if money answereth all things, it does so, as it were, behind the backs of many of the things and in spite of their social meanings. The market where exchanges of these sorts are free is a black market, and the men and women who frequent it are likely to do so sneakily and then to lie about what they are doing.

What Money Can Buy

What is the proper sphere of money? What social goods are rightly marketable? The obvious answer is also the right one; it points us to a range of goods that have probably always been marketable, whatever else has or has not been: all those objects, commodities, products, services, beyond what is communally provided, that individual men and women find useful or pleasing, the common stock of bazaars, emporiums, and trading posts. . . .

The market produces and reproduces inequalities; people end up with more or less, with different numbers and different kinds of possessions. There is no way to ensure that everyone is possessed of whatever set of things marks the "average American," for any such effort will simply raise the average. Here is a sad version of the pursuit of happiness: communal provision endlessly chasing consumer demand. Perhaps there is some point beyond which the fetishism of commodities will lose its grip. Perhaps, more modestly, there is some lower point at which individuals are safe against any radical loss of status. That last possibility suggests the value of partial redistributions in the sphere of money, even if the result is something well short of simple equality. But it also suggests that we must look outside that sphere and strengthen autonomous distributions elsewhere. There are, after all, activities more central to the meaning of membership than owning and using commodities.

Our purpose is to tame "the inexorable dynamic of a money economy," to make money harmless—or at least, to make sure that the harms experienced in the sphere of money are not mortal, not to life and not to social standing either. But the market remains a competitive sphere, where risk is common, where the readiness to take risks is often a virtue, and where people win and lose. An exciting place: for even when money buys only what it should buy, it is still a very good thing to have. It answereth some things that nothing else can answer. And once we have blocked every wrongful exchange and controlled the sheer weight of money itself, we have no reason to worry about the answers the market provides. Individual men and women still have reason to worry, and so they will try to minimize their risks, or to share them or spread them out, or to buy themselves insurance. In the regime of complex equality, certain sorts of risks will regularly be shared, because the power to impose risks on others, to make authoritative decisions in factories and corporations, is not a marketable good. This is only one more example of a blocked exchange; I will take it up in detail later. Given the right blocks, there is no such thing as a maldistribution of consumer goods. It just doesn't matter, from the standpoint of complex equality, that you have a yacht and I don't. . . .

The Marketplace

There is a stronger argument about the sphere of money, the common argument of the defenders of capitalism: that market outcomes matter a great deal because the market, if it is free, gives to each person exactly what he deserves. The market rewards us all in accordance with the contributions we make to one another's well-being. The goods and services we provide are valued by potential consumers in such-and-such a way, and these values are aggregated by the market, which determines the price we receive. And that price is our desert, for it expresses the only worth our goods and services can have, the worth they actually have for other people. But this is to misunderstand the meaning of desert. Unless there are standards of worth independent of what people want (and are willing to buy) at this or that moment in time, there can be no deservingness at all. We would never know what a person deserved until we saw what he had gotten. And that can't be right.

Imagine a novelist who writes what he hopes will be a best seller. He studies his potential audience, designs his book to meet the current fashion. Perhaps he had to violate the canons of his art in order to do that, and perhaps he is a novelist for whom the violation was painful. He has stooped to conquer. Does he now deserve the fruits of his conquest? Does he deserve a conquest that bears fruit? His novel appears, let's say, during a depression when no one has money for books, and very few copies are sold; his reward is small. Has he gotten less than he deserves? (His fellow writers smile at his disappointment; perhaps that's what he deserves.) Years later, in better times, the book is reissued and does well. Has its author become more deserving? Surely desert can't hang on the state of the economy. There is too much luck involved here; talk of desert makes little sense. We would do better to say simply that the writer is entitled to his royalties, large or small. . . .

HARD WORK

Equality and Hardness

It is not a question here of demanding or strenuous work. In that sense of the word, we can work hard in almost any office and at almost any job. I can work hard writing this book, and sometimes do. A task or a cause that seems to us worth the hard work it entails is clearly a good thing. For all our natural laziness, we go looking for it. But *hard* has another sense—as in "hard winter" and "hard heart"—where it means harsh, unpleasant, cruel, difficult to endure. . . .

This kind of work is a negative good, and it commonly carries other negative goods in its train: poverty, insecurity, ill health, physical danger, dishonor and degradation. And yet it is socially necessary work; it needs to be done, and that means that someone must be found to do it.

The conventional solution to this problem has the form of a simple equation: the negative good is matched by the negative status of the people into whose hands it is thrust. Hard work is distributed to degraded people. Citizens are set free; the work is imposed on slaves, resident aliens, "guest workers"—outsiders all. Alternatively, the insiders who do the work are turned into "inside" aliens, like the Indian untouchables or the American blacks after emancipation. In many societies, women have been the most important group of "inside" aliens, doing the work that men disdained and freeing the men not only for more rewarding economic activities but also for citizenship and politics. Indeed, the household work that women traditionally have done—cooking, cleaning, caring for the sick and the old—makes up a substantial part of the hard work of the economy today, for which aliens are recruited (and women prominently among them).

The idea in all these cases is a cruel one: negative people for a negative good. The work should be done by men and women whose qualities it is presumed to fit. Because of their race or sex, or presumed intelligence, or social status, they deserve to do it, or they don't deserve not to do it, or they somehow qualify for it. It's not the work of citizens, free men, white men, and so on. But what sort of desert, what sort of qualification is this? It would be hard to say what the hard workers of this or any other society have done to deserve the danger and degradation their work commonly entails; or how they, and they alone, have qualified for it. What secrets have we learned about their moral character? When convicts do hard labor, we can at least argue that they deserve their punishment. But even they are not state slaves; their degradation is (most often) limited and temporary, and it is by no means clear that the most oppressive sorts of work should be assigned to them. And if not to them, surely to no one else. Indeed, if convicts are driven to hard labor, then ordinary men and women should probably be protected from it, so as to make it clear that they are not convicts and have never been found guilty by a jury of their peers. And if even convicts shouldn't be forced to endure the oppression (imprisonment being oppression enough), then it is *a fortiori* true that no one else should endure it.

Nor can it be imposed on outsiders. . . . [T]he people who do this sort of work are so closely tied into the everyday life of the political community that they can't rightly be denied membership. Hard work is a naturalization process, and it brings membership to those who endure the hardship. At the same time, there is something attractive about a community whose members resist hard work (and whose new members are naturalized into the resistance). They have a certain sense of themselves and their careers that rules out the acceptance of oppression; they refuse to be degraded and have the strength to sustain the refusal. Neither the sense of self nor the personal strength are all that common in human history. They represent a significant achievement of modern democracy, closely connected to economic growth, certainly, but also to the success or the partial success of complex equality in the sphere of welfare. . . .

Dangerous Work

Soldiering is a special kind of hard work. In many societies, in fact, it is not conceived to be hard work at all. It is the normal occupation of young men, their social function, into which they are not so much drafted as ritually initiated, and where they find the rewards of camaraderie, excitement, and glory. It would be as odd, in these cases, to talk about conscripts as to talk about volunteers; neither category is relevant. . . .

Even when its true character is understood, however, soldiering is not a radically degraded activity. Rank-and-file soldiers are often recruited from the lowest classes, or from outcasts or foreigners, and they are often regarded with contempt by ordinary citizens. But the perceived value of their work is subject to sudden inflation, and there is always the chance that they will one day appear as the saviors of the country they defend. Soldiering is socially necessary, at least sometimes; and when it is, the necessity is visible and dramatic. At those times, soldiering is also dangerous, and it is dangerous in a way that makes a special mark on our imaginations. The danger is not natural but human; the soldier inhabits a world where other people—his enemies and ours, too—are trying to kill him. And he must try to kill them. He runs the risk of killing and being killed. For these reasons, I think, this is the first form of hard work that citizens are required, or require each other, to share. Conscription has other purposes too—above all, to produce the vast numbers of troops needed for modern warfare. But its moral purpose is to universalize or randomize the risks of war over a given generation of young men.

When the risks are of a different sort, however, the same purpose seems less pressing. Consider the case of coal mining. "The rate of accidents among miners is so high," wrote George Orwell in *The Road to Wigan Pier* ". . . that casualties are taken for granted as they would be in a minor war."[19] It isn't easy, however, to imagine this sort of work being shared. Mining may not be highly skilled work, but it is certainly very difficult, and it's best done by men who have done it for a long time. It requires something more than "basic training." "At a pitch," wrote Orwell, "I could be a tolerable road-sweeper, or . . . a tenth-rate farm hand. But by no conceivable amount of effort or training could I become a coal-miner; the work would kill me in a few weeks."[20] Nor does it make much sense to break in upon the solidarity of the miners. Work in the pits breeds a strong bond, a tight community that is not welcoming to transients. That community is the great strength of the miners. A deep sense of place and clan and generations of class struggle have made for staying power. . . .

Dirty Work

In principle, there is no such thing as intrinsically degrading work; degradation is a cultural phenomenon. It is probably true in practice, however, that a set of activities having to do with dirt, waste, and garbage has been the object of disdain and avoidance in just about every human society. The precise list will vary from one time and place to another, but the set is more or less common. In India, for example, it includes the butchering of cows and the tanning of cowhide—jobs that have a rather different standing in Western cultures. . . .

So long as there is a reserve army, a class of degraded men and women driven by their poverty and their impoverished sense of their own value, the market will never be effective. Under such conditions, the hardest work is also the lowest paid, even though nobody wants to do it. But given a certain level of communal provision and a certain level of self-valuation, the work won't be done unless it is very well paid indeed (or unless the working conditions are very good). The citizens will find that if they want to hire their fellows as scavengers and sweepers, the rates will be high—much higher, in fact, than for more prestigious or pleasant work. This is a direct consequence of the fact that they are hiring *fellow* citizens. It is sometimes claimed that under conditions of genuine fellowship, no one would agree to be a scavenger or a sweeper. In that case, the work would have to be shared. But the claim is probably false. "We are so accustomed," as Shaw has written, "to see dirty work done by dirty and poorly paid people that we have come to think that it is disgraceful to do it, and that unless a dirty and disgraced class existed, it would not be done at all."[21] If sufficient money or leisure were offered, Shaw rightly insisted, people would come forward.

His own preference was for rewards that take the form of leisure or "liberty"—which will always be, he argued, the strongest incentive and the best compensation for work that carries with it little intrinsic satisfaction:

> In a picture gallery you will find a nicely dressed lady sitting at a table with nothing to do but to tell anyone who asks what is the price of any particular picture, and take an order for it if one is given. She has many pleasant chats with journalists and artists; and if she is bored she can read a novel. . . . But the gallery has to be scrubbed and dusted each day; and its windows have to be kept clean. It is clear that the lady's job is a much softer one than the charwoman's. To balance them you must either let them take their turns at the desk and at the scrubbing on alternate days or weeks; or else, as a first-class scrubber and duster and cleaner might

> make a very bad business lady, and a very attractive business lady might
> make a very bad scrubber, you must let the charwoman go home and have
> the rest of the day to herself earlier than the lady at the desk.[22]

The contrast between the "first-rate" charwoman and the "very attractive"
business lady nicely combines the prejudices of class and sex. If we set
aside those prejudices, the periodic exchange of work is less difficult to
imagine. The lady, after all, will have to share in the scrubbing, dusting,
and cleaning at home (unless she has, as Shaw probably expected her to
have, a charwoman there, too). And what is the charwoman to do with her
leisure? Perhaps she will paint pictures or read books about art. But then,
though the exchange is easy, it may well be resisted by the charwoman
herself. One of the attractions of Shaw's proposal is that it establishes hard
work as an opportunity for people who want to protect their time. So they
will clean or scrub or collect garbage for the sake of their leisure, and
avoid if they can any more engaging, competitive, or time-consuming employment. Under the right conditions, the market provides a kind of sanctuary from the pressures of the market. The price of the sanctuary is so
many hours a day of hard work—for some people, at least, a price worth
paying.

   The major alternative to Shaw's proposal is the reorganization of
the work so as to change, not its physical requirements (for I'm assuming
that they are not changeable), but its moral character. The history of
garbage collecting in the city of San Francisco offers a nice example of this
sort of transfomation, which I want to dwell on briefly. . . .

   The San Francisco Scavengers   For the past sixty years, roughly
half of the garbage of the city of San Francisco has been collected and
disposed of by the Sunset Scavenger Company, a cooperative owned by its
workers, the men who drive the trucks and carry the cans. In 1978 the
sociologist Stewart Perry published a study of Sunset, a fine piece of urban
ethnography and a valuable speculation on "dirty work and the pride of
ownership"—it is my sole source in the paragraphs that follow. The cooperative is democratically run, its officers elected from the ranks and paid
no more than the other workers. Forced by the Internal Revenue Service
in the 1930s to adopt bylaws in which they are referred to as "stockholders," the members nevertheless insisted that they were, and would remain,
faithful to the program of the original organizers "who intended to form
and carry on a cooperative . . . where every member was a worker and
actually engaged in the common work and where every member did his
share of the work and expected every other member to work and do his
utmost to increase the collective earnings."[23] Indeed, earnings have increased (more than those of manual workers generally); the company has
grown; its elected officers have shown considerable entrepreneurial talent.
Perry believes that the cooperative provides better-than-average service to
the citizens of San Francisco and, what is more important here, better-
than-average working conditions to its own members. That doesn't mean
that the work is physically easier; rather, cooperation has made it more
pleasant—has even made it a source of pride.

In one sense, the work is in fact easier: the accident rate among Sunset members is significantly lower than the industry average. Garbage collecting is a dangerous activity. In the United States today, no other occupation has a higher risk of injury (though coal miners are subject to more serious injury). The explanation of these statistics is not clear. Garbage collecting is strenuous work, but no more so than many other jobs that turn out to have better safety records. Perry suggests that there may be a connection between safety and self-valuation. "The 'hidden injuries' of the status system may be linked to the apparent injuries that public health and safety experts can document."[24] The first "accident" of garbage collecting is the internalization of disrespect, and then other accidents follow. Men who don't value themselves don't take proper care of themselves. If this view is right, the better record of Sunset may be connected to the shared decision making and the sense of ownership.

Membership in the Sunset Scavenger Company is distributed by a vote of the current members and then by the purchase of shares (it has generally not been difficult to borrow the necessary money, and the shares have steadily increased in value). The founders of the company were Italian-Americans, and so are the bulk of the members today; about half of them are related to other members; a fair number of sons have followed their fathers into the business. The success of the cooperative may owe something to the easiness of the members with one another. In any case, and whatever one wants to say about the work, they have made membership into a good thing. They don't distribute the good they have created, however, in accordance with "fair equality of opportunity." In New York City, because of a powerful union, garbage collecting is also a widely desired job, and there the job has been turned into an office. Candidates must qualify for the work by taking a civil service exam.[25] It would be interesting to know something about the self-valuation of the men who pass the exam and are hired as public employees. They probably earn more than the members of the Sunset cooperative, but they don't have the same security; they don't own their jobs. And they don't share risks and opportunities; they don't manage their own company. The New Yorkers call themselves "sanitationmen"; the San Franciscans, "scavengers": who has the greater pride? If the advantage lies, as I think it does, with the members of Sunset, then it is closely connected to the character of Sunset: a company of companions, who choose their own fellows. There is no way to qualify for the work except to appeal to the current members of the company. No doubt the members look for men who can do the necessary work and do it well, but they also look, presumably, for good companions.

But I don't want to underestimate the value of unionization, for this can be another form of self-management and another way of making the market work. There can't be any doubt that unions have been effective in winning better wages and working conditions for their members; sometimes they have even succeeded in breaking the link between income differentials and the status hierarchy (the New York garbage collectors are a prime example). Perhaps the general rule should be that wherever work can't be unionized or run cooperatively, it should be shared by the citizens—not symbolically and partially, but generally. Indeed, when union or cooperative work is available to everyone (when there is no reserve army), other work just won't get done unless people do it for themselves. This is clearly the case with domestic cooking and cleaning, an area where jobs are increasingly filled by new immigrants, not by citizens. "Mighty few young black women are doin' domestic work [today]," Studs Terkel was told by a very old black woman, a servant all her life. "And I'm glad. That's why I want my kids to go to school. This one lady told me, 'All you people are gettin' like that.' I said, 'I'm glad.' There's no more gettin' on their knees."[26] This is the sort of work that is largely dependent on its (degraded) moral character. Change the character, and the work may well become un-doable, not only from the perspective of the worker but from that of the employer, too. "When domestic servants are treated as human beings," wrote Shaw, "it is not worthwhile to keep them. . . ."[27]

What is most attractive in the experience of the Sunset company (as of the Israeli kibbutz) is the way in which hard work is connected to other activities—in this case, the meetings of the "stockholders," the debates over policy, the election of officers and new members. The company has also expanded into land-fill and salvage operations, providing new and diversified employment (including managerial jobs) for some of the members; though all of them, whatever they do now, have spent years riding the trucks and carrying the cans. Throughout most of the economy, the division of labor has developed very differently, continually separating out rather than integrating the hardest sorts of work. This is especially true in the area of the human services, in the care we provide for the sick and the old. Much of that work is still done in the home, where it is connected with a range of other jobs, and its difficulties are relieved by the relationships it sustains. Increasingly, however, it is institutional work; and within the great caretaking institutions—hospitals, mental asylums, old-age homes—the hardest work, the dirty work, the most intimate service and supervision, is relegated to the most subordinate employees. Doctors and nurses, defending their place in the social hierarchy, shift it onto the shoulders of aides, orderlies, and attendants—who do for strangers, day in and day out, what we can only just conceive of doing in emergencies for the people we love.

Perhaps the aides, orderlies, and attendants win the gratitude of their patients or of the families of their patients. That's not a reward I would want to underestimate, but gratitude is most often and most visibly the reward of doctors and nurses, the healers rather than merely the caretakers of the sick. The resentment of the caretakers is well known. W. H. Auden was clearly thinking of the patients, not the hospital staff, when he wrote:

. . . the hospitals alone remind us of the equality of man.[28]

Orderlies and attendants have to cope for long hours with conditions that their institutional superiors see only intermittently, and that the general public doesn't see at all and doesn't want to see. Often they look after men and women whom the rest of the world has given up on (and when the world gives up, it turns away). Underpaid and overworked, at the bottom of the status system, they are nevertheless the last comforters of humanity—though I suspect that unless they have a calling for the work, they give as little comfort as they get. And sometimes they are guilty of those petty cruelties that make their jobs a little easier, and that their superiors, they firmly believe, would be as quick to commit in their place.

"There is a whole series of problems here," Everett Hughes has written, "which cannot be solved by some miracle of changing the social selection of those who enter the job."[29] In fact, if caretaking were shared— if young men and women from different social backgrounds took their turns as orderlies and attendants—the internal life of hospitals, asylums, and old-age homes would certainly be changed for the better. Perhaps this sort of thing is best organized locally rather than nationally, so as to establish a connection between caretaking and neighborliness; it might even be possible, with a little invention, to reduce somewhat the rigid impersonality of institutional settings. But such efforts will be supplementary at best. Most of the work will have to be done by people who have chosen it as a career, and the choice will not be easy to motivate in a society of equal citizens. Already, we must recruit foreigners to do a great deal of the hard and dirty work of our caretaking institutions. If we wish to avoid that sort of recruitment (and the oppression it commonly entails), we must, again, transform the work. "I have a notion," says Hughes, "that . . . 'dirty work' can be more easily endured when it is part of a good role, a role that is full of rewards to one's self. A nurse might do some things with better grace than a person who is not allowed to call herself a nurse, but is dubbed 'subprofessional' or 'non-professional.' "[30] That is exactly right. National service might be effective because, for a time at least, the role of neighbor or citizen would cover the necessary work. But over a longer period, the work can be covered only by an enhanced sense of institutional or professional place. . . .

We can share (and partially transform) hard work through some sort of national service; we can reward it with money or leisure; we can make it more rewarding by connecting it to other sorts of activity— political, managerial, and professional in character. We can conscript, rotate, cooperate, and compensate; we can reorganize the work and rectify its names. We can do all these things, but we will not have abolished hard work; nor will we have abolished the class of hard workers. The first kind of abolitionism is, as I have already argued, impossible; the second would merely double hardness with coercion. The measures that I have proposed are at best partial and incomplete. They have an end appropriate to a negative good: a distribution of hard work that doesn't corrupt the distributive spheres with which it overlaps, carrying poverty into the sphere of money, degradation into the sphere of honor, weakness and resignation into the sphere of power. To rule out negative dominance: that is the purpose of collective bargaining, cooperative management, professional conflict, the rectification of names—the politics of hard work. The outcomes of this politics are indeterminate, certain to be different in different times and places, conditioned by previously established hierarchies and social understandings. But they will also be conditioned by the solidarity, the skillfulness, and the energy of the workers themselves. . . .

POLITICAL POWER

Property/Power

Ownership is properly understood as a certain sort of power over things. Like political power, it consists in the capacity to determine destinations and risks—that is, to give things away or to exchange them (within limits) and also to keep them and use or abuse them, freely deciding on the costs in wear and tear. But ownership can also bring with it various sorts and degrees of power over people. The extreme case is slavery, which far exceeds the usual forms of political rule. I am concerned here, however, not with the actual possession, but only with the control, of people—mediated by the possession of things; this is a kind of power closely analogous to that which the state exercises over its subjects and disciplinary institutions over their inmates. Ownership also has effects well short of subjection. People engage with one another, and with institutions too, in all sorts of ways that reflect the momentary inequality of their economic positions. I own such-and-such book, for example, and you would like to have it; I am free to decide whether to sell or lend or give it to you or keep it for myself. We organize a factory commune and conclude that so-and-so's skills do not suit him for membership. You gather your supporters and defeat me in the competition for a hospital directorship. Their company squeezes out ours in intense bidding for a city contract. These are examples of brief encounters. I see no way to avoid them except through a political arrangement that systematically replaces the encounters of men and women with what Engels once called "the administration of things"—a harsh response to what are, after all, normal events in the spheres of money and office. But what sovereignty entails, and what ownership sometimes achieves (outside its sphere), is sustained control over the destinations and risks of other people; and that is a more serious matter. . . .

The Case of Pullman, Illinois   George Pullman was one of the most successful entrepreneurs of late nineteenth century America. His sleeping, dining, and parlor cars made train travel a great deal more comfortable than it had been, and only somewhat more expensive; and on this difference of degree, Pullman established a company and a fortune. When he decided to build a new set of factories and a town around them, he insisted that this was only another business venture. But he clearly had larger hopes: he dreamed of a community without political or economic unrest—happy workers and a strike-free plant.[31] He clearly belongs, then, to the great tradition of the political founder, even though, unlike Solon of Athens, he didn't enact his plans and then go off to Egypt, but stayed on to run the town he had designed. What else could he do, given that he owned the town?

Pullman, Illinois, was built on a little over four thousand acres of land along Lake Calumet just south of Chicago, purchased (in seventy-five individual transactions) at a cost of eight hundred thousand dollars. The town was founded in 1880 and substantially completed, according to a single unified design, within two years. Pullman (the owner) didn't just put up factories and dormitories, as had been done in Lowell, Massachusetts, some fifty years earlier. He built private homes, row houses, and tenements for some seven to eight thousand people, shops and offices (in an elaborate arcade), schools, stables, playgrounds, a market, a hotel, a library, a theater, even a church: in short, a model town, a planned community. And every bit of it belonged to him.

> A stranger arriving at Pullman puts up at a hotel managed by one of Mr. Pullman's employees, visits a theater where all the attendants are in Mr. Pullman's service, drinks water and burns gas which Mr. Pullman's water and gas works supply, hires one of his outfits from the manager of Mr. Pullman's livery stable, visits a school in which the children of Mr. Pullman's employees are taught by other employees, gets a bill charged at Mr. Pullman's bank, is unable to make a purchase of any kind save from some tenant of Mr. Pullman's, and at night he is guarded by a fire department every member of which from the chief down is in Mr. Pullman's service.[32]

This account is from an article in the *New York Sun* (the model town attracted a lot of attention), and it is entirely accurate except for the line about the school. In fact, the schools of Pullman were at least nominally run by the elected school board of Hyde Park Township. The town was also subject to the political jurisdiction of Cook County and the State of Illinois. But there was no municipal government. Asked by a visiting journalist how he "governed" the people of Pullman, Pullman replied, "We govern them in the same way a man governs his house, his store, or his workshop. It is all simple enough."[33] Government was, in his conception, a property right; and despite the editorial "we," this was a right singly held and singly exercised. In his town, Pullman was an autocrat. He had a firm sense of how its inhabitants should live, and he never doubted his right to give that sense practical force. His concern, I should stress, was with the appearance and the behavior of the people, not with their beliefs. "No one was required to subscribe to any set of ideals before moving to [Pullman]." Once there, however, they were required to live in a certain way. Newcomers might be seen "lounging on their doorsteps, the husband in his shirt-sleeves, smoking a pipe, his untidy wife darning, and half-dressed children playing about them." They were soon made aware that this sort of thing was unacceptable. And if they did not mend their ways, "company inspectors visited to threaten fines."[34]

Pullman refused to sell either land or houses—so as to maintain "the harmony of the town's design" and also, presumably, his control over the inhabitants. Everyone who lived in Pullman (Illinois) was a tenant of Pullman (George). Home renovation was strictly controlled; leases were terminable on ten days' notice. Pullman even refused to allow Catholics and Swedish Lutherans to build churches of their own, not because he opposed their worship (they were permitted to rent rooms), but because his conception of the town called for one rather splendid church, whose rent only the Presbyterians could afford. For somewhat different reasons, though with a similar zeal for order, liquor was available only in the town's one hotel, at a rather splendid bar, where ordinary workers were unlikely to feel comfortable.

I have stressed Pullman's autocracy; I could also stress his benevolence. The housing he provided was considerably better than that generally available to American workers in the 1880s; rents were not unreasonable (his profit margins were in fact quite low); the buildings were kept in repair; and so on. But the crucial point is that all decisions, benevolent or not, rested with a man, governor as well as owner, who had not been chosen by the people he governed. Richard Ely, who visited the town in 1885 and wrote an article about it for *Harper's Monthly* called it "unAmerican . . . benevolent, well-wishing feudalism."[35] But that description wasn't quite accurate, for the men and women of Pullman were entirely free to come and go. They were also free to live outside the town and commute to work in its factories, though in hard times Pullman's tenants were apparently the last to be laid off. These tenants are best regarded as the subjects of a capitalist enterprise that has simply extended itself from manufacturing to real estate and duplicated in the town the discipline of the shop. What's wrong with that?

I mean the question to be rhetorical, but it is perhaps worthwhile spelling out the answer. The inhabitants of Pullman were guest workers, and that is not a status compatible with democratic politics. . . .

Ely argued that Pullman's ownership of the town made its inhabitants into something less than American citizens: "One feels that one is mingling with a dependent, servile people." Apparently, Ely caught no intimations of the great strike of 1894 or of the courage and discipline of the strikers.[36] He wrote his article early on in the history of the town; perhaps the people needed time to settle in and learn to trust one another before they dared oppose themselves to Pullman's power. But when they did strike, it was as much against his factory power as against his town power. Indeed, Pullman's foremen were even more tyrannical than his agents and inspectors. It seems odd to study the duplicated discipline of the model town and condemn only one half of it. Yet this was the conventional understanding of the time. When the Illinois Supreme Court in 1898 ordered the Pullman Company (George Pullman had died a year earlier) to divest itself of all property not used for manufacturing purposes, it argued that the ownership of a town, but not of a company, "was incompatible with the theory and spirit of our institutions."[37] The town had to be governed democratically—not so much because ownership made the inhabitants servile, but because it forced them to fight for rights they already possessed as American citizens.

It is true that the struggle for rights in the factory was a newer struggle, if only because factories were newer institutions than cities and towns. I want to argue, however, that with regard to political power democratic distributions can't stop at the factory gates. The deep principles are the same for both sorts of institution. This identity is the moral basis of the labor movement—not of "business unionism," which has another basis, but of every demand for progress toward industrial democracy. It doesn't follow from these demands that factories can't be owned; nor did opponents of feudalism say that land couldn't be owned. It's even conceivable that all the inhabitants of a (small) town might pay rent, but not homage, to the same landlord. The issue in all these cases is not the existence but the entailments of property. What democracy requires is that property should have no political currency, that it shouldn't convert into anything like sovereignty, authoritative command, sustained control over men and women. After 1894, at least, most observers seem to have agreed that Pullman's ownership of the town was undemocratic. But was his ownership of the company any different? The unusual juxtaposition of the two makes for a nice comparison.

They are not different because of the entrepreneurial vision, energy, inventiveness, and so on that went into the making of Pullman sleepers, diners, and parlor cars. For these same qualities went into the making of the town. This, indeed, was Pullman's boast: that his " 'system' which had succeeded in railroad travel, was now being applied to the problems of labor and housing."[38] And if the application does not give rise to political power in the one case, why should it do so in the other?*

Nor are the two different because of the investment of private capital in the company. Pullman invested in the town, too, without thereby acquiring the right to govern its inhabitants. The case is the same with men and women who buy municipal bonds: they don't come to own the municipality. Unless they live and vote in the town, they cannot even share in decisions about how their money is to be spent. They have no political rights; whereas residents do have rights, whether they are investors or not. There seems no reason not to make the same distinction in economic associations, marking off investors from participants, a just return from political power.

Finally, the factory and the town are not different because men and women come willingly to work in the factory with full knowledge of its rules and regulations. They also come willingly to live in the town, and in neither case do they have full knowledge of the rules until they have some experience of them. Anyway, residence does not constitute an agreement to despotic rules even if the rules are known in advance; nor is prompt departure the only way of expressing opposition. There are, in fact, some associations for which these last propositions might plausibly be reversed. A man who joins a monastic order requiring strict and unquestioning obedience, for example, seems to be choosing a way of life rather than a

*But perhaps it was Pullman's expertise, not his vision, energy, and so on, that justified his autocratic rule. Perhaps factories should be assimilated to the category of disciplinary institutions and run by scientific managers. But the same argument might be made for towns. Indeed, professional managers are often hired by town councils; they are subject, however, to the authority of the elected councilors. Factory managers are subject, though often ineffectively, to the authority of owners. And so the question remains: Why owners rather than workers (or their elected representatives)?

place to live (or a place to work). We would not pay him proper respect if we refused to recognize the efficacy of his choice. Its purpose and its moral effect are precisely to authorize his superior's decisions, and he can't withdraw that authority without himself withdrawing from the common life it makes possible. But the same thing can't be said of a man or a woman who joins a company or comes to work in a factory. Here the common life is not so all-encompassing and it does not require the unquestioning acceptance of authority. We respect the new worker only if we assume that he has not sought out political subjection. Of course, he encounters foremen and company police, as he knew he would; and it may be that the success of the enterprise requires his obedience, just as the success of a city or a town requires that citizens obey public officials. But in neither case would we want to say (what we might say to the novice monk): if you don't like these officials and the orders they give, you can always leave. It's important that there be options short of leaving, connected with the appointment of the officials and the making of the rules they enforce. . . .

[T]he political community is . . . a common enterprise, a public place where we argue together over the public interest, where we decide on goals and debate acceptable risks. All this was missing in Pullman's model town, until the American Railway Union provided a forum for workers and residents alike.

From this perspective, an economic enterprise seems very much like a town, even though—or, in part, because—it is so unlike a home. It is a place not of rest and intimacy but of cooperative action. It is a place not of withdrawal but of decision. If landlords possessing political power are likely to be intrusive on families, so owners possessing political power are likely to be coercive of individuals. Conceivably the first of these is worse than the second, but this comparison doesn't distinguish the two in any fundamental way; it merely grades them. Intrusiveness and coercion are alike made possible by a deeper reality—the usurpation of a common enterprise, the displacement of collective decision making, by the power of property. And for this, none of the standard justifications seems adequate. Pullman exposed their weaknesses by claiming to rule the town he owned exactly as he ruled the factories he owned. Indeed, the two sorts of rule are similar to one another, and both of them resemble what we commonly understand as authoritarian politics. The right to impose fines does the work of taxation; the right to evict tenants or discharge workers does (some of) the work of punishment. Rules are issued and enforced without public debate by appointed rather than by elected officials. There are no established judicial procedures, no legitimate forms of opposition, no channels for participation or even for protest. If this sort of thing is wrong for towns, then it is wrong for companies and factories, too.

Imagine now a decision by Pullman or his heirs to relocate their factory/town. Having paid off the initial investment, they see richer ground elsewhere; or, they are taken with a new design, a better model for a model town, and want to try it out. The decision, they claim, is theirs alone since the factory/town is theirs alone; neither the inhabitants nor the workers have anything to say. But how can this be right? Surely to uproot a community, to require large-scale migration, to deprive people of homes they have lived in for many years; these are political acts, and acts of a rather extreme sort. The decision is an exercise of power; and were the townspeople simply to submit, we would think they were not self-respecting citizens. What about the workers?

What political arrangements should the workers seek? Political rule implies a certain degree of autonomy, but it's not clear that autonomy is possible in a single factory or even in a group of factories. The citizens of a town are also the consumers of the goods and services the town provides; and except for occasional visitors, they are the only consumers. But workers in a factory are producers of goods and services; they are only sometimes consumers, and they are never the only consumers. Moreover, they are locked into close economic relationships with other factories that they supply or on whose products they depend. Private owners relate to one another through the market. In theory, economic decisions are non-political, and they are coordinated without the interventions of authority. Insofar as this theory is true, worker cooperatives would simply locate themselves within the network of market relations. In fact, however, the theory misses both the collusions of owners among themselves and their collective ability to call upon the support of state officials. Now the appropriate replacement is an industrial democracy organized at national as well as local levels. But how, precisely, can power be distributed so as to take into account both the necessary autonomy and the practical linkage of companies and factories? The question is often raised and variously answered in the literature on workers' control. I shall not attempt to answer it again, nor do I mean to deny its difficulties; I only want to insist that the sorts of arrangements required in an industrial democracy are not all that different from those required in a political democracy. Unless they are independent states, cities and towns are never fully autonomous; they have no absolute authority even over the goods and services they produce for internal consumption. In the United States today, we enmesh them in a federal structure and regulate what they can do in the areas of education, criminal justice, environmental use, and so on. Factories and companies would have to be similarly enmeshed and similarly regulated (and they would also be taxed). In a developed economy, as in a developed polity, different decisions would be made by different groups of people at different levels of organization. The division of power in both these cases is only partly a matter of principle; it is also a matter of circumstance and expediency. . . .

NOTES

1. Robert Nozick makes a similar argument in *Anarchy, State, and Utopia* (New York, 1974), pp. 149–50, but with radically individualistic conclusions that seem to me to miss the social character of production.
2. Ralph Waldo Emerson, "Ode," in *The Complete Essays and Other Writings*, ed. Brooks Atkinson (New York, 1940), p. 770.
3. William James, quoted in C. P. Snyder and Howard Fromkin, *Uniqueness: The Human Pursuit of Difference* (New York, 1980), p. 108.

4. Karl Marx, *The German Ideology*, ed. R. Pascal (New York, 1947), p. 89.
5. Bernard Williams, *Problems of the Self: Philosophical Papers, 1956–1972* (Cambridge, England, 1973), pp. 230–49 ("The Idea of Equality"). This essay is one of the starting points of my own thinking about distributive justice. See also the critique of Williams's argument (and of an earlier essay of my own) in Amy Gutmann, *Liberal Equality* (Cambridge, England, 1980), chap. 4.
6. Jean-Jacques Rousseau, "A Discourse on Political Economy," in *The Social Contract and Discourses*, trans. G. D. H. Cole (New York, 1950), pp. 302–3.
7. Edmund Burke, *Reflections on the French Revolution* (London, 1910), p. 75.
8. Cf. David Hume, *A Treatise of Human Nature*, bk. III, part II, chap. 8.
9. The quotation is from the Greek geographer Pausanias, in George Rosen, *A History of Public Health* (New York, 1958), p. 41.
10. Simone Weil, *The Need for Roots*, trans. Arthur Wills (Boston, 1955), p. 21.
11. Charles Fried, *Right and Wrong* (Cambridge, Mass., 1978), p. 122.
12. Louis Dumont, *Homo Hierarchus: The Caste System and Its Implications* (revised English ed., Chicago, 1980), p. 105.
13. See Whitney North Seymour, *Why Justice Fails* (New York, 1973), especially chap. 4.
14. Bernard Williams, "The Idea of Equality," in *Problems of the Self* (Cambridge, England, 1973), p. 240.
15. See Robert Nozick, *Anarchy, State, and Utopia* (New York, 1974), pp. 233–35.
16. Thomas Scanlon, "Preference and Urgency," *Journal of Philosophy* 57 (1975): 655–70.
17. Arthur Okun, *Equality and Efficiency: The Big Tradeoff* (Washington, D.C., 1975), pp. 6ff.
18. Ibid., p. 20.
19. George Orwell, *The Road to Wigan Pier* (New York, 1958), p. 44.
20. Ibid., pp. 32–33.
21. Shaw, *Woman's Guide*, p. 105.
22. Ibid., p. 109.
23. Perry, *Scavengers*, p. 197.
24. Ibid., p. 8.
25. Ibid., pp. 188–91.
26. Studs Terkel, *Working* (New York, 1975), p. 168.
27. Bernard Shaw, "Maxims for Revolutionists," *Man and Superman*, in *Seven Plays* (New York, 1951), p. 736.
28. W. H. Auden, "In Time of War" (XXV), in *The English Auden: Poems, Essays, and Dramatic Writings 1927–1939*, ed. Edward Mendelson (New York, 1978), p. 261.
29. Everett Hughes, *The Sociological Eye* (Chicago, 1971), p. 345.
30. Ibid., p. 314.
31. Stanley Buder, *Pullman: An Experiment in Industrial Order and Community Planning, 1880–1930* (New York, 1967).
32. Ibid., pp. 98–99.
33. Ibid., p. 107.
34. Ibid., p. 95; see also William M. Carwardine, *The Pullman Strike*, intro. Virgil J. Vogel, (Chicago, 1973), chaps. 8, 9, 10.
35. Richard Ely, quoted in Buder, *Pullman*, p. 103.
36. Ibid.; see also Carwardine, *Pullman Strike*, chap. 4.
37. Carwardine, *Pullman Strike*, p. xxxiii.
38. Buder, *Pullman*, p. 44.

Marilyn Friedman

Feminism and Modern Friendship: Dislocating the Community

Feminists have sometimes been among the most forceful critics of liberalism. Its individualistic assumptions, many argue, betray an inherent gender bias, focusing on the writing of Sandel and MacIntyre. Friedman surveys these charges. While finding merit in the communitarian position, she nevertheless rejects certain features of that approach, especially its tendency to celebrate the traditional attachments and roles in which we find ourselves. Many of the communities to which we now belong, she stresses, are not "found" as Sandel and MacIntyre suggest but rather are "chosen"—a fact that leads to a more critical and self-reflective stance. While agreeing with many of the communitarians' criticisms of liberalism, Friedman wishes to transform the communitarian vision of self and community in a direction more congenial to feminism.

INTRODUCTION

A predominant theme of much recent feminist thought is the critique of the abstract individualism which underlies some important versions of liberal political theory.[1] Abstract individualism considers individual human beings as social atoms, abstracted from their social contexts, and disregards the role of social relationships and human community in constituting the very identity and nature of individual human beings. Sometimes the individuals of abstract individualism are posited as rationally self-interested utility-maximizers.[2] Sometimes, also, they are theorized to form communities based fundamentally on competition and conflict among persons vying for scarce resources, communities which represent no deeper social bond than that of instrumental relations based on calculated self-interest.[3]

Against this abstractive individualist view of the self and of human community, many feminists have asserted a conception of what might be called the "social self."[4] This conception acknowledges the fundamental role of social relationships and human community in constituting both self-identity and the nature and meaning of the particulars of individual lives.[5] The modified conception of the self has carried with it an altered conception of community. Conflict and competition are no longer considered to be the basic human relationships; instead they are being replaced by alter-

Reprinted with revisions by the author from *Ethics* 99 (January 1989). © 1989 by The University of Chicago. Reprinted by permission.

native visions of the foundation of human society derived from nurturance, caring attachment, and mutual interestedness.[6] Some feminists, for example, recommend that the mother-child relationship be viewed as central to human society, and they project major changes in moral theory from such a revised focus.[7]

Some of these anti-individualist developments emerging from feminist thought are strikingly similar to other theoretical developments which are not specifically feminist. Thus, the "new communitarians," to borrow political theorist Amy Gutmann's term,[8] have also reacted critically to various aspects of modern liberal thought, including abstract individualism, rational egoism, and an instrumental conception of social relationships. The communitarian self, or subject, is also not a social atom but is instead a being constituted and defined by its attachments, including the particularities of its social relationships, community ties, and historical context. Its identity cannot be abstracted from community or social relationships.

With the recent feminist attention to values of care, nurturance, and relatedness—values that psychologists call "communal"[9] and which have been amply associated with women and women's moral reasoning[10]—one might anticipate that communitarian theory would offer important insights for feminist reflection. There is considerable power to the model of the self as deriving its identity and nature from its social relationships, from the way it is intersubjectively apprehended, from the norms of the community in which it is embedded.

However, communitarian philosophy as a whole is a perilous ally for feminist theory. Communitarians invoke a model of community which is focused particularly on families, neighborhoods, and nations. These sorts of communities have harbored social roles and structures which have been highly oppressive for women, as recent feminist critiques have shown. But communitarians seem oblivious to those difficulties and manifest a troubling complacency about the moral authority claimed or presupposed by these communities in regard to their members. By building on uncritical references to those sorts of communities, communitarian philosophy can lead in directions which feminists should not wish to follow.

My paper is an effort to redirect communitarian thought so as to avoid some of the pitfalls which it poses, in its present form, for feminist theory and feminist practice. In the first part of the paper, I develop some feminist-inspired criticisms of communitarian philosophy as it is found in writings by Michael Sandel and Alasdair MacIntyre.[11] My brief critique of communitarian thought has the aim of showing that communitarian theory, in the form in which it condones or tolerates traditional communal norms of gender subordination, is unacceptable from any standpoint enlightened by feminist analysis. This does not preclude agreeing with certain specific communitarian views, for example, the broad metaphysical conception of the individual, self, or subject as constituted by its social relationships and communal ties, or the assumption that traditional communities have some value. But the aim of Part I is critical: to focus on the communitarian disregard of gender-related problems with the norms and practices of traditional communities.

In the second part of the paper, I will delve more deeply into the nature of certain sorts of communities and social relationship which communitarians largely disregard. I will suggest that modern friendships, on the one hand, and urban relationships and communities, on the other, offer an important clue toward a model of community which usefully counterbalances the family-neighborhood-nation complex favored by communitarians. With that model in view, we can begin to transform the communitarian vision of self and community into a more congenial ally for feminist theory.

THE SOCIAL SELF, IN COMMUNITARIAN PERSPECTIVE

Communitarians share with most feminist theorists a rejection of the abstractly individualist conception of self and society so prominent in modern liberal thought.[12] This self—atomistic, pre-social, empty of all metaphysical content except abstract reason and will—is allegedly able to stand back from all the contingent moral commitments and norms of its particular historical context and assess each one of them in the light of impartial and universal criteria of reason. The self who achieves a substantial measure of such reflective reconsideration of the moral particulars of her life has achieved "autonomy," a widely esteemed liberal value.

In contrast to this vision of the self, the new communitarians pose the conception of a self whose identity and nature are defined by her contingent and particular social attachments. Communitarians extol the communities and social relationships, including family and nation, which comprise the typical social context in which the self emerges to self-consciousness. Thus, Michael Sandel speaks warmly of:

> those loyalties and convictions whose moral force consists partly in the fact that living by them is inseparable from understanding ourselves as the particular persons we are—as members of this family or community or nation or people, as bearers of this history, as sons and daughters of that revolution, as citizens of this republic.[13]

Sandel continues:

> Allegiances such as these are more than values I happen to have or aims I "espouse at any given time." They go beyond the obligations I voluntarily incur and the "natural duties" I owe to human beings as such. They allow that to some I owe more than justice requires or even permits, not by reason of agreements I have made but instead in virtue of those more or less enduring attachments and commitments which taken together partly *define the person I am.*[14]

Voicing similar sentiments, Alasdair MacIntyre writes:

> . . . we all approach our own circumstances as bearers of a particular social identity. I am someone's son or daughter, someone else's cousin or

uncle; I am a citizen of this or that city, a member of this or that guild or profession; I belong to this clan, that tribe, this nation. Hence what is good for me has to be the good for one who inhabits these roles. As such, I inherit from the past of my family, my city, my tribe, my nation, a variety of debts, inheritances, rightful expectations and obligations. These constitute the given of my life, my moral starting point. This is in part what gives my life its own moral particularity.[15]

(An aside: It is remarkable that neither writer mentions sex or gender as a determinant of particular identity. Perhaps this glaring omission derives not from failing to realize the fundamental importance of gender in personal identity—could anyone really miss that?—but rather from the aim to emphasize what social relationships and communities contribute to identity, along with the inability to conceive that gender is a social relationship or that it constitutes communities.)

For communitarians, these social relationships and communities have a kind of morally normative legitimacy; they define the "moral starting points," to use MacIntyre's phrase, of each individual life. The traditions, practices, and conventions of our communities have at least a *prima facie* legitimate moral claim upon us. MacIntyre does qualify the latter point by conceding that:

> . . . the fact that the self has to find its moral identity in and through its membership in communities such as those of the family, the neighborhood, the city and the tribe does not entail that the self has to accept the moral *limitations* of the particularity of those forms of community. . . .[16]

Nevertheless, according to MacIntyre, one's moral quests must begin by "moving forward from such particularity" for it "can never be simply left behind or obliterated."[17]

Despite feminist sympathy toward a social conception of the self and an emphasis on the importance of social relationships, at least three features of the communitarian version of these notions are troubling from a feminist standpoint. First, the communitarian's metaphysical conception of an inherently social self has little usefulness for normative analysis; in particular, it will not support a specifically feminist critique of individualist personality. Second, communitarian theory pays insufficient regard to the illegitimate moral claims which communities make on their members, linked, for example, to hierarchies of domination and subordination. Third, the specific communities of family, neighborhood, and nation so commonly invoked by communitarians are troubling paradigms of social relationship and communal life. I will discuss each of these points in turn.

First, the communitarian's metaphysical conception of the social self will not support feminist critiques of ruggedly individualist personality or its associated attributes: the avoidance of intimacy, non-nurturance, social distancing, aggression, or violence. Feminist theorists have often been interested in developing a critique of the norm of the highly individualistic, competitive, aggressive personality type, seeing that personality type as more characteristically male than female and as an important part of the foundation for patriarchy.

Largely following the work of Nancy Chodorow, Dorothy Dinnerstein, and, more recently, Carol Gilligan,[18] many feminists have theorized that the processes of psycho-gender development, in a society in which early infant care is the primary responsibility of women but not men, result in a radical distinction between the genders in the extent to which the self is constituted by, and self-identifies with, its relational connections to others. Males are theorized to seek and value autonomy, individuation, separation, and the moral ideals of rights and justice which are thought to depend on a highly individuated conception of persons. By contrast, females are theorized to seek and value connection, sociality, inclusion, and moral ideals of care and nurturance.

From this perspective, highly individuated selves have been viewed as a problem. They are seen as: incapable of human attachments based on mutuality and trust, unresponsive to human needs, approaching social relationships merely as rationally self-interested utility maximizers, thriving on separation and competition, and creating social institutions which tolerate, even legitimize, violence and aggression.

However, a metaphysical view that all human selves are constituted by their social and communal relationships does not itself entail a critique of these highly individualistic selves, or yield any indication of what degree of psychological attachment to others is desirable. On metaphysical grounds alone, there is no reason to suppose that caring, nurturant, relational, sociable selves are better than more autonomous, individualistic, and independent selves. All would be equivalently socially constituted at a metaphysical level. Abstract individualism's failure would be not that it has produced asocial selves, for, on the communitarian view, such beings are metaphysically impossible, but, rather, that it has simply failed theoretically to acknowledge that selves are inherently social. And autonomy, independence, and separateness would become just a different way of being socially constituted, no worse nor better than heteronomy, dependence, or connectedness.

The communitarian conception of the social self, if it were simply a metaphysical view about the constitution of the self (which is what it seems to be), thus provides no basis for regarding nurturant, relational selves as morally superior to those who are highly individualistic. For that reason, it appears to be of no assistance to feminist theorists seeking a normative account of what might be wrong or excessive about competitive self-seeking behaviors or other seeming manifestations of an individualistic perspective. The communitarian "social self," as a metaphysical account of the self, is largely irrelevant to the array of normative tasks which many feminist thinkers have set for a conception of the self.

My second concern about communitarian philosophy has to do with the legitimacy of the communal norms and traditions which are supposed to define the moral starting points of community members. As a matter of moral psychology, it is common for persons to take for granted the moral legitimacy of the norms, traditions, and practices of their communities. However, this point about moral psychology does not entail that those norms and practices really are morally legitimate. It leaves open the question of whether, and to what extent, those claims might "really" be morally binding. Unfortunately, the new communitarians seem sometimes to go beyond the point of moral psychology to a stronger view, namely that the moral claims of communities really are morally binding, at least as "moral starting points." MacIntyre refers to the "debts, inheritances, *rightful* expectations and obligations"[19] which we "inherit" from family, nation and so forth.

But such inheritances are enormously varied. In light of this variety, MacIntyre's normative complacency is quite troubling. Many communities practice the exclusion and suppression of non-group members, especially outsiders defined by ethnicity and sexual orientation.[20] Aren't there "rightful expectations and obligations" *across* community lines? Don't whites, for example, have debts to Blacks and native Americans for histories of exploitation? Didn't Jews, Gypsies, Poles, Czeckoslovakians, and others have "rightful expectations" that Germany would not practice military conquest and unimaginable genocide? Didn't Germany owe reparations to non-Germans for those same genocidal practices? If the new communitarians do not recognize legitimate "debts, inheritances, rightful expectations and obligations" across community lines, then their views have little relevance for our radically heterogeneous modern society. If there are such inter-community obligations which override communal norms and practices, then moral particularity is not accounted for by communal norms alone. In that case, "the" community as such, that is, the relatively bounded and local network of relationships which forms a subject's primary social setting, would not singularly determine the legitimate moral values or requirements which rightfully constitute the self's moral commitments or self-definition.

Besides excluding or suppressing outsiders, the practices and traditions of numerous communities are exploitative and oppressive toward many of their own members. This problem is of special relevance to women. Feminist theory is rooted in a recognition of the need for change in all the traditions and practices which show gender differentiation; many of these are located in just the sorts of communities invoked by communitarians, for example, family practices and national political traditions. The communitarian emphasis on communities unfortunately dovetails too well with the current popular emphasis on "the family," and seems to harken back to the repressive world of what some sociologists call communities of "place," the world of family, neighborhood, school, and church, which so intimately enclosed women in oppressive gender politics—the peculiar politics which it has been feminism's distinctive contribution to uncover. Any political theory which appears to support the hegemony of such communities, and which appears to restore them to a position of unquestioned moral authority must be viewed with grave suspicion. I will come back to this issue when I turn to my third objection to communitarian philosophy.

Thus, while admitting into our notion of the self the important constitutive role played by social and communal relationships, we, from a standpoint independent of some particular subject, are not forced to accept as binding on that subject, the moral claims made by the social and communal relationships in which that subject is embedded or by which she is identified. Nor are we required to say that any particular subject is herself morally obliged to accept as binding the moral claims made on her by any of the communities which constitute or define her. To evaluate the moral identities conferred by communities on their members, we need a theory of communities, of their interrelationships, of the structures of power, dominance, and oppression within and among them. Only such a theory would allow us to assess the legitimacy of the claims made by communities upon their members by way of their traditions, practices, and conventions of "debts, inheritances, . . . expectations, and obligations."

The communitarian approach suggests an attitude of celebrating the attachments which one finds oneself unavoidably to have, the familial ties, and so forth. But some relationships compete with others, and some relationships provide standpoints from which other relationships appear threatening or dangerous to oneself, one's integrity, or one's well-being. In such cases, simple formulas about the value of community provide no guidance. The problem is not simply to appreciate community *per se*, but rather to reconcile the conflicting claims, demands, and identity-defining influences of the variety of communities of which one is a part.

It is worth recalling that liberalism has always condemned, in principle if not in practice, the norms of social hierarchy and political subordination based on inherited or ascribed status. Where liberals historically have applied this tenet at best only to the public realm of civic relationships, feminism seeks to extend it more radically to the "private" realm of family and other communities of place. Those norms and claims of local communities which sustain gender hierarchies have no intrinsic legitimacy from a feminist standpoint. A feminist interest in community must certainly aim for social institutions and relational structures which diminish and, finally, erase gender subordination.

Reflections such as these characterize the concerns of the modern self, the self who acknowledges no *a priori* loyalty to any feature of situation or role, and who claims the right to question the moral legitimacy of any contingent moral claim.[21] We can agree with the communitarians that it would be impossible for the self to question all her contingencies at once, yet at the same time, unlike the communitarians, still emphasize the critical importance of morally questioning various particular communal norms and circumstances one at a time.

A third problem with communitarian philosophy has to do with the sorts of communities evidently endorsed by communitarian theorists. Human beings participate in a variety of communities and social relationships, not only across time, but at any one time. However, when people think of "community," it is common for them to think of certain particular social networks, namely, those formed primarily out of family, neighborhood, school, and church.[22] These more typical communities also coincide with the substantive examples of community commonly invoked by Sandel and MacIntyre. Those examples fall largely into two groups. First, there are political communities which constitute our civic and national identities in a public world of nation-states. MacIntyre mentions city and nation, while Sandel writes of "nation or people, . . . bearers of this history, . . . sons and daughters of that revolution, . . . citizens of this republic."[23] Second, there are local communities centered around families and neighborhood, and which some sociologists call "communities of place." MacIntyre and Sandel both emphasize family, and MacIntyre also cites neighborhood along with clan and tribe.[24]

But where, one might ask, is the International Ladies Garment Workers' Union, the Teamsters, the Democratic Party, Alcoholics Anonymous, or the Committee in Solidarity with the People of El Salvador? Although MacIntyre does mention professions and, rather archaically, "guilds,"[25] these references are anomalous in his work, which, for the most part, ignores such communities as trade unions, political action groups, associations of hobbiests, and so forth.

Some of the communities cited by MacIntyre and Sandel will resonate with the historical experiences of women, especially the inclusive communities of family and neighborhood. However, political communities form a particularly suspect class from a feminist standpoint. We all recall how political communities have, until only recently, excluded the legitimate participation of women. It would seem to follow that they have accordingly *not* historically constituted the identities of women in profound ways. As "daughters" of an American revolution spawned parthenogenically by the "fathers" of our country, we find our political community to have denied us the self-identifying heritage of our cultural *mothers*. In general, the contribution made to the identities of various groups of people by political communities is quite uneven, given that they are communities to which many are subject, but in which far fewer actively participate.

At any rate, there is an underlying commonality to most of the communities which MacIntyre and Sandel cite as constitutive of self-identity and definitive of our moral starting points. Sandel himself explicates this commonality when he writes that, for people "bound by a sense of community," the notion of community describes:

> *not a relationship they choose (as in a voluntary association) but an attachment they discover*, not merely an attribute but a constituent of their identity.[26]

Not voluntary but "discovered" relationships and communities are what Sandel takes to define subjective identity for those who are bound by a "sense of community." It is the communities to which we are involuntarily bound to which Sandel accords metaphysical pride of place in the constitution of subjectivity. What are important are not simply the "associations" in which people "cooperate," but the "communities" in which people "participate," for these latter:

> . . . describe a form of life in which the members find themselves commonly situated "to begin with," their commonality consisting less in relationships they have entered than in attachments they have found.[27]

Thus, the social relationships which one finds, the attachments which are discovered and not chosen, become the points of reference for self-definition by the communitarian subject.

For the child maturing to self-consciousness in her community of origin, typically a complex of family, neighborhood, school, and church, it seems uncontroversial that "the" community is found, not entered; discovered, not created. But this need not be true of an adult's communities of mature self-identification. Many communities are, for at least some of their members, communities of choice to a significant extent: labor unions, philanthropic associations, political coalitions, and, if one has ever moved or migrated, even the communities of neighborhood, church, city, or nation-state might have been chosen to an important extent. One need not have simply discovered oneself to be embedded in them in order that one's identity or the moral particulars of one's life be defined by them. Sandel is right to indicate the role of found communities in constituting the unreflective, "given" identity which the self discovers when first beginning to reflect on herself. But for mature self-identity, we should also recognize a legitimate role for communities of choice, supplementing, if not displacing, the communities and attachments which are merely found.

Moreover, the discovered identity constituted by one's original community of place might be fraught with ambivalences and ambiguities. Our communities of origin do not necessarily constitute us as selves who agree or comply with the norms which unify those communities. Some of us are constituted as deviants and resisters by our communities of origin, and our defiance may well run to the foundational social norms which ground the most basic social roles and relationships upon which those communities rest. Thus, poet Adrienne Rich writes about her experiences growing up with a Christian mother, a Jewish father who suppressed his ethnicity, and a family community which taught Adrienne Rich contempt for all that was identified with Jewishness. In 1946, while still a high school student, Rich saw, for the first time, a film about the Allied liberation of Nazi concentration camps. Writing about this experience in 1982, she brooded:

> . . . I feel belated rage that I was so impoverished by the family and social worlds I lived in, that I had to try to figure out by myself what this did indeed mean for me. That I had never been taught about resistance, only about passing. That I had no language for anti-Semitism itself.[28]

As a student at Radcliffe in the late 'forties, Rich met "real" Jewish women who inducted her into the lore of Jewish background and customs, holidays and foods, names and noses. She plunged in with trepidation:

> I felt I was testing a forbidden current, that there was danger in these revelations. I bought a reproduction of a Chagall portrait of a rabbi in a striped prayer shawl and hung it on the wall of my room. I was admittedly young and trying to educate myself, but I was also doing something that *is* dangerous: I was flirting with identity.[29]

And she was doing it apart from the family community from which her ambiguous ethnic identity was originally derived.

For Sandel, Rich's lifelong troubled reflections on her ethnic identity might seem compatible with his theory. In his view, the subject discovers the attachments which are constitutive of its subjectivity through reflection on a multitude of values and aims, differentiating what is self from what is not-self. He might say that Rich discriminated among the many loyalties and projects which defined who she was in her original community, that is, her family, and discerned that her Jewishness appeared "essential"[30] to who she was. But it is not obvious, without question-begging, that her original community really defined her as essentially Jewish. Indeed, her family endeavored to suppress loyalties and attachments to all things Jewish. Thus, one of Rich's quests in life, so evidently not inspired by her community of origin alone, was to reexamine the identity found in that original context. The communitarian view that found communities and social attachments constitute self-identity does not, by itself, explicate the source of such a quest. It seems more illuminating to say that Rich's identity became, in part, "chosen," that it had to do with social relationships and attachments which she sought out, rather than merely found, created as well as discovered.

Thus, the commitments and loyalties of our found communities, our communities of origin, may harbor ambiguities, ambivalences, contradictions, and oppressions which complicate as well as constitute identity, and which have to be sorted out, critically scrutinized. In these undertakings, we are likely to utilize resources and skills derived from various communities and relationships, both those which are chosen or created, as well as those which are found or discovered. Thus, our theories of community should recognize that resources and skills derived from communities which are not merely found or discovered may equally well contribute to the constitution of identity. The constitution of identity and moral particularity, for the modern self, may well require the contribution of radically different communities from those invoked by communitarians.

The whole tenor of communitarian thinking would change once we opened up the conception of the social self to encompass chosen communities, especially those which lie beyond the typical original community of family-neighborhood-school-church. No longer would communitarian thought present a seemingly conservative complacency about the private and local communities of place which have so effectively circumscribed, in particular, the lives of most women.

In the second part of this paper, I will explore more fully the role of communities and relationships of "choice," which point the way toward a notion of community more congenial to feminist aspirations.

MODERN FRIENDSHIP, URBAN COMMUNITY, AND BEYOND

My goals are twofold: to retain the communitarian insights about the contribution of community and social relationship to self-identity, yet open up for critical reflection the moral particulars imparted by those communi-

ties, and identify the sorts of communities which will provide nonoppres-
sive and enriched lives for women.

Toward this end, it will be helpful to consider models of human
relationship and community which contrast with those cited by communitarians. I believe that modern friendship and urban community can offer
us crucial insights into the social nature of the modern self. It is in moving
forward from these relationships that we have the best chance of reconcil-
ing the communitarian conception of the social self with the longed-for
communities of feminist aspiration.

Both modern friendship and the stereotypical urban community
share an important feature which is either neglected or deliberately
avoided in communitarian conceptions of human relationship. From a liberal, or Enlightenment, or modernist standpoint, this feature would be
characterized as voluntariness: those relationships are based partly on
choice.

Let's first consider friendship as it is understood in this culture.
Friends are supposed to be people whom one chooses on one's own to
share activities and intimacies. No particular people are assigned by custom
or tradition to be a person's friends. From among the larger number of
one's acquaintances, one moves toward closer and more friendlike relationships with some of them, motivated by one's own needs, values, and attractions. No consanguineal or legal connections establish or maintain ties of
friendship. As this relationship is widely understood in our culture, its
basis lies in voluntary choice.

In this context, "voluntary choice" refers to motivations arising out
of one's own needs, desires, interests, values, and attractions, in contrast to
motivations arising from what is socially assigned, ascribed, expected, or
demanded. Because of its basis in voluntary choice, friendship is more
likely than many other relationships, such as those of family and neighborhood, to be grounded and sustained by shared interests and values, mutual
affection, and possibilities for generating reciprocal respect and esteem.

Friendship is more likely than many other relationships to provide
social support for people who are idiosyncratic, whose unconventional
values and deviant lifestyles make them victims of intolerance from family
members and others who are unwillingly related to them. In this regard,
friendship has socially disruptive possibilities, for out of the unconventional living which it helps to sustain there often arise influential forces for
social change. Friendship has had an obvious importance to feminist aspirations as the basis of the bond which is (ironically) called "sisterhood."[31]
Friendship among women has been the cement not only of the various
historical waves of the feminist movement, but as well of numerous communities of women throughout history who defied the local conventions
for their gender and lived lives of creative disorder.[32] In all these cases,
women moved out of their given or found communities into new attachments with other women by their own choice, that is, motivated by their
own needs, desires, attractions, and fears, rather than, and often in opposition to, the expectations and ascribed roles of their found communities.

Like friendship, many urban relationships are also based more on choice than on socially ascribed roles, biological connections or other non-voluntary ties. Urban communities include numerous voluntary associations such as political action groups, support groups, associations of co-hobbiests, and so on. But while friendship is almost universally extolled, urban communities and relationships have been theorized in wildly contradictory ways. Cities have sometimes been taken as "harbingers" of modern culture *per se*,[33] and have been particularly associated with the major social trends of modern life, such as industrialization and bureaucratization.[34] The results of these trends are often thought to have been a fragmentation of "real" community, and the widely-lamented alienation of modern urban life: people seldom know their neighbors; population concentration generates massive psychic overload;[35] fear and mutual distrust, even outright hostility, generated by the dangers of urban life, may dominate most daily associations. Under such circumstances, meaningful relationships are often theorized to be rare, if at all possible.

But is this image a complete portrait of urban life? It is probably true, in urban areas, that communities of *place* are diminished in importance; neighborhood plays a far less significant role in constituting community than it does in nonurban areas.[36] But this does not mean that the social networks and communities of urban dwellers are inferior to those of non-urban residents.

Much evidence suggests that urban settings do not, as commonly stereotyped, promote only alienation, isolation, and psychic breakdown. The communities available to urban dwellers are different from those available to non-urban dwellers, but not necessarily less gratifying or fulfilling.[37] Communities of place are relatively non voluntary; for example, one's extended family of origin is given or ascribed, and the relationships found as one grows. Sociological research has shown that urban dwellers tend to form their social networks, their communities, out of people who are brought together for reasons other than geographical proximity. Voluntary associations, such as political action groups, support groups, and so on, are a common part of modern urban life, with its large population centers and the greater availability of critical masses of people with special interests or needs. Communities of place, centered around family-neighborhood-church-school are more likely, for urban dwellers, to be supplanted by other sorts of communities, resulting in what the sociologist Melvin Webber has called "community without propinquity."[38] As the sociologist, Claude Fischer, has stated it, in urban areas, "population concentration stimulates allegiances to subcultures based on more significant social traits" than common locality or neighborhood.[39] But most importantly for our purposes, these are still often genuine communities, and not the cesspools of "Rum, Romanism, and Rebellion" sometimes depicted by anti-urbanists.

Literature reveals that women writers have been both repelled and inspired by urban communities. The city, as a concentrated center of male political and economic power, seems to exclude women altogether.[40] However, as literary critic Susan Merrill Squier points out, the city can provide women with jobs, education, and the cultural tools with which to escape imposed gender roles, familial demands, and domestic servitude. The city can also bring women together, in work or in leisure, and lay the basis for bonds of sisterhood.[41] The quests of women who journey to cities leaving behind men, home, and family, are subversive, writes literary critic Blanche Gelfant, and may well be perceived by others "as assaults upon society."[42] Cities open up for women possibilities of supplanting communities of place with relationships and communities of choice. Thus, urban communities of choice can provide the resources for women to surmount the moral particularities of family and place which define and limit their moral starting points.

Social theorists have long decried the interpersonal estrangement of urban life, an observation which seems predominantly inspired by the public world of conflict between various subcultural groups. Urbanism does not create interpersonal estrangement *within* subcultures but, rather, tends to promote social involvement.[43] This is especially true for people with special backgrounds and interests, for people who are members of small minorities, and for ethnic groups. Fischer has found that social relationships in urban centers are more:

> culturally specialized: urbanites were relatively involved with associates in the social world they considered most important and relatively uninvolved with associates, if any, in other worlds.[44]

As Fischer summarizes it, "Urbanism . . . fosters social involvement in the subculture(s) of *choice*, rather than the subculture(s) of circumstances."[45] This is doubtless reinforced by the recent more militant expression of group values and group demands for rights and respect on the parts of urban subcultural minorities.

We might describe urban relationships as being characteristically "modern" to signal their relatively greater voluntary basis. We find, in these relationships and the social networks formed of them, not a loss of community, but an increase in importance of community of a different sort from that of family-neighborhood-church-school complexes. Yet these more voluntary communities may be as deeply constitutive of the identities and particulars of the individuals who participate in them as are the communities of place so warmly invoked by communitarians.

Perhaps it is more illuminating to say that communities of choice foster not so much the constitution of subjects as their reconstitution. We seek out such communities as contexts in which to relocate and renegotiate the various constituents of our identities, as Adrienne Rich sought out Jewish community in her college years. While people in a community of choice may not share a common history, their shared values or interests are likely to manifest backgrounds of similar experiences, as, for example, among the members of a lesbian community. The modern self may seek new communities whose norms and relationships stimulate and develop her identity and self understanding more adequately than her unchosen community of origin, her original community of place.

In case it is chosen communities which help us to define ourselves, the project of self-definition would not be arising from communities in which we merely found or discovered our immersion. It is likely that chosen communities, lesbian communities, for example, attract us in the first place because they appeal to features of ourselves which, though perhaps merely found or discovered, were inadequately or ambivalently sustained by our *un*chosen families, neighborhoods, schools, or churches. Thus, unchosen communities are sometimes communities which we can, and should, leave, searching elsewhere for the resources to help us discern who we really are.

A community of choice might be a community of people who share a common oppression. This is particularly critical in those instances in which the shared oppression is not concentrated within certain communities of place, as it might be, for example, in the case of ethnic minorities, but, rather, is focused on people who are distributed throughout social and ethnic groupings and who do not themselves comprise a traditional community of place. Unlike the communities of ethnic minorities, women are a paradigm example of such a distributed group, and do not comprise a traditional community of place. Women's communities are seldom the original, non-voluntary, found communities of their members.

To be sure, non-voluntary communities of place are not without value. Most lives contain mixtures of relationships and communities, some given/found/discovered, and some chosen/created. Most people probably are, to some extent, ineradicably constituted by their communities of place, their original families, neighborhoods, schools, churches, or nations. It is noteworthy that dependent children, elderly persons, and all other individuals whose lives and well-being are at great risk, need the support of communities whose other members do not or cannot choose arbitrarily to leave. Recent philosophical reflection on communities and relationships not founded or sustained by choice has brought out the importance of these social networks for the constitution of social life.[46] But these insights should not obscure the additional need for communities of choice to counter oppressive and abusive relational structures in those non-voluntary communities by providing models of alternative social relationships and standpoints for critical reflection on self and community.

Having attained a critically reflective stance toward one's communities of origin, one's community of place, toward family, neighborhood, church, school, and nation, one has probably at the same time already begun to question and distance oneself from aspects of one's "identity" in that community, and, therefore, to have embarked on the path of personal redefinition. From such a perspective, the communities of place uncritically invoked by the communitarians appear deeply problematic. We can concede the influence of those communities without having unreflectively to endorse it. We must develop communitarian thought beyond its complacent regard for the communities in which we once found ourselves toward (and beyond) an awareness of the crucial importance of "dislocated" communities, communities of choice.[47]

NOTES

1. Cf. Carole Pateman, *The Problem of Political Obligation: A Critique of Liberal Theory* (Berkeley: Univ. of California Press, 1979); Zillah Eisenstein, *The Radical Future of Liberal Feminism* (New York: Longman, 1981); Nancy C. M. Hartsock, *Money, Sex, and Power* (Boston: Northeastern Univ. Press, 1983); Alison M. Jaggar, *Feminist Politics and Human Nature* (Totowa, N.J.: Rowman & Allanheld, 1983); Naomi Scheman, "Individualism and the Objects of Psychology," in Sandra Harding and Merrill B. Hintikka, eds., *Discovering Reality* (Dordrecht: D. Reidel, 1983), pp. 225–244; Jane Flax, "Political Philosophy and the Patriarchal Unconscious: A Psychoanalytic Perspective on Epistemology and Metaphysics," in Harding and Hintikka, eds., ibid., pp. 245–281; and Seyla Benhabib, "The Generalized and the Concrete Other: The Kohlberg-Gilligan Controversy and Moral Theory," in Eva Feder Kittay and Diana T. Meyers, eds., *Women and Moral Theory* (Totowa, N.J.: Rowman and Littlefield, 1987), pp. 154–177.
2. Cf. David Gauthier, *Morals by Agreement* (Oxford: Oxford Univ. Press, 1986).
3. Cf. George Homans, *Social Behavior: Its Elementary Forms* (New York: Harcourt, Brace and World, 1961); and Peter Blau, *Exchange and Power in Social Life* (New York: Wiley, 1974).
4. Cf. my "Autonomy in Social Context," in James Sterba and Creighton Peden, eds., *Freedom, Equality, and Social Change: Problems in Social Philosophy Today* (Lewiston, New York: Edwin Mellen Press, forthcoming).
5. Cf. Drucilla Cornell, "Toward a Modern/Postmodern Reconstruction of Ethics," *University of Pennsylvania Law Review*, vol. 133, no.2 (January 1985), pp. 291–380.
6. Cf. Annette Baier, "Trust and Antitrust," *Ethics*, vol. 96, no.2 (1986), pp. 231–260; and Owen Flanagan and Kathryn Jackson, "Justice, Care, and Gender: The Kohlberg-Gilligan Debate Revisited," *Ethics*, vol. 97, no.3 (1987), pp. 622–637.
7. Cf. Hartsock, op. cit., pp. 41–42; and Virginia Held, "Non-Contractual Society," in Marsha Hanen and Kai Nielsen, eds., *Science, Morality and Feminist Theory*, Supplementary Volume 13 (1987) of *The Canadian Journal of Philosophy*, pp. 111–138.
8. Amy Gutmann, "Communitarian Critics of Liberalism," *Philosophy and Public Affairs*, vol. 14, no.3 (Summer 1985), pp. 308–322.
9. Cf. Alice H. Eagly and Valerie J. Steffen, "Gender Stereotypes Stem From the Distribution of Women and Men into Social Roles," *Journal of Personality and Social Psychology*, vol. 46 (1984), pp. 735–754.
10. Cf. Carol Gilligan, *In A Different Voice* (Cambridge, Mass.: Harvard University Press, 1982).
11. In particular, Michael Sandel, *Liberalism and the Limits of Justice* (Cambridge: Cambridge Univ. Press, 1982); and Alasdair MacIntyre, *After Virtue* (Notre Dame, Ind.: Univ. of Notre Dame Press, 1981).
12. Contemporary liberals do not regard the communitarians' metaphysical claims (discussed below) to be a threat to liberal theory. The liberal concept of the self as abstracted from social relationships and historical context is now treated, not as a metaphysical presupposition, but, rather, as a vehicle for evoking a pluralistic political society whose members disagree about the good for human life. With this device, liberalism seeks a theory of political process which aims to avoid relying on any human particularities that might presuppose parochial human goods or purposes. Cf. John Rawls, "Justice as Fairness: Political Not Metaphysical," *Philosophy & Public Affairs*, vol. 14, no. 3 (1985), pp. 223–251; and Joel Feinberg, "Liberalism, Community, and Tradition," drafted excerpt from *Harmless Wrongdoing*, vol. 4 of *The Moral Limits of the Criminal Law* (Oxford: Oxford Univ. Press, 1988).
13. Sandel, p. 179.
14. Ibid.; italics mine.
15. MacIntyre, pp. 204–5.
16. Ibid., p. 205.
17. Ibid.
18. Dorothy Dinnerstein, *The Mermaid and the Minotaur: Sexual Arrangements and Human*

Malaise (New York: Harper & Row, 1976); Nancy Chodorow, *The Reproduction of Mothering* (Berkeley: Univ. of California Press, 1978); and Gilligan, op. cit.
19. Op. cit., 205; italics mine.
20. A similar point is made by Iris Young, "The Ideal of Community and the Politics of Difference," *Social Theory and Practice*, vol. 12, no.1 (Spring 1986), pp. 12–13.
21. Cf. Cornell, op. cit., p. 323.
22. This point is made by Young, op. cit., p. 12.
23. MacIntyre, op. cit., p. 204; Sandel, op. cit., p. 179.
24. MacIntyre, ibid.; Sandel, ibid.
25. MacIntyre, ibid.
26. Sandel, p. 150; italics mine.
27. Ibid., pp. 151–152.
28. "Split at the Root: An Essay on Jewish Identity," in Adrienne Rich, *Blood, Bread, and Poetry* (New York: W.W. Norton & Co., 1986), p. 107; reprinted from Evelyn Torton Beck, ed., *Nice Jewish Girls: A Lesbian Anthology* (Trumansburg, N.Y.: Crossing Press, 1982), pp. 67–84.
29. Ibid., p. 108.
30. This term is used by Sandel, op. cit., p. 180.
31. Martha Ackelsberg points out the ironic and misleading nature of this use of the term "sisterhood" in " 'Sisters' or 'Comrades'? The Politics of Friends and Families," in Irene Diamond, ed., *Families, Politics, and Public Policy* (New York: Longman, 1983), pp. 339–56.
32. Cf. Janice Raymond, *A Passion for Friends* (Boston: Beacon Press, 1986), esp. Chaps. 2 and 3.
33. Claude Fischer, *To Dwell Among Friends* (Chicago: Univ. of Chicago Press, 1982), p. 1.
34. Cf. Richard Sennett, "An Introduction," in Richard Sennett, ed., *Classic Essays on the Culture of Cities* (New York: Appleton-Century-Crofts, 1969), pp. 3–22.
35. Cf. Stanley Milgram, "The Experience of Living in Cities," *Science*, vol. 167 (1970), pp. 1461–68.
36. Fischer, op. cit., pp. 97–103.
37. Ibid., pp. 193–232.
38. Melvin Webber, "Order in Diversity: Community without Propinquity," in R. Gutman and D. Popenoe, eds., *Neighborhood, City and Metropolis* (New York: Random House, 1970), pp. 792–811.
39. Fischer, p. 273.
40. Cf. the essays in Catherine Stimpson, et al., eds., *Women and the American City* (Chicago: Univ. of Chicago Press, 1980, 1981); and the special issue on "Women in the City," *Urban Resources*, vol. 3, no. 2 (Winter 1986).
41. "Introduction" to Susan Merrill Squier, ed., *Women Writers and the City* (Knoxville: Univ. of Tennessee Press, 1984), pp. 3–10.
42. Blanche Gelfant, "Sister to Faust: The City's 'Hungry' Woman as Heroine," in Squier, ed., ibid., p. 267.
43. Fischer, op. cit., pp. 247–8.
44. Ibid., p. 230.
45. Ibid.
46. Cf. Baier, op. cit.; Held, op. cit.; and Pateman, op. cit.
47. I am grateful to Cass Sunstein and the editors of *Ethics* for helpful comments on an earlier version of this paper. This paper was written with the support of a National Endowment for the Humanities Summer Stipend and a grant from the Faculty Research Committee of Bowling Green State University.

John Rawls

Justice as Fairness: Political Not Metaphysical

In this essay John Rawls elaborates and refines some of the themes found in A Theory of Justice. He argues against those who see his work aspiring to universal truth or resting on a particular metaphysical view of the person. Justice as fairness is, he claims, only a political conception of justice: It can be expected to appeal to citizens of a constitutional democracy where people have widely differing conceptions of the good. It is not a comprehensive moral or philosophical theory. Its view of persons as free and equal, in virtue of their moral powers, is an account of how we view each other in the political context—as citizens—and not a metaphysical truth about persons in general. Rawls characterizes justice as fairness as a liberal political doctrine, and concludes with a discussion of liberalism's understanding of social unity and stability.

In this discussion I shall make some general remarks about how I now understand the conception of justice that I have called "justice as fairness" (presented in my book *A Theory of Justice*). I do this because it may seem that this conception depends on philosophical claims I should like to avoid, for example, claims to universal truth, or claims about the essential nature and identity of persons. My aim is to explain why it does not. I shall first discuss what I regard as the task of political philosophy at the present time and then briefly survey how the basic intuitive ideas drawn upon in justice as fairness are combined into a political conception of justice for a constitutional democracy. Doing this will bring out how and why this conception of justice avoids certain philosophical and metaphysical claims. Briefly, the idea is that in a constitutional democracy the public conception of justice should be, so far as possible, independent of controversial philosophical and religious doctrines. Thus, to formulate such a conception, we apply the principle of toleration to philosophy itself: the public conception of justice is to be political, not metaphysical. Hence the title.

I want to put aside the question whether the text of *A Theory of Justice* supports different readings than the one I sketch here. Certainly on a number of points I have changed my views, and there are no doubt others on which my views have changed in ways that I am unaware of. . . . For our purposes here, it suffices first, to show how a conception of justice with the structure and content of justice as fairness can be understood as political and not metaphysical, and second, to explain why we should look for such a conception of justice in a democratic society.

I

One thing I failed to say in *A Theory of Justice,* or failed to stress sufficiently, is that justice as fairness is intended as a political conception of justice. While a political conception of justice is, of course, a moral conception, it is a moral conception worked out for a specific kind of subject, namely, for political, social, and economic institutions. In particular, justice as fairness is framed to apply to what I have called the "basic structure" of a modern constitutional democracy. (I shall use "constitutional democracy" and "democratic regime," and similar phrases interchangeably.) By this structure I mean such a society's main political, social, and economic institutions, and how they fit together into one unified system of social cooperation. Whether justice as fairness can be extended to a general political conception for different kinds of societies existing under different historical and social conditions, or whether it can be extended to a general moral conception, or a significant part thereof, are altogether separate questions. I avoid prejudging these larger questions one way or the other.

It should also be stressed that justice as fairness is not intended as the application of a general moral conception to the basic structure of society, as if this structure were simply another case to which that general moral conception is applied. In this respect justice as fairness differs from traditional moral doctrines, for these are widely regarded as such general conceptions. Utilitarianism is a familiar example, since the principle of utility, however it is formulated, is usually said to hold for all kinds of subjects ranging from the actions of individuals to the law of nations. The essential point is this: as a practical political matter no general moral conception can provide a publicly recognized basis for a conception of justice in a modern democratic state. The social and historical conditions of such a state have their origins in the Wars of Religion following the Reformation and the subsequent development of the principle of toleration, and in the growth of constitutional government and the institutions of large industrial market economies. These conditions profoundly affect the requirements of a workable conception of political justice: such a conception must allow for a diversity of doctrines and the plurality of conflicting, and indeed incommensurable, conceptions of the good affirmed by the members of existing democratic societies.

Finally, to conclude these introductory remarks, since justice as fairness is intended as a political conception of justice for a democratic society, it tries to draw solely upon basic intuitive ideas that are embedded in the political institutions of a constitutional democratic regime and the public traditions of their interpretation. Justice as fairness is a political conception in part because it starts from within a certain political tradition. We hope that this political conception of justice may at least be supported by what we may call an "overlapping consensus," that is, by a consensus that includes all the opposing philosophical and religious doctrines likely to persist and to gain adherents in a more or less just constitutional democratic society.

II

There are, of course, many ways in which political philosophy may be understood and writers at different times, faced with different political and social circumstances, understand their work differently. Justice as fairness I would now understand as a reasonably systematic and practicable conception of justice for a constitutional democracy, a conception that offers an alternative to the dominant utilitarianism of our tradition of political thought. Its first task is to provide a more secure and acceptable basis for constitutional principles and basic rights and liberties than utilitarianism seems to allow. The need for such a political conception arises in the following way.

There are periods, sometimes long periods, in the history of any society during which certain fundamental questions give rise to sharp and divisive political controversy, and it seems difficult, if not impossible, to find any shared basis of political agreement. Indeed, certain questions may prove intractable and may never be fully settled. One task of political philosophy in a democratic society is to focus on such questions and to examine whether some underlying basis of agreement can be uncovered and a mutually acceptable way of resolving these questions publicly established. Or if these questions cannot be fully settled, as may well be the case, perhaps the divergence of opinion can be narrowed sufficiently so that political cooperation on a basis of mutual respect can still be maintained.

The course of democratic thought over the past two centuries or so makes plain that there is no agreement on the way basic institutions of a constitutional democracy should be arranged if they are to specify and secure the basic rights and liberties of citizens and answer to the claims of democratic equality when citizens are conceived as free and equal persons (as explained in the last three paragraphs of Section III). A deep disagreement exists as to how the values of liberty and equality are best realized in the basic structure of society. To simplify, we may think of this disagreement as a conflict within the tradition of democratic thought itself, between the tradition associated with Locke, which gives greater weight to what Constant called "the liberties of the moderns," freedom of thought and conscience, certain basic rights of the person and of property, and the rule of law, and the tradition associated with Rousseau, which gives greater weight to what Constant called "the liberties of the ancients," the equal political liberties and the values of public life. This is a stylized contrast and historically inaccurate, but it serves to fix ideas.

Justice as fairness tries to adjudicate between these contending traditions first, by proposing two principles of justice to serve as guidelines for how basic institutions are to realize the values of liberty and equality, and second, by specifying a point of view from which these principles can be seen as more appropriate than other familiar principles of justice to the nature of democratic citizens viewed as free and equal persons. What it means to view citizens as free and equal persons is, of course, a fundamental question and is discussed in the following sections. What must be shown is that a certain arrangement of the basic structure, certain institutional forms, are more appropriate for realizing the values of liberty and equality when citizens are conceived as such persons, that is (very briefly), as having the requisite powers of moral personality that enable them to participate in society viewed as a system of fair cooperation for mutual advantage. So to continue, the two principles of justice (mentioned above) read as follows:

1. Each person has an equal right to a fully adequate scheme of equal basic rights and liberties, which scheme is compatible with a similar scheme for all.
2. Social and economic inequalities are to satisfy two conditions: first, they must be attached to offices and positions open to all under conditions of fair equality of opportunity; and second, they must be to the greatest benefit of the least advantaged members of society.

Each of these principles applies to a different part of the basic structure; and both are concerned not only with basic rights, liberties, and opportunities, but also with the claims of equality; while the second part of the second principle underwrites the worth of these institutional guarantees. The two principles together, when the first is given priority over the second, regulate the basic institutions which realize these values. But these details, although important, are not our concern here.

We must now ask: how might political philosophy find a shared basis for settling such a fundamental question as that of the most appropriate institutional forms for liberty and equality? Of course, it is likely that the most that can be done is to narrow the range of public disagreement. Yet even firmly held convictions gradually change: religious toleration is now accepted, and arguments for persecution are no longer openly professed; similarly, slavery is rejected as inherently unjust, and however much the aftermath of slavery may persist in social practices and unavowed attitudes, no one is willing to defend it. We collect such settled convictions as the belief in religious toleration and the rejection of slavery and try to organize the basic ideas and principles implicit in these convictions into a coherent conception of justice. We can regard these convictions as provisional fixed points which any conception of justice must account for if it is to be reasonable for us. We look, then, to our public political culture itself, including its main institutions and the historical traditions of their interpretation, as the shared fund of implicitly recognized basic ideas and principles. The hope is that these ideas and principles can be formulated clearly enough to be combined into a conception of political justice congenial to our most firmly held convictions. We express this by saying that a political conception of justice, to be acceptable, must be in accordance with our considered convictions, at all levels of generality, on due reflection (or in what I have called "reflective equilibrium").

The public political culture may be of two minds even at a very deep level. Indeed, this must be so with such an enduring controversy as that concerning the most appropriate institutional forms to realize the values of liberty and equality. This suggests that if we are to succeed in finding a basis of public agreement, we must find a new way of organizing familiar ideas and principles into a conception of political justice so that the claims in conflict, as previously understood, are seen in another light. A political conception need not be an original creation but may only articulate familiar intuitive ideas and principles so that they can be recognized as fitting together in a somewhat different way than before. Such a conception may, however, go further than this: it may organize these familiar ideas and principles by means of a more fundamental intuitive idea within the complex structure of which the other familiar intuitive ideas are then systematically connected and related. In justice as fairness, as we shall see in the next section, this more fundamental idea is that of society as a system of fair social cooperation between free and equal persons. The concern of this section is how we might find a public basis of political agreement. The point is that a conception of justice will only be able to achieve this aim if it provides a reasonable way of shaping into one coherent view the deeper bases of agreement embedded in the public political culture of a constitutional regime and acceptable to its most-firmly held considered convictions.

Now suppose justice as fairness were to achieve its aim and a publicly acceptable political conception of justice is found. Then this conception provides a publicly recognized point of view from which all citizens can examine before one another whether or not their political and social institutions are just. It enables them to do this by citing what are recognized among them as valid and sufficient reasons singled out by that conception itself. Society's main institutions and how they fit together into one scheme of social cooperation can be examined on the same basis by each citizen, whatever that citizen's social position or more particular interests. It should be observed that, on this view, justification is not regarded simply as valid argument from listed premises, even should these premises be true. Rather, justification is addressed to others who disagree with us, and therefore it must always proceed from some consensus, that is, from premises that we and others publicly recognize as true; or better, publicly recognize as acceptable to us for the purpose of establishing a working agreement on the fundamental questions of political justice. It goes without saying that this agreement must be informed and uncoerced, and reached by citizens in ways consistent with their being viewed as free and equal persons.

Thus, the aim of justice as fairness as a political conception is practical, and not metaphysical or epistemological. That is, it presents itself not as a conception of justice that is true, but one that can serve as a basis of informed and willing political agreement between citizens viewed as free and equal persons. This agreement when securely founded in public political and social attitudes sustains the goods of all persons and associations within a just democratic regime. To secure this agreement we try, so far as we can, to avoid disputed philosophical, as well as disputed moral and religious, questions. We do this not because these questions are unimportant or regarded with indifference, but because we think them too important and recognize that there is no way to resolve them politically. The only alternative to a principle of toleration is the autocratic use of state power. Thus, justice as fairness deliberately stays on the surface, philosophically speaking. Given the profound differences in belief and conceptions of the good at least since the Reformation, we must recognize that, just as on questions of religious and moral doctrine, public agreement on the basic questions of philosophy cannot be obtained without the state's infringement of basic liberties. Philosophy as the search for truth about an independent metaphysical and moral order cannot, I believe, provide a workable and shared basis for a political conception of justice in a democratic society.

We try, then, to leave aside philosophical controversies whenever possible, and look for ways to avoid philosophy's longstanding problems. Thus, in what I have called "Kantian constructivism," we try to avoid the problem of truth and the controversy between realism and subjectivism about the status of moral and political values. This form of constructivism neither asserts nor denies these doctrines. Rather, it recasts ideas from the tradition of the social contract to achieve a practicable conception of objectivity and justification founded on public agreement in judgment on due reflection. The aim is free agreement, reconciliation through public reason. And similarly, as we shall see (in Section V), a conception of the person in a political view, for example, the conception of citizens as free and equal persons, need not involve, so I believe, questions of philosophical psychology or a metaphysical doctrine of the nature of the self. No political view that depends on these deep and unresolved matters can serve as a public conception of justice in a constitutional democratic state. As I have said, we must apply the principle of toleration to philosophy itself. The hope is that, by this method of avoidance, as we might call it, existing differences between contending political views can at least be moderated, even if not entirely removed, so that social cooperation on the basis of mutual respect can be maintained. Or if this is expecting too much, this method may enable us to conceive how, given a desire for free and uncoerced agreement, a public understanding could arise consistent with the historical conditions and constraints of our social world. Until we bring ourselves to conceive how this could happen, it can't happen.

III

Let's now survey briefly some of the basic ideas that make up justice as fairness in order to show that these ideas belong to a political conception of justice. As I have indicated, the overarching fundamental intuitive idea, within which other basic intuitive ideas are systematically connected, is that of society as a fair system of cooperation between free and equal persons. Justice as fairness starts from this idea as one of the basic intuitive ideas which we take to be implicit in the public culture of a democratic society.* In their political thought, and in the context of public discussion of political questions, citizens do not view the social order as a fixed natural order, or as an institutional hierarchy justified by religious or aristocratic values. Here it is important to stress that from other points of view, for example, from the point of view of personal morality, or from the point of view of members of an association, or of one's religious or philosophical doctrine, various aspects of the world and one's relation to it, may be regarded in a different way. But these other points of view are not to be introduced into political discussion.

We can make the idea of social cooperation more specific by noting three of its elements:

1. Cooperation is distinct from merely socially coordinated activity, for example, from activity coordinated by orders issued by some central authority. Cooperation is guided by publicly recognized rules and procedures which those who are cooperating accept and regard as properly regulating their conduct.

2. Cooperation involves the idea of fair terms of cooperation: these are terms that each participant may reasonably accept, provided that everyone else likewise accepts them. Fair terms of cooperation specify an idea of reciprocity or mutuality: all who are engaged in cooperation and who do their part as the rules and procedures require, are to benefit in some appropriate way as assessed by a suitable benchmark of comparison. A conception of political justice characterizes the fair terms of social cooperation. Since the primary subject of justice is the basic structure of society, this is accomplished in justice as fairness by formulating principles that specify basic rights and duties within the main institutions of society, and by regulating the institutions of background justice over time so that the benefits produced by everyone's efforts are fairly acquired and divided from one generation to the next.

3. The idea of social cooperation requires an idea of each participant's rational advantage, or good. This idea of good specifies what those who are engaged in cooperation, whether individuals, families, or associations, or even nation-states, are trying to achieve, when the scheme is viewed from their own standpoint.

Now consider the idea of the person.‡ There are, of course, many aspects of human nature that can be singled out as especially significant

*Although *Theory* uses this idea from the outset (it is introduced on p. 4), it does not emphasize, as I do here . . . , that the basic ideas of justice as fairness are regarded as implicit or latent in the public culture of a democratic society.

‡It should be emphasized that a conception of the person, as I understand it here, is a normative conception, whether legal, political, or moral, or indeed also philosophical or religious, depending on the overall view to which it belongs. In this case the conception of the person is a moral conception, one that begins from our everyday conception of persons as the basic units of thought, deliberation and responsibility, and adapted to a political conception of justice and not to a comprehensive moral doctrine. It is in effect a political conception of the person, and given the aims of justice as fairness, a conception of citizens. Thus, a conception of the person is to be distinguished from an account of human nature given by natural science or social theory.

depending on our point of view. This is witnessed by such expressions as *homo politicus, homo oeconomicus, homo faber,* and the like. Justice as fairness starts from the idea that society is to be conceived as a fair system of cooperation and so it adopts a conception of the person to go with this idea. Since Greek times, both in philosophy and law, the concept of the person has been understood as the concept of someone who can take part in, or who can play a role in, social life, and hence exercise and respect its various rights and duties. Thus, we say that a person is someone who can be a citizen, that is, a fully cooperating member of society over a complete life. We add the phrase "over a complete life" because a society is viewed as a more or less complete and self-sufficient scheme of cooperation, making room within itself for all the necessities and activities of life, from birth until death. A society is not an association for more limited purposes; citizens do not join society voluntarily but are born into it, where, for our aims here, we assume they are to lead their lives.

Since we start within the tradition of democratic thought, we also think of citizens as free and equal persons. The basic intuitive idea is that in virtue of what we may call their moral powers, and the powers of reason, thought, and judgment connected with those powers, we say that persons are free. And in virtue of their having these powers to the requisite degree to be fully cooperating members of society, we say that persons are equal. We can elaborate this conception of the person as follows. Since persons can be full participants in a fair system of social cooperation, we ascribe to them the two moral powers connected with the elements in the idea of social cooperation noted above: namely, a capacity for a sense of justice and a capacity for a conception of the good. A sense of justice is the capacity to understand, to apply, and to act from the public conception of justice which characterizes the fair terms of social cooperation. The capacity for a conception of the good is the capacity to form, to revise, and rationally to pursue a conception of one's rational advantage, or good. In the case of social cooperation, this good must not be understood narrowly but rather as a conception of what is valuable in human life. Thus, a conception of the good normally consists of a more or less determinate scheme of final ends, that is, ends we want to realize for their own sake, as well as of attachments to other persons and loyalties to various groups and associations. These attachments and loyalties give rise to affections and devotions, and therefore the flourishing of the persons and associations who are the objects of these sentiments is also part of our conception of the good. Moreover, we must also include in such a conception a view of our relation to the world—religious, philosophical, or moral—by reference to which the value and significance of our ends and attachments are understood.

In addition to having the two moral powers, the capacities for a sense of justice and a conception of the good, persons also have at any given time a particular conception of the good that they try to achieve. Since we wish to start from the idea of society as a fair system of cooperation, we assume that persons as citizens have all the capacities that enable them to be normal and fully cooperating members of society. This does not imply that no one ever suffers from illness or accident; such misfortunes are to be expected in the ordinary course of human life; and provision for these contingencies must be made. But for our purposes here I leave aside permanent physical disabilities or mental disorders so severe as to prevent persons from being normal and fully cooperating members of society in the usual sense.

Now the conception of persons as having the two moral powers, and therefore as free and equal, is also a basic intuitive idea assumed to be implicit in the public culture of a democratic society. Note, however, that it is formed by idealizing and simplifying in various ways. This is done to achieve a clear and uncluttered view of what for us is the fundamental question of political justice: namely, what is the most appropriate conception of justice for specifying the terms of social cooperation between citizens regarded as free and equal persons, and as normal and fully cooperating members of society over a complete life. It is this question that has been the focus of the liberal critique of aristocracy, of the socialist critique of liberal constitutional democracy, and of the conflict between liberals and conservatives at the present time over the claims of private property and the legitimacy (in contrast to the effectiveness) of social policies associated with the so-called welfare state.

IV

I now take up the idea of the original position. This idea is introduced in order to work out which traditional conception of justice, or which variant of one of those conceptions, specifies the most appropriate principles for realizing liberty and equality once society is viewed as a system of cooperation between free and equal persons. Assuming we had this purpose in mind, let's see why we would introduce the idea of the original position and how it serves its purpose.

Consider again the idea of social cooperation. Let's ask: how are the fair terms of cooperation to be determined? Are they simply laid down by some outside agency distinct from the persons cooperating? Are they, for example, laid down by God's law? Or are these terms to be recognized by these persons as fair by reference to their knowledge of a prior and independent moral order? For example, are they regarded as required by natural law, or by a realm of values known by rational intuition? Or are these terms to be established by an undertaking among these persons themselves in the light of what they regard as their mutual advantage? Depending on which answer we give, we get a different conception of cooperation.

Since justice as fairness recasts the doctrine of the social contract, it adopts a form of the last answer: the fair terms of social cooperation are conceived as agreed to by those engaged in it, that is, by free and equal persons as citizens who are born into the society in which they lead their lives. But their agreement, like any other valid agreement, must be entered into under appropriate conditions. In particular, these conditions must situate free and equal persons fairly and must not allow some persons greater bargaining advantages than others. Further, threats of force and coercion, deception and fraud, and so on, must be excluded.

So far so good. The foregoing considerations are familiar from everyday life. But agreements in everyday life are made in some more or less clearly specified situation embedded within the background institutions of the basic structure. Our task, however, is to extend the idea of agreement to this background framework itself: Here we face a difficulty for any political conception of justice that uses the idea of a contract, whether social or otherwise. The difficulty is this: we must find some point of view, removed from and not distorted by the particular features and circumstances of the all-encompassing background framework, from which a fair agreement between free and equal persons can be reached. The original position, with the feature I have called "the veil of ignorance," is this point of view. And the reason why the original position must abstract from and not be affected by the contingencies of the social world is that the conditions for a fair agreement on the principles of political justice between free and equal persons must eliminate the bargaining advantages which inevitably arise within background institutions of any society as the result of cumulative social, historical, and natural tendencies. These contingent advantages and accidental influences from the past should not influence an agreement on the principles which are to regulate the institutions of the basic structure itself from the present into the future.

Here we seem to face a second difficulty, which is, however, only apparent. To explain: from what we have just said it is clear that the original position is to be seen as a device of representation and hence any agreement reached by the parties must be regarded as both hypothetical and nonhistorical. But if so, since hypothetical agreements cannot bind, what is the significance of the original position? The answer is implicit in what has already been said: it is given by the role of the various features of the original position as a device of representation. Thus, that the parties are symmetrically situated is required if they are to be seen as representatives of free and equal citizens who are to reach an agreement under conditions that are fair. Moreover, one of our considered convictions, I assume, is this: the fact that we occupy a particular social position is not a good reason for us to accept, or to expect others to accept, a conception of justice that favors those in this position. To model this conviction in the original position the parties are not allowed to know their social position; and the same idea is extended to other cases. This is expressed figuratively by saying that the parties are behind a veil of ignorance. In sum, the original position is simply a device of representation: it describes the parties, each of whom are responsible for the essential interests of a free and equal person, as fairly situated and as reaching an agreement subject to appropriate restrictions on what are to count as good reasons.*

---

*. . . These constraints are modeled in the original position and thereby imposed on the parties: their deliberations are subject, and subject absolutely, to the reasonable conditions the modeling of which makes the original position fair. The Reasonable, then, is prior to the Rational, and this gives the priority of right. Thus, it was an error in *Theory* (and a very

Both of the above mentioned difficulties, then, are overcome by viewing the original position as a device of representation: that is, this position models what we regard as fair conditions under which the representatives of free and equal persons are to specify the terms of social cooperation in the case of the basic structure of society: and since it also models what, for this case, we regard as acceptable restrictions on reasons available to the parties for favoring one agreement rather than another, the conception of justice the parties would adopt identifies the conception we regard—*here and now*—as fair and supported by the best reasons. We try to model restrictions on reasons in such a way that it is perfectly evident which agreement would be made by the parties in the original position as citizens' representatives. Even if there should be, as surely there will be, reasons for and against each conception of justice available, there may be an overall balance of reasons plainly favoring one conception over the rest. As a device of representation the idea of the original position serves as a means of public reflection and self-clarification. We can use it to help us work out what we now think, once we are able to take a clear and uncluttered view of what justice requires when society is conceived as a scheme of cooperation between free and equal persons over time from one generation to the next. The original position serves as a unifying idea by which our considered convictions at all levels of generality are brought to bear on one another so as to achieve greater mutual agreement and self-understanding.

To conclude: we introduce an idea like that of the original position because there is no better way to elaborate a political conception of justice for the basic structure from the fundamental intuitive idea of society as a fair system of cooperation between citizens as free and equal persons. There are, however, certain hazards. As a device of representation the original position is likely to seem somewhat abstract and hence open to misunderstanding. The description of the parties may seem to presuppose some metaphysical conception of the person, for example, that the essential nature of persons is independent of and prior to their contingent attributes, including their final ends and attachments, and indeed, their character as a whole. But this is an illusion caused by not seeing the original position as a device of representation. The veil of ignorance, to mention one prominent feature of that position, has no metaphysical implications concerning the nature of the self; it does not imply that the self is ontologically prior to the facts about persons that the parties are excluded from knowing. We can, as it were, enter this position any time simply by reasoning for principles of justice in accordance with the enumerated restrictions. When, in this way, we simulate being in this position, our reasoning no more commits us to a metaphysical doctrine about the

misleading one) to describe a theory of justice as part of the theory of rational choice, as on pp. 16 and 583. What I should have said is that the conception of justice as fairness uses an account of rational choice subject to reasonable conditions to characterize the deliberations of the parties as representatives of free and equal persons; and all of this within a political conception of justice, which is, of course, a moral conception. There is no thought of trying to derive the content of justice within a framework that uses an idea of the rational as the sole normative idea. That thought is incompatible with any kind of Kantian view.

nature of the self than our playing a game like Monopoly commits us to thinking that we are landlords engaged in a desperate rivalry, winner take all. We must keep in mind that we are trying to show how the idea of society as a fair system of social cooperation can be unfolded so as to specify the most appropriate principles for realizing the institutions of liberty and equality when citizens are regarded as free and equal persons.

V

I just remarked that the idea of the original position and the description of the parties may tempt us to think that a metaphysical doctrine of the person is presupposed. While I said that this interpretation is mistaken, it is not enough simply to disavow reliance on metaphysical doctrines, for despite one's intent they may still be involved. To rebut claims of this nature requires discussing them in detail and showing that they have no foothold. I cannot do that here.*

I can, however, sketch a positive account of the political conception of the person, that is, the conception of the person as citizen (discussed in Section III), involved in the original position as a device of representation. To explain what is meant by describing a conception of the person as political, let's consider how citizens are represented in the original position as free persons. The representation of their freedom seems to be one source of the idea that some metaphysical doctrine is presupposed. I have said elsewhere that citizens view themselves as free in three respects, so let's survey each of these briefly and indicate the way in which the conception of the person used is political.

First, citizens are free in that they conceive of themselves and of one another as having the moral power to have a conception of the good. This is not to say that, as part of their political conception of themselves, they view themselves as inevitably tied to the pursuit of the particular conception of the good which they affirm at any given time. Instead, as

---

*Part of the difficulty is that there is no accepted understanding of what a metaphysical doctrine is. One might say, as Paul Hoffman has suggested to me, that to develop a political conception of justice without presupposing, or explicitly using, a metaphysical doctrine, for example, some particular metaphysical conception of the person, is already to presuppose a metaphysical thesis: namely, that no particular metaphysical doctrine is required for this purpose. One might also say that our everyday conception of persons as the basic units of deliberation and responsibility presupposes, or in some way involves, certain metaphysical theses about the nature of persons as moral or political agents. Following the method of avoidance, I should not want to deny these claims. What should be said is the following. If we look at the presentation of justice as fairness and note how it is set up, and note the ideas and conceptions it uses, no particular metaphysical doctrine about the nature of persons, distinctive and opposed to other metaphysical doctrines, appears among its premises, or seems required by its argument. If metaphysical presuppositions are involved, perhaps they are so general that they would not distinguish between the distinctive metaphysical views—Cartesian, Leibnizian, or Kantian; realist, idealist, or materialist—with which philosophy traditionally has been concerned. In this case, they would not appear to be relevant for the structure and content of a political conception of justice one way or the other. I am grateful to Daniel Brudney and Paul Hoffman for discussion of these matters.

citizens, they are regarded as capable of revising and changing this conception on reasonable and rational grounds, and they may do this if they so desire. Thus, as free persons, citizens claim the right to view their persons as independent from and as not identified with any particular conception of the good, or scheme of final ends. Given their moral power to form, to revise, and rationally to pursue a conception of the good, their public identity as free persons is not affected by changes over time in their conception of the good. For example, when citizens convert from one religion to another, or no longer affirm an established religious faith, they do not cease to be, for questions of political justice, the same persons they were before. There is no loss of what we may call their public identity, their identity as a matter of basic law. In general, they still have the same basic rights and duties; they own the same property and can make the same claims as before, except insofar as these claims were connected with their previous religious affiliation. We can imagine a society (indeed, history offers numerous examples) in which basic rights and recognized claims depend on religious affiliation, social class, and so on. Such a society has a different political conception of the person. It may not have a conception of citizenship at all; for this conception, as we are using it, goes with the conception of society as a fair system of cooperation for mutual advantage between free and equal persons.

It is essential to stress that citizens in their personal affairs, or in the internal life of associations to which they belong, may regard their final ends and attachments in a way very different from the way the political conception involves. Citizens may have, and normally do have at any given time, affections, devotions, and loyalties that they believe they would not, and indeed could and should not, stand apart from and objectively evaluate from the point of view of their purely rational good. They may regard it as simply unthinkable to view themselves apart from certain religious, philosophical, and moral convictions, or from certain enduring attachments and loyalties. These convictions and attachments are part of what we may call their "nonpublic identity." These convictions and attachments help to organize and give shape to a person's way of life, what one sees oneself as doing and trying to accomplish in one's social world. We think that if we were suddenly without these particular convictions and attachments we would be disoriented and unable to carry on. In fact, there would be, we might think, no point in carrying on. But our conceptions of the good may and often do change over time, usually slowly but sometimes rather suddenly. When these changes are sudden, we are particularly likely to say that we are no longer the same person. We know what this means: we refer to a profound and pervasive shift, or reversal, in our final ends and character, we refer to our different nonpublic, and possibly moral or religious, identity. On the road to Damascus Saul of Tarsus becomes Paul the Apostle. There is no change in our public or political identity, nor in our personal identity as this concept is understood by some writers in the philosophy of mind.

The second respect in which citizens view themselves as free is that they regard themselves as self-originating sources of valid claims. They think their claims have weight apart from being derived from duties or obligations specified by the political conception of justice, for example, from duties and obligations owed to society. Claims that citizens regard as founded on duties and obligations based on their conception of the good and the moral doctrine they affirm in their own life are also, for our purposes here, to be counted as self-originating. Doing this is reasonable in a political conception of justice for a constitutional democracy; for provided the conceptions of the good and the moral doctrines citizens affirm are compatible with the public conception of justice, these duties and obligations are self-originating from the political point of view.

When we describe a way in which citizens regard themselves as free, we are describing how citizens actually think of themselves in a democratic society should questions of justice arise. In our conception of a constitutional regime, this is an aspect of how citizens regard themselves. That this aspect of their freedom belongs to a particular political conception is clear from the contrast with a different political conception in which the members of society are not viewed as self-originating sources of valid claims. Rather, their claims have no weight except insofar as they can be derived from their duties and obligations owed to society, or from their ascribed roles in the social hierarchy justified by religious or aristocratic values. Or to take an extreme case, slaves are human beings who are not counted as sources of claims, not even claims based on social duties or obligations, for slaves are not counted as capable of having duties or obligations. Laws that prohibit the abuse and maltreatment of slaves are not founded on claims made by slaves on their own behalf, but on claims originating either from slaveholders, or from the general interests of society (which does not include the interests of slaves). Slaves are, so to speak, socially dead: they are not publicly recognized as persons at all. Thus, the contrast with a political conception which allows slavery makes clear why conceiving of citizens as free persons in virtue of their moral powers and their having a conception of the good, goes with a particular political conception of the person. This conception of persons fits into a political conception of justice founded on the idea of society as a system of cooperation between its members conceived as free and equal.

The third respect in which citizens are regarded as free is that they are regarded as capable of taking responsibility for their ends and this affects how their various claims are assessed. Very roughly, the idea is that, given just background institutions and given for each person a fair index of primary goods (as required by the principles of justice), citizens are thought to be capable of adjusting their aims and aspirations in the light of what they can reasonably expect to provide for. Moreover, they are regarded as capable of restricting their claims in matters of justice to the kinds of things the principles of justice allow. Thus, citizens are to recognize that the weight of their claims is not given by the strength and psychological intensity of their wants and desires (as opposed to their needs and requirements as citizens), even when their wants and desires are rational from their point of view. I cannot pursue these matters here. But the procedure is the same as before: we start with the basic intuitive idea of society as a system of social cooperation. When this idea is developed into a conception of political justice, it implies that, viewing ourselves as persons who can engage in social cooperation over a complete life, we can also take responsibility for our ends, that is, that we can adjust our ends so that they can be pursued by the means we can reasonably expect to acquire given our prospects and situation in society. The idea of responsibility for ends is implicit in the public political culture and discernible in its practices. A political conception of the person articulates this idea and fits it into the idea of society as a system of social cooperation over a complete life.

To sum up, I recapitulate three main points of this and the preceding two sections:

First, in Section III persons were regarded as free and equal in virtue of their possessing to the requisite degree the two powers of moral personality (and the powers of reason, thought, and judgment connected with these powers), namely, the capacity for a sense of justice and the capacity for a conception of the good. These powers we associated with two main elements of the idea of cooperation, the idea of fair terms of cooperation and the idea of each participant's rational advantage, or good.

Second, in this section (Section V), we have briefly surveyed three respects in which persons are regarded as free, and we have noted that in the public political culture of a constitutional democratic regime citizens conceive of themselves as free in these respects.

Third, since the question of which conception of political justice is most appropriate for realizing in basic institutions the values of liberty and equality has long been deeply controversial within the very democratic tradition in which citizens are regarded as free and equal persons, the aim of justice as fairness is to try to resolve this question by starting from the basic intuitive idea of society as a fair system of social cooperation in which the fair terms of cooperation are agreed upon by citizens themselves so conceived. In Section IV, we saw why this approach leads to the idea of the original position as a device of representation.

VI

I now take up a point essential to thinking of justice as fairness as a liberal view. Although this conception is a moral conception, it is not, as I have said, intended as a comprehensive moral doctrine. The conception of the citizen as a free and equal person is not a moral ideal to govern all of life, but is rather an ideal belonging to a conception of political justice which is to apply to the basic structure. I emphasize this point because to think otherwise would be incompatible with liberalism as a political doctrine. Recall that as such a doctrine, liberalism assumes that in a constitutional democratic state under modern conditions there are bound to exist conflicting and incommensurable conceptions of the good. This feature characterizes modern culture since the Reformation. Any viable political conception of justice that is not to rely on the autocratic use of state power must recognize this fundamental social fact. This does not mean, of course, that such a conception cannot impose constraints on individuals and associations, but that when it does so, these constraints are accounted for, directly or indirectly, by the requirements of political justice for the basic structure.*

Given this fact, we adopt a conception of the person framed as part of, and restricted to, an explicitly political conception of justice. In this sense, the conception of the person is a political one. As I stressed in the previous section, persons can accept this conception of themselves as citizens and use it when discussing questions of political justice without being committed in other parts of their life to comprehensive moral ideals often associated with liberalism, for example, the ideals of autonomy and individuality. The absence of commitment to these ideals, and indeed to any particular comprehensive ideal, is essential to liberalism as a political doctrine. The reason is that any such ideal, when pursued as a comprehensive ideal, is incompatible with other conceptions of the good, with forms of personal, moral, and religious life consistent with justice and which, therefore, have a proper place in a democratic society. As comprehensive moral ideals, autonomy and individuality are unsuited for a political conception of justice. As found in Kant and J. S. Mill, these comprehensive ideals, despite their very great importance in liberal thought, are extended too far when presented as the only appropriate foundation for a constitutional regime. So understood, liberalism becomes but another sectarian doctrine.

This conclusion requires comment: it does not mean, of course, that the liberalisms of Kant and Mill are not appropriate moral conceptions from which we can be led to affirm democratic institutions. But they are only two such conceptions among others, and so but two of the philosophical doctrines likely to persist and gain adherents in a reasonably just democratic regime. In such a regime the comprehensive moral views which support its basic institutions may include the liberalisms of individuality and autonomy; and possibly these liberalisms are among the more prominent doctrines in an overlapping consensus, that is, in a consensus in which, as noted earlier, different and even conflicting doctrines affirm the publicly shared basis of political arrangements. The liberalisms of Kant and Mill have a certain historical preeminence as among the first and most important philosophical views to espouse modern constitutional democracy and to develop its underlying ideas in an influential way; and it may even turn out that societies in which the ideals of autonomy and individuality are widely accepted are among the most well-governed and harmonious.

By contrast with liberalism as a comprehensive moral doctrine,

---

*For example, churches are constrained by the principle of equal liberty of conscience and must conform to the principle of toleration, universities by what may be required to maintain fair equality of opportunity, and the rights of parents by what is necessary to maintain their childrens' physical well-being and to assure the adequate development of their intellectual and moral powers. Because churches, universities, and parents exercise their authority within the basic structure, they are to recognize the requirements this structure imposes to maintain background justice.

justice as fairness tries to present a conception of political justice rooted in the basic intuitive ideas found in the public culture of a constitutional democracy. We conjecture that these ideas are likely to be affirmed by each of the opposing comprehensive moral doctrines influential in a reasonably just democratic society. Thus justice as fairness seeks to identify the kernel of an overlapping consensus, that is, the shared intuitive ideas which when worked up into a political conception of justice turn out to be sufficient to underwrite a just constitutional regime. This is the most we can expect, nor do we need more. We must note, however, that when justice as fairness is fully realized in a well-ordered society, the value of full autonomy is likewise realized. In this way justice as fairness is indeed similar to the liberalisms of Kant and Mill; but in contrast with them, the value of full autonomy is here specified by a political conception of justice, and not by a comprehensive moral doctrine.

It may appear that, so understood, the public acceptance of justice as fairness is no more than prudential; that is, that those who affirm this conception do so simply as a *modus vivendi* which allows the groups in the overlapping consensus to pursue their own good subject to certain constraints which each thinks to be for its advantage given existing circumstances. The idea of an overlapping consensus may seem essentially Hobbesian. But against this, two remarks: first, justice as fairness is a moral conception: it has conceptions of person and society, and concepts of right and fairness, as well as principles of justice with their complement of the virtues through which those principles are embodied in human character and regulate political and social life. This conception of justice provides an account of the cooperative virtues suitable for a political doctrine in view of the conditions and requirements of a constitutional regime. It is no less a moral conception because it is restricted to the basic structure of society, since this restriction is what enables it to serve as a political conception of justice given our present circumstances. Thus, in an overlapping consensus (as understood here), the conception of justice as fairness is not regarded merely as a *modus vivendi*.

Second, in such a consensus each of the comprehensive philosophical, religious, and moral doctrines accepts justice as fairness in its own way; that is, each comprehensive doctrine, from within its own point of view, is led to accept the public reasons of justice specified by justice as fairness. We might say that they recognize its concepts, principles, and virtues as theorems, as it were, at which their several views coincide. But this does not make these points of coincidence any less moral or reduce them to mere means. For, in general, these concepts, principles, and virtues are accepted by each as belonging to a more comprehensive philosophical, religious, or moral doctrine. Some may even affirm justice as fairness as a natural moral conception that can stand on its own feet. They accept this conception of justice as a reasonable basis for political and social cooperation, and hold that it is as natural and fundamental as the concepts and principles of honesty and mutual trust, and the virtues of cooperation in everyday life. The doctrines in an overlapping consensus differ in how far they maintain a further foundation is necessary and on what that further foundation should be. These differences, however, are compatible with a consensus on justice as fairness as a political conception of justice.

VII

I shall conclude by considering the way in which social unity and stability may be understood by liberalism as a political doctrine (as opposed to a comprehensive moral conception).

One of the deepest distinctions between political conceptions of justice is between those that allow for a plurality of opposing and even incommensurable conceptions of the good and those that hold that there is but one conception of the good which is to be recognized by all persons, so far as they are fully rational. Conceptions of justice which fall on opposite sides of this divide are distinct in many fundamental ways. Plato and Aristotle, and the Christian tradition as represented by Augustine and Aquinas, fall on the side of the one rational good. Such views tend to be teleological and to hold that institutions are just to the extent that they effectively promote this good. Indeed, since classical times the dominant tradition seems to have been that there is but one rational conception of the good, and that the aim of moral philosophy, together with theology and metaphysics, is to determine its nature. Classical utilitarianism belongs to this dominant tradition. By contrast, liberalism as a political doctrine supposes that there are many conflicting and incommensurable conceptions of the good, each compatible with the full rationality of human persons, so far as we can ascertain within a workable political conception of justice. As a consequence of this supposition, liberalism assumes that it is a characteristic feature of a free democratic culture that a plurality of conflicting and incommensurable conceptions of the good are affirmed by its citizens. Liberalism as a political doctrine holds that the question the dominant tradition has tried to answer has no practicable answer; that is, it has no answer suitable for a political conception of justice for a democratic society. In such a society a teleological political conception is out of the question: public agreement on the requisite conception of the good cannot be obtained.

As I have remarked, the historical origin of this liberal supposition is the Reformation and its consequences. Until the Wars of Religion in the sixteenth and seventeenth centuries, the fair terms of social cooperation were narrowly drawn: social cooperation on the basis of mutual respect was regarded as impossible with persons of a different faith; or (in the terminology I have used) with persons who affirm a fundamentally different conception of the good. Thus one of the historical roots of liberalism was the development of various doctrines urging religious toleration. One theme in justice as fairness is to recognize the social conditions that give rise to these doctrines as among the so-called subjective circumstances of justice and then to spell out the implications of the principle of toleration. As liberalism is stated by Constant, de Tocqueville, and Mill in the nineteenth century, it accepts the plurality of incommensurable conceptions of the good as a fact of modern democratic culture, provided, of course, these conceptions respect the limits specified by the appropriate principles of justice. One task of liberalism as a political doctrine is to answer the question: how is social unity to be understood, given that there can be no public agreement on the one rational good, and a plurality of opposing and incommensurable conceptions must be taken as given? And granted that social unity is conceivable in some definite way, under what conditions is it actually possible?

In justice as fairness, social unity is understood by starting with the conception of society as a system of cooperation between free and equal persons. Social unity and the allegiance of citizens to their common institutions are not founded on their all affirming the same conception of the good, but on their publicly accepting a political conception of justice to regulate the basic structure of society. The concept of justice is independent from and prior to the concept of goodness in the sense that its principles limit the conceptions of the good which are permissible. A just basic structure and its background institutions establish a framework within which permissible conceptions can be advanced. Elsewhere I have called this relation between a conception of justice and conceptions of the good the priority of right (since the just falls under the right). I believe this priority is characteristic of liberalism as a political doctrine and something like it seems essential to any conception of justice reasonable for this priority is characteristic of liberalism as a political doctrine and something like it seems essential to any conception of justice reasonable for a democratic state. Thus to understand how social unity is possible given the historical conditions of a democratic society, we start with our basic intuitive idea of social cooperation, an idea present in the public culture of a democratic society, and proceed from there to a public conception of justice as the basis of social unity in the way I have sketched.

As for the question of whether this unity is stable, this importantly depends on the content of the religious, philosophical, and moral doctrines available to constitute an overlapping consensus. For example, assuming the public political conception to be justice as fairness, imagine citizens to affirm one of three views: the first view affirms justice as fairness because its religious beliefs and understanding of faith lead to a principle of toleration and underwrite the fundamental idea of society as a scheme of social cooperation between free and equal persons; the second view affirms it as a consequence of a comprehensive liberal moral conception such as those of Kant and Mill; while the third affirms justice as fairness not as a consequence of any wider doctrine but as in itself sufficient to express values that normally outweigh whatever other values might oppose them, at least under reasonably favorable conditions. This overlapping consensus appears far more stable than one founded on views that express skepticism and indifference to religious, philosophical, and moral values, or that regard the acceptance of the principles of justice simply as a prudent *modus vivendi* given the existing balance of social forces. Of course, there are many other possibilities.

The strength of a conception like justice as fairness may prove to be that the more comprehensive doctrines that persist and gain adherents in a democratic society regulated by its principles are likely to cohere together into a more or less stable overlapping consensus. But obviously all this is highly speculative and raises questions which are little understood, since doctrines which persist and gain adherents depend in part on social conditions, and in particular, on these conditions when regulated by the public conception of justice. Thus we are forced to consider at some point the effects of the social conditions required by a conception of political justice on the acceptance of that conception itself. Other things equal, a conception will be more or less stable depending on how far the conditions to which it leads support comprehensive religious, philosophical, and moral doctrines which can constitute a stable overlapping consensus. These questions of stability I cannot discuss here. It suffices to remark that in a society marked by deep divisions between opposing and incommensurable conceptions of the good, justice as fairness enables us at least to conceive how social unity can be both possible and stable.